Middlemen of the Cameroons Rivers

The Duala and their Hinterland, c. 1600–c. 1960

The Duala people entered the international scene as merchant-brokers for precolonial trade in ivory, slaves and palm products. Under colonial rule they used the advantages gained from earlier riverain trade to develop cocoa plantations and provide their children with exceptional levels of European education. At the same time they came into early conflict with both German and French regimes and played a leading – if ultimately unsuccessful – role in anti-colonial politics. In tracing these changing economic and political roles, this book also examines the growing consciousness of the Duala as an ethnic group and uses their history to shed new light on the history of "middleman" communities in surrounding regions of West and Central Africa. The authors draw upon a wide range of written and oral sources, including indigenous accounts of the past which conflict with their own findings but illuminate local conceptions of social hierarchy and their relationship to spiritual beliefs.

RALPH A. AUSTEN is Professor of African History at the University of Chicago. His publications include *Northwest Tanzania under German and British Rule* (1969), *African Economic History* (1987) and *The Elusive Epic: The Narrative of Jeki la Njambe in the Historical Culture of the Cameroon Coast* (1996).

JONATHAN DERRICK is a journalist and historian specializing in West Africa. He taught at the University of Ilorin in Nigeria in the 1970s. His book *Africa's Slaves Today* was published in 1975, and he contributed a chapter to M. Njeuna (ed.), *Introduction to the History of Cameroon* (1989).

African Studies Series 96

A list of books in this series will be found at the end of this volume

Middlemen of
the Cameroons Rivers

*The Duala and their Hinterland,
c. 1600–c. 1960*

Ralph A. Austen and Jonathan Derrick

CAMBRIDGE
UNIVERSITY PRESS

PUBLISHED BY THE PRESS SYNDICATE OF THE UNIVERSITY OF CAMBRIDGE
The Pitt Building, Trumpington Street, Cambridge CB2 1RP, United Kingdom

CAMBRIDGE UNIVERSITY PRESS
The Edinburgh Building, Cambridge CB2 2RU, United Kingdom
http://www.cup.cam.ac.uk
40 West 20th Street, New York, NY 10011-4211, USA   http://www.cup.org
10 Stamford Road, Oakleigh, Melbourne 3166, Australia

First published 1999

Printed in the United Kingdom at the University Press, Cambridge

Typeset in Times 10/12pt [VN]

A catalogue record for this book is available from the British Library

ISBN 0 521 56228 7 hardback
ISBN 0 521 56664 9 paperback

DT
571
.D83
A92
1999

Contents

Tables

Preface

The writing of this book has occupied well over twenty years, although both authors have simultaneously been involved in numerous other projects. The research and writing of chapters 2–4 is entirely the work of Ralph Austen. Chapters 5 and 6 are based on research and drafts by Jonathan Derrick, with additional research and the final writing undertaken by Ralph Austen.

In the course of our efforts we have both become heavily indebted to a great number of oral informants, research assistants and colleagues. Help on specific matters is acknowledged in our many footnotes but recognition beyond these formal courtesies must be extended to at least some institutions and individuals. These include the staffs of the many Cameroonian, British, Dutch, French, German and Swiss archives (governmental, missionary and private) in which we worked (the archives are specified in the bibliography).

In Cameroon we both benefited from the help of various members of the History and Geography Departments of the University of Yaoundé as well as the staffs of the American Cultural Center and the Goethe Institute. In Douala, we both owe special thanks to Father Eric de Rosny, SJ for personal support of various kinds and, in Ralph Austen's case, to the Collège Alfred Saker, the Procure Catholique, Louis Bissek and Martin Njeuma for lodging and other help. Jonathan Derrick is similarly obligated to Jean-Emile Mba and the late Achidi Ndifang in Douala and Dierk Lange in Paris and especially to Xavérie Kobla (now Mrs. Derrick). Although most of our interviews were carried out directly in English, French or German (a direct benefit of the Duala middleman past) Ralph Austen's work in the Littoral hinterland could not have been possible without the help of his assistant and interpreter, the late Moukouri Ndoumbe "Papa" Mbambe.

In Chicago Elizabeth Dale, Sara Pugach, Heather Barrow and J. Shields Sundberg provided valuable assistance. Other academic colleagues whose help went far beyond the footnote references include Manga Bekombo Priso, the late Jean-René Brutsch, Andreas Eckert, Richard Joseph, Yvette

Monga, David Richardson, Rosalinde Wilcox and Albert Wirz. Finally, financial support for travel to Africa and Europe came from the Ford Foundation, two Fulbright grants, the Social Sciences Research Council and the (United States) National Science Foundation. A critical period of writing by Ralph Austen also took place during a fellowship at the Harry Truman Institute of the Hebrew University of Jerusalem.

Portions of several chapters have been published previously in somewhat different form. Permission has graciously been granted by the following: Berghahn Books, Oxford for use in chapter 4 of Ralph A. Austen, "Mythic Transformation and Historical Continuity: The Duala of Cameroon and German Colonialism, 1884–1914," in Ian Fowler and David Zeitlyn (eds.), *African Crossroads: Intersections between History and Anthropology in Cameroon* (1996); the editors of *Cahiers d'Etudes Africaines* for use in chapter 6 of Ralph A. Austen, "Tradition, Invention and History: The Case of the Ngondo (Cameroon)" (32 [1992]: 285–309).

Abbreviations

AA	Auswärtiges Amt [German Foreign Office]
ALME	Archive of Léopold Moumé Etia, Douala
ANC/FA	Archives Nationales du Cameroun, Fonds Allemands, Yaoundé
ANC/FF	Archives Nationales du Cameroun, Fonds Français, Yaoundé
ANSOM	Archives Nationales, Section d'Outre Mer, Aix-en-Provence, France
BFA	Bell Family Archives, Douala
BGF	Buea German Files, Cameroon National Archives, Buea
BMG	Basler Missionsgesellschaft archives, Basel, Switzerland
BMH	*Baptist Missionary Herald*
BMS	Baptist Missionary Society, London
Calprof	Calabar Provincial Files, Nigerian National Archives, Ibadan
CEA	*Cahiers d'Etudes Africaines*
CO	Colonial Office files, Public Records Office, Great Britain
CSO	Central Secretariat Office Files, Nigerian National Archives, Ibadan
FO	Foreign Office files, Public Records Office, Great Britain
ISH	Institut des Sciences Humaines, Yaoundé
JAH	*Journal of African History*
JME	Journal des Missions Evangéliques
JOC	*Journal Officiel du Cameroun*
NBC	Native Baptist Church
PMC	League of Nations, Permanent Mandates Commission
PP	Great Britain, Parliament, House of Commons, Sessional Papers
RFHOM	*Revue Française d'Histoire d'Outre Mer*
RKA	Reichskolonialamt files, Deutsches Bundesarchiv, Potsdam
RT	Germany, *Verhandlungen des Reichstags* [Reichstag debates and papers]
SMEP	Société des Missions Evangéliques de Paris
UPC	Union des Populations du Cameroun

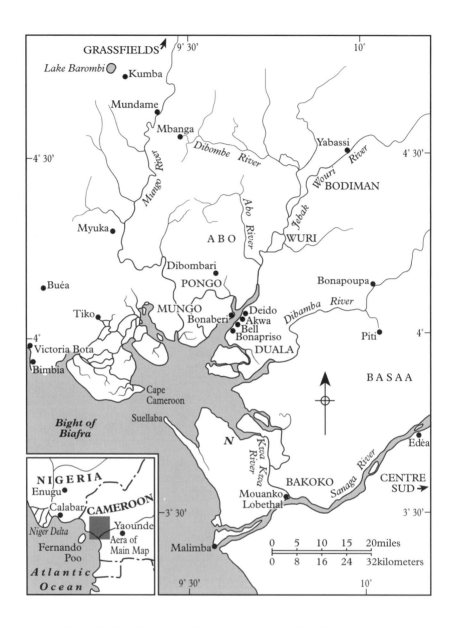

Map 1   The Cameroon Littoral, c. 1977. Reprinted by permission of the University of Wisconsin Press. Words in full capitals indicate ethnic groups.

1   Introduction

This book tells the story of a community which, even by African standards, has always been rather small. The people calling themselves Duala never numbered more than 20,000. Even if one adds another 30,000 members of neighboring ethnic groups with cultural and economic ties to the Duala, the total accounts for only 1 to 3 percent of the population and territory of Cameroon, itself not one of the largest states in Africa. Why then should two non-African historians devote so much effort to studying the history of the Duala? More to the point, why should an international audience bother to read the results of our efforts?

The most immediate significance of this history derives from the enduring position of the Duala as "middlemen" between the European-dominated Atlantic world and the hinterland of Cameroon. This role has been played out through a series of situations which, presented separately, would constitute rather conventional – some even old-fashioned – genres of Africanist historiography: "trade and politics on the X rivers"; "the X-people under German and French colonial rule"; and finally "the invention of tradition/construction of identity as a discourse of coloniality/postcoloniality." In the Duala case it is the possibility of combining these genres which allows us to create a whole which may, perhaps, transcend the sum of its parts.

The concept tying together all these episodes of Duala history is that of middlemen. What this term means in an empirical sense is quite evident. Throughout the approximately three centuries discussed here the Duala occupied a privileged position of intermediacy in European–African relations: first as merchant-brokers of precolonial trade; then as a colonial-era elite of educated évolués and planters; and finally as claimants to anti-colonial political leadership.

The division of chapters which follows is based upon the chronology of this evolving middleman role. From the time of their establishment in the Wouri estuary at the site of the present-day city of Douala (*c.* 1600) up until the full organization of a German colonial economy in the 1890s, the Duala provided Europeans with a variety of commodities brought from the interior: beginning with ivory, shifting to slaves in the late eighteenth and early nineteenth centuries, and for the latter three quarters of the nineteenth century shifting again to palm oil and palm kernels. The changes in the composition of exports produced alterations in the internal organization and scale of Duala middleman activities but the most basic function – control of riverain canoe trade and the products of inland labor – remained constant.[1]

During the colonial period the middleman role of the Duala moved from the arena of commerce to that of politics and culture. They lost their monopoly of trade on the rivers early in the era of German rule but took up new positions within the colonial establishment as "native chiefs," interpreters and clerks. They also served as clergy and teachers in the missionary school system, establishing Duala as a lingua franca of the Littoral (northern coastal) region of Cameroon. Their major economic role up until the Great Depression of the 1930s does not fit the normal definition of a middleman function: they produced food and export crops on inland plantations. However, this form of enterprise derived directly from the old commercial system, since the plantations were established along the rivers where the Duala had previously traded (and planted some food crops); the labor force also came from the same interior populations (and initially the same individuals) who had previously been purchased as slaves; and finally, this whole sector of the Duala economy also proved transitory, thus serving less to redefine the position of the Duala than as a model for other Cameroonian groups who eventually came to dominate export agriculture.

The Duala also played a pioneering but ultimately not very effective role in the development of Cameroonian nationalist politics. From quite early in the German period through the post-World War I French mandate and trusteeship administration they protested against various European policies and demanded greater autonomy for Africans within the colonial order. However, in all these endeavors the relationship between ethnic particularist and national goals and between scale of the claims and the possibility of their realization remained problematic.

Finally, during the 1930s but especially from the 1940s the Duala devoted much of their energy to redefining their own past and ethnic identity in order to shore up a declining economic, political and even demographic position. The account of the past embodied in the new/revived Ngondo organization and festival cannot be reconciled, in many particulars and on some very major points, with the record of Duala history developed through our own research. Nonetheless, such consciousness is itself part of Duala history just as it has become an element in the general study of African development. The Ngondo's focus on the *jengu* water-spirit cult represents an instructive reinterpretation of the critical role played by riverain navigation, migration, and related social hierarchies in earlier Duala middleman experience.

In comparison to other – commercially far more significant – middleman groups of precolonial Western Africa, the Duala are remarkable for their persistence into the twentieth century as a major factor in Cameroonian history. The absence of such continuity elsewhere in Africa may explain why so little attention has been paid to middlemen as a general historical phenomenon. What circumstances allowed the Duala to continue so long in their intermediary role will be explained at various points in the subsequent chapters. Ultimately, however, they failed to retain anything comparable to the dominance over external ties that they had enjoyed in the period up to the late 1800s. Yet, despite the decline of the Duala themselves, their historical role provides something of a paradigm for subsequent African elites. Moreover, their own perception of this long experience of mediation provides us with special insights into the meaning of modern history for African participants.

Had African political economy progressed clearly beyond the stage of middlemen towards substantially integrated modernization, then the history of the Duala would represent only a link with the past rather than a mirror of the present. However, postcolonial Africa remains heavily dependent upon resources controlled by industrialized countries in Europe, America and Asia. At the same time within the continent, local communities, whether still rural or shifted to urban and peri-urban settings, retain a certain degree of economic and cultural autonomy from the centers controlling modern resources. At such centers are elites whose status is notoriously difficult to define in orthodox Western or inherited African terms.

One concept frequently used to define the position of these new elites is that of "broker," a term which links the literal function of historical middlemen with a more metaphorical sense of what it means in contemporary Africa to be at once a client to external sources of power and wealth and a patron within a network of indigenous dependents. In their specific history the Duala do not, however, provide a case study for this entire range of middleman roles since they never achieved (except in the tenuous early colonial form to be discussed in chapter 4) control of an African state.[2] It is, of course, possible to link this history to the present in a more theoretical fashion, but for reasons of both personal inclination and considered judgment, we have not done so.

The continuing prominence of middleman functions in modern Africa speaks to larger development issues but does not suggest any ways to approach them. Whether observed from outside or experienced from within, the middleman role is essentially ambiguous. It does not define the vast and very uncontrollable poles of Africa and Europe but is rather defined by their separate and frequently incompatible dynamics.

Such situations of ambiguity lend themselves more readily to cultural than to economic theorization. The concept of "liminality" and its derivative notions of the trickster and carnivalesque directly address the "betwixt and between" position of both the Duala and the postcolonial elites whom they prefigure.[3] As will be seen especially in the last chapter, the Duala have often been perceived by both Europeans and fellow Africans as "tricksters" and a much-cited essay by a Cameroonian scholar has characterized the entire political culture of contemporary Africa as a perverse carnivalesque.[4] A more positive reading of such a position can be derived from Homi Bhabha's concept of "hybridity," which challenges the very notion of "authentic" African and European identities against which intermediaries such as the Duala are posited.[5]

We make no explicit use of any of these cultural concepts here, although one of us has done so in literary studies dealing with Cameroon and other regions of Africa.[6] For present purposes we considered it important to demonstrate that the Duala past had more potential for substantial achievement than such theories imply. Not all Duala efforts were unsuccessful and even those that ended in failure, tragedy or disillusion contain elements of heroic struggle, adversity and imagination which deserve to be taken seriously on their own terms before being deconstructed through postmodernist scrutiny.

Our ultimate justification for this study, therefore, is that any understanding of how either the political economy or the cultural situation of the modern African elite evolved requires a full examination of its historical forerunners. Among the most significant yet least systematically studied of these forerunners are middleman groups such as the Duala.

2 From fishermen to middlemen: the Duala inland and on the coast in the formative period, *c.* 1500–*c.* 1830

Nowhere do the multiple possibilities for constructing any history come into such obvious confrontation as in accounts of beginnings. In the case of the Duala, even more than for other African peoples, statements about the earliest stages of development appear most fully articulated in the form of oral traditions. Yet the references in Duala accounts to such distant centers as Egypt, Ethiopia, Moses at the Red Sea or even the more proximate Congo and Northern Cameroon savanna are difficult to accept in empirical terms. They seem rather to be attempts at establishing an identity in terms derived from a world encountered long after the events they claim to describe.[1]

Against the claims of these traditions, however, the evidence coming directly from the period prior to the 1800s is very thin: no indigenous texts, virtually no archeological materials, scattered and fragmentary European observations, and a few clues from comparative linguistics. Oral tradition, with all its ideological overtones, will thus have to be used as a major source for this chapter. Where it is most plausible and can be checked to some degree against other evidence, it may help reconstruct events. And where the ideology in such traditions derives from longstanding local experience, even as this includes contact with the outside world, it can be used even more fruitfully to comprehend the relationship between events and Duala historical consciousness.

The ethnographic present: *c.* 1850

The period upon which the earliest oral traditions along with all the European sources concentrate is one when the Duala had already taken up their role as commercial middlemen in the Atlantic trade. In order to understand something about the genesis of this role out of conditions that may initially have had an entirely different logic, it is necessary first to move in the opposite direction: to present an ahistorical "still photo" of the Duala situation in the better-known mid nineteenth century. In reality this period was no more stable than any other in Duala history and the next chapter will examine at some length the changes taking place between the end of the slave trade and the beginning of colonial rule. The present brief lapse into synchrony is intended to serve historical inquiry in several indirect ways. It will introduce the geographical and cultural landscape in which Duala history took place; it will indicate the kinds of questions one wants to ask about an earlier period; and it will inoculate us to some degree against asking these questions in the form dictated by the very situation whose beginnings they are supposed to explain. Once having established a context for (we hope responsible) speculation about the dimmer past, we can go on to look at what were unquestionably the two major events of this earlier period: the movement of the Duala from the interior to the coast, and the development of regular trading contacts with Europeans.

At the moment when they were first documented in any detail by the outside world, the Duala occupied the focal point of a trading network that extended from the Wouri estuary up the various river systems of the Cameroon Littoral: the Wouri itself with its Abo, Dibombe and other minor tributaries; the Dibamba,[2] the Kwakwa; and the Mungo (see map). The Duala themselves were concentrated within the location of the present city of Douala. Along the rivers lived other peoples, some linguistically and culturally related to the Duala (the Bodiman, Malimba, Oli/Ewodi/Wuri, Mungo, and Pongo) and some less closely related although partially assimilated (the Basaa, Bakoko and Abo).

The Duala engaged in fishing and in agriculture (the latter mostly carried on by slaves and women). However, their most lucrative activity was bartering goods obtained through canoe expeditions inland (in the nineteenth century mainly palm oil and kernels plus ivory) for imported commodities brought to Douala by European oceanic shippers.

Douala was politically independent of its European trading partners and likewise did not extend any formal sovereignty inland, except for a few agricultural settlements within ten miles of the port, occupied by Duala-owned slaves. Internally, Douala was divided into a number of residential centers ("towns") located on the high ground along the Wouri river banks and dominated by two major lineages, Bell (Bonanjo) and Akwa (Bonambela). The heads of the Bell and Akwa lineages were called "Kings" by Europeans and the rulers of several lesser locations (Deido/Bonebele: Joss/Bonapriso: Hickory/Bonaberi) were recognized as "chiefs" (see table 2.1). Contemporary European observers saw no evidence of any formal political structure uniting the Duala, although ritual societies exercised some influence across lineages and settlements.

Trading relations with both Europeans and inland peoples were

Table 2.1. *Duala political genealogy*

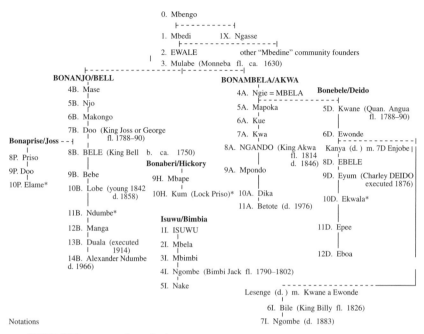

0. Mbengo
├ - - - - - - - - - ┤
1. Mbedi　　　　1X. Ngasse
├ - - - - - - - - - - - - - - - - ┤
2. EWALE　　　　other "Mbedine" community founders
3. Mulabe (Monneba fl. ca. 1630)
├ - - - - - - - - - - - - - - - ┼ - - - - - - - - - - ┤

BONANJO/BELL　　　　　　　　**BONAMBELA/AKWA**

4B. Mase　　　　　　　　　　4A. Ngie = MBELA　　**Bonebele/Deido**
├ - - - - - - - - - - - - - ┤
5B. Njo　　　　　　　　　　5A. Mapoka　　　　　5D. Kwane (Quan. Angua
　　　　　　　　　　　　　　　　　　　　　　　　　　　fl. 1788–90)
6B. Makongo　　　　　　　　6A. Kue

7B. Doo (King Joss or George　7A. Kwa　　　　　　6D. Ewonde
Bonaprise/Joss - - ┤ 　fl. 1788–90)　　　　　　　　　　　　├ - - - - - - - - - - - - - ┤
8P. Priso　　8B. BELE (King Bell b. ca. 1750)　8A. NGANDO (King Akwa　Kanya (d.) m. 7D Enjobe
　　　　　　　　　　　　　　Bonaberi/Hickory　　　fl. 1814　　8D. EBELE
9P. Doo　　9B. Bebe　　　　　9H. Mbape　　9A. Mpondo　d. 1846)　9D. Eyum (Charley DEIDO
10P. Elame*　10B. Lobe (young 1842　　　　　　　　　　　　　　　　　　　　　executed 1876)
　　　　　　　　d. 1858)　10H. Kum (Lock Priso)*　10A. Dika　　　10D. Ekwala*
　　　　　　　　　　　　　　　　　　　　　11A. Betote (d. 1976)
11B. Ndumbe*　　　　　**Isuwu/Bimbia**　　　　　　　　　　11D. Epee
12B. Manga　　　　　　1I. ISUWU
13B. Duala (executed　2I. Mbela　　　　　　　　　　　　　12D. Eboa
　　　　1914)　　　3I. Mbimbi
14B. Alexander Ndumbe　4I. Ngombe (Bimbi Jack fl. 1790–1802)
d. 1966)
　　　　　　　　　　5I. Nake　　　- - - - - - - - - - - - - - - - - -
　　　　　　　　　　　　　Lesenge (d.) m. Kwane a Ewonde

　　　　　　　　　　　　　6I. Bile (King Billy fl. 1826)
Notations　　　　　　　　7I. Ngombe (d. 1883)

– all UPPER CASE = eponymous lineage founders

– (d) = daughter of preceding figure

– names in parentheses or after ? are European or Pidgin rather than Duala versions

– names followed by * are signatories of 1884 Duala–German annexation treaty (the major Bell and Akwa lineages are
traced to the post-independence period; all others end with the rulers of the late nineteenth century)

– The Akwa lineage omits several rulers of brief tenure who were succeeded by brothers rather than sons.

managed through various forms of tribute, partnership, and marriage alliances. The internal political organization of the inland societies was even less centralized than that of the Duala. Some of these groups also engaged in fishing and canoe-borne trading, thus controlling portions of the navigable waters of their respective rivers. Others, such as the Abo, stayed on land, although they usually attempted to keep Duala merchants from travelling beyond their home areas.

This then is a bare sketch of the "classic" Duala political, economic and social situation. The description of institutions and relationships is very incomplete, but will be examined at much greater length in subsequent sections of both this chapter and the following one. The first historical question that has to be addressed, however, is how the Duala arrived at the position they were to occupy upon the nineteenth-century Cameroon coast.

The chronology of settlement: non-written sources

In attempting to describe such an apparently straightforward process as the movement of the Duala to their present geographical location, we are confronted with all the problems of limited and questionable evidence. What is popularly assumed to be the "primordial" base of African social change, the ethnic-linguistic identities of the peoples concerned is itself, for the Cameroon Littoral, as elsewhere in the world, a product of historical change.

The populations in this region are all Bantu-speaking which implies that they may have ultimately migrated from some common point of demographic dispersion. Linguistic evidence suggests that the latter is not far from the Cameroon coast in space, although the time gap of close to two millennia and the available archeological record of iron and ceramic artefacts do not permit an easy link between Bantu origins and historical accounts of contemporary Central African populations.[3]

Among the accepted categories of local groups, the Basaa and Bakoko are more numerous and have been in the Wouri estuary for a longer time than the entire set of Sawa (coastal) Bantu-speakers (the Duala and those most closely related to them). Although their own oral traditions refer back over what may be great periods of time to migrations from unspecified distant regions, the Basaa and Bakoko are mainly cultivators who are seen, in the relatively recent past, as more stable than the aquatic Sawa Bantu. Moreover, it was assumed for some time that the Duala language had particular affinities to Bakota and Lingala in Gabon and the Congo and that the Sawa Bantu had therefore migrated to Cameroon from the more southern regions of Central Africa.[4]

Lexostatistical analysis by contemporary linguists suggests that Sawa Bantu is, in fact, much more closely related to Basaa and Bakoko than to any Gabon-Congo languages.[5] Moreover, the most reliable Duala oral traditions say nothing specific about any movement from a point beyond a relatively recent homeland, Piti, which is located only a short distance from Douala on a creek linked to the Dibamba River (see table 2.2). We are thus left with little basis for postulating any origin for the Duala outside of Cameroon which is, after all, the presumed starting point of the general Bantu-speaking dispersion into the Congo-Ogowe Basin and points south and east.[6]

The Duala oral traditions that were recorded earliest and appear least influenced by external motifs are summarized in table 2.2 (for references to the genealogical position of named individuals, see table 2.1). With the partial exception of the two most recent versions, all give the point of origin for the Duala as Piti or its environs. The narratives all begin with events leading from Piti to the present site of Douala, with the longest genealogies going back seven to ten generations from Bele/King Bell (8B) who begins the list of figures we can trace through written sources.

These accounts also reinforce, to varying degrees, the belief that the Duala and all the Sawa Bantu speaking peoples of the Cameroon Littoral are descended from a single ancestor, Mbedi (0) s/o Mbongo (1) who lived at Piti. Ewale a Mbedi (2) is the eponymous ancestor of the Duala ("Dwala") proper and migrated from Piti to Douala, which was then dominated by the Basaa and/or Bakoko. Here Ewale himself or one of his descendants first made contact with Europeans (it is significant to note that the Basaa/Bakoko traditions make no claim to initiating such contacts).[7] About six generations after the time of Ewale, the leadership of the Duala was divided between the major segments of Bell/Bonanjo and Akwa/Bonambela. After this point, the contact between Duala and Europeans became so close that we do not need to rely on oral tradition as our major source of narrative data, a condition that the informants who supplied the earliest accounts seem to have acknowledged by supplying little information on the time after the ascendance of the first "King Akwa" (8A).

The focus of the present chapter is thus the period described most fully by Duala oral tradition. If we had to rely entirely on that source, we could still be confident of possessing at least some sense of historical events in the era covered. The tradition presents an account of the Duala past which is quite plausible because it is not very pretentious in either chronological or ideological terms. In both a positive and negative sense it is more of a history (or at least a genealogical chronicle) than a myth. The space encompassed by the migration of Ewale is precisely the kind of local trajectory that critics have alleged lies behind the tales of distant origins in other oral traditions of this region, at least as they appertain to the present millennium.[8] The time frame is also rather limited and lacks the gap between original ancestor and more recent figures that is characteristic of more lofty foundation stories.

Heroic themes are not only absent from Duala oral traditions but their possibility actually appears to be suppressed. Thus neither Mbedi, Ewale or any of the migration leaders are endowed with any larger-than-life qualities and the reasons given for their departure from Piti are not very dramatic or consistent. While some accounts do state that the Basaa/Bakoko were forced out of Douala, there is little sense here of "conquest"; several Duala traditions even concur with Bakoko accounts

Table 2.2. *Variants of the Duala oral tradition*

Date recorded	Inland origin(s)	Generations (Mbongo to Mbedi Bele)	Sons of	Reasons for departure	Relations with Basaa/Bakoko	Encounter Europeans
Smith[1] 1863	West of Mt. Cameroon		Koli, Dualla		"Expelled the Basas from their dwellings on the Cameroons river"	
Grenfell[2] 1882	Lungassi (near Piti)			Expelled by Lungassi people, move to Estuary, learn to fish	Move to source of floating plantain skins, trade for fish, then drive Basaa into forest	
Pauli[3] 1884	Lungassi	5				
Flad[4] c. 1890	Masongo → Piti	10	Kole, Duala, Bojongo, Balimba, Ewori, Bakoko, Ebonji	Wanderlust (from Masongo); Kole-Duala quarrel over chicken and canoe prow (Piti)	Trade fish w. Bakoko and settle peacefully; eventually use force to take land	Ndoko of Bonambela allows Bonaberi to deal w. Europeans but Ngando Akwa claims same status
Halbing[5] c. 1905	Pitti	7	Duala	Duala marries daughter of uncle who forces all sons of Mbedi out		Duala and Bojongo meet Europeans, send Mapoka s/o Duala to Europe
	Kole, Bojongo			Mbongo war w. Lungassi; Piti either short of food or Duala quarrels w. Mbedi over first imported cloth	Settle peacefully w. Basaa, then cheat them at trade	First encounter before leaving Piti; Bojongo meets ship while fishing but Duala, as senior, controls trade

	No.	Groups (order of migration)	Group	Reason for migration	Settlement / relations with hosts	Notes
Ebding, 1[6] 1902		Duala, Babimbi (near Lungassi), Piti	Kole, Bojongo			Much detail, no names
Ebding, 2[7] 1901–14	4	Kole, Piti, Duala, (Bojongo?)		Attracted by trade of fish for food w. Bakoko	Settle peacefully but Bakoko fear large numbers; Duala conceal migration, eventually impose unfair trade, then warfare enslavement, political rule	
Ebding, 3[8] 1901–14		Duala, Piti	Bojongo	Bojongo discovers Bakoko, then Europeans	Establish market at Bomobko; s/o Bojongo wounds Bomboko	Bojongo and son flee, meet Europeans
Ekolo[9] c. 1910	6	Babimbi, Piti, Kole	Duala	Duala marries daughter of Uncle; Bojongo leaves first	Settle peacefully but quarrel over who resides on high ground. Duala secretly kill Basaa to drive them off	
		Bojongo, Dibongo	Ewodi	Seek better trade	Settle peacefully; Duala later conquer surrounding territory	Proverb: "Bojongo found the Europeans, Bonambela [= Duala] took them over." Mapoka s/o Duala to Europe
Mpundo Dika[10] 1914	7	Piti, Kole, Bojongo	Ewale			
IBB[11] 1930s +	8	Bantu–Muslim war, Bongele, Kole, Piti, Bojongo, Moo, Dibongo	Duala	Trade; Duala marriage with niece leads to warfare w. uncle	Peaceful at first but Basaa accuse Duala of killing them by witchcraft	Bojongo discovers Europeans but wants to kill them; Duala decides on trade, takes over, sends son Mapoka to Europe

Table 2.2. (*cont.*)

Date recorded	Inland origin(s)	Generations (Mbongo to Mbedi Bele)	Sons of	Reasons for departure	Relations with Basaa/Bakoko	Encounter Europeans
Ngaka Akwa[12] 1940s		7(?)		Mortality in home village, Ngiye Mulobe cannot stay with maternal uncle gets land for fish, marries Basaa daughter; Mapoka, nephew of Ngiye, also marries Basaa and must give son Kuo to them temporarily	Bojongo killed in encounter w. Europeans; Ngiye saves Europeans from revenge "Bonambela took them over." Mapoka to Europe	
Buhan[13] (Bakoko traditions) 1976, 1979	Congo, Pitti				Duala arrive at night and secretly kill Bakoko; establish settlements in order to take over; Duala are savage, dirty and do not respect Bakoko's "fear of incest, sexual modesty, penchant for secrecy."	

[1] Robert Smith, Cameroons report, *BMH*, 1863: 123.

[2] George Grenfell, "The Cameroons District, West Africa," *Proceedings of the Royal Geographical Society* 4 (1882): 589.

[3] Dr Pauli, "Anthropologisches und Ethnologisches aus Kamerun," *Correspondenz-Blatt der Anthropologische Gesellschaft* (Munich), 32 (1901): 112–17.

[4] Flad, "Zur Geschichte der Vergangenheit der Dualla," *Mitteilungen aus den Deutschen Schutzgebieten* 4 (1891): 39–47.

[5] Aug Halbing, "Genealogie des Duala, Sohns des Mbedi," *Mitteilungen des Seminars für Orientalischen Sprachen* 9, part III (1906): 259–77.

[6] Friedrich Ebding, "Die Geschichte des Duala-Stammes/miango ma tumba la Duala," ms., Duala Arbeiten, Ebding Nachlass, Seminar für Afrikanische Sprachen und Kulturen, Hamburg (these manuscripts, in both German and Duala, were copied by Ebding from an original notebook labeled "Kole" which has not been found).

[7] "Die Geschichte des Duala-Volkes," ibid.

[8] "Geschichte des Duala Mberi, des Bodjongo Mberi oder Wie die Duala und die Weissen nach Kamerun kamen," ibid.

[9] Josef Ekolo, "Wege der Duala" (Mangea ma Duala). Ernst Dinkelacker Nachlass, Johannes Ittmann Papers, Basel. Mission Society, Basel.

[10] Ludwig Mpundo Dika to Governor Ebermeier, n.d. [c. Jan.–Mar. 1914], ANC/FF TA (Traductions allemandes), 6 (Mpundo gives as his source for this information "le tam-tam" presumably indicating the praise names encoded in drum language and thus accounting for the completeness of his genealogy).

[11] Idubwan Ebele Bele, an historical association founded in Bonaberi during the 1930s. More or less identical translations of their manuscript history (with some post-World War II emendations) can be found in René Bureau, "Ethno-Sociologie religieuse des Duala et apparentés," *Recherches et Etudes Camerounaises* 7/8 (1962–64): 319–39; René Gouellain, *Douala: ville et histoire* (Paris: Institut d'ethnologie, 1975), 56–64, 70–5.

[12] Gouellain, *Douala*, 75–80.

[13] Christine Buhan with Etienne Kange Essiben, *La mystique du corps: jalons pour une anthropologies du corps, les Yabyan et les Yapeke, Bakoko (Elog-Mpoo ou Yamben-Ngee) de Dibombari au Sud-Cameroun* (Paris: L'Harmattan, 1979), 93, 420–2 (the authors indicate as their main informants for these accounts Toto Kange and Njo Esobe).

(Buhan in table 2.2) of how coastal territory was appropriated by under-handed means. Apart from the stories of their descent from Mbedi, the Duala and related coastal peoples share another major oral narrative, the epic of Jeki la Njambè, an explicitly heroic story whose apparent evocation of local historical themes is consistently denied by virtually all inform-ants.[9] The most intense portion of the Duala historical tradition, that dealing with the Bell–Akwa split, does contain considerable elements of violence but, as will be seen when it is examined more closely below, this is both a reflection of real, relatively recent events and an explanation more of political weakness than of strength.

One of the most ideologically positive – but empirically questionable – elements of the claim to descent from Mbedi of Piti is its diffusion through-out the Douala hinterland. The prevalence of these accounts among peoples connected in a hierarchical relationship to the Duala must be treated with the same suspicion as recent Duala statements about their own ultimate origin in Ethiopia, Egypt or Arabia. Not only do these stories reflect the trade structure of the nineteenth century but, in their twentieth-century versions, they echo a new kind of regional hegemony exercised by the Duala in the early decades of colonial rule. It is certainly hard to believe many of the details of genealogy and migration by which peoples linguistically related to the Duala trace their history back to Piti, to say nothing of similar statements within communities that are clearly Basaa and Bakoko.[10]

On the other hand, there are Sawa Bantu speaking communities in this region, the Kole, Bakwiri, and Batanga who were not part of the nine-teenth-century trading network or its colonial administrative aftermath and yet claim similar connections to the Piti center. The Kole, of Rio del Rey in the extreme southwest corner of Cameroon, arrived in their present location well before the Douala-centered network had developed to any wide extent, but their eponymous ancestor is mentioned in six of the Table 2.2 narratives and the Kole themselves maintain a complete version of the Piti tradition.[11] The Bakwiri of the Mount Cameroon region, linguistically belonging to a distinctive subgroup of the Sawa Bantu agglomeration, have incorporated into their speech forms an honorific term equating freeborn status with descent from Mbongo (either the father of Mbedi or one of the brothers of Ewale).[12] It is nevertheless possible that the inser-tion of even these communities into the Mbedine lineage is the result of general Duala prominence in the colonial era.[13] We can trace such a shift in the case of the Batanga, who (like the Bakwiri) are totally absent from early Duala accounts of the sons of Mbedi and only began to add this item to their own oral traditions sometime after World War I.[14]

Thus Piti may be an even less significant center of migration to the coast than is asserted in the already modest Duala oral histories. In both the limitations and the extensions of their claims to a major position in the past, the Duala do suggest that its basis is less a long-established superiority to other coastal Cameroon peoples than the relatively recent attainment of a strategic position in relation to Europeans. It is thus not inappropriate that in attempting to construct a more precise account of early Duala history, we turn to European documents.

The chronology of migration: European sources

European accounts of Douala before the 1820s, limited as they are, still provide us with a valuable check upon the indigenous oral tradition (see table 2.3). The advantage of these sources is obviously that they are preserved for us in the form in which they were recorded during the period of early contact between Europeans and Duala. They are most valuable for the simple, often unreflective, statements they make about conditions at these moments rather than for any conscious efforts at narrative or analysis. Unfortunately, the fragments of accounts that we have up to the 1780s are not very rich in descriptions of the Duala themselves. They are mainly concerned with the business of navigation and ivory and slave trading rather than the politics, social organization or culture of the African areas that provided these goods. Moreover, when Europeans do attempt comments it is usually in general travel books at one or more removes from the primary sources of contact, filtered through considerable layers of ignorance, fantasy, and prejudice. Nonetheless, if used critically, these records can allow us to specify some of the dates of the Duala movement to the coast and also the changing relationship between Duala and other coastal locations as a center of Atlantic trade.[15]

The earliest reports of European navigation along the Cameroon coast are Portuguese accounts from the early sixteenth century, which say little about either the Wouri estuary or its African trading peoples, since there was apparently almost no contact with either. The first identifications of inhabitants of this region come from early-seventeenth-century Dutch sources.[16] It is only with the Leers/Blommaert description, probably referring to observations of the 1630s, that we have the name of a ruler at Douala, "Monneba," and the sample vocabulary of a language that is almost certainly Duala. Ardener and others have identified Monneba with Mulobe a Ewale in the Duala oral tradition (table 2.1, no. 3). If we accept this very reasonable inference, we can then date Mulobe's father, Ewale a Mbedi, and the migration from Piti at about 1575–1600. This chronology places Ewale at, or just before, the first European trade in the estuary. More importantly, it lends credence to Duala oral tradition, since the

Table 2.3. *Early European accounts*

Date of voyage	Observer/author reference[1]	Area described	Comments
1503–4	Pereira, Duarte Pacheco, *Esmeraldu in Situ Orbis* (George Kimble trans.). London, 1937	Rio del Rey, Coast, Estuary	Slave, pepper, ivory trade but none in Estuary
1510s	Jao de Lisbon. *Ho Tratado de Aguhla de marear in de Brito Rebello. Livro de Marinharia.* Lisbon: 1903	Rio del Rey, Coast, Estuary	Estuary difficult to navigate
1528–9	Duarte Rodrigues to Lisbon, May 10, 1529 in Antonio Brasio (ed.) *Monumenta Missionaria Africana, Africa Ocidental* (Lisbon, 1954), IV, 144	Ambos (island off coast)	Small amount of trade
1529	Jao de Lobato to Lisbon, March 13, 1529, in *Brasio* 1 (1952): 505–18	Fernando Po, Coast	Use of oars to navigate (i.e., difficult)
1590s	Cornelius Claesz, *Intinerario . . . van Jan Hugens van Jan Linschoten.* Amsterdam, 1596	Coast around Fernando Po	Advise navigators to avoid it by sailing outside the island
1600	Pieter de Mareez, *Description . . . de Gunea . . .* Amsterdam: 1605	Coast around Fernando Po	Dangers of being caught "behind the islands of Fernando Po." Nothing to trade there
1603–4	*Andreas Ulsheimer, unpublished ms[2]	Cameroons R.	Europeans initially attacked, eventually buy "many elephant tusks" using sign language
1608	Samuel Brun. *Schiffarten.* Basel: 1624/Amsterdam: 1913	Rio del Rey, Ambas Bay, Cameroons R.	Rio del Rey trades slaves captured from "enemies";[3] otherwise only akori beads available
1618	Gaspar da Rosa to Lisbon, *Brasio* 6 (1955): 346–50	Cameroons R.	Dutch trading there generally. Portuguese buy slaves

Table 2.3. *(cont.)*

1630s	Samuel Blommaert in Arnout Leers. *Pertinente Beschryvinge van Africa . . .* Rotterdam: 1665	Douala, Rio del Rey	Details on trade, rulers (Monneba), town and language
1660s	Dr. O. Dapper. *Naukeurige Beschrijvinge der Afrikanische Gewesten . . .* Amsterdam: 1688	Same as above	Same as above. Samson down, Monneba up, Old Calabar active
1650s	*Anon, Dutch maps, Rijksarchief, Hague (Marine 2334, Leupe 145) and Bibliothèque Nationale, Paris (H794)	Details of Estuary Walleba, Tande	Confirm above plus Betebe, Gat, Monnebaes Gat, Oute Gat

[1]With the exception of the two items marked with an asterisk (*) all references here can also be found in Joseph Bouchaud, *La côte du Cameroun dans l'histoire et la cartographie* (Douala: IFAN, 1952) and Edwin Ardener, "Documentary and Linguistic Evidence for the Rise of Trading Polities between the Rio del Rey and Cameroons, 1500–1650," in I.M. Lewis (ed.), *History and Social Anthropology* (London: Tavistock, 1968), 81–126.
[2]Original and translation with annotations in Adam Jones, *German Sources for West African History, 1599–1669* (Wiesbaden: Franz Steiner, 1983), 18, 25–26, 343–4.
[3]See English translation and notes in Jones, *German Sources* 69.

translation of the genealogical list of rulers (ten to twelve generations from the late nineteenth century) would, by allowing twenty-five years to a generation, take us back to about the same date for Mulobe as does the first identification of Monneba.

The early European sources suggest some delay in Douala's rise to prominence as the main trading center on the Cameroon coast. Portuguese and Dutch navigators were first drawn to more accessible coastal inlets, such as the misnamed Rio del Rey and the coast and islands opposite Fernando Po (Santa Isabel). It was only with further exploration of the region, spurred by an increasing demand for African goods, that the difficult but more rewarding outlets of the inland rivers (Old Calabar in present-day Nigeria, with its link to the Cross River, as well as Douala) were penetrated. Ulsheimer's 1603–04 references to armed hostility and dumb barter suggest a very early, but also lucrative, Douala trading system. Even in the second two decades of the seventeenth century, when there are indications of a slave and ivory trade from "Rio de Camerones" (the estuary), it is fairly clear that Rio del Rey remained a more important place, with its ruler "Samson" receiving somewhat higher customs dues

Table 2.4. *Early Cameroon overseas trade*

Period	Nationality	Exports	Quantity	Location	Sources
1. 1500–1600	Portuguese pepper	Slaves, ivory	Small	Coast, Rio del Rey	See table 2.3
2. 1600s	Dutch	Ivory, slaves, accories	Small	Rio del Rey, Douala	See table 2.3
3. 1700–50s	Dutch	Slaves, ivory	Ivory, some substantial (11MCC voyages. @ 5,113 lb per voyage = 56,243 lb + other unrecorded)	Douala only	Middleburgh Commercial Company[1]
4. 1752–1807	British, some Dutch, American	Slaves, some ivory	30–40,000 slaves; ivory not tabulated (substantial)	Douala and some Bimbia	See table 3.4
5. 1807–84	British, Spanish, German	Slaves, palm oil/kernel, some ivory	6,000 slaves	Douala and some Bimbia	See tables 2.5 and 3.2

[1]Ralph A. Austen with K. Jacob, "Dutch Trading Voyages to Cameroon, 1721–59," *Annales de la Faculté des Lettres et Sciences Humaines, Université de Yaoundé* 6 (1974): 1–27; on trade by the Dutch West India Company up to 1725, see Harvey M. Feinberg and Marion Johnson, "The West African Ivory Trade during the Eighteenth Century," *International Journal of African Historical Studies* 15/3 (1982): 435–53 (as noted on p. 440 of this article, the actual coastal origins for Dutch ivory imports in this period are not given in available documents, although Cameroon is one of the likely sources).

than Monneba.[17] Dapper's summary of conditions in the mid-1600s describes Samson as routed from his Rio del Rey base (by invaders who possibly included the Duala-related Kole); it is now that Old Calabar and Douala come into their own. The coast between Rio del Rey and the estuary receives little further mention during the next century except for indications that it attracts little trade. The pattern of commerce in this period is confirmed by contemporary Dutch maps, which include detailed indications of the various landmarks within the estuary, centering on "Monneba's village" and referring to the Dibamba River as "Monneba's Creek" (*Monnebasa Gat*).[18]

For the years 1732 to 1739 we have a series of correspondence and ships' logs from Dutch vessels trading for ivory at Douala, but these give virtually no data on the Duala themselves other than their immediate behavior in market transactions (see below and table 2.4). During all this time Douala is still referred to as "Monneba's" and the single-mindedness with which the Dutch directed their ships there, by-passing all other points on the Cameroon coast, indicates a very complete Duala domination of the local market.

The rationale of coastal settlement: from fishing to trade

The usual explanation for the movement of the Duala from the Cameroon interior to the coast is the attraction of European trade. This is the assertion in several (but not most) of the Duala oral traditions in table 2.2[19] and it is also taken up by modern scholars (even a very critical one such as Ardener). Such an argument treats the outcome of a process as its intention, always a tempting yet dangerous assumption for historians. Moreover, as noted above, neither the oral traditions of the Duala's predecessors on the Wouri, the Basaa and Bakoko, nor the earliest European records in table 2.3 (which coincide with the period of Duala migration from Piti) suggest that there was any oceanic commerce in the estuary at the time. By recognizing that the later trading system of the Cameroon rivers was probably a result, not a cause, of the Duala presence on the coast, we can provide not only a more plausible account of events in this region during the sixteenth and seventeenth centuries but also some insight into the nature of the Duala middleman position.

The logical basis for understanding the genesis of this coastal role – migration as well as the development of trade – is the prior occupational specialization of the Duala: fishing. Such an analysis draws upon the excellent studies of Alagoa, Harms, Horton, and Jones, which have demonstrated how other Western African trading societies emerged from fishing economies.[20] The Duala case is not identical with these situations but the comparison is valuable even where it points out differences. In any case, there is good reason to see the needs of fishing as the basis for initial Duala migration and, perhaps more importantly, the social organization and cultural idiom of fishing as the basis upon which the later middleman role of the Duala was defined.

When the Duala resided at Piti, it is likely that their fishing activities resembled those of other inland African communities, making their living this way from antiquity up to more recent times.[21] Fishing on inland waterways is relatively easy, not necessarily requiring much movement away from home. At the same time, the scale of population or the range of specialization and exchange of fish for other goods is limited in such a situation. The Duala in particular, as a linguistic and cultural minority in a Basaa-Bakoko dominated region, could hardly expand their sphere of territorial control in the immediate vicinity of Piti.

The Duala might, of course, simply have remained at Piti or (as most other Sawa-Bantu speakers apparently did) migrated to other riverain locations of a similar character. Piti itself is clearly not a location that could support even as large a population as the river sites occupied by the Bodiman, Mungo, Pongo and Wuri. It is a small creek without good access to the neighboring rivers. If the entire set of peoples claiming descent from Mbedi once lived here, it is not surprising that they migrated out in different directions. If only the Ewale a Mbedi branch were at Piti and the others merely claimed it as a point of origin later, it is still understandable that an outward movement eventually took place. That this movement was directed toward the coast need not have resulted from an initially positive incentive. Several of the Duala traditions in table 1.2 portray the departure of Ewale as the involuntary result of internecine quarrels. Such accounts may be read as projections of later Duala segmentary politics upon the distant past; but they are also consistent with conditions in that past as well as with patterns of small-scale migration all over Bantu-speaking Africa.[22] It is those "Mbedine" peoples settled inland (sometimes portrayed as descended from more senior branches of the lineage than Ewale) who carry on most directly the tradition of their putative common ancestor. The Duala moved, possibly not by choice, into a higher-risk fishing area.

The lack of any heroic dimension to the accounts of Ewale's installation in the Basaa/Bakoko territory of Douala can thus be explained in a number of ways. First, as already noted, by the time these accounts were recorded, the emphasis of Duala identity had so shifted to trade with Europeans that achievements within the more restricted realm of fishing tended to be forgotten or at least placed in a sphere (as they were in contemporary Duala life) apart from the activities of the elite. Secondly, it probably did not require significant force of any kind to gain a place close to the water's edge in Basaa territory, since the Basaa were not interested in fishing but, rather, in cultivating the extensive and well-watered (through rainfall) lands farther inland. Duala conceptions of status later came to be expressed in, among other terms, the contrast of *mudongo* (high land close to a river/realm of the free, male, noble populations) with *kotto* (inland agricultural areas/realm of slaves, women, subject peoples). As will be seen in analyzing a later portion of the tradition, the Basaa could thus be equated with slaves. However, this imputed lower status derives from the lifestyle of the Basaa and perhaps from their failure to attain the commercial success of the Duala, and not from any heroic conquest by Duala fisher-invaders.

Fishing on the Cameroon coast does have its heroic qualities, which one can imagine being incorporated into conquest myths in the same way that the idiom of the hunt has been used in other African oral traditions. The Duala share in the rich cosmology that has developed around the rewards and dangers of seeking local aquatic life, with its focus on the placation of *miengu* (sing. *jengu*), the spirits that control the fate of both humans and animals in Cameroon's oceanic waters.[23] As will be seen, one form of *jengu* association came to play a major role in the exercise of authority by the "true" Duala elite.

However, there are two interesting complications here. While the Duala looked down upon peoples who did not fish at all, like the Basaa, as well as those members of their own society (women and slaves) who could only fish for crabs and shrimp in shallow waters, they also recognized their own limitations in this area. Duala pursuit of herring in the relatively protected estuary did not compare in heroism to the feats of neighboring peoples who chased after whale and *mukabo* (salt-water pike) in the *munja a tube* (true sea).[24]

Further, both fishing and the *jengu* cult are less closely associated with the main Duala lineages and their leaders than with the communities closer to the ocean and its more perilous modes of fishing, such as the Balimba, Batanga and Wovea. More critically, among the Duala themselves the central locale of the *jengu* cult is the island of Jebale, a politically and geographically marginal site, but one very closely associated with trade in fish rather than European goods. The Jebale community claims to be descended from an older brother of Mbedi, Male, but takes its name from Male's *jengu* wife, whom he encountered near Malimba.[25] In this context fishing and the *jengu* cult are identified with an autochthonous, feminized population rather than the dominant Duala "conquerors." Such a division between invasive secular political power and aboriginal "earth priests" who control the reproductive forces of the local environment is common throughout Africa.[26] But in the Duala case the critical role of middleman trade complicated the position of the "fisher king,"[27] who simultaneously represented categories of domination and subordination. The relationship between local status hierarchies and occupational/gender positions would become even more ambiguous with late-colonial attempts to draw on the *jengu* cult for a new form of "tradition."[28]

What we must conclude, therefore, is that the Duala did not see their shift from inland fishing to the higher stakes of exploiting the Wouri estuary as an action of heroic choice. It may well have been forced upon them as one of the few opportunities left after they were squeezed out of (or into) Piti. But the combination of extending their fishing ventures beyond inland waters while still retaining access to these waters would make the fortune of the Duala.

As Robert Harms has shown most clearly in his study of the Bobangi of the Congo Basin, extended fishing expeditions provide an excellent social basis for the organization of long-distance, water-borne trade.[29] For the Duala, as with other African peoples in similar situations, the central institution of fishing was the dugout canoe. During more recently recorded annual fishing ventures to temporary camps on the islands and peninsulas of the Wouri estuary, the crews of these boats (four to six men) would be divided into elites and servitors. The former owned the vessels and nets and undertook the prestigious tasks of deep water fishing. The latter – younger men and, later, slaves – were responsible for more routine work such as paddling, maintaining living quarters and food supplies at the camps, processing and preserving the daily catch of herring, and fishing for crabs near the camp. Fishing of this kind was not predictable, and different crews could, according to skill or luck, achieve very different results. At the same time, in a large and complex area such as the estuary, the Duala as a collective entity could constantly expand the points that provided a favorable combination of camping facilities and access to fish.[30]

The analogy with later trading expeditions is quite clear. These also centered around canoes (much larger than fishing vessels, carrying trading capital of far greater value than nets) with a similar division of status and labor among the crews. Here the prestigious tasks were negotiation with inland partners. The routine chores again consisted of paddling, and now carrying goods and providing physical protection for the leaders in cases of dispute. Again, there were possibilities for very differential success as well as a collective impulse to open up an ever-widening range of commercial routes.

The great advantage of the estuary, as opposed to fishing in the open waters and archipelagos of the external Cameroon coast, is that it does connect with a wide range of inland waterways, which could thus be exploited for trade. It is not clear to what extent the Duala were on the coast long enough to develop such trade simply on the basis of exchanging fish for inland food products. Unlike coastal peoples in Nigeria, the Duala had easy access to agricultural products in their own residential areas. Moreover, there is no evidence in sources for the early period of trade in sea salt, which would have greatly increased the value of coastal commerce for inland peoples. Oral traditions collected relatively recently at Jebale and among the Pongo of Dibombari state that fish did precede imported goods as an item of Duala (or possibly pre-Duala) trade in at least one section of the rivers system.[31] However, the narrators may here be simply transporting a contemporary hierarchy of exchange enterprises into chronological form. More likely, extensive inland trade of Duala fish developed more or less simultaneously with the somewhat sporadic early stages of European commercial contact. In any case, the organization of these two kinds of enterprise is highly compatible and thus with or without experience of trading at long distances inland, the Wouri estuary fishermen were well prepared to take on their role of Atlantic middlemen.

The remainder of this chapter will examine two, apparently contradictory, aspects of the early development of this role. First we will look at the immediate records of European trade as an indication of the increasing ability of the Duala to supply export goods. Secondly, we will consider the political transformation of Douala represented in the one phase of the oral tradition that does take on heroic dimensions but also indicates a failure (later to prove very costly) to transcend the segmentary structure of the original fishing society.

European ivory and slave trade

As already indicated, the earliest European documents of trade in Cameroon do not give us very much information about Duala society. However, by the eighteenth century, when this trade had become more regular and intensive, its records do tell us something about local politics as well as the economic context of broader social change.

For the first two centuries of European presence (phases 1 and 2 of table 2.4) we do not have enough economic data to make positive inferences of any kind about Duala history. What we can assume, however, is that the Portuguese probably did not trade with the Duala at all while the first Dutch to make contact with "Monneba" did so on a very irregular basis. It is not even clear from these sources in what proportion the two main commodities mentioned, ivory and slaves, were purchased. All we do learn is that by 1650 Douala was put quite literally on the maps of European commercial ventures in Africa and the rudiments of a system for carrying on barter – identification of a chief and a level of customs payments – had been established.

It is only with the recorded voyages of the Dutch MCC (Middelburgh Commercial Company) between 1732 and 1759 that we first get a detailed and continuous record of Duala overseas trade. Even here, description of frustrations in the log of the earliest voyage suggests that commerce with Europeans may not yet have been fully regularized. However, the account books of the eleven ships from 1743 onward, with their large cargoes of ivory, imply that the Duala had by now become quite efficient suppliers of a major and valuable export.

The absence of political comment in the MCC records may be read as testimony to the smoothness of this trade. The Dutch captains did not concern themselves with giving the personal names of the successors of Monneba nor recording the amounts of customs paid. Presumably these were now routine matters that had no effect upon the overall profit balance of each venture. The accounts do indicate a steady rise in the price of Douala ivory, a process one would expect given the increasing and (as indicated by the reference to other shipping in the later MCC logbooks) competitive European demand for African commodities. The emphasis on ivory rather than slaves in this early commerce is itself indicative of less social tension on the African side of the trade and conducive to few of the difficulties over credit arrangements which, as will be seen below, characterized later stages of Duala trade. It is also not surprising that the calm period of Dutch domination over a quite active commerce has made no impact upon Duala oral tradition.

With the arrival of the British and a shift from predominantly ivory to an at least equal emphasis upon slave trading, the story becomes more complicated. As indicated in table 2.4, the British first began to trade regularly in Cameroon at the same time as the Dutch ivory trade was reaching its peak. While ivory prices had begun to rise by this time, the area attracted British merchants because of the low cost of slaves compared to established trading centers on other portions of the western African coast.[32] Table 2.5, however, notes the growing intensity and competitiveness of slave trading at Douala, from which we may infer (as a few ships' accounts also state) that the prices eventually rose to the levels of the general Atlantic market.

The late but then quite energetic entry of the Duala into the Atlantic slave trading system can be explained to a considerable extent by factors of supply. The majority of slaves exported via Douala originated in the Cameroon Grassfields to the northwest of the Littoral. This is one of the most densely settled regions of West Africa, which developed an internal system for exploiting surplus population by exporting unlucky individuals into the Atlantic slave markets via both the Cameroon estuary and the Cross river route to Old Calabar.[33] The slave trade thus marks the first phase of a movement of peoples from the Grassfields (generally referred to as Bamileke) to the rather thinly populated coastal areas. This migration would continue well beyond the slave trade era, through many other forms of *le dynamisme Bamiléké*, as one of the major themes in Duala and general Cameroonian history.

The estimates of the numbers of slaves exported through Douala during the entire period of this commerce is presented in table 2.5 on a rather tentative basis. The problems with deriving statistics from the available documents are discussed in the comments column of the table itself. The data do clearly indicate that the bulk of this trade took place between 1760 and 1807 with a significant tail in the period between abolition and 1860, when the general Atlantic slave trade came to an end. The estimated Cameroon total, even at its highest range of 46,000, does not represent a very significant portion of the general Atlantic slave trade (11.5–12 million) or even of the estimates for the less intensive trans-Saharan human exports during the same period (1.5–2 million), which also drew on the Cameroon Grassfields.[34] Still, for Cameroon, which could not have had a population of more than 2 million at the time, this figure (which must be at least doubled for the Grassfields slaves sold through Old Calabar) represents a substantial drain. Even if we assume that political and demographic pressure on the Grassfields would have produced some kind of migration without the pull of the slave trade, the settlement of a greater number of these peoples in the Littoral (where, as later nineteenth- and twentieth-century developments show, there was plenty of room for them) would have produced a very different pattern of development than what occurred in the later eighteenth and early nineteenth centuries.

For the Duala themselves, the slave trade did not represent a demographic loss as we can assume that even in this period a considerable number of imported slaves also stayed within the coastal region. Since the Duala in this period probably numbered slightly less than the 20,000 who were counted at the end of the nineteenth century (see below), the revenues generated by the sale of something like 675 slaves per annum, plus significant (if not enumerated) amounts of ivory, must have provided dramatic new levels of wealth. The formerly impoverished fishermen of Piti had now become the major economic force in their portion of Western Africa. We must now inquire into the means by which such material good fortune was sustained, expanded, and absorbed into the existing political and social organization.

Table 2.5. *The Cameroon[1] slave trade, 1600–1860*

	Dates	No. of voyages	No. of slaves	Comments
A. Data: 1600–1750[1]				
1. General descriptions	1600s			See table 2.3; the accounts referred to here describe a small slave trade but give no statistics.
2. Dutch West India Co.[2]	1637–45	?	432	Slaves from Cameroons and Rio del Rey reported from Gold Coast (Ghana) posts, where they were transshipped to the New World.
3. Account of the Limits and Trade of the Royal African Company[3]	c. 1672	?	?	Includes "the Bite, whither many ships are sent to trade at New and Old Calabar for slaves and teeth, which are there to be had in great plenty, and also in the rivers Cameroons and Gaboons which are near, but no factories, those places being very unhealthy."
4. Middleburgh Com. Co.[4]	1732–50	5	17	Voyages primarily for ivory; captains instructed to sell slaves to other nationalities to make room for tusks.
1. Middleburgh Com. Co.	1750–56	5	62	See previous comment.
2. N.Y. Sloop "Polly"[5]	1755	1	c. 30	Arrives in Charleston, S.C. with slaves and redwood.
3. Liverpool Port Records	1755–59	5	710	This is the largest single set of statistics available. However the information is based upon announced destinations and official capacities of each ship; some of these ships may never have reached Cameroon, and many probably took less slaves there than indicated.[19] Moreover, the years covered here are those of relatively high general slave trading rates; we have no continuous data for Cameroon in the low periods of 1776–82, 1793. On the other hand, the list does not include the less numerous but still significant non-Liverpool ships buying slaves here (cf. B4–7 below).[20] On balance, the totals here should be somewhat discounted.
	1760–76[11]	58	13,810	
	1784–87[12]	19	4,920	
	1798[13]	2	565	
	1799[14]	1	161	
	1806–7[15]	10	2,685	

Source	Year	Ships	Slaves	Notes
4. General observations[6]	1752–91	32	?	Ships reported in various sources as slaving at Cameroons and Bimbia but without statistics. It should be noted that at least 10 of these (plus all 4 vessels in B6) are not from Liverpool.
5. Davenport Papers[7]	1765–84	26 (15)	3,430	The 15 of these voyages that report ships from Cameroons selling slaves in the West Indies are our most reliable single source of data. However, they do not account for slave deaths in the middle passage nor is it always clear that all the slaves sold actually came from Cameroon.
6. Rogers Papers[8]	1785–90	4 (1)	232	?Our only non-Liverpool (Rogers was a Bristol merchant) series and the only full account of slave purchasing in Douala and Bimbia (the final cargo included another 47 slaves from Old Calabar). Also reports 100 slave deaths on another, unnamed, ship.
7. Anonymous observations[9]	1782	4	1,424	British ships at Cameroon. The account also indicates that in 1782 and 1783 respectively 339 and 331 slaves were "buried" in Cameroon.
	1783	2	857	
8. Parliamentary Papers	1770–72[16]	2	360	Reports of 1770–72 are of purchases before crossing, based on memory. 1789–1806 are West Indian arrival records; figures marked with an asterisk include mortality in the middle passage, which varies from 5% to 34%. Thus the 7 1789–90 voyages are undercounted. However, other voyages may be overcounted because they included slaves not purchased in Cameroon.[21] At the same time the list cannot be considered exhaustive for Cameroon trade since, in most years, the African ports of half or more of the ships are not given.
	1789	3	408	
	1790	4	782	
	1791[17]	3	906*	
	1792	1	300*	
	1793[18]	1	322*	
	1797	1	277*	
	1798	1	279*	
	1799	1	138*	
	1804	1	245*	

Table 2.5. (*cont.*)

	Dates	No. of voyages	No. of slaves	Comments
9. Illegal slave trade[10]	1815–37	21 (23)	5,331+	Ships reported (usually captured) by the British Royal Navy. Because Douala and Bimbia were particularly visible to British patrols in this period, the 21 cargoes listed probably constitute our most reliable large set. However they are also unrepresentative: the ships were not British and had to deal with new conditions of illegal slaving. In estimating the total scale of slaving in this period, account must also be taken of 2 ships with unknown numbers in the reported series and a few slavers who must have entirely escaped the very imperfect system of British detection, especially between 1808 and 1815. Moreover, we have evidence of small amounts of continued Cameroon slave exporting for at least 4 years after 1837.[22] Thus a more realistic total for the illegal slave trade is 6,500–7,000.

C. Estimates

1. Ships per annum (1760–1807): 3.5

B3	1760–75	16 years	56 voyages
B7	1782–83	2 years	6 voyages
B3	1785–86	2 years	14 voyages
B8	1791	1 year	6 voyages
B3	1798–99	2 years	3 voyages
B3	1806–7	2 years	10 voyages
aggregate	25		95 = 3.8 p.a.

This calculation is based mainly on Liverpool port records and only for years in which reports seem to be complete. There is thus an under-count, due to the omission of non-Liverpool ships but also an over-count due to Liverpool ships that may not have arrived in Cameroon and known years of low general slave trade (1776–81, 1793) that are not reported. Thus the final working figure has been adjusted downward.

2. Slaves per ship (1760–1807): 245

B3a	1760–76	13,810	slaves on	58 ships = 238.1
B7	1782–83	2,281	slaves on	6 ships = 380.2
B3b	1784–87	4,920	slaves on	19 ships = 272.1
B3c	1798–1807	3,411	slaves on	13 ships = 262.4
B5	1765–84	3,430	slaves on	15 ships = 228
B6	1790	232	slaves on	1 ship = 232
B8a	1770–72	360	slaves on	2 ships = 180
B8b	1789–1804	3,775*	slaves on	16 ships = 235.9 (*adjusted for mortality undercount)
B9	1815–37	5,331	slaves on	21 ships = 253.9
aggregate		37,550		151 = 248.6

A reduced aggregate average appears more realistic than the one actually calculated for the following reasons: (1) the largest component of this data set (B3) is probably an exaggerated capacity estimate; (2) the entire eighteenth century series is somewhat weighted towards higher tonnage/capacity Liverpool vessels.[23]

3. Total estimate: 46,000–56,000[24]
1760–1807: 3.5 ships p.a. at 245 slaves per ship = 857.5 slaves per annum
48 years at 857.5 slaves per annum = 41,160 (37,000–45,000)

1808–1860 (see B9): 6,500–7,000
1750–59 (B1–B3 = 100 p.a.) 1,000
1600–1750 (A = 10–20 p.a.) 1,500–3,000

4. Cameroon as percentage of total slave trade:[25]

	Cameroon p.a.	Atlantic p.a. (Cameroon %)	Guinea p.a. (Cameroon %)
1760–1807	857.5	56,805 (1.5%)	33,082 (2.6%)
1811–1837	255	56,056 (0.6%)	20,360 (1.3%)

Table 2.5. (cont.)

[1] The data presented here is based mainly on voyages to "Cameroons," which probably means Douala, as well as some documents that refer explicitly to Bimbia and (much less frequently) Rio del Rey.

[2] Ernest van den Boogaart and Pieter C. Emmer, "The Dutch Participation in the Atlantic Slave Trade, 1596–1650," in Henry A. Gemery and Jan S. Hogendorn (eds.), The Uncommon Market: Essays in the Economic History of the Atlantic Slave Trade (New York, 1979), 360; some seventeenth-century accounts do not distinguish Rio del Rey from Old Calabar but this one has a separate (and very large) entry for "Calabari;" more material on the Cameroon slave trade could probably be found in the archives of the various Dutch West India Companies, but work done on these sources indicates that such traffic was quite limited: Johannes Menne Postma, The Dutch in the Atlantic Slave Trade, 1600–1815 (Cambridge: Cambridge University Press, 1990), 106–8.

[3] Great Britain, Public Record Office, Calendar of State Papers, Colonial Series, vol. 7 (London: HMSO, 1889), 413.

[4] Austen and Jacobs, "Dutch Trading Voyages," 10–12.

[5] Philip Hamer (ed), The Papers of Henry Laurens (Columbia: U. of S. Carolina, 1968), vol. 1, 295.

[6] Sources include MCC (see Austen and Jacobs, "Dutch Trading Voyages,") and various documents cited in notes 14–16, 18 below; it should be noted that there are no references to slaves from Cameroon in the very exhaustive work of Jean Mettas, Repertoire des Expéditions Négrières françaises au XVIIIieme siècle, 2 vols. (Paris: Société Française d'Histoire d'Outre-Mer, 1978, 1984).

[7] William Davenport Papers, University of Keele Library, account books of voyages of ships Badger, Fox, Henry, King of Prussia, Preston, William (copies of relevant sections provided by James Rawley of the University of Nebraska); see also, David Richardson, "Profits in the Liverpool Slave Trade: the Accounts of William Davenport," in Anstey and Hair, 60–90.

[8] James Rogers Papers, PRO, Chancery Masters Exhibit C. 107, especially Bundles 5 (1) and 10 re voyage of brig Sarah to Bimbia and Douala (photocopies as well as catalogue of contents provided by the Perkins Library, Duke University).

[9] John Rylands Library, Manchester, MSS. 517, f. 2 (provided by David Richardson).

[10] Great Britain, Foreign Office records (data compiled and supplied by David Eltis).

[11] Great Britain, Public Records Office, BT 6/3 (data compiled and supplied by David Richardson, University of Hull).

[12] Liverpool Record Office, Holt and Greeson Papers 942 HOL, Vol. 10, 449–88 (data compiled and supplied by David Richardson).

[13] Gomer Williams, The Liverpool Privateers with an Account of the Liverpool Slave Trade (London: Heinemann, 1897), 381–5.

[14] A Genuine "Dickey Sam," An Historical Account of the Liverpool African Slave Trade (Liverpool: Bowker, 1884), 122–3.

[15] Gore's Liverpool Directory; for the Year, 1807, appendix, 97–100.

[16] Great Britain, Parliament, House of Commons, Sessional Papers (hereafter PP), 1789, XXV (635–645), Minutes of Evidence Presented before the Committee on the Abolition of the Slave Trade, Testimony of Thomas King, London, 232–38. See also general observations of ships in Cameroon in ibid. XXVI (646A), Part 1, Report of the Lords of the Committee in Council, 50–58.

[17] In 1791 six ships are reported as trading in Cameroon but without statistics of slaves purchased, Great Britain, House of Lords, Sessional Papers. 1798–99, II, 338–46 (data supplied by David Richardson).

[18] PP 1792, Accounts and Papers, XXXV, 767, 1–7; ibid, 1795–96, XLII, 849, 1–10; for 1790 3 ships from "Africa" are assumed to be from Cameroon because they were described as buying slave there by the captain of the *Sarah* (see note 8 above).

[19] For six of the 1784–87 voyages Richardson (see note 7) provides data on West Indian arrival cargoes; all are below the projected Cameroon capacity, four of them by very wide margins (16% to 43%). These disparities could be accounted for entirely by losses of slaves on the coast and in the middle passage (see B7 and B8) but it is more likely that such high numbers in a random sample (the average loss from West Africa in this period was below 10%) indicate smaller purchases than estimated. See also note 20 below.

[20] D. P. Lamb, "Volume and Tonnage of the Liverpool Slave Trade, 1772–1807," in Roger Anstey and P. E. H. Hair (eds.), *Liverpool, the African Slave Trade, and Abolition* (Liverpool: Historic Society of Lancashire and Cheshire, 1976), 91–112.

[21] Comments on B6 above and the account of the Boston sloop *Friend*, which in 1768 was abandoned at Cameroon and there transferred its cargo of 63 Gold Coast slaves to a Liverpool ship (included in B3) for transport to Barbados, Elizabeth Donnan, *Documents Illustrative of the Slave Trade to America* (New York: Octagon, 1969), II, 74–5.

[22] For details on this point and the general process of British abolitionist efforts, see below, the first section of chapter 3.

[23] According to Lamb, "Volume and Tonnage," 98–103, Liverpool vessels increased their tonnage after 1776, as reflected in figures for this period in C2; however, the series under-represents non-Liverpool vessels both in the generally lower-capacity pre-1776 period (when London and Bristol had an over 40% share of the slave trade) and between 1776 and 1804 (the share of these ports declined significantly only after 1792), when their average tonnage increased at a smaller rate than that of Liverpool ships.

[24] We are providing a range of estimates here since the data are, at best, incomplete and the actual figures calculated represent both an assumption of slave trading which is not reported and (as indicated in several places above) a conservative treatment of those figures that are available.

[25] Atlantic 1761–80 and West African figures: Paul E. Lovejoy, "The Volume of the Atlantic Slave Trade: a Synthesis," *JAH* 23 (1982): 473–501. Atlantic 1781–1840: David Eltis, *Economic Growth and the Ending of the Atlantic Slave Trade* (New York: Oxford University Press, 1987), 249.

European trade and Duala politics

From European sources we can trace not only shifts in the type, quantity and price of goods traded at Douala, but also something of the mechanisms for managing overseas commerce and the tensions that arose when these devices broke down. Evidence for such tensions coincides with a phase in the Duala oral tradition that chronicles internal conflicts and major political realignments. The collation of these two forms of evidence provides a preliminary understanding of the changes involved in this first stage of a major middleman role and also something of the Duala perception of the process.

The detailed records of eighteenth-century Dutch ivory trade cited in table 2.4 reveal a rather simple and straightforward bartering process. The Europeans paid a certain amount of customs duty to open the trade; ivory was then brought on board and exchanged for various assortments of imported goods. Reports of occasional haggling and the pattern of prices (a general rise and higher payments per pound for larger tusks) indicate a normal market process. The only difficulties reported were shortages of ivory or brief delays in providing it, which were weighed by the ships' captains against the cost of remaining in the estuary and the possibly better opportunities at nearby ports, such as Gabon. It is significant to note that, in comparison to a later period, the Middelburgh merchants never seem to have considered advancing trade goods to the Duala in order to procure ivory still held by other Africans in the interior.

The Dutch sources say nothing about these interior sources, although one of their maps labels a small waterway leading to the Mungo River as "Tanden Gat" (Tusk Creek).[35] However, the general impression conveyed is that ivory was not too difficult or complicated to procure. Indeed, in the more complicated negotiations of the subsequent slave trade, ivory tusks were sometimes given to European captains as a form of collateral against trade goods that had been advanced for the eventual production of human cargo. Ivory probably did not reach the Duala from any great distance during this period since its sources do not seem to have been under the control of any other specialized long-distance traders such as the Hausa, who dominated the flow of this commodity to the coast in the latter part of the nineteenth century (see below chapter 3). The great advantage of ivory, however procured, over later export commodities was that it could be carried and stored according to any schedule that suited the existing market. Slaves and palm oil were less easily managed commodities, thus producing greater problems for large scale barter arrangements.[36]

The evidence for complication in slave trading that foreshadows the better-documented later difficulties of the palm oil and kernel trade consists mainly of complaints about credit arrangements. There are general indications of problems of this kind in the instructions given British captains during the later eighteenth century, admonishing them not to advance goods to Africans.[37] We know from the general history of Afro-European trade in this period that credit was a necessity for procuring slaves. This situation applied particularly in the Bight of Biafra, which included Cameroon, the main source of West African slaves during the later eighteenth century but a region where Europeans had established no permanent on-shore trading stations.[38]

For Cameroon, we have two detailed accounts of trade for 1788 and 1790 which make it very clear that ivory tusks as well as human "pawns" from the Duala and Bimbia population were regularly taken by European merchants as guarantees for credit advances.[39] The 1788 account also reports in some detail the measures taken by British captains to speed up the delivery of slaves, including one ship that sailed off with its Duala pawns and sold them in the West Indies. The Duala, in order to force the return of their own people, took a number of captains from other British ships captive.[40]

Obviously the supply of slaves to Europeans presented the Duala with far greater problems than the supply of ivory. The slaves exported via the Cameroon coast came from a long distance inland, well beyond the limits of navigability of the rivers within the Littoral trading system (and the Duala, by the early nineteenth century, had not even reached the farthest navigable points of the Mungo and the Wouri).[41] Moreover, at the point where Grassfields slaves entered the coastal zone, they could be moved either southeast to Douala or southwest (by the longer but more direct Cross River route) to Old Calabar. Given this competitive and remote market for the purchase of commodities which were, after all, human beings and not inanimate goods, it is not surprising that advances of goods were needed to bring slaves to the coast. It is no less surprising that the slaves were often not delivered on schedule, leading to changes in the assigned destinies of ships and disputes over the payment of credit.

It is also highly probable that disputes on the coast were paralleled in the relations between the Duala and secondary middlemen in the interior. The known delays on the coast must have been linked to similar problems further along the chain of transactions. In their oral traditions the Duala and interior peoples still preserve accounts of quarrels over marketing arrangements. The most famous deals with a Pongo giant, Malobe, who is said to have threatened the Dibombari market until he was defeated by Engomga a champion recruited by the Duala from among the Bakoko of Japoma. Although it is a bit difficult to relate to a specific period of Duala history, the story is remembered in sufficient detail among various groups to be based on some real incident (or repeated set of incidents) before the period of oil trade and a continuous European presence. The story always concludes with Malobe being sold into slavery.[42] Even if details of this last point and the connection of the entire story with the founding of the Ngondo are questionable,[43] the fact that some Duala slaves came from among related inland peoples suggests that trading relations occasionally broke down, leading to the sale of pawns or the capture of individuals through seizure or full-scale warfare. As will be seen in examining the nineteenth-century palm products trade, such conflicts were certainly common in a later phase of overseas commerce.

The main Duala oral traditions reach their greatest level of narrative intensity in describing events that take place in the fourth through eighth generations of descent from Mbedi (see table 2.6). Using terms derived from the analysis of similar traditions among other coastal peoples in Western Africa, we may designate this sequence as a "middle period" between the somewhat vague era of the founding ancestors and the time when political and social structures familiar to the narrator are already in place. The middle period encompasses the immediate formation of this contemporary order and is thus full of references to extremely significant historical events, yet often presents them in terms that are not entirely plausible and (in variants of the tradition) contradict one another.[44]

To achieve a critical historical understanding of this climactic phase of the early Duala past, we must first restate the story as it is understood within the tradition, and then confront this account with the now quite considerable body of relevant (if not explicitly parallel) data from contemporaneous European observations. The major underlying theme in all instances is the division of the Duala polity into its two major segments, the Bonanjo (Bell) and Bonambela (Akwa). The conflicts between these two groupings, linked to critical defections among sub-lineages supposedly subordinate to each, constitute the major motif of nineteenth-century Duala politics.

In table 2.1 the division between the Bell and Akwa is traced back to the fourth and fifth generations after Mbedi when the descendants of Njo a Mase (5B) and Ngie a Mulobe (4A), also known as Mbela (= "Eagle"), formed two separate lines. This particular genealogy has been chosen because it includes the names vital to all versions of Duala history. However, there is no way of deriving an objectively "true" account from the many recorded traditions (see table 2.2[45]) nor is it useful for present purposes to lay out all the variations. The important point is that the different sources are in agreement over the major events and personalities leading to a definitive split of what is remembered as a previously single Duala polity.

Table 2.6. *Oral traditions and the Duala crisis*

	Bell	Akwa
Flad (Bell)	Bele a Do is peaceful, but Priso is violent (cites canoe song: "Priso a Doo, here comes warfare"). Priso robs everyone, finally killed at Bimbia	Kuo is irreligious, separates from brother Njo, marries into "subjugated population"; Ngando serves as house servant for Bele to learn white men's trade
Halbing (Bell)	No Priso story. Bele educates Ngando but protests his elevation	Kuo is demi-slave (*etumbi*) Ngando is greedy and usurps "King" title
Ebding, 1 (Akawa?)	Very long story; Bele is adopted son of Doo Makongo, seized for unpaid debt from interior. Betrays Priso a Doo Makongo (great warrior and thief) to Europeans, flees to Bonaberi, populates it with Priso's captives but succeeds to chieftainship	Nothing on Akwa
Ebding, 2 (Bell)	Nothing	ditto
Ebding, 3 (Bell)	Priso kills a European and Europeans kill Sopo a Lobe	ditto
Ekolo	Same story; Doo chooses Bele because of Priso's horrible behavior; P. forces B. to flee to Bonaberi. Later Bele and Priso ally against Bakoko of Bonaberi. Bele trade prospers vs. Priso	ditto
Mpundu	Akwa descent = direct from founding line, w/o "slave"	All tradition is Akwa, no conflict
IBB	Same Bele-Priso story but Doo complicit in betrayal of Priso to Europeans (*nb*: nail in ear to mast). Priso killed by mukwiri at Subu. Bele demands north of Subu as recompense	Mapoka 2 sons: Njo = legitimate, Kuo "considered to be a slave." Ngando forbidden to speak Basaa and insults Bele as slave and Bele son threatens him, recalls his servile ancestry → separation (Ngondo motif stressed)
Ngaka	Usual story; includes Ngando residence chez Bele and complicated marriage politics	Njie = powerful; Mapoka gives Kuo to Basaa ("bakom") as part of marriage agreement. Kwane succession problem → Ngando

Note: For full references to the sources cited, see table 2.2.

The key figures in this change are: on the Bell side, the two sons of Doo a Makongo (7B), Priso (8P) and Bele (8B); and on the Akwa side, Ngando a Kwa (8A). Doo was apparently recognized as the senior chief of his generation and Priso, as his eldest son, should logically have succeeded him. Bele and Ngando, on the other hand, both bear the ultimate Duala stigma of possible servile origin. Bele is universally acknowledged as the natural offspring of a Mungo man from the interior rather than of Doo; the latter adopted Bele after seizing his mother (or pregnant mother-to-be) in compensation for an unpaid debt: thus Bele's epithet "*yom'a moto a Mongo ewu onola etom* (miserable Mungo, paid as a debt)."[46]

In Ngando's case, his grandfather Kuo (6A) was either an adopted slave of Mapoka a Ngie (5A), or connected through maternal descent, marriage or residence, to a Basaa community. On this basis the Bonanjo coined the more widely used epithet "*Bonakuo Bakom* [the Akwa [descendants of Kuo] are slaves]." At the time of Doo the most powerful figure among the Bonambela appears to have been not Ngando's father or grandfather but rather his great uncle, Kwane a Ngie (5D).

Priso apparently lost his birthright because of his overly violent behavior, which included robbing and killing European merchants. The Europeans are even said to have imprisoned him for a time, with the connivance of his brother (and possibly father). Bele himself was forced to flee Priso either before or after being named successor by the dying Doo. He moved from the main, left bank, Douala settlement to the right bank of the Wouri (now named after him Bonaberi = Bona Bele).[47] Eventually he re-established himself at the present left bank Bell center of Bonanjo while Priso and his successors retained control over their own neighboring and supposedly subordinate area, Bonapriso.

Ngando is said to have begun his career in the household of Bele at Bonaberi. His return to the left bank of the Wouri is connected with the early death of Ewonde (6D) son of the powerful Kwane. Ngando not only claimed the Bonambela succession but, probably in reaction to the problems in the succession to Doo, now insisted on equal status to Bele. Meanwhile Kwane's line created a secondary Bonambela position for itself through Ewonde's daughter, Kanya married an Abo captive/immigrant, Enjobe (7D); their son Ebele (8D), become the first ruler of Bonebele ("Bona Ebele") or, in Pidgin, "Deido," which eventually become the third major trading center on the left bank of the Wouri.[48]

Although the oral accounts of these conflicts all center around claims to succession from the founding ancestors, it is clear that the two major winners, Bele and Ngando (to say nothing of Ebele's line), have very compromised genealogies. Their relationships to previous Duala authorities remain important but the decisive element in these struggles is recognition by Europeans. What Doo a Makongo already had and what Ngando a Kwa sought was the title of "King" (*Kine* in Duala[49]) and the possession of a *kalati* (trade book in which written records of credit were kept).

The Europeans represented as conferring these prerogatives in the oral traditions are presented in terms that are often hard to reconcile with written records. For one, almost all these merchants are described as Portuguese.[50] Duala accounts of the first arrival of Europeans (see table 2.2) frequently equate this event with the established Atlantic trade of the eighteenth and nineteenth centuries. The insistence that an early ancestor, Mapoka, was sent to Europe may reflect a real eighteenth or even seventeenth-century occurrence, but could also be based on the only European record of such a journey, which took place in the latter nineteenth century.[51]

European written sources, on the other hand, can be used to confirm the chronology of internal Duala history in this period as well as to illuminate its critical relationship to Atlantic commerce. The surviving records of these foreign traders provide two valuable kinds of information about Douala: the names of prominent local figures at specified moments of observation and, in cases where negotiations of various kinds are detailed, some idea of the relative status of these figures.

For the first 150 years of European–Duala trade, we unfortunately have only one name, Monneba, which ceases to be of any chronological value after its first evocation. Some of the other names on seventeenth-century and early eighteenth-century maps ("Beteba," "Walleba") may be of some significance, but it is difficult to relate them to Duala oral tradition and they may just be "ghost terms" attached to areas around Douala that the Dutch did not actually visit.[52]

From 1788 onward, however, we have working records as well as maps and travel accounts which give us many critical details of internal Duala developments, as well as the related affairs of Bimbia (Isuwu) which became an important (if secondary) Cameroon trading center at this time. The two main Douala records are again the reports of the pawning crisis of 1788 and the account books of the brig *Sarah* in 1790.[53] These indicate that the British recognized one figure in Douala, "King George," as pre-eminent ruler, giving him not only a unique title but a form of customs duties not related to any particular transaction. "George" appears to be Doo a Makongo (7B) since he has beneath him "Preshaw" (Priso a Doo, 8P), "Bell" (Bele a Doo, 8B) and "Peter a doe" (Priso again?).[54]

The other prominent names in these records are "Angua" (1790) or "Quan" (1788), both probably identical with Kwane a Ngie (5D). In the 1788 reports it is "Quan" rather than "the King" who takes the most decisive action in forcing the remaining British captains to seek the return

of Duala pawns from the West Indies. In the very revealing list of payments made by the *Sarah* in 1790, we see a similar pattern: King George is
given the most goods because he is paid both "customs" and a "dash"
(bonus gift) for forty slaves. Angua, however, sells fifty slaves and receives
a much bigger dash than George. "Angua's People" also get quite a
considerable dash. The third largest dash goes to Preshaw and Bell gets a
fairly small amount.

We thus have a rather detailed confirmation of the situation described in
the Duala oral tradition for this crucial period of transition. There is a
single recognized "King" of the Bonanjo line, Doo a Makongo, but his
counterpart from the Bonambela line, Kwane a Ngie, is comparably
prominent in practical affairs, which involve some elements of violence.
There is nothing to indicate, however, the violent role of Priso a Doo.
Moreover, according to the information about Bimbia in the 1790 account
books of the *Sarah* and in Danish negotiations for a plantation off the
coast in 1800[55] the ruler here is either "King Mercer" (Mbimbi, I3?) or
Bimbi Jack (Ngombe Mbimbi, I4) with no mention of Kwane a Ewonde
who was supposedly forced to Bimbia by Priso's actions against the line of
his grandfather, Kwane a Ngie.

The events that disrupted the order of the 1788–90 period are first
referred to by written sources in travel accounts of the early 1800s.[56]
Robertson, reporting on the situation in about 1810, finds only "King
Bell" ruling at Douala. In the period described by Bold (*c.* 1822) there is
already a division between King Bell and King Akwa. Jackson, in the
journal of his 1826 visit to Douala, gives very precise information that may
not be literally accurate, but indicates connections (both substantive and
ideological) between the events described in eighteenth-century documents
and internal Duala change: Bell is now about eighty years old; in 1792,
Bell's unpopular older brother (presumably Priso a Doo) was overthrown
in a very violent episode involving the intervention of European captains;
as a result of the weakened "monarchy" Akwa, in 1814, declared himself
an independent ruler, equivalent (if somewhat junior) to Bell. Jackson also
says that "Preese," a relative of Bell, is carrying on piracy at the entry to
the estuary. Similar piracy (without identification of its perpetrator) is
reported by Homan for 1828. According to Jackson, Bimbia was by this
time under a monarchy related to the Duala, probably that of Bile a
Kwane (8I), the descendant of the formerly senior Bonambela line.

The European documents thus confirm that in the decades spanning the
end of the eighteenth century and beginning of the nineteenth, the Duala
political system underwent a major change, from a single paramountcy to
a situation in which two major and a number of minor segments competed
for power. But the presence of European observers during these events is

not a mere coincidence. We must therefore look next for the connection between the growth of European trade and the shift in Duala political structure.

One of the least plausible elements in the Duala oral tradition is its statements about early encounters with Europeans; nonetheless, the intensification of the narrative in the period beginning with the generations after Njo and Ngie accurately reflects the broad chronology of increased overseas trade from the early eighteenth century. Moreover, from what we know of this trade through European documents, it began to be conducted in a less orderly fashion precisely towards the end of the eighteenth century, when the Duala political system split.

The immediate cause of this disorder was, as already seen, the irregularities in the disbursal and redemption of credit. It was the European traders, far in space and climate from home with their precious trade goods at risk, who were most immediately concerned about credit. As the correspondence already cited indicates (and this theme will echo well into the colonial era of Duala economic affairs), European merchants recognized the riskiness of advancing goods to Africans and, in principle, were all opposed to the practice. However, the market for slaves and ivory in Africa was a very open one, with many British, as well as some continental and American shippers competing for the purchase of goods. Such an atmosphere drove up prices and, in combination with international wars not unconnected to control of the Atlantic sugar system, increased the risks of making no profit on voyages.[57] Thus merchants could neither afford to refuse credit, for fear of losing out to competitors, nor could they easily afford to give it, since a few defaulters could wipe out their entire profit margins, usually not very great in any case. The result was the disorderly trading system described in the documents, with Europeans supporting their commercial claims by sporadic intervention in African politics.[58]

The problems for the Duala in this situation were not identical to those of Europeans. Competition among shippers and high prices meant greater profits for Africans. However the supply of slaves at Douala was limited owing to the distance from the Grassfields sources of major accessible populations, the already mentioned competition for this supply of slaves from Old Calabar, as well as a lesser degree of competition from Bimbia, which reemerged as an alternate Cameroon port sometime after 1759 (the date of the last recorded MCC voyage).

It is not possible to link the resulting conflicts within Douala to the immediate influence of Europeans competing for local trading partners or seeking to enforce credit arrangements. There is simply no evidence for such a direct tie between external and internal affairs even, as will be seen in the next chapter, for the much better documented Duala conflicts of the nineteenth century. What does seem clear is that the relatively peaceful, unheroic character of political and economic life ascribed by the oral tradition to the formative stages of Duala society now shifts into a more violent mode. Priso a Doo represents a warrior figure who is rejected as heir to the senior Bonanjo/Bell line. However, the newer Bonambela/Akwa major segment identifies very consciously with a more violent image of leadership, as symbolized in both the career of Ngando a Kwa and the names of the two most prominent Akwa figures: Mbela ("Eagle") and Ngando ("Caiman/Alligator").[59] The ambivalence with which this violent dimension is incorporated into the tradition suggests that it derives less from Duala conquest of their own environment than from intervention by outsiders, Europeans who could not ultimately be controlled by the Duala. The "heroic era" of Duala history thus presents a heroism of middlemen, who are never fully masters of the worlds they straddle.

Internal development in the formative period: state vs segmentation

The political events discussed in the previous section represent the external dimensions of change: a division of power among African leaders, their relationship to the European presence, and the image of these developments in the public chronicles of the Duala. What we need to examine in the concluding sections of this chapter is the internal dimension of this same change: the structures that link politics to society and the relationship of this system to the Duala role in the interior of the Cameroon Littoral.

Viewed from the exterior, the Duala political system appears to be highly segmentary. Under changing conditions, instead of central institutions becoming stronger, they split into multiple, roughly equivalent, units. To confirm or qualify this impression, however, we have to look more closely at the internal institutions of Duala political life at the level of the entire community, the individual "chiefdoms," and the extended household. To what extent did the changes of the formative period produce stable and effective organization within each of these domains?

This issue has produced a certain amount of controversy in the literature on Duala history. Duala authors argue, with occasional support from European researchers, that there was some form of state in nineteenth-century Douala, focused at the communal level around a central judicial council, the Ngondo, and at the level of chiefdoms around a hierarchy of hereditary offices. Non-Duala scholars (the present authors included) have tended to view the surface of segmentation as an indicator of little real cohesion at either the communal or chiefdom level of Duala political life.

But such an assertion requires the careful examination of arguments for a more centralized system.

The most elaborate of the centralist arguments are made at the communal level around the emergence of the Ngondo as a Duala general assembly or court.[60] According to these accounts, the Ngondo was founded by Ngando a Kwa to deal with the case of the Pongo giant Malobe (see pp. 33–34 above) who had been disturbing inland Duala markets. The other major historical acts attributed to the Ngondo are the trial and execution of Eyum a Ebele (Charley Deido, 9D) in 1876 and the signing by all the major Duala chiefs of the annexation treaty with Germany in 1884. While Harter and Doumbé-Moulongo (a Wuri with Bell connections) content themselves with arguing for an undefined institutional continuity in these (and several other) collective actions by Duala chiefs, a very prominent Akwa intellectual insists that from its creation the Ngondo was surrounded by an elaborate and formal array of offices, rituals and cosmology.[61]

The evidence against any political centralization at the level of the entire Duala community after the division into multiple chiefdoms is of two kinds.[62] In the first place, none of the oral traditions collected before World War II, including two by rather convinced and ideologically articulate Akwa partisans, mentions the Ngondo.[63] Secondly, no references to the Ngondo are found in the observations by Europeans present at the various nineteenth-century events linked to the Ngondo in post-World War II accounts: the execution of Eyum a Ebele, the German annexation, and the various meetings of the "Court of Equity" or "Cameroons Council" by which the British and later German consuls attempted to bring chiefs and European merchants together in some kind of judicial-consultative body (see chapter 3 below). The Ngondo is named after a beach in Douala that separates the Bell and Akwa quarters and where the execution of Eyum Ebele, as well as quite possibly some other collective events, did take place. Its conception as a major communal ruling institution is linked to developments of the 1930s and 40s which will be discussed at considerable length below.

The role of *jengu* in the "revived" Ngondo of the 1940s and afterwards suggests another set of unquestionably very real institutions, the *losango* cult associations, which may have functioned as political instruments cutting across segmentary units within Douala and possibly even to other related inland groups. Cults of various kinds did play this role among the coastal trading peoples and their inland trading partners in eastern Nigeria with one, *ekpe*, even extending into western Cameroon via the Cross River almost to the Duala trading zone.[64] However, the *losango* of the precolonial Littoral seem only to have accentuated the division between Bell and Akwa within Douala, to say nothing of freemen and slaves, and

Duala and interior peoples. There is no evidence that they functioned to regulate trade or other public affairs and much indication that the ideology of the *jengu* cult, from which the Akwa appear to have been excluded, reinforced the fishing-is-to-farming as slave-is-to-free equation that has already been cited in describing the construction of Duala identity.[65]

If it is difficult to find any institutions at the communal level that held Duala society together in a formal manner, what of the units that emerged from each stage of segmentation, the chiefdoms? Again, there is a set of Duala authors, narrower but with a longer lineage than those arguing for the historical role of the Ngondo, who insist that despite the widespread adaptation of the European term "King" the Duala had their own titles and offices of rulership. The more recent authors dealing with the Ngondo have also elaborated their notion of the role and structure of these offices although the common denominator of all accounts is that they expressed a relationship of succession to the supreme political position of *mokoledi* or *niaziam*. Again, before the first recorded reference to these offices in 1908 there is no mention of them in oral traditions nor do they appear in European accounts of Duala political organization at any period. When first asserted by Mpondo Akwa they were disputed by a German Catholic missionary linguist, Father Hermann Nekes, who claimed that no contemporary Dualas had ever heard of them.[66] The circumstance under which Mpondo probably invented these titles, especially the patently European one of *biscompta*, will be examined in chapter 4 below.

It is only when we move from the level of the chiefdom to that of the extended household that we find a set of terms and relationships which seem to have governed the actual organization of precolonial Duala life. This concept of the *mboa* with its constituent units of smaller households built around wives, junior sons and various groupings of slaves has been well described by Bekombo and others.[67] The problem here is how we can make use of these concepts to understand the operations of systems that obviously maintained some kind of coherence beyond the level of what is normally understood as a household. The terms used for more powerful figures in the nineteenth century are confusing: "King" and "chief" imply a hierarchy of recognition by Europeans, a matter of great importance for the Duala, but these titles indicate nothing about the internal institutional content of the positions so designated. The Duala *sango* (usually translated as "lord") can apply to anything from the Judaeo-Christian-Muslim God to the head of an insignificant household. *Janea* or *mwanedi*, usually translated as "chief," can likewise apply to a very local authority or the superior relationship of one "King" to another.

While there are certainly some notions of what constitutes a legitimate ruler over a large segment of Duala society (to be discussed in the next chapter in relation to free-slave populations), we have to accept the fact that virtually no formally articulated institutions did separate the most insignificant *sango mboa* from a ruler such as King Bell or King Akwa: thus the constant process of segmentation. Nonetheless, the scale of followers over whom the major rulers could exercise command clearly distinguished them from mere household heads. Perhaps the most useful definition of such a political system is Jan Vansina's application to this entire African region of the South Pacific anthropological term "Big Man."[68] The successful Duala leaders were those who could mobilize an entourage of followers, both kin and strangers, slave and free, for purposes of long-distance canoe trading inland and negotiation with Europeans at Douala. This definition implies that there was no need for a state among the Duala. However, as will be seen in the next chapter, the absence of any central political authority was to cause great difficulties in the mid- and late-nineteenth century. Moreover, the insistence by many Duala historians on greater precolonial centralization than the documentary evidence seems to support suggests at least a retrospective indigenous recognition of such a need. We thus have to take a final look at the formative stage of Duala history and, in comparison with other similar African societies, inquire under what conditions a state might have developed here and why it ultimately did not.

Early Duala political development in comparative perspective

Despite the very controversial nature of the literature on early state formation in Africa, it is possible to identify four conditions which have been utilized most effectively (often in combination) to explain such change: (1) the pressure of populations upon subsistence resources; (2) the threat or reality of external conquest; (3) diffusion of cultural models from pre-existing states; (4) control over markets for high value surplus goods.[69] Of these conditions, the first three clearly do not apply to the Duala and can be discussed very briefly. The last, however, seems to describe their middleman position and thus its failure to induce fuller state formation is worth more lengthy contemplation.

The migration of the Duala from Piti did possibly result from a subsistence crisis, but one that was resolved without the need for major social change. New fishing areas were easily found by the Duala and those other Sawa peoples who actually migrated. Even during the later processes of segmentation within Douala, new chiefdoms could easily find empty land somewhere along the banks of the Wouri and thus replicate the society they had left rather than finding new means to control the same resources. Even assuming a limited amount of space available for continuing the form of food production to which the Duala were committed, the population of Douala does not appear to have grown very much during the nineteenth century (and presumably in the immediately preceding period) due to the health and fertility costs of an urban existence under African epidemiological conditions.[70]

The Duala movement into Basaa territory cannot be characterized as any form of "conquest," nor were the Duala afterwards threatened with domination by any other peoples. Despite some of the violent animal symbolism attached to the Bonambela lineage conquest is thus a theme notably absent from Duala culture in both its organizational and expressive dimensions.

The Wouri estuary is also distant from major sites of African state formation, such as the Sudan, Benin, or the Congo Basin, which might have provided models for political centralization even without an intense impetus from local social needs. Europe, by the sixteenth and seventeenth centuries, did of course possess highly developed political institutions and the prestige of the Pidgin/English title "King" among the Duala has already been noted. However the representatives of European culture who first reached Douala were not state agents but the captains and crews of mutually competing sailing vessels who offered a model of political behavior closer to segmentary anarchy than centralization. Attempts by other Europeans, from the mid nineteenth century, to impose elements of their political culture on the Duala raised further problems, as will be seen in the next chapter.

The Duala did, however, occupy a strategic point in a major long-distance trading system and the failure of this condition to bring about more intense political development, while not exactly a paradox, does require some explanation. The relationship between politics and the political economy of Atlantic African trade is best explored by comparing the Duala situation to that of other societies engaged in similar riverain commerce from the Niger Delta to the Congo River.[71] Among these societies it is possible to observe a scale of political centralization that declines as we move east and south. The Kalabari, Nembe (Brass), and Ibani (Bonny) traders of the Niger Delta did develop kingship with some structure of authority at the communal level. The Efik of Old Calabar and their Igbo trading partners had no central monarchy, but used cult organizations (*ekpe* and, for the Igbo, the Aro shrine) as a basis for some form of collective governance at both the communal and the trade network level. At the other extreme, the Bobangi of the Congo River were organized only into "Big Man" canoe units whose relative power rose and fell entirely according to their fluctuating commercial successes. The Duala fall somewhere between the middle and the bottom of this scale since they had no articulated central political institutions but also retained some sense of genealogical continuity in the leadership and the constellation of their dominant segments. Moreover, as will be seen in the next chapter, the social mobility of Duala slaves was ultimately limited.

It is possible to correlate these differences in political development with varying conditions of commerce.[72] Such a comparison does not fully explain the distinctions between African cases (particularly between the Duala and the Bobangi), and in the following chapter more attention will be given to cultural factors which, in certain respects, operated independently to shape responses to economic needs and opportunities in these areas. However for the formative period, when it is difficult to establish any chronology for beliefs or even kinship structures, the economic side of the comparison can be developed most easily.

Jones and Horton argue that the presence of European traders, offering income and status to African authorities, provided the key impetus towards political centralization in the Niger Delta. However, we have seen that for the Duala, and also for the Efik, competition among merchant ships could just as easily encourage segmentation. Within the economic sphere, therefore, the critical variable determining the direction of political change seems to have been relations with the internal rather than the external sphere of middleman operations.

As already noted in discussing fishing in the estuary, the enterprise of controlling an inland zone of exploitation can be seen as both a collective undertaking involving the community as a single entity, or an area of competition between different segments with their separate canoe-based organizations. Whether a society stressed one or the other of these approaches to trade depended upon both the geography of the region being exploited and – more directly – upon the degree of competition from any neighboring community. In the case of the Niger Delta Kalabari, Nembe, Bonny, and various lesser trading communities were in intense competition with one another for control of mutually-accessible waterways and this conflict forced each "city state" to maintain some degree of unified organization around a monarch. The contradiction, in later-nineteenth century Bonny, between economic success and political-economic status led to a kind of segmentation, when the slave merchant Ja Ja withdrew from the town. However, he immediately established an entirely new settlement, Opobu, where he revived the role of monarch.[73]

In the Cross River region between the Niger Delta and the Wouri estuary lay Old Calabar which, by the late seventeenth century, dominated local overseas trade. However, control of the densely populated inland region did lead to conflicts. Along the western axis of this trade, the Aro Igbo were able to meet the challenge of coastal incursions by forming their own proto-statal ritual-trading network.[74] To the east, along the Cross River itself, Efik traders from Old Calabar overcame the political factionalism of their home base by submitting to the discipline of the *ekpe* cult organization, which was also joined (and possibly even formed) by inland trading partners.[75]

The Duala interior trading situation did not demand any such collective controls. In diametrical opposition to the Niger Delta, the Duala enjoyed virtually exclusive access to an extensive network of rivers connecting the coast to the interior. Seen from an historian's wide-ranging perspective, there was clearly a major level of competition between Douala and Old Calabar for the slave exports of the Cameroon Grassfields. But, given the geographic separation of the ports and even of the Cross River from the Mungo (especially before the Duala reached the navigable limits of the latter), there was no consciousness of such rivalry on either side.[76] Bimbia, by the later eighteenth century, represented some alternative to Douala for traders coming to Cameroon. However, Bimbia's location did not give it the same access as Douala to the main waterways bringing commodities from inland and, as indicated in both oral traditions (Priso a Doo's death at Bimbia) and accounts of European observers (especially Jackson in 1826) relations between the two communities seem to have been peaceful.

In principle, the Duala might have shared a common interest in pushing their canoe expeditions up to the limits of navigability of each of the main Littoral rivers. As will be seen, this did become an issue in the nineteenth century, although one pursued by individual Duala segments rather than the community under any single leadership. This lack of collective action is not surprising, given the passive nature of the threat from the inland groups, which were far too small to compete with the Duala beyond their own individual territories. Moreover, the multiplicity of Cameroon coastal rivers allowed a geographic expression of Douala domestic segmentation to extend itself into the hinterland. The fact that the Bells specialized in trade along the Mungo, which offered the richest commodities with the least effective indigenous resistance to Duala expansion, would have consequences in the nineteenth and twentieth centuries that will have to be explored later. But in the formative period of the Duala middleman role, the physical and human structure of the Littoral provided no incentive to political centralization.

Compared with the trading societies of the neighboring Nigerian coast and hinterland, the Duala transformation from fishermen to middlemen seems not to have been a very intensive process. There is a neat match between the lower statistical contribution to the slave trade and the limited development of any centralized political institutions. On the other hand, the more relaxed response of the Duala to their role as intermediaries in

Atlantic trade is also a function of their more assured control over coastal access to the interior of Cameroon than was the case with any of the Eastern Nigerian trading states. As a result the Duala, despite their small numbers, would survive much more effectively into the colonial and post-colonial period as a major element in territorial/national development, and thus provide us with a unique opportunity to explore the ramifications of the middleman phenomenon.

3   Hegemony without control: the Duala, Europeans and the Littoral hinterland in the era of legitimate/free trade, *c.* 1830–1884

For our understanding of the Duala as a middleman community, the nineteenth century is the classical era. In strictly chronological terms, these decades constitute a middle period between the establishment of an autonomous Duala trading position on the Cameroon coast and its displacement by European colonial rule. It is also from this time, as indicated previously, that most of our information about the precolonial Littoral world is derived. Finally, the nineteenth century saw the full articulation of a hierarchical structure descending from Europeans who crossed the ocean, through the Duala on the coast and the Littoral river system, down to the peoples of the Littoral hinterland.

During the nineteenth century the volume of trade and its spatial boundaries constantly expanded, with the initiative always reflecting the hegemonic position of Europeans over Duala and Duala over the interior. At the same time no political structures evolved to convert this hegemony into orderly control over any of the key points of commercial exchange. But in the complex discourse of middleman historiography, this very absence of control and order has been converted into another form of hegemony, that of cultural identity. From a European perspective, the nineteenth-century Duala represent a failure of legitimacy and freedom: they could not conform to the model of capitalistic self-management proffered by post-slave trade liberal policies and thus had eventually to be incorporated via colonialism into the political system of their overseas trading partners. At the same time the Duala interpreted their growing contacts with Europeans as a mandate for identifying themselves against interior peoples in terms diametrically opposed to European liberal values: the Cameroonians not in direct contact with the ocean were generically *bakom* (slaves) even when (as was usually the case) not literally enslaved; the Duala themselves were free to exercise a monopoly over a widening trade zone in which there was no possibility of any but defensive competition.

The chapter that follows will attempt both to transcend and to reconstruct the hegemonic cultural models embodied in the relatively abundant sources (particularly European ones) for this period. It will begin by delineating the major changes defining the era: shifts in European export demand from slaves to palm products; Duala commercial expansion into the interior; and the new European merchant, government and missionary presence on the coast. Next, the political economy of the hierarchical trade network linking coast and interior will be analyzed. Finally, we will deal with internal Duala politics and their relationship to the German annexation of 1884 as well as the larger question of the viability of a stateless middleman regime.

From slave trade to "legitimate" export goods

Among the European ideological motifs that have produced misunderstandings of African history, none is more problematic than the early nineteenth-century attack upon the slave trade.[1] Nevertheless, we must recognize that for a variety of reasons the shift from slave to non-human exports on the Western African coast did mark a significant watershed in local development. In Cameroon, as elsewhere, the change did not come abruptly and slave *imports* from the interior continued and possibly increased. European market demands by no means dictated abolition of slave exports[2] but they did make possible the general growth of African overseas commerce encompassing entirely new categories of commodities, which in West Africa meant mainly vegetable oils. The procurement of these goods (and the slaves to cultivate, process and transport them) greatly expanded African internal markets, creating new needs for their social and cultural management.

Britain, the almost exclusive slave trading partner of the Duala in the later eighteenth century, officially ended its own participation in this traffic in 1807. However, despite the Royal Navy's efforts at suppression, an illegal slave trade continued up to 1860 at a pace comparable to that of the eighteenth-century peak.[3] Cameroon, as shown in table 2.4, was no exception. The mainly Brazilian, Portuguese and Spanish ships actually observed trading clandestinely here between 1815 and 1837 arrived less frequently than their legal predecessors but took aboard a slightly larger number of slaves per voyage. However, despite the sustained demand for servile African labor in the sugar and coffee plantations of Brazil, Cuba and Puerto Rico, Douala and the surrounding areas on the Cameroon coast ceased exporting significant quantities of slaves several years before signing the abolition treaties of 1840–1848 listed in table 3.1.

This termination of human exports does not seem to have sprung from any distinction between the values of the Duala and those of merchants or rulers of societies elsewhere in Africa who continued for many decades

Table 3.1. *Nineteenth-century European treaties*[1]

	Cameroonian site	European state	Subject	Cameroonian signatories[2]
1840 (March)	Douala	Britain regulation	Trade, credit Aqui[3]	King Bell, King
1840 (June)	Douala	Britain	Preliminary slave trade abolition	King Acqua, King Bell
1841 (May)	Douala	Britain	Slave trade abolition, 5-year payment	King Bell, King Acqua
1842	Batanga[4]	France	Sovereignty ceded	3 Banoko Kings
1842	Douala[5]	Britain	Human sacrifice	A'Lobah King Bell, Gandoh King Aqua
1844	Bimbia	Britain	Slave trade abolition, 1 payment, MFN (most-favoured-nation)	King William and 5 chiefs
1845	Batanga[6]	France	Slave trade abolition, legitimate trade protection	3 Banoko or Batanka chiefs
1848	Bimbia	Britain	Human sacrifice	King William and 8 chiefs
1848	Malimba[7]	Britain (France can join)	Slave trade abolition, MFN	King Pass and 5 chiefs
1848	Boquah[8]	ditto	ditto	King Dick Mondah and Mate
1848	Batanga[9]	ditto	ditto	King William, King John Batanga, King Batanga
1850	Douala	Britain	Trade regulation, return fugitive slaves	King Bell, King Acqua, Ned Dido, 14 chiefs
1850	Bimbia	Britain	ditto	King William and 6 chiefs
1852	Douala[10]	Britain	Human sacrifice, missionaries	King Acqua

Year	Place	Country	Purpose	Signatories
1855	Bimbia, Boobee	Britain	Bimbia sovereignty, Boobee not molested	King William, 2 Boobee, 4 Bimbia chiefs
1855	Douala	Britain	Settling disorders	King Acqua (Ned, Charley Dido = Acqua chiefs), King Bell, 12 chiefs
1856	Douala	Britain	End of Akwa–Deido war	John Acqua, Ned Dido (King Acqua, Ned Dido = witnesses)
1856	Douala	Britain	Court of Equity (22 articles)	King Bell, King Acqua, Charley, Ned Dido, 6 chiefs
1858	Douala (Akwa)	Britain	Abolish Makoko and Manganga "country custom"	King Acqua, 4 chiefs, 2 slave chiefs
1859 (Feb.)	Douala[11]	Britain	Purity of oil	Unspecified
1859 (July)	Douala	Britain	Human sacrifice, disputes arbitrated by Europeans	Bonny Bell, Josse, Prieso Bell, King Acqua
1860	Batanga[12]	Britain	Trade regulation, recognition of 2 kings, shipwrecks	King John, King William
1861	Douala	Britain	Murder for reprisal or "barbarous custom"	Bonny Bell, King Acqua, Prieso Bell
1862	Bimbia (Dikolo Town)	Britain	Outrages against missionaries	Dick Merchant and 4 local chiefs
1862	Douala	Britain	Court of Equity (19 articles)	Preso Bell, King Bell, King Acqua (Charley Dido also court member)
1869	Douala	Britain	Court of Equity (3 articles, reference to 1856 treaty)	King Bell, King Akwa, Charley Dido, Priso Bell
1869	Batanga[13]	France	Renewal of previous treaties	Banoko chiefs
1871	Douala[14]	Britain	Court of Equity (7 articles, reference to 1856 treaty)	King Bell, Charley Dido, Prince Acqua, Black Acqua, Preso Bell
1874	Douala[15]	Britain	End of Akwa–Bell–Joss war	Bell, Akwa chiefs
1878	Douala[16]	Britain	Akwa succession, sacrifice, order, pilotage	Jim Acqua, Court of Equity
1880	Batanga[17]	Britain	Trade regulation	King William, King John
1883	Douala[18]	Britain	13 articles re consul, chiefs, Court of Equity	King Bell, King Acqua

Table 3.1. (cont.)

Date	Cameroonian site	European state	Subject	Cameroonian signatories[2]
1883	Batanga[19]	France	Renewal of previous treaties	Banoko chiefs
1883 (April 19)	France[20]	French protection, MFN, territory ceded	King Passal	
1883 (Nov. 19)	Campo[21]	France	Protection	2 chiefs
1884 (July 11)	Bimbia[22]	Germany	Protections	22 chiefs
1884 (July 11)	Douala[23] (Deido)	Germany	Protection Deido chiefs	Jim Ekwalla
1884 (July 12)	Douala[24]	Germany	(See chapter text for discussion) Bell, 20 Akwa	King Aqua, King Bell, Joss chiefs
1884	E. Cameroon[25]	Germany	Protection chiefs, including Malimba, Batanga	Various coastal (July–Aug.)
1884 (Aug.–Sept.)	W. Cameroon	Britain	Protection	18 local chiefs
1884 (Oct. 3, 4)	Campo[26]	France	Confirmation of previous treaty	12 chiefs

[1] Source, unless otherwise indicated, Shirley G. Ardener, *Eye-Witnesses to the Annexation of Cameroon, 1883–1887* (Buea, Ministry of Primary Education and West Cameroon Antiquities Commission, 1968). Appendices A and B: "treaties" include official agreements of various kinds as well as formal treaties.

[2] The names, orthography, and order of signature are those of the original documents.

[3] Names are given here as they appear on the treaties. For reference to the indigenous names of Duala rulers, see table 2.1.

[4] M. de Clercq, *Recueil des traités de la France* (Paris: Amyot, 1865), IV, 617–18.

[5] Papers Relating to the Niger Expedition, PP 1843, XLVIII, 62.

[6] De Clercq, *Recueil*, V, 402.

[7] Lewis Hertslet, *Hertslet's Commercial Treaties* (London: H. Butterworth, 1851), VIII, 43–4.

[8] Ibid., 47–8.

[9] Ibid., 17–18.

[10] Copy deposited, signed Consul Beecroft, April 29, 1852, Calprof 5/7/1 (this archival series, entitled "Treaties," contains a number of formal agreements that were apparently not forwarded as such to the Foreign Office).

[11] Consul Hutchinson report, Feb. 23, 1859, Calprof 4/2/1.

[12] Ibid., XIV, 967–8.

[13] Treaty not found in de Clercq but reported in unspecified file of French Foreign Ministry archives in Philippe Laburthe-Tolra, "Christianisme et ouverture au monde, Cameroun, 1845–1915," *RFHOM* 75 (1988): 210.

[14] PRO FO 84/1343, Hopkins to FO, June 6, 1871.

[15] Copy dated Sept. 25, 1874, signed Consul Hartley, Calprof 5/7/1.

[16] Copy dated Jan. 19, 1878, signed Acting Consul Holder, Calprof 5/7/2.

[17] Hertslet, *Hertslet's Commercial Treaties*, XV, 538–9.

[18] Copy deposited, signed Consul Hewett, Mar. 29, 1883, Calprof 5/7/2.

[19] See note 13 above.

[20] M. de Clercq and Jules de Clercq, *Recueil des traités de la France*, (Paris: Durand et Pedone-Lauriel, 1886), XIV, 309.

[21] Ibid., 314.

[22] Ardener, *Eyewitnesses*, 23, 58.

[23] Ibid.

[24] Original in DZA RKA 4447; see appendix.

[25] Original in RKA 4447; see also Alexandre Kum'a Ndumbe III, "Les traités camerouno-germaniques (1884–1907)" in ibid. (ed)," *L'Afrique et l'Allemagne: de la colonisation à la coopération, 1884–1986 (Le cas du Cameroun)* (Yaoundé: Africavenir, 1986), 57–8.

[26] De Clercq and de Clercq, *Recueil*, XIV, 419–20.

longer to produce slaves for the Atlantic as well as the trans-Saharan and Indian Ocean slave trades.[4] Our best early account of Douala (from 1826) records the chiefs complaining about the decline in the slave trade;[5] there is also documentation for small numbers of illegal and unfree labor going, after 1837, both to the Americas and to European plantations on off-shore African islands.[6]

The key to the cessation of the Cameroon slave trade was the intensification of British efforts at interdiction during the later 1830s. The most effective of these measures was the stopping of Portuguese and Spanish ships equipped for the illegal trade, whether or not they had slaves aboard. As a secondary step, Royal Navy officers were ordered to present coastal African rulers north of the equator with standardized treaties banning local slave trade and promising orderly and open conditions for other local commerce. Despite accompanying offers of compensatory payments, the British met resistance in some of the most active slave-exporting areas such as Bonny in the Niger Delta, where only positive trade agreements were initially signed.[7]

There is evidence of such delay in Douala. As indicated in table 3.1, a commercial treaty was signed here several months before any agreement to end the slave trade. However by some constructions, both the 1840 Duala preliminary declaration and the full 1841 Duala anti-slave trade treaty were the first such West African accords to remain effectively in force.[8] Moreover, the accounts by Naval officers of these negotiations indicate very little difficulty in obtaining the consent of the Bell and Akwa rulers, despite some efforts to protect an apparently minor Spanish slave trade still going on up to 1841.[9]

The ease with which the slave trade ended in Cameroon as compared to other parts of the Guinea coast must again be attributed in considerable portion to British efforts. In 1827 Britain established a settlement on the island of Fernando Po that served as a base for various forms of naval, missionary and, from 1849 to 1872, consular anti-slavery activities in the Bights of Biafra and Benin.[10] Because Fernando Po was so close to the Cameroon estuary, Douala received British attention out of proportion to its statistical significance in either slave or subsequent palm product commerce. However, it is certainly the growth of palm oil exports that allowed, even if it did not directly inspire, Duala abandonment of the slave trade.

The slave trade had played a critical role in transforming the internal political and social organization of Douala during the eighteenth century. On the broader Atlantic market, however, Cameroon had always been a very minor slave supplier (see above table 1.5). In contrast to its relative poverty in population, the hinterland of Douala was rich in those natural resources deemed appropriate, for a "legitimate" nineteenth-century overseas trade.

Ivory, the first commodity to bring the Duala into regular contact with Europeans, remained significant as an export up to the early colonial period. Indeed, the demand for this item in both Europe and Asia increased constantly throughout the 1800s, and Cameroon was noted as a major source.[11] However, not only were ivory supplies in any part of Africa ultimately quite limited, but the Atlantic ports of Cameroon competed for tusks during the same period with an expanding trans-Saharan caravan network.[12] The result, as shown in table 3.2, is an actual decline in Douala ivory exports during the course of the century.

The commodity with the greatest capacity for expansion was palm produce, first only in the form of oil extracted from the fruit of the palm tree, *Elaeis guineensis* and later combined with the kernels of this fruit. The oil palm is indigenous to Africa and its product has been a mainstay of local diets since the earliest period of sedentary civilization in the West and Central African forests.[13] In the early nineteenth century a new and rapidly expanding market developed in Europe, where an industrializing society needed vegetable oils for lubricating machinery and manufacturing candles and soap. From the 1850s petroleum took over the lubrication and illumination role of palm oil and in the last quarter of the century new sources of vegetable fats and animal tallow also cut into the demand for its use in soap-making. A new market for palm kernels in the 1870s, arising out of margarine manufacturing and tin plating, compensated somewhat for this decline in demand, but the real impact of these additional uses was not felt until after 1900.[14] Thus from the 1860s a stagnation and then decline in palm produce prices would play as great a part in Douala "trade and politics" as had the original rise in "legitimate" exports.

Because the nineteenth-century history of Cameroon is so much better documented than any previous period, it is difficult to compare closely the impact of the two periods of trade upon internal developments. Of the major commodities reaching the coast from the hinterland two, ivory and slaves, were no less significant before 1800 than afterwards. The sources of both appear to be so far in the interior that we have little direct information about how they were procured even in the latter period. Palm oil and kernels, on the other hand, had a very dramatic and visible impact on the Duala middleman role.

Owing to their perishability (at least for oil) and low value-to-bulk ratio, these products had to be gathered in large quantities from relatively near the coast. Profitability in the palm goods trade thus depended upon efficient utilization of the inland waterways connecting various portions of the Cameroon Littoral as well as manipulation of political and social relations between Duala merchants and the local communities occupying the space between Douala and the immediate points of oil palm cultivation. The expansion and price shifts of palm product exports created

Table 3.2. *Nineteenth-century "legitimate" exports (in British long tons; % = proportion of West African exports; * = Liverpool imports only)*

	Ivory	Palm oil	Palm kernel	Sources
1810	25–40 (30%)[1]	50–60 (4.8%)		Robertson, *Notes*, 323; Marion Johnson, "Ivory and Nineteenth Century Transformation in West Africa," in G. Liesegang et al., *Figuring African Trade* (Berlin: D. Riemer, 1986), 113; PP 1845, XLVI, 481
1822		60 (2.1%)		Bold, *Guide*, 83; PP 1845, XLVI,481
1845*		360 (22.5%)		PP 1850, IX, 219–21
1847*		1,183 (6.2%)		ditto
1848*		1,487 (8.2%)		ditto
1849*		1,288 (7.0%)		PP 1852, XLIX, 451–5
1850*		1,796 (11.0%)		ditto
1851*		1,334 (5.6%)		Ibid., pp. 460–61
1855–68	2,100 (11%)	(5%)[2]		Johnson, "Ivory," 115; "Abstracts of Reports on Trade," PP 1857, XVI (2201), 437–41
1864		2,000 (7.3%)		Burton report, April 15, 1864, FO 84/1221
1875	7.6	3,000 + 200 "cocoa nuts"	200	Mersmann to McKellor, Nov. 29, 1875, NNA CalProf 3/1
1883	8.0	2,600 (8.6%) +100 cocoa	1,800	Hewett report, Dec. 17, 1883, PP 1884–85, LV (4279), 19

[1] Ivory export percentages are based on British imports only.
[2] A lower proportion is given for Cameroon in Martin Lynn, "Change and Continuity in the British Palm Oil Trade with West Africa," *JAH* 22 (1981): 341–2, but the Customs Bills of Entry used for Lynn's calculations are not very clear about the origins of cargoes; they could produce a better series than presently available if checked against other knowledge of ships that went to Cameroon.

tensions along the entire hierarchy of coast-to-interior trade and also intensified rivalries among internal Duala political segments. All of these problems reached a peak level shortly before the colonial annexation of 1884, with which the present chapter will end. However, to understand these affairs as something more than petty local squabbles or remote imperialist maneuvers, it is first necessary to place them in their regional African context.

The geography and politics of inland trade

The Cameroon estuary is fed by a complex system of rivers and creeks extending throughout the Littoral. As with most of Africa, the distance that can be travelled between the ocean and the interior in a large dugout canoe is limited by rapids or cataracts, in this case all occurring within seventy miles of the coast. Large areas of oil palm growth – an outcome but not always a continuous responsibility of human settlement – could be found along the banks or within easy transport distance of all these waterways.

The Duala themselves neither cultivated nor harvested any of the local palm trees. The closest they came to direct control of such production was to establish satellite villages of slaves in relatively close and accessible inland locations. As early as 1842 and 1843 villages of this kind belonging to both Lobe Bell and Ngando Akwa are described ten miles or so up the Wouri River and along the Kwa Kwa.[15] By 1884, according to one report, there were fifteen such settlements, nine belonging to Akwa and six to Bell.[16] However, the greatest portion of the palm products exported by the Duala were purchased from independent interior groups who were often themselves not the original producers.

As noted in the previous chapter, Duala access to the Littoral waterways was never challenged by any other coastal group. Neither did European merchants, dissatisfied as they were with Duala management of the local trading system, seriously seek to move inland themselves.[17] Thus the Duala could theoretically extend their interior commercial network as freely as they had earlier expanded their fishing camps in the estuary. With the exception of the Sanaga, Duala canoes and trading stations had, by the 1880s, reached the limits of navigability of the major coastal rivers. However the achievement of this goal required adaptation not just to a landscape and natural resources but also to inland communities with their own interests in controlling relations between producers and middlemen. The socio-economic institutions by which these relationships were managed parallel those established between Europeans and Duala on the coast and will be discussed below. For the present we will concentrate upon the more immediate and exclusively African questions of access to interior markets. Because the only contemporary records of this process come from rare European inland travellers, the chronology must remain uncertain. However, from the combination of these sources, very early colonial documents, and local oral traditions, we can learn something about the geographical extent and limitations of Duala regional hegemony.

The ideal trading partners for the Duala were populations living near easily accessible waterways but content with specializing in the role of agricultural producers. Such groups could be found along the lower reaches of the Wouri just above the point where it flowed past Douala into the Cameroon estuary. Here the Duala settled the largest number of their own slaves in agricultural villages and other groups of Basaa cultivators had "converted" to Duala ethnicity.[18]

The only autonomous inland community to meet Duala needs so unproblematically were the Pongo, a Sawa-Bantu speaking people located immediately northwest of Douala on the Bomono and Dibombari creeks. Pongo–Duala trade probably goes back well before the nineteenth century since the two groups share traditions of early exchanges of fish for agricultural products and possibly slaves. The beginnings of this trade are linked to the Duala community on the Wouri island of Jebale, located near the entrance to the Bomono creek.[19] The significance of the Pongo in the slave trade is more questionable, since it is based on the story of the giant, Malobe, who was allegedly despatched to the New World for disrupting local markets.[20] Despite the implausibility of some of the details, there is reason to accept the Malobe legend as a reference to some kind of pre-nineteenth-century commerce since it is distinguished in oral tradition from a nineteenth-century quarrel with the Duala over palm kernel measures.[21] More importantly still, the longevity of the Duala–Pongo relationship and even the character of the conflicts that punctuate its memory suggest a securely established paradigm of partnership between aquatic middlemen and terrestrial producers. The same cannot be said of trading relations along more remote waterways.

The terminal point of Wouri river navigability, Yabassi, is inhabited by a Basaa community also historically dedicated to agriculture. However, between the farthest inland Duala servile settlements and Yabassi are two Sawa-Bantu speaking groups, the Wuri (or Ewodi/Oli) and Bodiman whose own dedication to fishing and canoe transport challenged Duala hegemony over the Wouri trade routes. There is no remembrance of any conflict between the Wuri and the Duala over movement between the estuary and the Wuri territory itself. However our earliest travel account on this region suggests that the otherwise friendly Wuri were anxious to keep outsiders from "going to the Budiman's country."[22] According to missionary reports of 1872 and 1875, this same Bodiman territory was said to mark the outer limits of Duala trade routes.[23] Some time shortly after this period a lengthy war broke out between the Wuri and Bodiman. Although the ostensible issue was control of territory on the immediate borders between the two peoples, the underlying cause seems to have been trade to both Yabassi and the communities along the Dibombe river (see below) which itself formed the Wuri–Bodiman boundary. The Duala were drawn into this quarrel on the side of the Wuri thus apparently obtaining direct access to Yabassi. However, the Wuri–Bodiman conflicts continued into the first years of the colonial era, making commerce on this part of the river quite precarious.[24]

The territory of the Wuri people is bounded on both sides by tributaries of the Wouri river, the Dibombe to the north and the Abo to the south. These secondary waterways provide alternate routes to the country of perhaps the most populous agricultural group in the Littoral, the Abo. Being neither aquatic nor Sawa-Bantu speaking, the Abo would appear to fit very neatly into the role of inland complement to Duala trade. Up until the later nineteenth century the Duala merely came to the Abo from the south, as they had to the Pongo, and there seem to have been no critical complications.[25] However in the 1880s Duala inland commercial expansion set off rivalries among the various Abo towns and threatened collective Abo control over access to trade goods coming from farther inland.

The details or even an adequate outline of nineteenth century politics within Abo country are far too complicated to recount here.[26] However, major control of palm products as well as slaves coming overland from the rich Mungo and Grassfields region appears to have been controlled by the towns of Mandouka and Miang located at the westernmost points of the Abo region. Duala traders had two possible means of using their canoes to bypass this Abo position: one via the Dibombe tributary of the Wouri to the north, the other via the Mungo in the West.

The Dibombe route, apparently the simplest, was also the site of the Wuri–Bodiman war and is perceived to this day as a dangerous area associated with hippos, pirates and legendary giant crocodiles.[27] The Duala did not trade there until after the establishment of German rule in 1884.[28] Even this change appears to have been the cause of a violent war between the Wuri town controlling this new route, Bangseng, and the Abo of Mandouka that ended only after extensive colonial intervention.[29] However, even before the outbreak of the Dibombe–Bangseng quarrels, the rulers of Miang and Mandouka had made it clear to visiting Germans that they were enraged at the Duala for having "ruined" their trade by establishing direct contacts with the peoples of the upper Mungo.[30]

The extension of Duala trade routes to the navigable limits of the Mungo can be dated fairly precisely to 1882, when a son of King Ndumbe Lobe Bell accompanied the Baptist missionary Joseph Jackson Fuller to visit a mission station already established at Bakundu by James Richardson.[31] During the eighteenth and early nineteenth century the Mungo region was in the Bimbia trading zone but with the internal near-collapse of Bimbia during the 1850s, local exports went directly to Douala.[32] However, for most of the nineteenth century both Bimbia and Duala Mungo trade had been confined to the mouth of the river; further inland the Mungo, Balong and Abo peoples acted as middlemen while coastal merchants were not allowed to buy "even a chicken."[33] It is ironic that the Baptists gave the Duala their entrée into this portion of the interior, since Bell had previously feared Richardson as a rival and refused him all help on the Mungo, thus forcing the missionary to reach Bakundu via an overland route. By 1884, however, the Bells had established trading positions not only at Bakundu but beyond it to Mombo Beach immediately south of the cataracts, which bar further canoe passage inland.[34]

The Bell commercial coup on the upper Mungo created considerable hostility among not only the Abo but also the Balong[35] as well as (see below) between the Bells and other Duala groups. At the same time, this accomplishment revealed quite clearly the geographical limits of Duala trading potential, since all explorers to the upper Mungo in the mid-1880s found the region extensively penetrated by Efik merchants from Old Calabar.[36]

South of Douala in the estuary itself are two rivers used for trade to the east. We know less about the nineteenth-century history of trade relations in this part of the Littoral since few precolonial travellers went there and the Germans gave it less early attention than the west, where their position was more threatened by British activities.

The closer of the rivers going eastward, the Dibamba, could be traveled into well-populated Basaa country as far as Bonapoupa. At some point before 1875 Akwa traders – possibly exploiting the Basaa connections of their group's founder, Kuo Mapoka – had established themselves along the entire navigable length of the Dibamba. However, it is not clear how active commerce was along this axis, since a missionary explorer in 1875, who had also been on the Wouri, Abo and Mungo, described Dibamba "trading life" as "of the slenderest."[37]

Farther south from Douala lay the Kwa Kwa River, connecting the estuary to the largest of the Cameroon coastal waterways, the Sanaga, which is navigable through Bakoko country as far inland as Edea. Unlike in the west, precolonial Duala merchants never succeeded in thwarting local controls over this route. Their penetration here was thus restricted to the Kwa Kwa itself, which became an arena of rivalry between Bell and Akwa.[38] Sanaga trade, meanwhile, remained in the hands of the Bakoko, who transferred goods to both the Duala on the Kwa Kwa and to merchants from an alternative oceanic outlet at the less accessible estuary of Malimba.[39]

The European presence

The only Europeans to visit Douala during the seventeenth, eighteenth and early nineteenth centuries were ivory and slave traders, who carried on their business directly from the decks of the ships that brought them in and out of the estuary. As shown in the previous chapter, negotiations even under these circumstances could sometimes involve complicated credit arrangements and produce episodes of violence. It is the records of these encounters that provide us with our most reliable evidence of early Duala history. On the other hand, because European contact with the Duala was so limited during this period, historians are neither the beneficiaries nor victims of a coherent account of local development from these sources.

During the nineteenth century, both the scale and character of European activity in Douala changed considerably. Merchant vessels not only arrived more frequently but representatives of trading firms began to maintain permanent residence on off-shore trading stations constructed from the hulks of abandoned sailing vessels. Moreover, the estuary was visited at frequent intervals by British naval vessels, either alone or escorting representatives of the Foreign Office, whose mandate was both to regulate commercial affairs and suppress the slave trade, along with other local abuses of what contemporary Europeans perceived as fundamental human rights. Finally overseas merchants and proconsuls were joined by a small group of British and African-American Baptist missionaries, with an entirely unprecedented program for transforming local society.

Because these various European groups are all so much better documented than the Duala, to say nothing of the peoples of the Littoral interior, there is some danger that the telling of their story may draw attention away from local African history. This danger is at least partially mitigated by the inverse relationship between substantive significance and consciously articulated goals among the Europeans present at Douala. It is the merchants who were most continuously and effectively – for better or worse – in contact with the Duala, but they have left us little commentary on these activities. With the official British representatives in this period, as for their colonial successors, we encounter Europeans intent upon exercising a degree of control over the African world, although in the nineteenth century the limitations of such ambitions are also quite obvious. The goals of missionaries in this period approach an almost total cultural hegemony but as will be seen, they enjoyed very little success among the Duala.

a.   *Merchants*

Among their more literate government and missionary compatriots, European merchants on the nineteenth-century West African coast were often characterized as "palm oil ruffians." Such men were regarded by British officials as little different from their slave-trading predecessors, and castigated specifically in Cameroon for "showing them [local Africans] every day examples of fraud, drunkenness and violence accompanied by the most infamous and abusive language."[40] The paucity of records from the merchants themselves makes it difficult to counter this view or, more importantly, understand fully the European side of nineteenth-century trading relationships.

Given this historiographic situation, even the chronology of change at Douala from European merchants as a series of transient ships' companies to a community of continuous residents remains somewhat obscure. From what we do know, the shift seems to have been very gradual and sometimes ambiguous. First, it should be noted that even in the slave trade era, ships remained at Douala for many weeks at a time and were turned into temporary "factories" by the lowering of their sails and the construction of mat roofs upon their decks.[41] This "floating" or "transit" trade seems to have continued up through at least the first decades of the palm oil period.[42] One British merchant, John Lilley, did establish his own "town" at Bonaberi in the 1830s and again in the 1860s but this example of assimilation to Duala culture neither endeared Lilley to British officials (who accused him of slave trading, murder and general incitement to disorder) nor provided a model for other European commercial representatives.[43]

From the mid nineteenth century, British naval and consular reports generally refer to the individuals responsible for the local commerce of various commercial houses as "supercargoes" a term that does not always distinguish them from ships' captains. By 1852, however, the first allusion is made to the "resident agent" of a local British firm and his establishment offshore in the Wouri river on a "hulk."[44] Cameroon did, however, appear to lag behind the busier "Oil Rivers" ports of Nigeria in the permanence as well as the number of these retired vessels used as places of residence and business for European merchants.[45] In 1864 there was still only one hulk at Douala although three had earlier been seen; in 1868 there may have been none; around 1882 there were four; and in 1884 there were seven.[46] It is also likely that some of the vessels in Douala described as hulks were not permanently anchored in the Wouri but rather operated in a "relay" or "rotation" system, whereby ships with skeleton crews were left in West African harbors to take on local produce until replaced by vessels belonging to the same firm bringing out new European trade goods.[47]

Along with the hulks, merchants in this era also kept "keg houses" on land for storing and processing oil before repacking it for shipment to Europe.[48] In Cameroon as elsewhere these terrestrial establishments grew in size and function during the latter decades of the century; by 1884 the largest local firm, Woermann, had already abandoned its hulk for a factory building at Akwa, where agents both lived and transacted business.[49]

The use of permanent trading stations in Cameroon was further facilitated by the inauguration, from the early 1850s, of regular steamship service between Europe and West Africa.[50] At Douala, unlike ports such as Old Calabar, this innovation did not significantly increase the number of European firms entering local trade. During the 1840s there appear to have been four to five British trading houses and one Dutch firm active in Cameroon;[51] in 1856 and again in 1864 six firms, all British, are listed;[52] in 1873 the fall in oil prices left only three firms, two British and one German;[53] by the time of the German annexation in 1884 the number of trading houses had risen to eight, of which six were British and two German.[54]

In addition to the European personnel (numbering about fifty by 1884), the resident expatriate merchant community at Douala included African employees of the commercial firms (mainly Liberian Kru manual laborers but also some mission-trained artisans and junior clerks from the Gold Coast).[55] As elsewhere in West Africa after 1850, the possibility of purchasing small amounts of shipping space on steam vessels also allowed Creole African entrepreneurs from Sierra Leone and especially Fernando Po to set up as independent merchants. One such entrepreneur, Jonathan Scott, was the subject of a major controversy at Douala as early as 1852.[56] In 1864 Consul Richard Burton reports (with considerable disapproval) the local presence of small businesses run by Sierra Leone Creoles "and other liberated [African] men."[57] However, Creole merchants seem to have disappeared from Douala by 1884 so we may assume that some combination of the trade problems of the 1870s and their concentration at the more hospitable British community of Victoria in what later became West Cameroon removed them from competition with Europeans.[58]

Competition among merchants at Douala thus seems to have been much less intense than in the Nigerian palm product trade. The major disturbance to the domination of Liverpool and Bristol firms (some of them continuing from the slave trade era) was the arrival of the German Woermann house in 1868 and the establishment at Cameroon of a separate operation by the former Woermann agent, Johannes Thormählen, in 1875.[59] Nonetheless, Burton described Douala in 1864 as "perhaps the most troublesome place on the coast."[60]

The troubles Burton refers to derive less from direct friction between European merchants than from their varying relationships with internally competing Duala political segments. The specific nature of these problems will be dealt with below. But first it is necessary to examine the link between merchants and the other elements of the European presence at Douala.

b.   *Naval and consular authority*

During the nineteenth century Douala, along with the general West and East African coast, fell firmly within the sphere of British "informal empire." Despite the establishment of several French colonial posts from Gabon to Senegal, a Portuguese presence to the south and formal Spanish control of Fernando Po, the British Royal Navy was clearly the dominant force in this region. A naval squadron was kept in West Africa to enforce anti-slavery measures and in 1849 the Foreign Office created a Consular District of the Bights of Benin and Biafra (separated from Benin in 1853), with its headquarters at Fernando Po until 1872 and afterwards at Old Calabar.

Evidence of this hegemony can be found in the many agreements and treaties signed by Britain in Cameroon between 1840 and 1884 (see table 3.1), as well as the frequent interventions of the Royal Navy and consuls in local affairs. What the documents of these events reveal only indirectly (by the repeated efforts to accomplish the same things) is the limited control achieved through these measures over developments within West African societies or even their relations with European merchants.

To stress such failures of the official British presence at Douala assumes that Britain had articulated a set of objectives in West Africa whose attainment can be measured in terms of control. This is not the place to discuss at length the complex issues of British overseas policy in the liberal era.[61] Suffice it to say that explicit goals existed, but that these quickly proved to be mutually incompatible. The most profound contradiction can be found in the two most prominent policy objectives, replacement of slaving with legitimate trade and the promotion of British economic interests. With slave trade abolition Britain incurred the material costs not only of maintaining its West African squadron but also of alienating major New World trading partners. The compensation was expanded access to African markets, more fully activated by the production and transport of large quantities of vegetable products than by the export of relatively few but highly valuable slaves. However, the limitations of these markets became painfully evident through the fall of vegetable oil prices in the later nineteenth century.

Of more immediate relevance to control over Douala affairs was the contradiction between British commitment, on the one hand, to classical liberal principles of free trade and minimal public expenditure and, on the other, to the suppression of slave trading and the maintenance of orderly conditions in West African trading ports. The presence of the navy and the consuls in West Africa represented a recognition that free trade in this area of the world depended upon active government intervention. However, the resources allocated were far too limited to deal with the crises that kept occurring at each trading center. To achieve minimal control without undertaking further political responsibility, the British attempted to organize local European merchants and major African traders into Courts of Equity.

These courts were expected to assemble regularly on shore, adjudicate through majority vote all cases of commercial dispute (including acts of fraud and violence), and call in the consul only as an instance of higher appeal and administrator of sanctions beyond monetary fines. The model for this institution was a less formal but apparently effective assembly of supercargoes and chiefs recognized in a treaty by Royal Navy officers in 1836 at Bonny in the Niger Delta.[62] The first British consul in the Bights, John Beecroft, convened a similar body at Douala in 1852 to vote for the replacement of the then King Akwa.[63] However, the establishment in 1856 of official Courts of Equity for the Cameroons and the other Oil Rivers proved problematic, as indicated in table 3.1 by the repeated reconstitution of the Douala Court in the treaties of 1862, 1869, 1871 and 1883. Indeed, the very legitimacy of such jurisdiction under British law was left in doubt until a full Order in Council of 1872 provided the consuls with the necessary authority.[64]

There is evidence that the Douala Court of Equity functioned to some degree before its first "revival" in 1862, but it does not seem to have been operative again until a further, non-formalized, reorganization in 1868.[65] During the next decade or more meetings were held and some cases settled (particularly right after the 1871 reorganization when one merchant member claimed that the Court "ruled the river").[66] But for the most part the Court was ineffective in its judicial role. Instead, it seems to have become an arena for airing, but not resolving, more essential disputes about export price agreements among Europeans, the relations of British consular authority to German merchants, the political role of missionaries, and the separation of disputes among Africans from those involving Europeans. This last consideration meant that even in the brief periods when the Court did become an active local force it risked the loss of external support: "Her Majesty's Government can hardly approve of missionaries and traders becoming native rulers."[67]

After falling back into total disuse from at least 1880, the Court was revived (in conjunction with a much stronger definition of his own role) by Consul Edward Hyde Hewett in 1883. For the next year and a half it met frequently (if not regularly or always on land) to hear a wide range of cases involving disputes between Europeans and Duala, among the Duala themselves, and between the Duala and inland peoples.[68]

"Too Late" Hewett is, of course, the consul notorious for the failure of his 1884 efforts to annex Cameroon to the British Empire rather than allowing it to fall into German hands. Thus the period when both the official British representative and his chosen local instrument operated most harmoniously in Douala is also the time when informal imperialism was clearly coming to an end. The degree to which this termination can be attributed to African as opposed to international causes will be discussed below. However, the failure of consular authority to establish any acceptable means of control over local affairs prior to the institution of formal colonial administration tells its own story about the limits of nineteenth-century British hegemony.

A more revealing dimension of these frustrations, if one less germane to practical British concerns, is revealed by the repeated references in treaties and despatches to the practice of human sacrifice by Duala rulers.[69] The number of people killed in these actions, mainly undertaken by local rulers shortly after the deaths of their predecessors, were few. The social meaning of such events lay rather in the confirmation of a concept of human worth that placed slaves and inland peoples (the inevitable sacrificial victims) on a lower level than freeborn Duala. Given its historical basis, this concept was only reinforced by a hegemonic European presence on the coast, despite the stated humanitarian goals of such a presence. This paradox will have to be explored more fully below when the organizational and cultural links between various levels of the nineteenth-century Littoral trading system are examined. But first it is necessary to look at the most articulated of the contemporary British attempts to redefine Cameroon in hegemonic terms.

c.   *The Baptist mission*

If it is difficult to discern any vision of legitimate trade in the European merchant presence in nineteenth-century Douala, and if the vision guiding the official British presence remains contradictory, that of their missionary compatriots is abundantly clear. For the London Baptist Missionary Society (hereafter BMS) that entered Cameroon in 1841, the material achievements of European industrial civilization were inseparable from a set of religious beliefs and a secular lifestyle which were to be imposed upon existing African culture. If measured in terms of these well-articulated goals, the Baptist mission was a much greater failure than British informal empire. However, this failure itself helps us to understand the Duala middleman role, while the special presence of the BMS further shaped that role in ways often contradictory to missionary intentions.

BMS evangelical endeavors in the nineteenth-century Littoral were extensively documented by the missionaries themselves and have subsequently been translated into coherent and detailed narratives by a number of European and Cameroonian historians.[70] We need thus only abstract from this story (which conveniently ends in 1886, when the Basel Missionary Society replaced the BMS) the relationship between goals and achievement and then consider why missionization had such a limited effect among the nineteenth-century Duala and their neighbors.

The immediate goal of the BMS was to convert the Duala to a general model of Christianity and Victorian Civilization.[71] Their secondary aim was to eliminate from Duala culture specifically objectionable practices such as slavery, polygamy, human sacrifice and *losango* cults. As an alternative to the transformation of what they finally came to see as a hopelessly corrupt Duala middleman establishment, the missionaries also sought to create an autonomous Christian base among some combination of former slaves and "unspoiled" inland peoples.

The outcome of the primary BMS conversion project can be assessed fairly precisely through statistics of church membership and also more impressionistically in its influence on the lifestyles of the Duala elite. At the moment of Basel takeover in 1886, the Baptist churches in and around Douala (excluding the Creole settlement of Victoria) reported a total of 164 full members, and 262 school pupils.[72] Assuming a population in Douala alone of about 20,000, this represents a less than 1 percent conversion rate. Moreover, the most dedicated of this tiny band of converts were slaves; the Duala rulers and notables, even when friendly to the missionaries (or even educated in Britain under their influence, as was the case of the Bell heir, Manga Ndumbe[73]) remained devoted to all the "pagan" practices the BMS sought to extirpate.

The general continuation among the Duala of slavery, human sacrifice, polygamy and *losango* attest further to the weakness of missionary efforts. The only real progress made in this regard occurred in the somewhat isolated Duala quarter of Bonaberi, on the right bank of the Wouri. Here in 1879 the very devoted African-American missionary, Joseph Jackson Fuller, convinced the local ruler to suppress the *jengu* and *mungi* cults.[74] But *losango*, as will be seen, proved to be a very protean element in Littoral culture which survived many apparent disappearances. More generally, Duala rulers attempted to assimilate the missionary presence to their own secular purposes. The missionaries were considered valuable allies against merchants in the Court of Equity[75] and the Bell, Akwa and Deido rulers jealously sought to play host to mission stations as a status symbol comparable to (and closely linked with) their ownership of European houses, furniture and clothing.

The failure of the BMS in their direct assaults on Duala "paganism" are not difficult to understand from a broader historical perspective. Unlike situations in which Africans turned to missionaries as guides to a world already altered by very direct European domination, the Duala in the nineteenth century felt no need to adapt their culture to such radically disruptive teachings.[76] The Baptist missionaries themselves recognized this situation both implicitly and explicitly and thus sought little more than tolerance from the Duala rulers while directing their main efforts at other groups. The implicit alternative to conversion "from the top" was an assault from the margins, via ex-slaves and Creoles, groups that always constituted the base of the BMS effort in Cameroon. Among the early missionaries themselves were individuals such as Joseph Merrick, Fuller and the Richardsons, recruited from among recently emancipated African-Americans in Jamaica.[77] The first African BMS Christian community, founded at Fernando Po and later transferred to Victoria, consisted of Creoles either coming from already established commercial centers such as the Gold Coast or recaptured by the Royal Navy from illegal slaving vessels. As already indicated, former slaves (sometimes refugees but usually purchased from their masters by missionaries) constituted a key element in the Douala Baptist congregations.[78]

However, even the deployment of their own cultural middlemen produced only limited results for the BMS. The Fernando Po community started out with great promise but soon shrank drastically in size despite (or, as Martin Lynn has argued, because of) the success of its Creole members in the local palm oil trade.[79] Likewise in Douala the prominence of slaves among the Baptist converts is less striking than their small numbers, given general estimates that well over half the local population was in a servile condition.[80] Thus despite the many tensions existing in Douala between merchants of various kinds and slave versus *wonja* Duala, the alienation among those in less advantageous positions does not seem to have been sufficiently strong or clearly defined so as to attract a significant proportion of them to the Christian communities fostered by the BMS.

The assimilation of once devout Christian Creole merchants to the more worldly culture of the European "palm oil ruffians" suggests a positive dynamism to the trading world of the West African coast which, in the case of Duala–BMS relations, translated into cultural transfers of a kind very different from what the missionaries intended. At a very obvious level, the BMS offered the Duala training in artisanal skills as well as the writing and speaking of standard (versus Pidgin) English, all appreciated for their usefulness in the trading economy.[81] A major portion of missionary energy was also devoted to the study of the Duala language, ostensibly for evangelical purposes.

The relationship of such undertakings to the spiritual goals of the mission was questioned within the BMS itself, where a major controversy raged during the 1860s and early 1870s around the founding figure of the Cameroon church, Alfred Saker.[82] What even Saker's sharpest critics did not appreciate was the extent to which the acquisition of European formal education and even more the early attainment of literacy in their own language would serve to institutionalize Duala middleman hegemony in both commercial and cultural realms. However the full realization of this role had to await the colonial era.

In the last decade before German annexation BMS missionaries became disillusioned with the Duala, "a cunning, impudent set of rascals,"[83] and began an effort to "get away to the people inland of better promise."[84] In this spirit Fuller, Richardson, Grenfell and other Baptist agents attempted to establish contacts as far into the Cameroon interior as possible. From an evangelical perspective the results were mediocre at best. Even the Richardsons' heroic settlement at Bakundu on the upper Mungo never produced more than seven converts and was not continued under the Germans.[85] Neither local European merchants nor the British consuls supported the missionaries in this program of inland penetration.[86] The Duala, as indicated above, actively opposed any European movement beyond the coast, but eventually profited more from the Bakundu mission than did the BMS.

The most immediate cause for the departure of the British Baptists from Cameroon in 1886 was undoubtedly political tension arising out of German colonial occupation (see next chapter). However, BMS discouragement with evangelical efforts among the Duala, expressed in the efforts to reach the Cameroon interior during the 1870s, had also directed much of the Society's African energies towards an entirely new field, the putatively "unspoiled" Congo.[87] For the BMS, a people like the Duala were more than uncontrollable: they had become positively repugnant. Yet without the extraordinary efforts of the BMS in Cameroon it is hard to imagine that the initial commercial position of the Duala could have developed into such a broad and durable middleman role.

The institutions of hegemonic free trade

The narrative of developments in the nineteenth-century Littoral presented so far has been dominated by two apparently incompatible themes:
first, a constant expansion of commerce across European–Duala–interior
boundaries; and second, the failure to establish any mechanism for regulating these exchanges. The relationship between this situation and the
eventual colonial annexation of Cameroon will be discussed in the final
section of the chapter. First, however, it is necessary to take into account
the ability of the participants in this trading system to maintain active
relationships over more than half a century despite the absence of effective
political authority.

The arrangements that provided some basis for order in the Littoral
world all center around the universal process of commercial exchange but,
as presented here, move progressively outward into the particularistic
realms of society and culture.[88] They begin with a market for export and
import goods, which is directly supported by a system of credit; credit in
turn depends upon a set of tributary/partnerships relations, which are
themselves reinforced by intermarriage; finally all such transactions operated within mutually understood currency values and market languages.
These institutions, more than any other aspect of the nineteenth-century
coast–Littoral trading system, embody that combination of heirarchy and
anarchy which was its central characteristic.

a.   *The market*

The hegemonic motor of "legitimate" trade in Cameroon was the European demand for vegetable oils, which has already been discussed at some
length. Limited as are our statistics for palm product exports in the
nineteenth century, those for European goods imported into Cameroon
during this period are even worse.[89] The closest surrogates are found in
table 3.3. But at the very least these sources, as well as several other less
precisely quantified accounts of Cameroon commerce,[90] make it clear that
in contrast to the slave trade era the Duala now imported fewer "trinkets,"
more textiles, and considerably greater quantities of alcoholic beverages,
tobacco and salt. Otherwise nothing had changed very much, nor was
Douala much distinguished in this respect from other ports on the West
African coast.[91]

According to formal economic theory, no truly competitive market can
be hegemonic, since all buyers and sellers are free to make the best bargains
possible given the resources they bring with them to the place of exchange.
Douala, from the early eighteenth century onward, had been a competitive

Table 3.3. *Composition of nineteenth-century Douala imports (ad valorem)*

A.

1823[1]	Total £190:	Salt	Textiles	Munitions	Brass pans	Misc. (beads, iron, lead chests, hardware, earthenware)
		7.9%	20%	42.6%	7.9%	16.3%

B.

1884[2]	Spirits	Tobacco	Cloth	Salt	Brandy	Wood	Misc.
	22%	10%	40%	5%	5.3%	5%	18%

C.

1891–2[3]	Total (Reichsmarks)	Textiles	Alcohol/tobacco	Munitions	Metals/metal goods	Foods	Salt	Consumer goods[4]	Capital goods	Misc.
1891	4,114,270	32.7%	19.0%	12.9%	6.5%	2.6%	3.9%	10.9%	10.5%	1.0%
1892	4,111,675	22.3%	18.9%	8.3%	6.9%	4.1%	3.5%	12.9%	22.1%	0.9%
1891–92	8,225,945	27.5%	18.9%	10.6%	6.7%	3.3%	3.7%	11.9%	16.3%	1.0%

[1] *Source*: Captain John Adams, *Remarks on the Country Extending from Cape Palmas to the R. Congo . . .* (London: Whittaker, 1823), 251 (this is not a record of actual trade but rather a statement by an experienced merchant of what cargo would be required to purchase a given quantity of export goods).

[2] *Source*: Edward Schmidt report on German trade with Cameroon, Aug. 1, 1884, CSO 6/3/5; the two German firms at Douala in this period accounted for slightly over half the local trade (see Hewett report, Dec. 17, 1883, PP 1884–85, LV), but the omission of British imports distorts the list in favor of spirits and against munitions and possibly textiles (on distribution of imports between Britain and Germany, see Voss report, n.d. [1884], CSO 6/3/5).

[3] *Source*: *Deutsches Kolonialblatt*, 1892, supplement: 15; ibid., 1893: 302; in both original tables, imports into "Kamerun" (presumably Douala) are separated from those into Victoria. The German administration published import data for previous years, but only in terms of quantity, which does not allow for any meaningful comparison between different categories of goods. The effect of early colonial rule on this data is probably most evident in the high figure for capital goods, much of it equipment for the use of the government and expanding merchant firms (note the increasing proportion of this item over the two years). Otherwise the picture is probably quite close to the preceding nineteenth-century period. For an analysis of this and subsequent German trade data for Cameroon, see Leonard Harding, "1884–1984: cent ans de relations commerciales," in Kum'a Ndumbe (ed.), *L'Afrique et l'Allemagne*, 392–413.

[4] Most of this category is unspecified and probably includes a good deal of food, particularly stockfish, which is cited by Voss in 1884 as a major German import.

market and the subsequent history of its commerce provides ample evidence that the local merchants knew how to negotiate effectively with their European counterparts. The Duala did enjoy something of a monopoly over interior markets, but it has already been shown that there was competition here between different Duala groups and also, as will be noted below, important bargaining assets under the control of "bush" palm product suppliers.

Nonetheless, both contemporary and more recent European and African observers have perceived the commercial process in Cameroon and nineteenth-century Africa as generally very one-sided: an exchange of low quality industrial products for valuable local raw materials.[92] The obvious truth behind these observations is that Europe in this period was industrialized and thus had a wide range of goods to offer Cameroonians, whose own economy could produce only a few items of interest to Europe and did so at considerable expenditure of labor. It must be kept in mind, however, that in pure market terms Africans benefited as much as Europeans from industrialization, since the declining production costs of European goods lowered their price in relationship to raw material exports, i.e. the barter terms of trade for African goods improved steadily throughout the eighteenth and at least the first half of the nineteenth century.[93]

The larger historical issue, which is difficult to incorporate into a discussion of markets, is whether the economic and social changes resulting from such cross-cultural exchange ameliorated or exacerbated the inequalities between the two partners. In cases where exports constituted vital and wasting assets, such as slaves and ivory, one can argue that the market was pushing Africans towards a literal "dead end."[94] However the palm products marketed at Douala in the nineteenth century were a renewable resource, whose production involved further investments in labor organization and transport which, at least in local terms, must be characterized as elements of positive growth.[95]

More problematic perhaps is the prominence of salt[96] and the growing role of stockfish on the nineteenth-century import lists, suggesting that the Duala were now unable to supply from their own industry even those items in whose production they had specialized at the time of their arrival at the coast. Evidence of this kind was constantly used by Europeans to depict the Duala as lazy and parasitical. However, despite the continuing import of "neptune" distilling pans from Europe, the Duala had never been in a position to produce salt very efficiently. Fishing did become a less common and certainly less prestigious local activity as trading opportunities increased, but such a preference (as well as a taste for varieties of fish not available locally) should have been understandable to expatriate observers, themselves often professional merchants and consumers of imported foods. Moreover, the fisheries of the Cameroon estuary have never declined in activity during modern times, even if the participants became increasingly non-Duala.[97]

Despite the "rational choice" behavior of everyone in the Littoral market system, it is difficult not to assume some immediate effect of the unequal access to capital and information among the various levels of participants. The transformation of this situation into a form of hegemony is most obvious in the secondary transactions, beginning with credit arrangements, which will be discussed immediately below. Within the market itself, our best test of the relationship between asymmetry and hegemony is the response of Europeans, Duala and inland suppliers to changes in the prices of palm oil exports. In abstract market terms, such a decline is the ultimate evidence of the superior position of Europeans, who had developed access to so many sources of vegetable fat (or substitutes for it) throughout the world that they no longer depended upon suppliers in any one region such as West Africa. However, the European economy had also become heavily dependent on the smooth functioning of this international market, so that the later-nineteenth-century decline in overseas supplier prices, i.e. a shift of the terms of trade in favor of manufactures, contributed to a major depression in the metropoles.[98] Moreover, at Douala the immediate casualties of the price declines were European merchant firms, several of whom (as noted above) disappeared from the scene in the 1870s.

The weapon used by both the Duala and their inland suppliers to deal with this market shift was a series of "trade stoppages," i.e. a simple refusal to provide goods for reduced returns. During the first period of price declines, in the 1860s, this device seems to have worked quite well as European firms proved unable to combine for any counter-boycott.[99] The 1870s witnessed a series of reversals indicating some sort of balance: first, the three surviving European houses forced the Duala to accept lower prices; then the representative of a new Bristol trading firm entered the river and restored part of the old oil price in the form of bonuses to large-volume sellers.[100]

What we can perceive in these price struggles is that the survival of Cameroon African societies did not depend on the continuation of export-import trade in the same way as did that of specialized European business organizations. The major initiators of stoppages were inland peoples, the least committed to the market of all the major participants. The political difficulties of the Duala at this time may be linked to commercial pressures, but this is again a question that will have to be taken up below. In the restricted arena of the market place, the Duala emerged from this crisis as the major winners since they managed to cut the costs of palm oil by moving closer to the original supply sources (see above), expanded their trade by including increasing quantities of palm kernels, and forced Europeans to pay more for exports than they had originally offered. However, the most persistent conflicts between merchants in the Littoral did not focus directly upon prices, but rather on the more complex issues of credit and partnership agreements.

b.   *Trust*

Those same economic axioms which tell us that a competitive market must eventually reach equilibrium also indicate that no such market can deal in large quantities of goods over great distances without considerable outlays of credit. The European merchants trading at Douala, to say nothing of the secondary suppliers and manufacturers who provided them with equipment and trade goods, all operated on the basis of borrowed capital, supplied by bankers and various forms of commercial paper. The Duala middlemen met most fixed capital needs (mainly canoes and servile labor) out of their own resources; however, the seasonal journeys toward scattered interior sources of palm goods required that essential working capital – the import commodities for which these goods were exchanged – be advanced directly from their European trading partners.

As noted in the previous chapter, such a credit system became a regular feature of Douala trade by the later eighteenth century, when slaves had replaced ivory as the principal export. Under the common term of "trust" it was a feature of virtually all West African coastal trade in the nineteenth century. Colin Newbury argues further that this kind of credit arrangement functioned as a major instrument of control by "monopolistic" European firms attempting to keep smaller competitors, particularly Creole Africans, out of the palm oil markets.[101] Undoubtedly, their lack of ability to make large advances hindered Creoles in the Douala market, but probably a greater factor – as already suggested – was their relative inability to fight price wars. Moreover, from the eighteenth century onward European merchants, and especially British and German officials presumably looking after their interests, consistently decried what Burton called "the gambling dishonest system of trust."[102] Periodic attempts by European merchants to operate without trust, however, proved impossible.[103] British–Duala treaties, beginning with the first in 1840, thus recognized the institution as a normal, if disturbing, element of local commerce.[104]

The unilateral flow of credit from Europeans to Duala and Duala to the interior is thus a clear marker of hegemony in the Littoral trading system but not necessarily an instrument of control over that system. Indeed, the bad reputation of trust among Europeans reveals the difficulty of maintaining such hegemony on a purely economic basis. Trust agreements at Douala were inscribed by writing in "books" or *kalati*,[105] copies of which were retained by both Europeans and Duala. The recording of goods advanced by Duala merchants to their inland partners usually remained in oral form although sometimes these transactions were symbolized by marking banana leaves or bundling sticks and grass so as to indicate quantities of debt.[106] In substance there was little distinction between the books and the leaves or bundles, since no neutral authority existed to enforce the contracts.

The need to enforce contracts arose out of failures to repay debts at all levels of trade. Europeans tended to explain such default and delay as the result of willful Duala chicanery, which may well have been the case at times; the Duala in turn blamed the ignorance and greed of the "bushman" for failures to deliver goods. However, price disagreements and the unforeseeable circumstances of any business operation extending across such boundaries must have played at least as great a role as the personal shortcomings of African participants. Early British treaties (see table 3.1, 1840) attempted to make Duala "kings" responsible for enforcing debt repayment, but since the local rulers were not only weak but frequently themselves the debtors in question, this device did not prove very effective. After 1856 the arbitration of such disagreements was supposed to fall under the jurisdiction of the ill-fated Court of Equity.

In the absence of central authority, debt regulation had to be enforced by the trading partners themselves. As seen in the accounts of slave-trading, this recourse could operate on a basis of mutual understanding whereby "pawns" of persons or ivory tusks were deposited as guarantees for the eventual "washing" of trust. Such practices continued in the nineteenth century, both at Douala and inland, but with even less satisfactory results than previously. There are thus countless incidents of pawns not being returned as expected and, more often, apprehended unilaterally by creditors, producing violent counter-reactions on the part of alleged debtors.[107] None of these occurrences reached quite the spectacular level of the events of 1788 (see above, p. 33) but there were many nineteenth-century instances of rulers and other prominent traders being imprisoned in hulks and even beaten, as well as seizures of principal European agents by African authorities.

Disturbing as these "trust palavers" may have been, they were apparently accepted by merchants at all levels as one of the costs of doing what was still a quite profitable business.[108] Unlike prices, credit did not become any more problematic in the course of the nineteenth century and, as will be seen, the trust system continued well into the colonial era. However, it is clear that market forces alone could not provide all the conditions needed to maintain credit relationships, even at the level of reliability found in precolonial Douala.

c.   Partnership and intermarriage

If the Cameroon Littoral in the nineteenth century can be conceptualized as an integrated sector of an impersonal international market, relatively little of the trade taking place here was transacted between anonymous buyers and sellers. First of all, any carrier of large quantities of foreign goods entering either the Douala harbor or interior rivers would require some form of permission from local authorities who, in the prevailing circumstances, would themselves also be direct participants in whatever trade ensued. Secondly, the necessity of advancing import goods in order to procure palm produce dictated that incoming merchants establish long term bonds with their suppliers, whoever these might be. If European demand and European capital provided the economic basis for these bonds, their terms ultimately had to take into account local African conceptions of social obligation and even intimacy.

The element of these relationships most apparent to Europeans and one that British–Duala treaties attempted to regulate on a market basis, was the payment of tribute (comey) to Duala rulers. From the European perspective comey was, like the fees paid to local pilots for guiding European vessels into the estuary, a charge for specific services. In this case the services included provisions of anchorage, access to food and water, and space for caskhouses or factories at the "beaches" in the various Douala quarters. The treaties went so far as to calibrate the rates of comey to the tonnage of the vessels involved and set a maximal amount for land rental.[109]

Such a conception is more appropriate to the "dash" paid by transient ship captains in the eighteenth century (and still offered, under this name, as a bonus for specific deliveries of palm produce) than to the sums proffered by merchants with long-term ties to Duala rulers. Even the British treaties recognized that "in special cases, or those of resident agents, their comey [is] to be according to as they may arrange it." From the schedule of comey obligations recorded at three different periods, it is clear that the varying payments made to local rulers by European houses regularly represented at Douala depended not upon volume of traffic but, rather, the principal area of trade and protection of the firms as well as the political status of the rulers.[110] Pilotage was likewise controlled by the rivalries of the two major Duala lineages, Bell and Akwa.[111]

It is thus obvious that trade relations at Douala were inseparable from local politics, just as the power and prestige of Duala rulers depended upon their ties to both merchants and, to a lesser extent, missionaries. It is more difficult to learn in detail from available documents about the social and personal ties between traders and Duala rulers. On the one hand, it appears that European merchants, living upon their hulks, kept a certain physical and presumably also social distance from the Duala. Unlike other areas of the West African coast such as Old Calabar, Europeans did not become members of local cult societies nor did the *losango* associations, widespread as they were throughout the Littoral, ever become a basis for partnership between Duala traders and inland suppliers.[112]

On the other hand, we know from various sources that European residents in Douala (along with Creole Africans and more transient merchants and sailors) had frequent sexual relations with local women.[113] In the perception of European observers, these relations were again seen as essentially commercial i.e. a form of prostitution. While it is certain that in the cases of longer-resident Europeans (none of whom except missionaries ever brought their wives) more than prostitution was involved, it is hard to determine the full social significance of such sexual bonds.

In only two instances, those of John Lilley in the 1830s and 1840s and the Woermann agent Eduard Schmidt in 1884, are European merchants reported to have formed lasting bonds with local women, and both cases are also distinguished by the fact that the men resided on land. We have little information about the transactions by which these relationships were established although the women appear to have been of servile status and thus probably did not create anything like kinship bonds between their European mates and major Duala trading partners.[114] Two other British merchants of the 1870s and 1880s are known to have had children by the daughters of apparently free, but not prominent Duala families but again we know little more about the circumstances.[115] Buchner does, however, describe the household servants in the Woermann factory as "mainly the sons of the most noble lineages, full of hope . . . To be a 'boy' was honorable and at the same time a good education . . ."[116]

What to make of these European–Duala household ties may become clearer by comparison with the bonds between Duala merchants and their inland partners/hosts. Written sources on this aspect of the Littoral trading system are scarce and superficial, but they do reveal Duala agents residing inland for extended periods in modest residences, i.e. on much more intimate and egalitarian terms with local peoples than was the case with Europeans at Douala.[117] Information from African oral sources is less specific about matters of political economy than about politics; however, informants do state that payments were generally made to the rulers of the interior rivers and that less trade took place in open markets than through protected transactions between the big men of each side. We do learn a great deal from these records about a pattern of hypergamous intermarriage, i.e. like Europeans in Douala, Duala in the interior took local women but did not recognize such unions by the usual criterion of giving their own women in return.[118]

Such marriage patterns have very deep resonance in the local understanding of non-political hegemony in the Littoral. As explained by the Duala, they were in part simply a counter-gift from hosts to prestigious visiting merchants, like women given to Europeans at Douala. However, unlike Europeans, Duala fathers formally recognized the children of these unions and retained them in their own households. If male, such offspring could be sent back to carry on trade in the homeland of their mothers where they enjoyed a special status of *mulalo* (matrilineal nephew).[119] At one level this mulalo relationship can be seen as nothing more than the local variant of a widespread African practice by which sisters' sons enjoyed a degree of license in their uncles' households. The pattern is found throughout the Littoral and specifically in intra-Duala marriages.[120] However as instituted unilaterally across trading boundaries, it expresses and supports a sense of Duala superiority, even of an exploitative variety. Inland informants regularly explained the lack of marital reciprocity with the phrase "they called us *bakom* [slaves]." Even in the otherwise ahistorical Jeki epic, shared throughout the Littoral, a frequent theme is the hero's capture and killing of various wild beasts by the trick of claiming to be their *mulalo*.[121]

Within the closely shared African culture of the Littoral, hypergamous intermarriage thus expresses in subtle yet powerful form the status of the Duala as middlemen. It is not surprising that social ties with Europeans are less clearly articulated. The degree of contact between "natives" and expatriate merchants at Douala was far more restricted than the activity required to gather palm produce at myriad points in the interior. Moreover, the superior resources of the Europeans spoke for themselves in the commercial context and were reinforced, even if not with any orderly effect, by gunboats, consuls and missionaries. Even so, the limited transfer of women and perhaps the more explicit apprenticeship of children reinforce, as do hypergamous marriages in the interior, the characteristic regional pattern of hegemonic yet autonomous exchange.

d.   *Currencies and market language*

In order to carry on trade of the regularity and scale developed in Cameroon, a market and personal relationships were not sufficient. It was also necessary for the participants to share at least a minimal system of cultural representations and a recognition of the values they embodied.

Table 3.4. *The Douala currency system, c.* 1884

1 crew (*eloko, etoloki,*	= 10–20 shillings in import goods
etotoki, etroki)	(10 imperial gallons/100 kilo oil)
	= 2 *esuku, idoma, mbom*
	= 4 keg (*keki*)
	= 8 piggen (*mbengilan*)
	= 20 (24) bar (*bema, yamposo, kurikenge*) (1 shilling)
	= 40 (48) *esungu a yoma*

Source: adapted from Wirz, *Vom Sklavenhandel*, 75; additional sources: Helmlinger, *Dictionnaire*; Transcripts ANC/FA Court Records, 1902/2/246; Peter Makembe, "Duala Texte," *Zt. f. Eingeborenen-Sprachen* 11 (1921): 179–80. It should be noted that these sources are not always mutually consistent so that the currency system was probably less stable (and certainly more open to negotiation in any given transaction) than indicated here.

For nineteenth-century Douala, this shared culture extended beyond the minimal, but not as far as it did in other regions of West Africa. Barter trade was mediated by a currency system but without much use of money; Pidgin English on the coast and Duala in the interior allowed merchants to communicate on matters of immediate concern but not to discourse much beyond this; Christianity and local *losango* cults were widely recognized, but not practiced in such a way as to create cross-ethnic bonds.

The Douala currency system is noted by almost all observers of nineteenth-century trade in this region (see table 3.4). Its basic unit, the crew, is clearly not a tangible entity but rather a fictitious measure of value whose very etymology remains a mystery (the Duala equivalent term apparently derives from an Efik name for brass rod currency).[122] Keg and piggen (picken = Port./Sp. pequeño = small) are explicit units of export commodity measurement, as is the more ambiguous "big ting." Only the next-to-smallest unit, the bar, refers to a commodity usable as money, in Cameroon as at other points on the coast. Both nineteenth-century reports and contemporary oral evidence indicate that actual metal bars were used as currency in the Littoral interior during this period, although they had become anachronistic in Douala itself.[123]

There is no reason to expect that large-scale exchanges of import and export goods should be transacted in anything but fictitious units of equivalent value in nineteenth-century Africa any more than in modern international trade. Monetization, as a measure of market integration and cultural change, is mainly to be sought in smaller transactions of consumer goods. Iron bars would always have been too bulky and expensive to play this role. Instead, in eighteenth- and nineteenth-century Africa generally, cowrie shells, imported in very large quantities from the Indian Ocean, functioned as the major consumer money.[124] It has been noted that the Duala imported cowries during the eighteenth century but ceased doing so in the nineteenth. Probably these shells, along with the various forms of glass beads purchased in much greater quantities during this early period, were passed on to the interior, perhaps even to slave producers of the Sudanic cowrie zone; a Duala proverb even recalls that "the tribes of the interior carried on trade by means of cowries and beads."[125]

Europeans and their employees who needed to buy small quantities of consumer goods at Douala in the 1800s apparently did so with what were referred to as "little tings" (more or less synonymous with *esungu a yoma* in table 3.4). These consisted of import goods which, unlike "big tings" (mainly powder and guns), could be broken up into small allotments and bartered for eggs, yams, chickens, woven mats, etc. A certain quantity of British coinage, paid out to African sailors and Douala merchant house employees, also served such purposes but the main standard by which local consumption items were measured continued to be their bar or (at most) piggen equivalent in imported commodities.[126] However, for both Europeans and Duala, most items of daily consumption do not seem to have been purchased on the local market but rather supplied either from overseas (for Europeans) or by the labor of their own retainers (water and wood for Europeans, almost everything for the Duala or any expatriates with local women in their households).

The limited integration of domestic African economies into local systems of international trade has inspired some scholars to perceive the monetary terms of the latter as "fixed equivalencies" which inhibited the exposure of African societies to market forces. This concept has been used to argue both for and against the hegemonic character of international trade: either Europeans and middlemen unilaterally manipulated market factors in their favor or they were forced to adapt to indigenous anti-market values.[127] In the case of the Cameroon Littoral, this entire assumption is difficult to defend. It has already been demonstrated that competition among European merchants and changes in international prices stimulated market responses among African sellers and producers of exports. The local currency system often registered these changes without shifts in formal prices by altering the content or substantive size of a given unit. The well-reported bargaining among Europeans and Duala thus involved both the quality of import goods and subtleties of their quantity (e.g. the folding of cloth) as well as the amounts of dash and terms of credit added to each immediate exchange. In the interior, the key variable appears to have been the size of containers making up a given unit. Contemporary European observers accused the Duala of manipulating such measures to their advantage,[128] but it is unlikely that interior suppliers could not perceive the price changes involved in such shifts. In fact, during the early 1870s (a time of price pressures on the coast) the Duala and their usually least problematic suppliers, the Pongo, entered into a violent conflict that is remembered in songs still current today as the affair of "Keki Mukudi" (the false measure).[129]

If the system of market values in the Littoral, like the market itself, seems essentially neutral, the language in which these values as well as general market communication were expressed does represent – in several senses of this verb – the cultural hegemony of both Europeans and Duala. Very few European merchants on the coast ever learned West African languages, forcing their local trading partners to speak a form of English (with some Portuguese admixture) now known as Pidgin.[130] The Duala in turn imposed their language as the medium of internal trade. As with everything else in this larger commercial zone, linguistic hegemony gave no immediate powers of control to native speakers of the dominant idiom; indeed, it could be argued that the Duala or their own inland partners (when these did not already speak a language very close to Duala) had actually gained something by acquiring a second tongue. Early accounts of the fact that Duala rulers could speak "English" are meant to be complimentary.[131]

More will be said in later chapters about the role of the Duala language as an element of internal hegemony, when this issue is joined to the questions of colonial education policies. However, the effect of Pidgin in European–Duala relations is already evident in the nineteenth century. Not only did such linguistic practice strengthen a general sense of Europe as the source of all empowerment, but it also forced the Duala to accept nomenclature for themselves that Europeans could then mock ("the so-called kings") or that directly expressed condescension and even racist contempt ("Charley Dido," "Looking Glass Bell," "Hickory [= Niggery] Town"). Had Cameroon Pidgin developed into a fuller "Creole" language,[132] it might have been possible for the Duala to transcend this early position of linguistic subservience; but for reasons connected with the colonial experience it has remained an idiom of secondary usage, bearing within it the stigma of incomplete mastery of a dominant culture.

The politics of disorder

In the course of the nineteenth century Douala became notorious for the frequent outbreaks of violent conflict involving every level of the local trading system: Duala vs. Europeans; Duala vs. inland peoples; major chiefdoms (Akwa, Bell, Deido) vs. one another; and between groups within each chiefdom (succession struggles, town vs. town, slave vs. free).

A detailed chronology of these clashes would make for tedious and largely meaningless history. What we need to understand instead is their relationship to both change and stability in the world of the Littoral. Most obviously, the myriad struggles over power and wealth must be linked to the commercial development which is the central dynamic of this era. At the same time, the very petty and repetitive nature of the affairs in question implies the survival of an inherited segmentary political system. Finally, we have to examine the connections between politics within Douala during the free trade era and the imposition of European colonial rule upon Cameroon.

Political competition and political economy

If Duala politics in the nineteenth century had any positive direction, we must look for it first in the most obvious place: the competition between those chiefdoms (Bell, Akwa and Deido) with some claims to centralized authority. For better or worse these entities became the vehicles for mediating and exploiting trading relations between the coast and interior as well as defining the position of lesser towns and slaves within Douala itself. It has already been made clear that no Duala rulers were able to fulfill such a role very effectively. But before dismissing their efforts as either re-enactments of pre-state social patterns or preludes to colonialism, it is important to consider seriously the rise and fall of rulers who did, at the very least, play an important part in the expansion of the Littoral trade network.

If we view these politics in chronological terms they fall into three major periods: (1) the establishment of a Bell-Akwa equilibrium; (2) the rise and check of Deido; and (3) the reassertion of Bell hegemony (see above table 1.1). The successes and failures implicit in this periodization depend a great deal upon personalities, but also upon more abstract and less parochial issues of social organization.

In the previous chapter we traced the shift in Duala politics from a single center of authority to a dual one: the "classical" opposition of Bell and Akwa, with Bonaberi as a lesser polity (without a "king") on the opposite river bank. In that story Akwa, represented by Kwane and Ngando a Kwa, clearly played the more active role. Akwa's position grew out of a weakness in the more "legitimate" Bell line (an uncontrollably violent Priso a Doo and a less vigorous Doo a Makongo and Bele a Doo). However, Akwa claims to ascendancy remained tainted by both the recency of their emergence as well as their descent from the "slave" Kuo a Mapoka. Even in the late nineteenth century, they were excluded from the *jengu* cult by the Bells, thus implying a not-wholly-free status.[133]

The dynamic of this relationship is the familiar one of slightly marginalized groups pursuing new economic opportunities to advance themselves beyond the existing establishment. In fact Akwa had a larger population than Bell throughout the nineteenth century and did enjoy, as noted, some advantage in trading relations with Basaa and Bakoko peoples as well as the founding of inland servile villages. However the general possibilities for expansion during the earlier decades of this period seem to have obviated any need for mutually destructive competition. In the records of the 1820s through 1840s Bell and Akwa rivalries only become politically sensitive at moments of succession, when British intervention would be sought both by rivals within the Akwa camp and by the king of the opposing sector, claiming violations of treaties against human sacrifice.[134]

This equilibrium was upset during the middle decades of the century by the rise of Deido as an even less legitimate and more dynamic trading center than Akwa. When first heard of in 1845 under its apparently founding ruler, Ebule Ebele (Ned Deido; D2 in table 1.1), Deido is an important center of trade ("Ned" is said to have visited Britain), which is even making a play for Baptist mission patronage, but does not yet seriously challenge Akwa (under whose authority it theoretically lies) or Bell.[135] By the 1850s "Ned Dido" is a regular signatory of treaties on a level just below the two main rulers (as "chief" or "headman" rather than "king");[136] at the same time, he is facing an internal challenge from his junior half-brother, Eyum (Charley Deido). In 1856 Deido was already a sufficient threat to the main Douala rulers that it was violently attacked by Akwa, possibly in league with Bell.[137] Twenty years later, in 1876, Eyum was apparently in sole control of Deido but, upon refusing to punish a homicide by one of his subordinate chiefs, he was attacked by the combined forces of Bell and Akwa, captured, and then publicly executed.[138]

Because it involved all the local rulers, the execution of Eyum Ebele/Charley Deido has become a focal event in the explanation of precolonial Duala history and political development. We will return shortly to the institutional aspects of this historiography. In terms of a simple struggle for power, it marks a return to equilibrium: Eyum, the oldest and possibly most violently ambitious trader on the river[139] is kept in check although Deido remains an autonomous and important force in the Littoral political-economic universe. In fact, immediately after Eyum's death the Deido merchants were able to negotiate their re-establishment in Douala by using their place of inland refuge as a base for blocking all trade to the coast.

If the rise of Deido can be associated with the general expansion of oil trade during the middle decades of the century, its restriction coincides with the fall in prices of the last decades before annexation. The most effective positive response available to the Duala in such a situation was the expansion of inland networks so as to lower prices paid to suppliers. In such an endeavor the Deido merchants may have labored at a disadvantage, since they did not have satellite slave villages and relations with interior peoples comparable to those of the longer-established Bell and Akwa. Akwa in turn suffered from the difficulty of expanding into the Sanaga against energetic Bakoko competition, and also because of the personal limitations of its rulers during this period, Mpondo and Dika (translated as "stingy").[140] Ndumbe Lobe Bell and his English-educated son Manga, on the other hand, were well qualified to take the steps necessary for expanding trade, particularly, as already seen, in the rich Mungo region. King Bell had even succeeded, during the late 1870s, in exploiting Akwa trust quarrels with Kwa Kwa traders so as to enter into the commerce of this river for the first time.[141]

The limited ascendancy of Bell in the decade preceding annexation is reflected in the relative comey payments to each chief. In the 1860s all major rulers received the same amount, but by 1878 Bell was paid 80 crew by each merchant house and Akwa only 60. In 1884 the total allotted to Bell was 500 crew, while that of Akwa amounted to just 300. However, these last figures only reflect the number of merchants (and presumably the quantity of produce) present at the respective Douala quarters. Each trader was now required to pay Bell and Akwa the same sum (80 crew if anchored there, 10 crew if only trading; Deido received only 50 crew for anchored vessels but the one Bonaberi hulk also paid 80 crew).[142] This information suggests that the trade advantage of Bell had not been converted into any kind of formal recognition (or re-recognition) as a paramount Duala ruler. But to consider this issue we must examine the changes, if any, that occurred in the Duala political system during the nineteenth century.

Institutional change and stasis

Attentive readers of the previous chapter will already know that the present analysis of internal Duala competition will not conclude with any argument for the emergence of a more centralized state structure. However, a re-examination of nineteenth-century events in terms of the potential for change will provide both a clearer sense of what segmentary politics is about as well as a final prelude to the critical moment of colonial annexation.

There are two issues in nineteenth-century Douala politics that suggest at least the possibility of movement towards centralization: the European

Court of Equity and the collective Duala action against Eyum Ebele/Charley Deido. In indigenous twentieth-century historiography, these issues have been linked through the concept of the Ngondo or General Assembly of the Duala People.[143]

The failure of European efforts at organizing Douala merchants and chiefs into an effective judicial, to say nothing of administrative, body have already been discussed. All that needs to be added here is that this failure grew largely out of the segmentary nature of the merchant presence: a series of mutually competing firms which (in the case of the two German houses) could even split off into a greater number of units when the market expanded. Conceivably the combination of political instability and price decline could have produced a consolidation of these units or their take-over by an ambitious outside force, as occurred to some extent in the case of Sir George Goldie's United/National African Company in the Niger Delta.[144] However, just as Goldie met considerable resistance from established British firms in the future Nigeria, so these and similar firms in Cameroon undermined efforts of British consuls to bring them closer together before 1884. Moreover, as will be seen in the next chapter, even the more politically conscious German firms refused after 1884 to go along with Bismarck's schemes to make them govern the new colony. The only effective authority at Douala in the nineteenth century was the British combination of gunboats and consuls, but this remained too sporadic a presence to transform local institutions.

Eyum Ebele's execution does represent a unique instance of collective action by the other Duala rulers, precisely at a moment when the Court of Equity had been warned against taking upon itself the role of "native rulers."[145] There is some evidence that the European merchants had informally encouraged the sanctioning of the Deido ruler because his refusal to punish violence within his own territory (as well as his previous behavior) represented a particularly blatant threat to the order of local trading affairs.[146] The term Ngondo can be linked to these accounts only as the name of the sandbar between the Bell and Akwa territories where Eyum's death actually took place. The missionary observer George Grenfell records a contemporary Duala explanation for the choice of this terrain that provides some cultural, if not historical, basis for the later elaboration of the Ngondo concept: the sandbar was neutral ground which prevented Eyum from petitioning, "according to country fashion," either Bell or Akwa for sanctuary (and apparently Bell was inclined to make such an offer).[147]

If the 1876 Deido affair neither manifested nor brought about the existence of any collective Duala political organization, it does at least represent a momentary transcendence of segmentary political behavior.

However, the events immediately leading to this act represent segmentary politics at its most extreme i.e. a conflict between two "towns" within the Deido chiefdom, where the followers of the late Ebule/Ned had apparently not yet accepted the authority of Eyum/Charley. Moreover Bell and Akwa seem to have used the occasion of this internal Deido struggle to reassert the political system that had prevailed previously rather than either of them allowing the other to gain a long-term advantage by alliance with the energetic Deido merchants.

The more direct rivalry between Bell and Akwa took a similarly segmentary form, with units splitting off at strategic moments from whichever party seemed to be gaining in strength. The very emergence of an autonomous Deido during the lifetime of Ngando a Kwa, a period of Akwa ascendence, may be interpreted in these terms. An 1872–74 set of "wars" between Bell and Akwa centered around the attempt of a subordinate Bell unit, Bonapriso (Joss), to secede to the now weaker Akwa. During this conflict Deido sided with Bell, although no major battles were fought and much of the difficulty (from the viewpoint of the reporting British consuls) appears to be confused with trade stoppages resulting from price issues.[148] Finally, on the very eve of German annexation, in 1882–83, three of King Bell's brothers entered into a violent quarrel with him and found support from both Akwa and another of Bell's supposed subordinates, the ruler of Bonaberi on the opposite Wouri bank.[149]

What all this splintering suggests about the underlying relationship between "trade and politics" is that the limited paramount status of a Bell or Akwa was not reinforced by the functional needs of mercantile ventures. For purposes of effective trade the critical unit was not a more centrally organized chiefdom but rather a group of related households constituting the "towns" which in turn comprised the (often dissident) sub-units of the Bell, Akwa and Deido chiefdoms.[150] Ebule/Ned and Eyum/Charley Deido appear to have based their political claims upon mobilization of such trading units. In the late 1870s King Ndumbe Lobe Bell and his son Manga combined rulership and commerce much more effectively than did Kings Mpondo or Dika Akwa, neither of whom organized the major trading operations within the Akwa quarter. However, the success of a "royal" Bell trading establishment along the Mungo could arouse just as much jealousy among lesser towns supposedly subject to Bell sovereignty as those outside it, resulting in the kinds of splits that have been observed.

A further line of tension or potential transformation within the individual trading units was the division between *bakom* (slaves) and *wonja* (freeborn Duala).[151] British intervention on the West African coast had done nothing to inhibit the flourishing internal slave trade, and various treaties signed with the Duala (see table 3.1) explicitly recognized local property rights in slaves. Within nineteenth-century Duala society, slaves were the key element in constructing an effective commercial organization but suffered both socially, by their limited possibilities for advancement, and physically, when they became the victims of petty warfare and rituals of sacrifice and plunder. Although abolitionist-minded European observers tended to exaggerate the strains arising from servile institutions, the idiom of slave-free clearly pervaded much of the indigenous discourse on relationships between groups in the Littoral. It is also possible to link the role of slaves with a general theme of morbidity and witchcraft in the entire middleman role of the Duala, a people who drew on the reproductive forces of the interior not only to enrich themselves in overseas trade of different kinds but also to maintain the stagnant demography of Douala itself.[152]

In the immediate nineteenth-century context, however, there were severe limits to the impositions that could be placed upon Duala slaves. By most counts slaves constituted the majority of the population in Douala throughout the period, and the only groups among them to be under anything like close surveillance were those in the relatively privileged positions of household retainers and the crews of trading expeditions. The greatest number worked in agriculture or as auxiliary fishermen in relative autonomy from their masters. We do have reports of slave uprisings in 1858, 1859 and 1870 as responses to particularly onerous abuses in both Akwa and Bell. Rather than demonstrating any need for transformation, however, these events reveal how the slaves could defend their interests and thus maintain social equilibrium.[153]

For purposes of resisting excessive exploitation, slaves drew upon the same instruments as those used by their "free" Duala master: *losango* cults (in the case of slaves drawn from nearby inland areas, specifically Abo in 1858 and 1859). The followers of Eyum Ebele/Charley Deido, stigmatized as descendents of slaves, had likewise threatened "to buy our own *Elong* elsewhere" when sanctioned by one of the major Duala *losango* with this name.[154] The consciousness being expressed here seems less one of class or caste than of a simultaneously hierarchical and segmentary social order in which the lower ranked groups could use the same devices as the higher ones to defend and even advance their position. Thus, if the other peoples of the Littoral were *bakom* to the Duala, these communities held numerous slaves of their own from farther in the interior, particularly the over-populated Grassfields. As with so many issues in Duala development, attempts to transcend or transform these relationships would only occur when all of the groups involved were confronted by a common external threat, something which did not occur here until after the establishment of colonial rule.

Internal crises and colonial annexation

Along with a reputation for exceptional disorder, Douala is distinguished among the nineteenth-century oil trading centers of West Africa for the unsolicited letters written by its rulers requesting British sovereignty. The obvious conclusion drawn by historians from this evidence is that the strains of the middleman role had caused a complete breakdown of local society and that colonialism was the only available solution.[155] In reconsidering this judgment and at last concluding the present chapter we must address three sets of questions: to what extent had the Duala system really broken down by the 1880s? What did Duala rulers understand by British (or later German) sovereignty? And what is the connection between local developments of any kind and the European decisions to annex Cameroon? In sum, could the hegemonic system of relations in the Littoral have continued to meet either European or African needs without the imposition of some central authority?

The failure of various efforts to assert political control over the trading world of Douala has been the central theme of this entire chapter. However, such failure is not itself evidence of crisis; on the contrary, it is conceivable that the prevailing system of "trade and politics" resisted radical transformation precisely because it could go on without it. A review of the problems arising within this system suggests that, if not resolved, they had at least receded by the 1880s.

The previous narrative has identified several issues that, in varying degrees of significance, underlay the specific problems arising at Douala: first, the violent competition among local rulers for pre-eminence; second, declining produce prices; and last (and probably least, except in its relation to the first) social tensions between freeborn and slaves. The decade of the 1870s witnessed the simultaneous eruption of all these issues in a form that brought local disorder to its peak. Bell and Akwa fought their only real wars during this period although the response to the challenge and internal disorder of Deido probably occasioned a higher level of violence, especially if the deaths of freeborn elites are given greater weight than those of slaves. This is also the period when declining palm oil prices became a permanent fact of local economic life leading to extended African export stoppages and a decline in the number of local expatriate purchasers. 1870 also marks the last slave uprising in Douala, despite the fact that slaves were to be the major casualties in the ensuing local wars.

During the half-decade preceding colonial annexation it appears that most of these problems had considerably subsided. Political conflicts continued to take place among the Duala, but these mainly involved defections within the Bell and Akwa camps rather than direct confrontations between major political units. Palm oil prices fluctuated but immedi-

Table 3.5. *Douala shipping, 1878–84 tonnage of cargo ships entering (fig-ures in parentheses = total no. of ships)*

1878	1879	1880	1881	1882	1883	1884[1]
16,729	19,600	12,129	18,097	29,115	38,742	59,802
(19)	(23)	(17)	(25)	(31)	(35)	(35)

[1]Through July only.
Source: Eduard Schmidt report, August 1, 1884, CSO 6/3/5.

ately around 1883–84 they recovered somewhat and the volume of trade increased (see table 3.5). More importantly, palm kernels now supplement-ed oil as a major export and the number of European firms at Douala was at a new peak. The price issue had also been alleviated by Duala success in establishing more direct contact with remote inland suppliers, thus causing new political difficulties with secondary middlemen such as the Abo and possibly the Bodiman. It is difficult to consider these last conflicts as a crisis: rather they were a challenge that might have stimulated greater collective action by the Duala but instead only became absorbed into their internecine disputes.[156]

Even if, from a historical observer's perspective, there seems to have been no critical deterioration of the Douala situation in the 1880s, it is possible to see the requests for British sovereignty by the Bell and Akwa rulers as evidence that the key African actors in this arena no longer found their situation bearable. The documentation of these requests is not all that historians would desire and their accounts have thus sometimes been confused.[157] But there can be little doubt that the well-known letters from King Akwa in 1879 and Kings Bell and Akwa in 1881 were preceded by less formal statements of similar sentiments possibly going back as far as 1857.[158] In 1881 Bell and Akwa put their position in what appear to be very unambiguous terms: "We are tired of governing this country our-selves; every dispute leads to war and often to great loss of lives."[159]

The full historical meaning of these statements does, nonetheless, re-main ambiguous. We can agree with Ardener and Wirz that the 1879 and 1881 letters express the sentiments of their authors rather than the dis-guised ambitions of merchants and consuls.[160] Wirz has noted the prob-able role of Baptist missionaries in composing the texts and even inspiring their content; but, as already seen, the Baptists were not powerful enough at Douala to influence such major political initiatives by local rulers. The problem in explicating these demands for British rule lies rather in the concept of sovereignty held by the authors and its relationship to previous nineteenth-century developments in and around Douala.

The only references to sovereignty in the Bell and Akwa letters are, not surprisingly, rather vague. Dika Akwa, in his 1879 request for British rule, states that he wants Douala "to be like Calabar now." Since Calabar was, at this time, not a colony at all but had become the headquarters of the British Consul for the Bight of Biafra, we might infer that the Duala rulers sought no greater change in their political status than a strengthening of the Court of Equity, enforced and regulated by a constant consular presence. On the other hand, the references to the failure of their own rule, based particularly on the disorderly experience of the 1870s, imply a more serious transformation.

There are also specific statements of change in non-political areas that suggest readiness for a major break with the past. Dika Akwa and his chiefs thus declare themselves ready, in 1879, to "have every fashion altered." In a meeting with Consul Hewett in early 1883 all the kings and chiefs insisted upon their desire for British rule, even if it meant giving up domestic slavery, "country custom" (losango and related cults), polygamy and their monopoly of trade with the interior.[161]

In the final balance, however, it appears that the Duala rulers did not expect to lose very much from the acceptance of foreign sovereignty. Their own experience of a constantly segmenting balance of mutual power demonstrated that even a highly successful Bell could not achieve any real control over affairs within Douala. The previous British presence, punctuated by treaties promising (but never imposing) many of the conditions threatened by Hewett in 1883 (and compromised even by him in the same year[162]) had brought them increased prosperity. More of the same would mean primarily the arbitration of quarrels and the limitation of violence from which none had gained and that had little value in the historical self-conception of the Duala. Even the "surrender" of monopoly over inland trade was less than threatening, since the middleman role of the Duala depended more upon their own increased access to the interior than it did upon excluding European merchants, who had never shown much inclination to move off their hulks, let alone beyond the coast. In short, the Duala had profited from a relatively free market and seem to have envisaged British sovereignty in classical liberal terms, as an instrument of arbitration that would protect their comparative advantage while releasing them from a prisoner's dilemma of competing for unattainable and economically valueless political domination.

If the Duala conception of British rule centered around a continuation of the established middleman position, the European decision to undertake such responsibility still retains the aura of a major political shift, which has been subject to endless historiographic debate. While it is not appropriate to enter extensively into this controversy here, it should be noted that the recent consensus appears to support a "big bang" rather than a "steady state" interpretation of the annexation process. It seems to have been driven more by Great Power politics and internal socio-economic anxieties within Europe than by the logic of ongoing relationships in Africa.[163] Such a conclusion is consistent with the lack of awareness by Duala leaders of what would come from their appeals for an enhanced local European presence.

It is difficult to specify the motivations of Europeans immediately involved in establishing colonial rule over Cameroon, since they were always reacting both to local developments and messages from a larger theater of political action where "the Scramble for Africa" had already begun. Particularly important here are the actions of France in challenging the British position on the Niger and in the Congo. There had never been any significant French presence in Cameroon up to 1883 but in March of that year, essentially as a by-product of the Niger and Congo questions, France signed a protectorate treaty with one of the chiefs at Malimba, located immediately to the south of Douala.[164]

For British and German trading firms in Douala, the perspective of domination by France, an alien power known for its protectionist interference with commerce, must have seemed a sufficient reason to demand counter-moves on the part of their own respective governments. In the case of the British merchants, it is difficult to find any evidence of interest in taking formal control over Cameroon prior to the emergence of the French threat. Metropolitan responses to the "Great Depression" had stimulated new interest in African commerce generally during the late 1870s but these were never directed specifically at Cameroon and, in any case, had receded during the early 1880s, to be revived only in the context of Congo affairs later in the decade.[165]

On the German side, it was Eduard Schmidt, resident agent of the Woermann firm, who actually signed the initial protectorate treaties with the Duala. There can also be no doubt that Schmidt's Hamburg chief, Adolf Woermann, was a major force behind the metropolitan policies supporting this move.[166] It is also possible to find a basis for such colonialism in earlier nationalistic sentiments and expressions of dissatisfaction with informal British hegemony among German merchants at Douala. Thormählen, Woermann's first agent in Cameroon, was even excluded from the Court of Equity in the late 1860s. However, from this date onward available records indicate that the Germans were treated by British consuls on an equal footing with their own countrymen.[167] Indeed, by 1883 the two German firms in the Wouri had, between them, over half the local export trade.[168]

In July 1883 the Hamburg Chamber of Commerce sent the government a memorandum specifically requesting both a German consular-naval presence in West Africa and a colony in Cameroon. However, this document also makes reference to both the French at Malimba and the fair treatment hitherto received from British representatives.[169] Woermann seems to have been won over to formal colonialism only under the pressure of French and British initiatives; as late as 1879 and 1881, he responded to domestic German colonial propaganda with only cautious endorsement and a vigorous defense of free trade (including the trust system).[170] Since it was Germany that actually annexed Cameroon, the lack of clear colonial goals by German merchants already active there would have complex results for the later fate of the Duala.

Of all the local participants in colonial partition it was only the British consul Hewett and the Baptist missionaries who appear to have been consistently motivated by a vision of altering the existing system of Littoral trade. The Baptists had little influence over policies in Cameroon (they would quickly be expelled by the Germans, see next chapter). But Hewett, despite the eventual failure of his annexation efforts, was an important factor in the German decision to act in this region. Hewett's energetic responses to the 1881 requests for protection from Bell and Akwa precede the French treaty with Malimba and make a very clear argument for breaking with the existing system:

> If not actually stated, it certainly must have been intended by those who framed the Commercial Treaties with the various Kings along the coast, that while we employed them as our middlemen they should do the best for trade; but in this . . . they have proved themselves sadly remiss. I cannot therefore but think that steps should be taken to prevent their continuing to be obstacles in the way of extending our trade . . .[171]

The implementation of a policy that would allow such changes was costly, probably far too much so for it ever to have been pursued on the basis of protecting the marginal existing trade with Cameroon or gambling on the very uncertain rewards of more direct contacts with the interior. However, the exogenous "big bang" of heated international rivalry provided the extra incentive for European governments to take such risks in the mid-1880s. The Duala middlemen had thus proved themselves capable of responding – even if in characteristically non-heroic fashion – to the economic demands of free trade. They would now be tested in a new context created by politics remote from the affairs of the Cameroon Littoral.

4 Mythic transformation and historical continuity: Duala middlemen and German colonial rule, 1884–1914

There is no period of the Duala past so fully documented in both written records and oral memory as the thirty years during which Germany occupied the Cameroon Littoral. Yet, for reasons closely connected to the existence of such materials, both European and African historical imagination have endowed the events and personalities of this relatively recent era with an aura of mythic heroism and tragedy far beyond that ascribed to more distant precolonial times.[1]

The established accounts of the German–Duala encounter are constructed around not one but three, somewhat contradictory, myths. The first is a Faustian myth of the German *Sonderweg* (exceptional historical path), rooted in the role of Germany as the dynamic yet dark center of modern European development and underscored by the exceptionality of an African colonial experience distinguished from the "ordinary" rule of Britain and France. Secondly, there is the myth of extreme colonial oppression, based upon the catastrophic climax of German rule in Douala in which the leading local chief, Rudolf Duala Manga Bell, was executed for high treason. Finally there is the Golden Age myth, cultivated among the Duala with adult experience spanning the German and subsequent French mandate periods, which contrasts the prominence and prosperity achieved during the former era with the relative obscurity that followed.[2]

We refer to these presentations of the Duala–German relationship as myths not because they are completely untrue (all can be supported with extensive evidence) but rather because the only way in which their various truths can be reconciled is to recognize an ambiguity and also a banality in colonial history that the myths themselves obscure. Nonetheless, one cannot simply dismiss such one-sided and inflated presentations of an important era in the past. First of all, they persist as a subtext that indicates the relevance of the German experience for Duala historical identity and explains the fascination of this period for both historians and the lay public. Secondly, both the internal contradictions among these myths and their joint contrast with "real" history point to the central ambiguity that makes the German era so important: it represents the moment when

Europeans, shifting from hegemony to formal control, were to redirect the course of African development in their own terms; yet it reveals the absence of the means, the will or even the very terms necessary to carry out such a transformation.

The colonial order in Cameroon was specifically dedicated to creating a territorial entity in which the kind of political, economic and cultural middleman role exercised by the Duala would cease to exist: Europeans and not Africans were to be the political sovereigns; the economy of the hinterland was to be opened up to direct domination by European merchants and, eventually, producers; and the values and idioms guiding such changes were to come from Europe rather than Africa. But in all these spheres of activity, the Germans found that they had to rely upon African, and more specifically Duala, intermediaries. Thus despite losing their autonomy and ultimately their central position within Cameroon, the Duala found themselves occupying political offices more powerful than those existing in the past, enjoying new opportunities for economic enterprise, and acting as cultural brokers between Europe and an expanded hinterland. To understand this further unfolding of the middleman paradox we first need to examine the various arenas in which the Duala struggled to maintain themselves both against and with the Germans and then pursue the conflicts around the control of urban space that created such a dramatic final confrontation between the Duala people and their earliest European rulers.

The Duala and the German state

At the level of politics, German colonial rule in Africa diverged from that of Britain or France through two important characteristics: first, the lack of an historical model for the administrative organization of overseas territories; and second, the very active involvement of the metropolitan parliament, the Reichstag, in colonial affairs. Both of these peculiarities can be traced to the sudden manner in which Germany entered the ranks of the European Great Powers. No further explanation is needed for the lack of colonial experience but the Reichstag role, which became figuratively and literally fatal for the Duala, requires some comment.

This unusual level of legislative colonial concern did not derive from the substantive interest in Africa among German strategic or economic interest groups but was rather an artifact of the general position of the Reichstag in the Wilhelmian state. This national body was elected, from its inception, by universal manhood suffrage and thus represented a wide range of sophisticated ideological positions; however, the conservative Prince Otto von Bismarck had designed the new political system so as to deprive the Reichstag of real control over such critical issues as the selection of the chancellor (prime minister), the military budget, and the internal affairs of the supposedly subordinate state of Prussia (covering most of Germany). The Reichstag thus devoted a disproportionate amount of its considerable energies to those matters (including the colonies) left fully under its jurisdiction, partly as a device for eventually widening such jurisdiction.[3]

In a specific locale such as Douala, the political role of any colonial regime was to provide the central authority needed to resolve endemic disputes over "trade and politics." However, it took the Germans considerable time even to put in place the European apparatus needed to establish minimal order in the Cameroon Littoral, let alone integrate this region into a structure embracing the entire territory of Cameroon. This process involved not the elimination of Duala indigenous rulership but rather its definition in a more powerful, if externally constrained, form. But in the German case, external constraint also opened a metropolitan arena for African politics, with dramatic results even before the cataclysmic expropriation crisis.

German administration: defining a colonial entity

For Germany to rule the Duala, it was first necessary to establish both the organizational basis for political domination and its relationship to wider territorial control. The German achievement of such a definition required often painful passage through a series of unplanned stages: first retreat to a modified version of the previous British consular system, then a more formal government limited to the Littoral, third a disorderly advance into the interior, and finally a "reformed" regime which culminated in the crisis of Douala expropriation.

Neo-consular rule, 1884–1885

Had the goals of colonial expansion been evident at the time of Cameroon's annexation, a model for ruling the new territory might quickly have suggested itself to the Germans. However, it immediately became evident that both the Berlin government and the Hamburg merchant firms already active on the coast were clear only about what they wanted to avoid when a local government was established.

What Chancellor Bismarck did *not* want in the recently acquired colonial territories was a "French" practice of costly bureaucratic structures. Beside the immediate budgetary burdens of such a system, Bismarck correctly foresaw the political advantages it would give to opposition parties in the Reichstag. Instead, he attempted to follow a supposedly

"British" method of delegating the tasks of colonial rule to private bodies with immediate economic interests in the overseas territories. On this basis, Bismarck negotiated with the firms of Woermann and Jantzen & Thormählen who, together with several other German merchant houses, formed a "Syndikat für Westafrika" that was to govern both Cameroon and the other German West African territory of Togo.[4] The firms steadfastly refused to accept such a burden, but they and Bismarck seem to have tacitly agreed that at least in the short run, German needs could be met by a permanently stationed official with powers similar to that of the earlier peripatetic British consul.[5] However, events on the spot quickly made this run much shorter than anticipated.

The unfurling of the imperial banner not only failed to solve any of the Duala political divisions but added to them a far more explosive issue: the polarization of local forces around Anglo-German rivalry. At an international level, Britain never challenged Germany's claims to the Wouri estuary. However, the Foreign Office did attempt for a time to retain the Baptist settlement at Victoria and also solicited new "protectorate" treaties with rulers in the West Cameroon hinterland (see above table 3.1). Within Douala, British merchants also continued to outnumber representatives of German firms. Efforts to replace the Court of Equity with a German-dominated Cameroons Council met with a British boycott, amidst rumors of plots by merchants and Baptist missionaries to undo the new colonial arrangements. The German Imperial West African Commissioner, Gustav Nachtigal, emulated his British predecessors by departing from Douala soon after signing the annexation agreements, but he did leave behind a makeshift permanent representation in the person of his deputy, the physician Max Buchner.[6]

Under such circumstances, it is not surprising that those Duala segments dissatisfied with both the continued ascendancy of Bell and the new arrangements made with Germany should undertake violent action. The center of this dissent was Bonaberi ("Hickory"), the Duala quarter located across the Wouri river from the main town and theoretically subordinate to Bell. One of King Ndumbe Lobe Bell's major motives in seeking European protection was to prevent the kind of defections that had been attempted in the 1870s and early 1880s by segments of his following, including Bonaberi. However, Kum a Mbape (Lock Priso), the Bonaberi ruler, was the only significant Duala chief not to have signed a German protectorate treaty in July 1884. Believing (probably with some local European encouragement) that he would have the support of the British, Kum attacked and burnt Belltown in December 1884. This effort was supported by the ruler and inhabitants of Bonapriso (Joss), a community that had been at the center of earlier internecine Bell politics and subsequent Akwa–Bell warfare (see above, p. 86).[7]

Table 4.1. *German governors of Cameroon*

1885–1890	Julius Freiherr von Soden
1891–1895	Eugen von Zimmerer (acting governor 1890)
1895–1907	Jesco von Puttkamer
1907–1910	Theodor Seitz
1910–1911	Otto Gleim
1912–1915	Karl Ebermaier

Note: for concise biographies of these governors, see Hausen, *Deutsche Kolonialherrschaft*, 306–8.

Buchner reacted to these events by calling in the small naval squadron that had been patrolling West Africa to back up German interests in the volatile Scramble process. Gunners and marines from the ships quickly suppressed the revolt by destroying both Bonaberi and Bonapriso. The fighting cost the life of Woermann's Belltown European agent as well as twenty-five or more Duala (including a brother of the Bonapriso chief). In Duala terms this was a major war and one that ended any efforts at military challenge to European rule. For the Germans, the rebellion demonstrated the need to move beyond the methods of informal empire. The ineffectual (but for historians, very informative) Buchner immediately surrendered local authority to Admiral Knorr, commander of the West African squadron, who remained in charge until July 1885, when the first colonial Governor, Julius Freiherr von Soden, arrived at Douala.[8]

Restricted formal administration, 1885–c. 1900

In principle Soden and his immediate successors (see table 4.1) possessed the full accoutrements of a colonial state: a civil bureaucracy, a military force, and at least the beginnings of a modern transport link between the coast and interior in the form of several small steam vessels. The new order was physically represented by its quarters on the Joss plateau, confiscated for government use from the rebels of December 1884. However, even after the collapse of Bismarck's "British" model and the departure from power of Bismarck himself, the Reich was not committed to large-scale political investment in its colonies. The European administrative staff thus remained small; military organization grew slowly and was based mainly on African recruits (first foreign *Polizeitruppen* and only after 1895 a Cameroonian *Schutztruppe*); mechanized travel and effective administration remained limited to the coast and Littoral river system.

This apparatus was sufficient to inhibit the Duala from any direct contestation of German rule, but was kept very busy asserting its authority over small inland rulers, especially along the Wouri, Abo and Sanaga rivers.[9] Modest as it was in territorial extent, the conquest of the coast also incurred political costs in the Reichstag. Deputies of the liberal and socialist left made considerable capital out of the scandals surrounding a mutiny by Dahomean police conscripts and the extreme mistreatment of inland chiefs and villagers.[10]

The relevance for Duala commerce of these campaigns, as well as the more ambitious German expeditions towards Yaoundé and the West Cameroon Grassfields, will be discussed below. From a political perspective, the Duala found themselves collaborating with the Germans against peoples they had never been able to overcome on their own and thus refused to take sides with either the Dahomean mutineers or inland rulers.[11] The Germans, in turn, formalized this relationship by delegating official powers to chiefs who accepted their authority, which meant primarily the Duala.[12] Although no official representative or judicial body brought together government officials, European merchants, missionaries and African chiefs, the small scale of the colonial bureaucracy and the fact that it was centered in Douala meant that much of the political style of the earlier consular regime survived on an informal basis.[13]

The Puttkamer era, c. 1897–1907

The most radical shift in the administrative status of Douala occurred under the aegis of the one colonial governor who would embody all the mythic qualities of German rule, Jesco von Puttkamer.[14] Although Puttkamer had begun his colonial career at Douala as *Kanzler* (second in command) under Governor von Soden in 1885–87 and presided over a restricted coastal regime during the first years of his own lengthy governorship he began, even before his second tour in Cameroon, to formulate several projects that would dramatically shift the focus of Cameroon development: first the establishment of large-scale European plantations in the area of Mount Cameroon; second the granting of vast northwest and south Cameroon forest zones to parastatal concession companies; and finally the extension of political control over the densely populated savannah regions of the Grassfields and Adamawa.[15] None of these policies worked out in the way Puttkamer and his allies had planned, but their combined permanent effect was to shift the focus of German policy away from the coast. This process of interior expansion gained additional strength from the single uncontested success of Puttkamer's concessionary policy, the private construction between 1906 and 1911 of Cameroon's first full-size railroad, the Nordbahn, from Bonaberi via the Mungo valley to Nkongsamba.

The most obvious political change in the Littoral resulting from this inland expansion was the abandonment of Douala as the colonial capital. In 1901 Puttkamer transferred his headquarters to Buea on the side of Mount Cameroon for health as well as administrative reasons.[16] Both the plantation controversy and later railroad construction (the Mittelandbahn from Douala to Eseka was begun in 1910 and completed by 1913) soon raised questions about the appropriateness of Buea as the site of central administration. However, pleas from Douala Africans and Europeans for the governor's return to their own city were rejected in favor of a possible location still farther inland such as Baré, Bertoua or the present-day Cameroon capital of Yaoundé.[17] In administrative terms Douala and its surroundings were thus reduced to the status of a territorial sub-unit and placed under the supervision of a *Bezirksamtmann*, the German equivalent of the classic District Commissioner or *Commandant du Cercle*. However, as the port of entry for an ever-expanding commerce and in particular the starting point of Cameroon's two railroad lines, Douala actually gained in urban stature during this period.[18] To meet the demands of this new role, the German administration began to intervene more directly in local society, first undertaking a campaign to modernize streets and housing in the main indigenous quarters of the city, then introducing direct taxation, and finally expropriating land required by the new railroad installations.[19]

Metropolitan political involvement in Cameroon affairs reached its peak during the Puttkamer era, mainly around the land, labor and trade controversies aroused by plantations and concession companies. However the strains of urban development in Douala also produced conflicts that culminated in 1906 with special judicial hearings in Cameroon and the calling of both Puttkamer and the Bezirksamtmann, Eduard von Brauchitsch, before a Colonial Office investigator in Berlin. It is difficult to determine the relative weight of these various issues (along with the official charge of forging a pass for his demi-mondaine mistress) in the ultimate dismissal of Puttkamer from his governorship. However, when the Duala side of the urban questions is discussed below, it is important to keep in mind the general political context of these local affairs.

The era of "reform," 1907–1914
The years of German colonial administration immediately preceding its termination by World War I are generally cited as a period when, under the leadership of Colonial Secretary Bernhard Dernburg, the irresponsible policies of figures such as Puttkamer gave way to more rational development which paid special attention to the interests of African "natives."[20] This period receives only brief treatment here not because it is insignificant but precisely because its importance for the Duala requires lengthier examination in the final section of the present chapter.

Insofar as post-Puttkamer adminstration concentrated on strictly economic issues, the Duala did benefit. Further railroad construction gave greater value to all activity in Douala and the new emphasis on indigenous rather than expatriate plantation agriculture allowed the regime to recognize a major new dimension of Duala commercial enterprise (see below). The governor who immediately succeeded Puttkamer, Theodor Seitz, also proposed political reforms that would give Douala the status of a self-governing municipality in which both Africans and Europeans enjoyed rights of representation. However, this plan met with opposition from both the Colonial Office and the Europeans-only Cameroon Government Council that had been introduced by Berlin decree in 1904.[21] For the Duala, therefore, the political legacy of the reform era was not improvement but rather the expropriation crisis in which all power within the local administration was to be abandoned in a desperate play for both Reichstag and interior Cameroon support.

Segmentary politics and colonial chiefdom

The continuing – indeed growing – importance of the small Duala population in German colonial politics can be traced to a combination of the peculiarities of German rule in Africa as a whole and the specific circumstances of Cameroon. It is the German element in this situation that explains the rather ambiguous role assigned to Duala rulers in the new colonial state as well as the ability of these rulers to bring their local grievances to the attention of the Reichstag.

It would have been difficult, even under a more articulated British-type indirect rule system, for colonial administrators to find a place for coastal middlemen chiefs. The authority of Duala "kings," it must be recalled, rested not upon a visible state apparatus, which colonialism might have coopted, but rather on control over informal networks of inland trade, which colonialism sought to dissolve. As it turned out, the Duala maintained more of their precolonial influence in the era of European rule than did the coastal middleman states of that indirect rule model, British Nigeria.[22] In terms of colonial geopolitics, this persistence can be explained by the difficulty of extending European administration into the more populous inland regions of Cameroon as well as to the continuation of Douala, even after the interior was effectively penetrated, as the major commercial center of the territory.

It is difficult to trace clear "stages" of development through the confusion surrounding the political position of the Duala in German Cameroon. Indeed, as already reiterated, the climax of this process cannot be dealt with until after economic and cultural issues have been examined. However it is necessary to lay out the interplay between German policy and Duala politics in the first decades of colonial rule so as to establish at least the formal basis for later, more dramatic, clashes.

From segmentation to formal jurisdiction

The mini-war between the Germans and Bonaberi-Joss in December 1884 represented the last eruption of classical Duala segmentary politics, in which the potential hegemony of one faction (in this case Bell) was countered by the defection of its own subordinate units. With their military actions of 1884 and the subsequent installation of a colonial state appar- atus, the Germans not only insured themselves against further armed Duala resistance, but also determined that intra-Duala competition would no longer reach such levels of violence or complexity.[23]

Given the budgetary constraints under which it operated, the colonial regime could not substitute its own bureaucratic agents for the African chiefs it had now pacified. The politics of the Littoral during the first decades of German rule thus centered around the negotiation of a role for local rulers that would be both self-supporting and consistent with the goals of European rule.

The most immediate and continuous issue in these negotiations re- mained the question of financial support. The income of Duala rulers in the precolonial period had come principally from their inland trading enterprises and the comey (tribute) paid to them on the coast by European merchants. The changes in the entrepreneurial role of chiefs will be dis- cussed below but for present purposes it is only necessary to note that the Germans never contemplated expanding it in such a way as to eliminate the need for sources of revenue more directly connected with political functions. These sources consisted of salaries, court fees and fines, and a share of direct tax revenues.

As a general policy the Germans in Cameroon never followed the British practice of paying regular salaries to recognized African chiefs.[24] How- ever, the major Duala authorities did receive such compensation on the basis of their previous comey rights. These rights had been guaranteed in the 1884 protection treaty and for the first three years of German rule, the merchants continued to pay comey at the same rate as in the immediate precolonial era. However, after extensive discussion with the German firms, the administration agreed that as of 1888 it would take over direct responsibility for such disbursements, allowing overseas merchants to meet their obligations through the payment of government export/import fees.[25]

Establishing the political role as well as the income of African chiefs through judicial functions held a special appeal for German colonial bureaucrats, almost all of whom had qualified for their positions by legal studies in preparation for the state *Assessor* examination. However during most of the administration of the first German governor, von Soden, the basis upon which Duala political authority was organized still followed the model of the consular-era Court of Equity. Soon after his arrival Soden attempted to set up yet another version of this body, in which representatives of the chiefs as well as the merchant houses would regularly meet.[26] The records indicate that the procedures, like their predecessors, degenerated into an *ad hoc* and frustrating intervention of the administration into local quarrels.[27] As already noted, the European merchants had no formal role in government for the first two decades of German rule; when this situation changed with the establishment of a territorial Gouvernmentsrat (government council), the remedy was more legislative (on a theoretically advisory basis) than judicial and Africans were excluded.

For Africans, the German government decided in 1890 to recognize officially the separate judicial powers of Duala chiefs and followed this two years later by creating a second level of *Eingeborenen-Schiedsgerichte* (Native Appeals Courts) which eventually extended throughout the Littoral. The chiefs' courts were only empowered to deal with civil and criminal cases involving very limited sums (100 marks), fines (300 marks) or periods of imprisonment (6 months), while appeals courts could both retry such cases and serve as the first instance for any other matters not involving penalties of more than two years imprisonment or death. The Schiedsgerichte were required to keep records for the inspection of the German administration, to which, in turn, further judicial appeal was allowed.[28]

Native courts of this kind not only constituted the most formal public function that the German regime was to grant Duala and other Littoral chiefs, but they also provided additional income through the sharing of fees and fines. Officially the most lucrative form of this compensation, that accruing to the Schiedsgerichte, did not go to chiefs but rather to individuals named by the governor as court members. However these nominees were always linked to particular chiefdoms within the appeals courts' jurisdiction, and their relative weight within a given court was perceived as a major political issue.[29]

Direct taxation was not introduced by the Germans into Cameroon until 1903, and up to 1907 the new tax regulations applied only to the Douala district. From the beginning, the Douala administration experienced great difficulty in collecting the expected sums despite offering chiefs 5 to 10 percent of the revenue (the higher figure being for greater rates of return).[30] Instead of strengthening the financial position of the chiefs, this measure proved so unpopular with their constituents that it ultimately entered the agenda of major political disputes between African and European authorities.

The tax collection problems are symptomatic of more general contradictions in the new conception of Duala rulership. The German goal had been to transform the chiefs from factional leaders into the depoliticized instruments of low-cost colonial administration. However, by the very act of creating a basis of authority more powerful than anything that had previously been known in the Littoral, the European regime raised the political stakes of occupying even a circumscribed chiefly office. The Duala rulers thus experienced not only the general dilemma of colonial intermediacy – being caught between European demands and African resistance – but also an enlarged, if less direct, reconstitution of their earlier segmentary conflicts.

Segmentary politics with a German accent: Akwa vs. Bell, 1885–1911

The establishment of German rule in Douala was accompanied – if not caused – by the expressed willingness of both leading indigenous rulers, Ndumbe Lobe Bell and Dika Mpondo Akwa, to give up full autonomy in return for more orderly settlement of the endless conflicts at all levels of local political life.[31] The Bell faction can be seen as the more immediate beneficiary of this change, since their recent economic successes were threatened by rebellious subordinates. However the Akwa chiefs made the same requests for European intervention and proved more uniformly willing to sign the German annexation treaty. Yet, by the early 1900s Bell ascendancy had become so obvious that the Akwas launched a series of protests that culminated in the first explosive eruption of Duala and German politics into one another's realms.

The German–Akwa conflicts contributed as much to the mythologization of this era as did the later execution of the Bell ruler. The Akwas even have their own martyr, Mpondo Dika, the self-styled Prince who spent most of this period in Germany and later died mysteriously while interned by the Germans in Northern Cameroon. The main antagonist of the Akwas was none other than Governor von Puttkamer, for whose subsequent deposition the Duala took credit.

To understand these developments in fuller historical terms it is necessary, first of all, to recognize in them a continuity of earlier Duala politics that the Germans neither cultivated (despite arguments that they resulted from colonial "divide and rule" policies[32]) nor had the power to overcome. The disturbance that sent this process into a new orbit was the rise of the Bells, which itself emerged less from the logic of either Duala tradition or European colonial policy than from the contingencies of personality and unplanned economic change.

Personality factors are always the easiest to introduce into a political narrative and in the Duala–German case they provide critical, if not sufficient, explanations for the rise of Bell over Akwa. European accounts of Douala during the decades immediately preceding and following colonial annexation are almost uniform in praising Ndumbe Lobe Bell and his British-educated heir-apparent, Manga. Dika Mpondo Akwa, on the other hand, was generally despised by Europeans and his son Mpondo, a generation younger than Manga, was to become the target of European scorn and even ridicule in both Douala and Germany.[33] Bell, as seen above, received a considerably higher comey than Akwa, as a result of his greater commercial success (especially in the Mungo region). On the other hand, various German censuses of Douala always recognized that the Akwa faction represented a far larger portion of the local population than did the Bells.[34]

The position of the Bells suffered a setback during the administration of the first German Governor, von Soden, who favored the Akwas and exiled Manga Bell to Togo for two years. Personality factors also seem to have been at work here, since Soden was very annoyed at complaints raised in Germany by Alfred Bell, a nephew of the ruler sent there for European education.[35] The governor was also influenced in these matters by his official interpreter, David Meetom (Mwange Ngondo), himself a secondary Akwa chief.[36] The exile of Manga was never tied to any specific issues; Soden simply called him a "bad influence," responsible for generally uncooperative Bell attitudes towards the government.[37]

It is possible, however, to see some policy considerations behind this shift in the fortunes of the two Duala factions. Soden had committed himself, both in his official and private capacity, to European commercial penetration of the area northwest of Douala which constituted the main Bell trading zone. The governor presented his proposals for eliminating the entire Bell chiefdom in direct connection with a project of the Jantzen and Thormählen commercial firm and the explorer, Eugen Zintgraff, involving plantations and a trading station on the Mungo River.[38]

The long-term ascendancy of the Bells can be dated from the moment of Soden's departure in 1890. While in exile Manga Bell had established a good relationship with the German commissioner of Togo, Eugen von Zimmerer, who then took over the governorship of Cameroon. Apparently chastened by his punishment, Manga subsequently took care to cultivate all the important German officials in the Littoral, including Karl Leist (notorious for provoking the Dahomean Polizeisoldat mutiny), Seitz (during the period when that later governor served under Puttkamer in Douala) and especially the long-tenured Douala Bezirksamtmann, von Brauchitsch.[39] Meanwhile in 1894 the government interpreter, Meetom, was detected in gross abuses of his powers and eventually shot while fleeing German justice, thus depriving the Akwas of a major tie to the colonial authorities.[40]

Under Zimmerer's governorship the Germans also gave up their efforts at commercial penetration of the interior via the Mungo Valley, thus returning this region to unchallenged Bell influence. Instead, the Europeans now undertook a conquest of the Sanaga and the establishment of their trading firms at Edea. At first this policy opened up new commercial opportunities for the entire Duala merchant community. However the closing of the Sanaga in 1895 to all African coastal traders especially hurt the Akwa, since this was a Bakoko-Basaa region where they would have enjoyed particular benefits.[41]

Despite the advantages gained (or regained) by the Bells in the early 1890s, German policy in this period did not deliberately privilege one Duala faction over the other. The system of native appeals courts established between 1892 and 1897 sought rather to balance Bell and Akwa within Douala (each took turns in providing the president of the local court[42]) and to define the various inland regions as political entities under German control and separate from the Duala.[43]

The special role of the Bells became apparent, however, when Ndumbe Lobe ("King Bell") died in December 1897 and the status of Manga as his successor had to be defined. The responsible German official, Seitz, immediately determined that Manga would inherit his father's comey compensation as a "salary" (at a slightly reduced level), in return for undertaking greater responsibility over his subjects and supplying the government with porters. A similar status (but at still lower rates of compensation) was then granted to the three other principal Duala chiefs.[44] However, a few months later Seitz took the even more radical step of assigning to Manga a new and lucrative appeals jurisdiction over the entire non-Duala Littoral.[45] The distinction that this measure created between Bell and Akwa became apparent within the same year when Mpondo Dika (the beneficiary of several years' study in Germany) was threatened with exile by Seitz for claiming comparable authority among the Abo.[46] Moreover at Manga Ndumbe Bell's death in 1908 the same jurisdiction was transferred to his son, Duala Manga Bell, a contemporary of Mpondo.[47]

The formalization of Bell ascendancy coincided with the shift in the German colonial presence from a coastal to an interior focus. For the Duala as a whole this was a stressful period, when they seemed to be losing influence within Cameroon while confronting an intensified European interference in their immediate urban realm. In this new context both Bell and Akwa rulers found it necessary to assert their position through direct appeals to the metropolitan German government. However, it was the Akwas who pushed such efforts the farthest, with results that further damaged their own position but also revealed the fault lines in the whole local colonial regime.

The major occurrences in Duala–German political relations during the first decade of the twentieth century have been very fully chronicled by Adolf Rüger. The present account will not, therefore, provide a detailed narrative but rather an outline of events and an analysis of their relevance to understanding the redefinition of authority in the Littoral. Again some attention has to be paid to the contingency of personalities but these now played out their roles in a context of not only Duala segmentary rivalries but also the systemic imperatives of urban modernization and the structure of domestic Wilhelmian politics.

The political story of this era may be summed up as follows: in 1902–3 Manga Bell and Dika Akwa personally presented complaints and requests to the colonial authorities in Germany; between 1903 and 1906 the Douala Bezirksamt undertook extensive street, sanitation and housing renovations in the city; in 1905 the Akwa chiefs despatched a list of twenty-four complaints to Berlin for which act they were twice put on trial and convicted; in 1911 Mpondo returned to Douala and was himself arrested for illicit commercial-political organization.[48]

The journeys of Bell and Akwa to Germany reveal a continuing degree of parity among the two Duala rulers: both were able to undertake the voyage accompanied by sons (Rudolf Duala Manga Bell and August Mpondo Akwa) who had been educated in Germany; moreover their basic complaints (against government prestations, brutalities by local officials, remoteness from the governor in Buea, restrictions on Sanaga trade, loss of elephant hunting rights) were the same. However, financial problems prevented Dika Akwa from arranging his departure as quickly as Manga Bell and so he was received later and more casually by the Berlin authorities. Moreover, Dika's complaints included (or, according to the receiving official, were mainly motivated by) the favoritism shown Bell.[49]

Despite strong initial objections by Puttkamer, some of these grievances were actually dealt with both for the Duala as a whole and for Manga personally (he received back the very valuable elephant license). For the Duala leaders this success indicated that appeals to the metropole could have some affect. However, it is unlikely that they took into account the broader political circumstances that made even such minimal victories possible; the journeys to Berlin coincided with the first major attacks in the Reichstag and the Kolonialrat (Colonial Advisory Council) against the plantations and concession companies comprising the "System Puttkamer."[50]

The key figure in the efforts initiated in 1903 to modernize Douala was not Puttkamer but Brauchitsch, who served as Bezirksamtmann from 1900 to his death in 1908.[51] Because of his role in both urban and agricultural improvements, Brauchitsch remains a legendary figure in Duala oral memory.[52] However, the records of his actions in Douala indicate that the

Bezirksamtmann (who came to this post from a military rather than a juridical-civil service background) strayed well outside the bounds of correct German administrative deportment.[53] In the investigation of Akwa charges against him Brauchitsch provided very inconsistent statements, finally having to confess partiality towards Manga Bell, brutality towards the Akwas, and the purchase of a young Duala woman for sexual purposes.[54]

The positive Duala memory of Brauchitsch can be justified by his energetic pursuit of a clearly very difficult task. In order to meet its new commercial role, Douala essentially needed streets with proper drainage. However, the elevated riverbank settlements that constituted Bell, Akwa and Deido "towns" are divided from one another by swampy depressions, so that the construction of a continuous road system demanded considerable labor. The Bezirksamt had only limited funds to pay for such work and spent all of it on the first stage of construction in the Bell sector of Bonanjo, leaving nothing over for the more difficult efforts within the larger Akwa sector and across the lowland boundary zones. The project also called for the removal without compensation of many houses and fruit-bearing trees from the path of the roadways.

Of the twenty-four complaints in the Akwa petition of 1905, only four referred directly to the modernization project,[55] although this seems to have been the most continuous factor in raising political tensions to this new level. Two more immediate issues must also be considered, however, not only in explaining the sequence of events but also because they accentuate the underlying issue of Bell–Akwa rivalry. The first is the 1905 condemnation of Dika Akwa to five months, penal labor for claiming (and fraudulently exercising) rights to oil wells found in several Basaa villages. This humiliation wounded not only the Akwa chief's person, but also his claim to any jurisdiction beyond Douala itself, even in an area where his lineage, and not that of the Bells, had previously held commercial and informal political hegemony.[56]

The other circumstance critical to the translation of these complaints into a formal petition was the renewed residence of Mpondo Akwa in Germany, where he had stayed after his father's 1902 journey. Mpondo continued to concern himself with Duala politics and first suggested the Reichstag as a target of protests in 1904; however, it was only his own 1905 imprisonment that induced Dika Akwa to undertake such a provocative measure.[57]

While it is impossible to assess the importance of the Akwa petition in comparison with the other controversies contributing to Puttkamer's ouster from Cameroon, it is clear that the Reichstag gave considerable attention to this affair.[58] The Akwa chiefs achieved the dignity of having their

1905 condemnation for libel and defamation against the Cameroon administration reviewed in the following year by a German judge not connected with the local regime. However, the result was only a second conviction with a somewhat milder prison sentence. Moreover, the other Duala chiefs, particularly Manga Bell, emphatically distanced themselves from the Akwa complaints, thus further strengthening Bell hegemony in the Littoral.[59]

The final effort at recovering Akwa authority came from Mpondo Akwa, who used his time in Germany after 1906 to plan some kind of large-scale trading venture. The economic basis for this project must have been weak at best, since Mpondo's career in Germany was marked by financial embarrassments as well as public attacks upon his personal life.[60] Following his 1911 return to Cameroon, Mpondo attempted to raise money in Douala and the Littoral hinterland for what appeared as much a political as a commercial undertaking. These activities were the grounds for his arrest by the Germans, who then exiled him to Northern Cameroon until his obscure death during World War I.[61]

Mpondo, whom Seitz describes (on the basis of encounters during the 1890s) as "the very caricature of a human being,"[62] seems to have embodied the mythic aspects of Duala–German relations in both tragic and comic forms. A German music hall routine of this era featured "Prinz Akwa," a monocled black dandy usually accompanied by a white female "Cousinchen"; the latter was easily identified by those in the know with Puttkamer's mistress whose false representation as an aristocratic relative had been the official cause for the governor's dismissal.[63] Mpondo, for his own part, seems to have invented a precolonial Duala state structure replete with titled offices designated in terms of which some at least appear African (*Nyiaziam*) and others are of unquestionable European origin (*Biscompta*).[64]

If it was the Bells who managed early colonial politics so as to achieve an unprecedented ascendancy in the Littoral, it was the Akwas who played upon the widest possibilities of the German presence. Up to 1911 it still looked like the Bell approach was more realistic, particularly because it was built upon a substantial, if also modest, transformation of the Duala economic base.

The Duala colonial economy: from merchants to planters

The economic issues of the German–Duala encounter are central to both negative and positive myths of this era. On the negative side is the view (supported by many statements of the Germans themselves) that a central function of the new European regime was to destroy the Duala commercial position in the Littoral. But this picture is opposed by the well-documented and well-remembered success of the Duala during this same period in creating a new economic role for themselves as cocoa planters. One may also combine these two aspects of the Duala early colonial experience to produce yet another of those accounts so beloved by a recent generation of economic historians in which an African instantiation of the universal human entrepreneurial spirit triumphs over the obstacles created by colonial racial prejudice.[65]

In many respects the Duala plantation efforts do represent such a triumph since the Germans experienced particular difficulty in appreciating the constructive potential of African economic endeavors. However, as the last section of this chapter will demonstrate, in a colonial situation European racism could always find ways to overcome African entrepreneurship. More importantly, it was not just the raw repressive power of white rulers that circumscribed the commercial efforts of the Duala; their economic innovation ran up against structural boundaries that reveal how difficult it has been for any African elites in the modern era to move beyond a middleman role, even when shifting from their classical merchant function to that of direct commodity producers.

The struggle over trade

In the annexation treaty signed with the Duala chiefs as well as an accompanying agreement stating "the Wishes of the Cameroons People," the Germans had contracted to respect all the established interests of local rulers; these included: comey (tribute) payments; the distribution of trust credit; "that white men should not go up to trade with the Bushmen . . . they must stay here in this river"; and "our cultivated ground must not be taken from us."[66]

In retrospect, the preceding list reads like an agenda for precisely those incursions upon Duala economic concerns that the Germans would eventually attempt. With the exception of the land question (to be discussed in a later section) they are also issues centering around trade, the basis of the Duala middleman role and thus the first target of German efforts at "opening up" Cameroon. To accomplish this goal Europeans had, above all else, to establish direct contact with the interior sources of export goods. However the earliest changes attempted by the colonial regime related to comey and trust, which we must thus consider first.

The coastal marketplace
Comey can be treated briefly here, since it was already dealt with in discussing the political status of Duala chiefs.[67] It should be noted that the

original agreement with the Duala had also stated that "We need no Duty or Custom house in our country" thus theoretically excluding the source for the revenue used by the German government to replace local firms in making annual payments to local rulers.

The termination of comey did not explicitly violate Duala interests, since the chiefs continued to receive an income, but it met a strong European merchant demand for freedom from any recognition of indigenous authorities as their protectors in carrying on trade. By taking over these payments the colonial authorities also eliminated the one set of European–African transactions still measured in local crew currency terms. As Rüger has noted, this power was then used to reduce the real value of the comey payments by declaring a 40 percent lower ratio between the crew and the Reichsmark.[68] However a Reichsmark system did correspond to the free trade conditions that the Germans claimed to support and from which, in principle, the Duala would benefit as much as their European trading partners. In that era of the international gold standard, the Reichsmark was freely interchangeable with other major world currencies (most relevantly here, British sterling) at a fixed ratio. Thus neither the new currency system nor, as it turned out, the import duties introduced by the Germans gave significant privileged protection to firms of their own nationality; protectionism in Cameroon would have been costly to German merchants, who did most of their business in neighboring British colonies, and British commercial houses continued to play a very important role in Cameroon trade up to the end of German era.[69]

One of the great illusions in German attempts to transform precolonial hegemony into thorough control over the Cameroon economy was the belief that trust – the advancement of goods from European importers to African middlemen – could be abolished. As noted throughout the previous chapter, much of the disorder in nineteenth-century Douala centered around "trust palavers"; yet the movement of export goods from the interior could not have taken place without credit arrangements of this kind.[70]

The difficulty in managing the often violent disputes arising from trust explains the hostility toward this system regularly expressed by British consuls. Not surprisingly German colonial officials, whose arrival was accompanied by an unprecedented rise in unpaid Duala trust,[71] took an even stronger stand against the granting of such credit, "the very disease of Cameroons."[72] However, the European trading firms in Douala maintained their precolonial ambivalence over this issue. Of the two main German houses, Jantzen & Thormählen had earlier attempted to operate without advances to their African partners and, soon after the annexation, urged the colonial regime to officially outlaw trust. The other German firm, Woermann, along with several of the local British houses, took the position that any efforts to restrict credit would constitute unwarranted government interference with commerce. The quarrel over trust helped break up the Syndicate for West Africa, an event that was itself a victory for Woermann's free trade principles.[73]

The actions taken against trust by the first German governor, von Soden, closely resembled the efforts at trade regulation by his peripatetic British predecessors. In December 1885 European trade agents and Duala chiefs were summoned to a meeting on board a German warship and induced to sign an agreement (subsequently published as an official decree) settling immediate debts and outlawing future trust advances.[74] A few months later, not only had the European heads of Woermann and the largest British Cameroon firm, R. & W. King, expressed their opposition to the prohibition of trust but the Duala also declared a total stoppage of trade with Europeans in protest against the low prices now being offered for their exports.[75]

The presence of the German government explains why neither the massive outstanding trust nor the trade boycott produced new outbreaks of violence. However, in other respects there is striking continuity with precolonial trade relations. The colonial authorities would make numerous further efforts at either abolishing or regulating African credit, all of which imposed some cost on African traders (after 1908 the latter were even required to buy official licenses[76]) but did little to restrict their activities beyond whatever became the frontier of European commercial presence.[77] European firms (including Woermann) all confessed to dissatisfaction with the system but none could restrain themselves from offering advances and merchants in Douala remained, as late as 1913, steadfastly opposed to the formal abolition of trust.[78]

Similarly, the firms were unable to counter African boycotts of the 1880s or general African bargaining advantages with any effective collusion of their own. These failures did not arise out of a principled commitment to free trade. European counter-boycotts against Duala trade stoppages were attempted in 1887 and 1888; but in both cases Woermann and some of the British houses broke ranks, forcing the governor to negotiate compromises with the Duala at least on the amounts of export products to be delivered for trust advances made at earlier price levels.[79] In the remaining years before World War I, the firms entered into numerous agreements to eliminate price competition and credit advances for palm products, timber rubber and other Littoral export goods.[80] However, as indicated in the records of two of the main European houses operating in Cameroon during this period, the immediate pressures of commerce inevitably overcame the elaborate regulations laid down in the agreements and, despite constant complaints, business does not seem to have suffered in the long run.[81]

In the much-beleaguered realm of trading relations, therefore, the principles of the market appear to have overcome the combination of European ill-will and colonial power. These same principles, however, were evoked against the Duala by Europeans seeking direct commercial access to the Littoral hinterland. Here the colonial regime would effect change but at a slower pace and in less disastrous form than existing accounts have suggested.

The inland rivers

The Germans spoke more vehemently about the Duala trading monopoly than they did of any other economic issue confronting them at the beginning of their rule in Cameroon, However, neither the means available at this early stage of colonial administration nor the logic of the European mercantile interests in Cameroon impelled a very rapid movement beyond the coast. We may thus divide the process by which the Duala position was overcome into three stages roughly corresponding to the political evolution of the German colonial era: first, up to about 1895, a series of military expeditions into the immediate hinterland; then the establishment of European trading stations at the navigable limits of the Littoral rivers; and finally the operation from 1911 onwards of railroads that by-passed the Littoral entirely as the focal region of Cameroon commercial development. Duala middleman trade actually benefited from the first phase of German efforts; it weakened but took on new dimensions in the second; and in the third it finally declined into total marginality.

The small power-driven vessels and the police troops available to the Germans during the first decade of their administration were regularly deployed along the river routes that constituted the Littoral trading network. In attacking the chiefdoms of the Abo and upper Wouri regions, the Germans neutralized local centers of authority that had blocked free Duala passage to the sources of palm products. Moreover, after having struggled with the Duala on the coast over the need to accept lower prices for export goods whose value had fallen on European markets, the colonial authorities could now pass the same message on to interior secondary middlemen and producers, thus shifting some of the burden of reduced profits from the Duala.[82]

The most dramatic change in favor of the Duala came in the Sanaga river, between its link to Douala via the Kwa Kwa and the Edea waterfalls, a route that had been dominated by local Bakoko traders throughout the precolonial period. In 1892 the Germans launched an expedition against the Bakoko in which the seventy-six-man police troop was augmented by an auxiliary force of 1,300 Duala and 600 Malimba men. The success of this and subsequent campaigns opened up the Sanaga zone for the first time to Duala traders, although simultaneously allowing the establishment of European inland factories.[83]

We may thus treat 1895 as the high point of Duala middleman trade since in the early part of that year coastal African merchants remained active on all the rivers where they had previously been established, operated more securely (and perhaps for the first time) in such places as Yabassi at the terminus of Wouri navigability, and finally broke the barrier of Bakoko resistance to their movement along the Sanaga. The Germans expected their Littoral expedition to damage what they saw as a restrictive Duala commercial system and regularly informed the interior communities whom they contacted that they could now bring their goods directly to the coast. The Duala apparently saw such communications as a threat to their own interests, since interpreters were sometimes caught by missionaries deliberately mistranslating them:[84] but on the whole changes in this direction do not appear to have been the main issue. The occasional presence of agents from European firms along some of the inland waterways did cause more serious problems; a petition of the Duala chiefs to the government in 1892 begins with a complaint about the difficulty of collecting trust when Europeans offered higher prices to suppliers.[85] But until the expatriate firms had permanent stations inland, the Duala would continue to be the main carriers of export products to the coast and thus the main beneficiaries of colonial "pacification."

The definitive European replacement of the Duala in the trade of the Littoral rivers can be dated from mid-1895, when Duala merchants were expelled from Edea on the Sanaga. It would be quite easy to see this event as the direct culmination of the intentions, articulated since 1884 by various official and unofficial German colonial spokesmen, for making the kind of moves into the interior that would put the Duala out of business. These intentions were, indeed, acted upon well before 1895 but economic conditions in Cameroon turned out to be far more resistant to such radical transformation than the Germans had imagined.

The logical positions for placing European trading establishments within the Littoral interior were the end points of navigability on each of the main rivers: Mundame for the Mungo, Yabassi for the Wouri and Edea for the Sanaga. Early German efforts at such penetration focused on Mundame and Edea. The choice of these locations over Yabassi can be explained partly in terms of coastal commerce; the Wouri seemed more clearly under Duala control than the two flanking waterways. But merchant entry into both Mundame and Edea followed the wake of major military-exploration expeditions with the larger ambition of connecting the coast with the fabled and contested Muslim regions of Northern Cameroon. The valleys of the Mungo and Sanaga seemed more promising for this purpose than the Wouri.[86]

The explorer behind the Mundame maneuver was Eugen Zintgraff, who had formulated his plans for a caravan route from the upper Mungo to Adamawa as early as 1887. Zintgraff's subsequent efforts to create a staging post at Barombi (present-day Kumba) and form an alliance with the Bali chiefdom in the Bamenda grassfields inspired the firm of Jantzen & Thormählen to establish a factory at Mundame in 1889. Over the next three years this German merchant house and Zintgraff formally combined their projects for expansion into the northwest, aided initially by the active support of Governor von Soden.[87]

Despite the great political investment in this effort, it produced no lasting change in the pattern of coastal trade. The circuitous water route connecting the upper Mungo with the coast favored African canoe transport over European power vessels. Jantzen & Thormählen's efforts to purchase palm products, ivory and rubber in this region were thus outbid by both the Bells of Douala, who had well-established stations and alliances along the entire Mungo, and Efik traders from Calabar in Nigeria, who drew goods from north of Mundame via the Cross River. The Bell efforts were aided by trust advances from British firms who were excluded from direct entry into the Mungo under the monopoly rights granted there to Jantzen & Thormählen. The Mundame European factory was finally abandoned in 1892, mainly due to its economic failure, but also because Soden's successor as governor, von Zimmerer, based his own policy upon a combination of support for the Bells in the Mungo and more aggressive pursuit of European trade on the Sanaga.[88]

The expeditions of the late 1880s into southern Cameroon of Richard Kund, Hans Tappenbeck and Curt Morgen had all combined an interest in developing a strategic post at the distant inland location of Yaoundé with a concern for commercial control over Edea on the Sanaga. This effort met resistance from both the Bakoko around Edea and the Malimba on the coastal portion of the Sanaga; but the possibilities of trade in this region encouraged Woermann to sponsor yet another expedition in 1890, in return for which he received his own monopoly over direct access to Edea.[89] Although Woermann immediately founded an Edea factory, the position of his agents here was not secure until after the major campaign against the Bakoko of 1892.

In contrast to Jantzen & Thormählen at Mundame, Woermann enjoyed lasting success in his Edea enterprise.[90] The route up the Sanaga, once secured militarily, was quite suitable for European craft and the hinterland was densely populated and not connected by any other rivers to the coast.

Nonetheless, Duala traders, again supported by trust from the excluded European competitors of Woermann, were able to develop their own commerce on this river.[91] In 1895, however, the Duala were expelled entirely from the Sanaga on the grounds that they had sold munitions (specifically percussion caps) to the still-dangerous Bakoko. The evidence for this behavior is thin, especially in consideration of the historically hostile relations between the Duala and the Bakoko. It is more likely that the Germans simply sought a legal pretext for an action that was described by the new governor, von Puttkamer, as "extraordinarily useful for Sanaga trade."[92] The absence of strong local connections in the Sanaga also made it difficult for the Duala to resist such expulsion. As already seen, the main sufferers from this loss were the Akwas and their allies in Josstown.[93] If Bell interests had been more seriously involved, it is possible that the Germans would have acted less harshly.[94]

The installation of European merchants at Yabassi represents somewhat of a middle ground between the situations in Mundame and Edea. During the early years of the German administration conflicts between the Duala and local Abo, Wuri and Bodiman peoples had required several expeditions to the upper Wouri river, but these were organized without great fanfare, using the resources regularly available to the government.[95] The first attempts at European installations in this part of the river were undertaken during the mid-1890s, initially by Jantzen & Thormählen, then by the administrators Seitz and Puttkamer (the latter had ideas of both setting up plantations here and using Yabassi as the jumping-off point for the long-sought north).[96] Nothing came of any of these efforts but suddenly, between 1898 and 1900, all eleven of the merchant firms in Douala purchased land for stations in Yabassi. At the same time, however, sites along the river here were sold to Manga Bell and his servile step-brother, the very successful merchant David Mandessi Bell.[97]

Seitz offers what is probably a sufficient explantion for the timing of this shift; the number of European firms had now reached a critical mass, inducing competition for more efficient access to export goods.[98] If market factors rather than political ambitions thus governed the European move to Yabassi, it is understandable that Duala merchants would continue to find a niche there. With the exception of Europeanized merchants such as Mandessi, the Duala role at Yabassi did not involve competing with European on the Wouri route to the coast but rather in procuring goods from points still farther inland. This presence was important enough to warrant a series of lengthy and infuriated accounts by the German administrator of Yabassi, Oberleutnant Buthut, who complained that the political alliances and market advantages of Duala traders, regarded by ignorant local peoples as "Herren des Landes," were responsible for limiting economic growth, maintaining all the evils of the trust system, and hiding the entire process from European eyes through the continued use of crew currency.[99]

As already indicated, there was little that German colonial legislation could do to end the trading system so deplored by both Buthut and, ostensibly, the very firms that kept giving out trust at Yabassi.[100] Buthut's reports attest, among other things to the futility of trading licenses in limiting Duala activity in local commerce; indeed, the issuance of such licenses serves only to provide us with documentation of the large number of Duala who remained active in this sphere up until World War I.[101] In addition to their secondary middleman role, the Duala also continued to trade independently and even on a newly extended basis along the lesser Littoral rivers such as the Dibamba.[102]

However, the movement of coastal factories inland to Yabassi and Edea made evident the imbalance between the capital resources and organization of European firms and African merchants within Cameroon. This asymmetry became even more apparent with the building of the first railroads to the interior. While Duala chiefs and a few wealthy traders such as Mandessi Bell and Sam Deido had been able to compete to some degree with Europeans by purchasing their own power vessels for riverain travel, there was no way for them either to appropriate any part of the technology embodied in rail transport or to play a significant role in the wide new markets created by such infrastructural change.[103]

The full impact of railroads on the economy and politics of Cameroon would not be felt until the French mandate era after World War I. However, as early as 1912, with completion of the Nordbahn and the first stages of the Mittelandbahn, the marginality of all commercial operations in the Littoral rivers system was already obvious even to such a successful operator as Woermann.[104] Had the Duala depended entirely upon trade, this would have marked the eclipse of their economic middleman role. However during the early 1900s a significant number of Duala entrepreneurs had found a new outlet for their energies in commercial agriculture.

Founding an African plantation system[105]

Among the prime articles in the standard German indictment of Duala laziness was an evident disdain for farming. There is some basis for such a charge: the Duala system of social classification placed agricultural labor in opposition to manhood and freedom as the domain of women and slaves. However, far from discouraging the precolonial Duala merchant elite from taking an interest in cultivation, this attitude accounts for their establishment of satellite villages immediately up the Littoral rivers where slaves were settled to produce both food and palm oil.[106]

The German vision of agricultural enterprise, however, focused less upon the established consumption and export crops of Cameroon than upon the introduction of new and more profitable items, particularly cocoa. During the 1890s various German capitalists, including the major merchant firms in Douala, invested considerable sums in the development of large-scale cocoa plantations in the region west of the Mungo River extending from the coast to the slopes of Mount Cameroon. The controversies surrounding these plantations have been examined at length elsewhere.[107] For the Duala their significance lay not so much in the well-publicized conflicts over labor recruitment and land appropriation but rather in the realm of market competition and demonstration effect. Would the emergence of this new sector of the Schutzgebiet's economy further marginalize the trading enterprises of the Littoral waterways or would it stimulate new African undertakings in the immediate Douala hinterland?

There can be no question that it was the first result which German authorities (especially Puttkamer) both intended and assumed as the automatic outcome of any insertion of racially superior Europeans into the Cameroonian agricultural landscape.[108] During the first stage of plantation development little effort was made to prevent Africans from cultivating their own cocoa and thus extensive, if not statistically significant, farms were laid out, mainly by the Creole community around Victoria. By the early 1900s, however, diseases of European cocoa bushes were being blamed upon the carelessness of African competitors and restrictive measures began to be taken against indigenous growers, at least in the West Cameroon region. Ironically, investigators soon ascertained that the main cause of blight in European cocoa plantations around Mount Cameroon was the unsuitability of this extremely damp region for such a crop. Both this discovery and a leveling off of cocoa prices well below the peaks that had inspired massive European investments eventually produced a shift in German practice and policy: the plantations changed over to other crops in which economies of scale gave them a market advantage (palm products, hevea rubber and bananas) while the government now sought to encourage cocoa as a tropical *Volkskultur* i.e. a product to be grown by African peasants.

The entry of the Duala into cocoa growing did not derive from this change of heart by the Germans nor, as will be seen, did the subsequent *Volkskultur* policies have Duala agriculture in mind. Duala success here did not even owe much to the Basel Missionary Society, a vocal champion of African rights against plantation interests and also a link between

Cameroon and the model colony of African-grown cocoa, the British Gold Coast (Ghana). However it would also be wrong to present the Duala as the quintessential autonomous African entrepreneurs, finding their way into the colonial market despite all prejudiced colonialist obstacles. The initiation of major Duala cocoa production required both the right economic incentives and some critical support from sympathetic Europeans.

Cocoa was known to the Duala from before the colonial era and German administrators attempted to encourage at least Manga Bell to grow it on a commercial scale from the early 1890s.[109] But these first efforts never took hold, probably because the risks of an unfamiliar agricultural practice that could yield no income until after plants had matured for several years appeared unattractive when compared to still expanding trade opportunities.[110]

We have no direct account of how the Duala finally committed themselves to more extensive and continuous cocoa cultivation. The best chronological evidence comes from 1911, when the first recorded German notice of large Duala cocoa farms on the Mungo River reports that significant portions of them had been planted as much as ten years earlier.[111] Soon after this date, the Duala chiefs would attribute the establishment of cocoa plantations to two factors that also suggest a date around 1901: first, a recognition by the Duala that since their expulsion from Edea in 1895, "trading interests . . . were set within limits"; and secondly the role of von Brauchitsch (Bezirksamtmann since 1900) who "spared nothing" in his efforts at "teaching the preparation of the soil, plantation enterprize and the expansion of fisheries . . . "[112] Brauchitsch himself only left a report in early 1908 of having, presumably quite recently, laid out large plantations on the Mungo with Manga Bell.[113]

The slight incongruity in these records suggests that some of the first Duala plantation expansion may have taken place without direct – or at least acknowledged – German participation. The obscurity surrounding an undertaking that was so strongly supported by Brauchitsch and others can probably be explained by the issue of slavery. There is considerable evidence that the early stages of Duala commercial cocoa-growing depended upon the labor of slaves, both transferred to the Mungo from established Wouri oil-palm villages and freshly purchased from the interior. Under theses circumstance the Duala could hardly expect any support in their new enterprises from missionaries. Instead, the Baslers mounted a campaign against what they did see, a renewal of the slave trade, and pressured the colonial authorities to enforce dormant anti-slave trade legislation that dated back to 1895. In 1902 slavery itself was finally abolished in Cameroon but on terms that, like the tolerant treatment of Manga Bell's agricultural undertakings, did not interfere much with Duala social relations.[114] The more open German accounts of Duala plantations from 1908 on may reflect the ability by this time of such farms to attract free labor, a process that will be discussed more fully in the next chapter.[115]

From about 1908 and especially after 1912 there seems to have been a kind of land rush among small and medium Duala entrepreneurs attempting to enter cocoa growing. This rapid growth can be seen statistically from descriptions of the ages of bushes within various farms, which are given as approximate years in the 1911 Mattner report or as "old" vs. "young" in Inspektor Frommhold's larger 1913 survey; in both cases newer plantings are in the overwhelming majority.[116] From 1908 on the Cameroon archives also contain numerous letters from Duala merchants as well as government clerks asking government permission to purchase land for cocoa-growing.[117]

The more positive attitude of German authorities towards Duala cocoa cultivation from 1908 is consistent with new policy orientations emanating from the reforms of Colonial Secretary Dernburg and the replacement of Puttkamer by Seitz as Cameroon governor.[118] However, the official "discovery" in 1911 of extensive Duala cocoa growing on the Mungo as well as in West Cameroon seems to have been a totally unexpected by-product of land disputes instigated by local European plantation companies.[119] Prior German discussions of how to develop native agriculture in Cameroon had both explicitly and implicitly excluded cocoa growing. Beginning in 1912 the Germans did lend some support to African planters by creating a cocoa inspectorate and also pursuing closer cooperation with missionaries, in particular asking the Baslers for advice on Gold Coast precedents.[120]

If the Germans had not been expelled in 1914, it is possible that these new measures might have aided the Duala in furthering their agricultural efforts. But in the short time actually available, little could be accomplished; in fact, the major target of agricultural officials in the Littoral seems to have been the indigenous populations of the Wouri and Dibombe rivers, who were reprimanded for not emulating the exemplary cocoa growing efforts of Duala settlers in their region.[121] Moreover, simultaneous German efforts to expropriate Duala urban landholdings suggest an ultimate failure of the colonial authorities to accept fully the new form of African entrepreneurship represented by expanded commercial agriculture. We will return to this question below when discussing the expropriation crisis.

Within Duala society, the development of cocoa production did appear to strengthen precisely those Bell elements who had most effectively come to political terms with the Germans. As already indicated, it was Manga Bell and his followers in their Mungo trading sphere (as well as in the Tiko plains on the eastern edge of the West Cameroon plantation zone) who pioneered large scale African cocoa cultivation. In 1913, when the most complete survey of Littoral cocoa farms was made, the Mungo region, almost exclusively Bell, accounted for nearly 70 percent of the total of 572 while another 20 percent were laid out along the Akwa-dominated Dibamba river and the rest, along the Wouri, Dibombe, etc. were divided up among various groups including many Deidos.[122] This division corresponds very closely to the trading spheres established in the later nineteenth century and obviously represents a capitalization of gains made at that time by King Ndumbe Lobe and Manga Bell.

This advance from "merchant" to "producer" capitalism is impressive in the terms used by both liberal and Marxian historians to analyze African economic development. On the ground, however, the cocoa plantations, even when as large as 200 hectares, did not require major transformations of the social organization that had been inherited from the previous era. The Germans had exaggerated the complications of growing cocoa, just as they had underestimated the agricultural dimensions of precolonial Duala enterprise. We have already shown how the new plantations system grew out of previous inland farms as well as the Duala riverain trading networks. In at least one case, Bell slaves previously settled on the Wouri were moved to the Mungo to grow cocoa.[123] The land on which cocoa was planted initially came into Duala hands through the same kind of personalized transactions as were used to establish earlier commercial relationships.[124] And finally the proprietors of these recently acquired landholdings combined their innovative cocoa production with the provision of more traditional goods – mainly macabo (cocoyam), plantain, and timber – for the Douala market.

The integration of Duala commercial agriculture into the local economy constituted its major competitive advantage over European plantations. But this kind of entrepreneurship did not assure the Duala elite of any power in those urban sectors that controlled the new political system of Cameroon and required forms of material and human capital that were often inappropriate to the African countryside. But through their experience as middlemen the Duala recognized such needs and thus linked their increased commitment to the economy of the Littoral interior with an equally intensified involvement in European culture.

Cultural brokerage and colonial middleman identity

All colonial regimes in Africa were compelled, by practical manpower needs as well as the imperatives of ideological legitimation, to promote education and support missionary activities – often combining the two.

Because of their established position on the coast the Duala became the major Cameroonian collaborators in such activities during the German period, a role that added European culture to the repertoire of imports which they now distributed to the hinterland.

In assuming such a function the Duala raised for themselves, for various categories of German authority, and for other Cameroonians some basic questions of identity. In the precolonial era we have seen how the Duala defined themselves less through any specific set of political structures or even language than by their position within a hierarchy descending from hegemonic Europeans to the *bakom* (slaves) of the hinterland. However, the social and cultural distance between Europeans and Duala had always remained much greater than that between the Duala and the inland peoples, with whom they lived on very intimate terms.

Following the establishment of colonial rule the possibility of a coastal elite becoming culturally "European" increased greatly; but, particularly in the case of the Germans, so did the assertion of racial boundaries emphasizing the divide between white rulers and all black Africans. At the same time the process of acculturation could, both literally and figuratively, take the form of "translation" in which new content would be given to hegemonic relations among African communities. The Duala exemplify this process far more profoundly than the present study can examine, since their language and music have become a vehicle for African popular culture extending beyond the colonial period and even outside Cameroon. The pages immediately following focus upon the issues of culture and identity raised – often very vehemently – in the German colonial context; we will attempt to link these concerns to earlier phases of Duala middleman history while suggesting questions which will be taken up in later chapters as well as – we hope – subsequent research by more appropriately equipped scholars.

The German perspective: Kulturkampf in Kamerun

Comparative judgment of colonial regimes conventionally gives special attention to the measurable social benefits – including both education and health – provided for African subjects. In these terms the thirty years of German rule in Cameroon come out fairly well. One strength of this system was the ability of government and missionary societies to work together, thus allowing a more efficient use of existing resources than in the case of neighboring French territories.[125]

However, such a cooperative effort in the Cameroonian context brought its own problems with which, as will be seen, the French would also have to struggle in the subsequent mandate period. Like republican France, imperial Germany brought to Africa its own domestic burdens of conflicts between religious and national allegiances. In the German case the classical *Kulturkampf* of the Bismarckian era had pitted a Protestant Prussian hegemony against Roman Catholicism. In Cameroon this relationship was to be reversed; Catholic missionaries, once admitted into the Schutzgebiet, proved more subservient to government and even plantation policies than the Protestants. However, the underlying issue of Germanization vs. Christianization as a goal of education remained the same at home and in Africa. Duala cultural identity entered this conflict via the classical nationalist question of what language or languages were to become the vehicles of literate communication in the new territory.

The basic narrative of these struggles is fully presented in other works and need only be summarized here.[126] The British Baptist Missionary Society, which had been the only long-term European presence on land in Douala departed a year after colonial annexation because of both its alleged implication in Duala resistance to German rule and its acknowledged preference for an interior Congo field over the "corrupt" Duala middlemen. The main missionary effort in the Littoral then fell to the Protestant successors of the BMS, the Basel Evangelical Mission Society. This organization was not as far outside the Reich as its name and Swiss headquarters imply, but it did emerge from a South German (Würtemberg) pietist tradition somewhat alien to the Prussian spirit. The Baslers immediately had to deal with ecclesiastical competition in the Littoral from Victoria Creoles and a small group of Duala Christians who, loyal to the Baptist tradition, first formed an independent church, then invited in the German Baptist Mission, and subsequently divided into mission and "Native" Baptists.[127] A German Catholic mission, of the Pallotine Order, entered Cameroon in 1890 and concentrated its main efforts in the Sanaga and South Central regions of the territory, although a Douala urban base was established in 1898.[128]

The dialogue over education policy in German Cameroon took place essentially between the Baslers and the government although the presence of Baptist and especially Catholic missions somewhat weakened the Basel position. This position remained consistently in favor of using schools to promote literacy in regional languages, which would then become the basis for African churches securely rooted within their own communities. The first German governor, von Soden (himself a Würtemberger) worked closely with the Baslers in establishing two government schools in Douala. The schoolmaster, Theodor Christaller, a seconded Basel missionary had Soden's firm support in producing teaching materials that would develop Duala as the principal language of both education and general communication in the expanding sphere of African contact with the coast.

The first conflicts over this policy occurred early in the regime of von Puttkamer, who used the context of education issues to express his regret that the Germans had not taken advantage of the Bonaberi and Dahomean mercenary uprisings to "annihilate or remove the Duala." As for their language, it "like all Negro dialects, in itself expresses very suitably the character of the people . . . despite all Bible translations and reading primers it is scarcely possible to excise from it the spirit of the lie."[129]

The main avenue through which Puttkamer acted upon his anti-Duala feelings and also came into conflict with the Baslers was not, however, education but rather the installation of plantations and concession companies in regions outside the Littoral. The more serious confrontations over schools and language policy occurred after 1906 when Puttkamer's reformist successors, Seitz and Ebermaier, negotiated the terms under which mission education would receive government subsidies. The government insisted that such support would depend directly upon the achievements of African pupils in learning German. The question that remained open was the degree to which literacy in local languages would be supported, even indirectly, and if so, which languages.

The Basel mission had clearly committed itself by this time to a policy of developing regional languages (Duala throughout the Littoral, Bali in the Grassfields, possibly Basaa along the Sanaga). It was also obvious that government opposition to any measures which might strengthen the influence of the Duala extended well beyond the stigmatized Puttkamer. Seitz, while serving in the Colonial Office prior to his return to Cameroon as governor, had characterized Duala as "this miserable, criminal, this low-class cunning language."[130] In later negotiating with Seitz over the school ordinance that would determine the status of mission establishments teaching in Duala, the Baslers needed to push very hard to achieve a compromise that limited the spread of Duala but allowed it "as a language of instruction and a subject of instruction" in the entire zone extending from Rio del Rey in the southwest, through Buea, Kumba and Yabassi in the north to Edea in the southeast.[131] The Baslers were thus allowed to continue their teaching practices and the production of Duala-language literature, a policy that incurred significant financial sacrifice in the form of subsidies lost to Catholic educators, who put much greater emphasis upon German.[132]

It would be misleading to present the positions of the government and missionaries on either language or the more general role of the Duala as diametrically opposed. Although the Baslers did envisage African languages as the basis for rooting Christianity in local culture, their sensibility here was itself rooted in an abstract romanticism that evoked little sympathy towards a specific culture such as that of the Duala. Instead, the missionaries concurred in much of the government criticism of the Duala language as a vehicle for "the spirit of conceitedness, impudence, and treachery" displayed by Duala traders.[133] Most missionary inquiries into Littoral beliefs and practices grew out of efforts to replace them with a more orthodox Christian way of life.[134] Unlike their Baptist predecessors the Baslers did choose to continue working through the Duala rather than shifting to an interior base, but this decision was founded less upon any positive appreciation for Duala culture than from a recognition of Duala influence. Hostility to the Duala or (as Governor Zimmerer suggested) abandonment of them to the newly-arrived German Baptists would only undermine Basler influence in the farther interior because "what the Duala does sets an example for the other tribes."[135] If the Baslers did effectively strengthen the middleman role of the Duala it was because they were forced to accept the results of an historical process whose present status, both economic and cultural, they found distasteful.

On their own side, had German officials found the Duala language useful as a tool of the secular colonial project it is likely that they would have overcome their scruples and used it in the same way that Swahili, despite all its implications of Islamic-middleman opposition to European rule, was adopted in German East Africa.[136] As it turned out, no German administrator, even one so close to the Duala as Brauchitsch, ever mastered their language; not only is Duala, with its tonal system, difficult for Europeans to learn but English or, still more, Pidgin provided a much readier lingua franca for this region.[137] However when Pidgin, Hausa, Beti/Fang and even Swahili were considered in one way or another as candidates for the role of officially endorsed "*Einheitssprache in Kamerun*" none proved acceptable. Despite nationalist pressures at home, the widespread teaching of German in Cameroon also came to be seen as both impractical and, from a political and social viewpoint, undesirable.[138]

German education policy, whether laid out by government or missionaries, thus expanded the cultural dimensions of the Duala middlemen role but did so only with great reluctance. But what opportunities and definitions of the middleman situation did colonial culture provide for the Duala themselves?

New Duala elites of the German era

It is far easier to catalogue the positions opened up by literacy within the colonial hierarchy than to probe the consciousness created by this experience. Nonetheless, both tasks must be attempted here because it is the process of mediating between European and African worlds which is the most lasting legacy of those coastal Cameroonians who first – but only temporarily – dominated the ranks of "modern" occupations.

That the Duala did exercise such domination throughout the German period is obvious from documents like the enrollment figures in German government schools where, as late as 1914, Dualas constituted the clear majority of the pupils on the coast and an overwhelming plurality of those throughout Cameroon.[139] We do not have similar figures for missionary schools but the fact that the Baslers, with their commitment to Duala language instruction in the Littoral, maintained the largest operation in Cameroon throughout this period assured a similar result.

The most immediate goal of formal education from both a government and mission viewpoint was to train an African auxiliary cadre. In the government case, this meant clerk-interpreters whose position in a colonial structure gave them considerable power over both Africans and Europeans. We have already discussed the problematic political role of the first generation of such interpreters, David Meetom and Conrad Elame, English-speaking pupils of the BMS.[140] As more such individuals, educated in German, became available, the government could control them somewhat more effectively although, as will be seen below, European officials remained vulnerable to at least espionage by their African subordinates.

Some of the most successful pupils in both government and mission schools remained there as teachers and a small number of those in the Basel system attained ordination as pastors.[141] Duala school graduates were slower, however, to penetrate the clerical and artisanal ranks of the merchant firms in the Littoral, who preferred Gabonese, Togolese or Gold Coast employees to Cameroonians.[142] Possibly these enterprises saw some conflict between the continuing role of the Duala as primary or (more frequently) secondary middlemen in the interior and the interests of European trade. However, just as there had been no significant Creole presence among the merchants in late precolonial Douala, so the foreign African employees of private firms seem to have made little impact on the local scene during the early colonial era.

Indigenous school leavers, however, constituted an important petty bourgeois elite within Duala society. They were less wealthy than the Bell chiefs or the few really successful merchants such as Mandessi Bell, Jacob Kaya, Jong Boneyum and Sam Deido who had extensive inland plantations and built impressive masonry houses in Douala.[143] But the clerks, teachers and pastors also invested the savings from their relatively high salaries in cocoa farms and, as will be seen below, felt no less threatened than their more affluent compatriots by German plans for expropriating urban land. Compared to the Africans of a more developed colonial port-city such as Lagos, the German-era Duala lacked a stratum of higher-educated professionals such as doctors and lawyers but they nevertheless began to develop a consciousness of themselves as a new kind of middleman elite.[144]

The question of the content of such a consciousness is raised, perhaps prematurely, by the participation of the Duala elite in extended resistance to the German expropriation efforts described below. But what evidence can we find in the culture, as opposed to the clearly ambiguous politics, of the Duala elite to help define their new identity? Unfortunately, the sources available to the present authors for this period are so heavily embedded in their European provenance that they reveal more about the culture of colonial hegemony than of African consciousness. However, these documents at least tell us something about the life styles and literary self-expression of the German-era Duala and may help other scholars towards a more thorough pursuit of this issue.

Our most detailed and informed reports on Duala life-style come from missionaries, who lived more closely with local Africans than any other Europeans but constantly evaluated what they saw in terms of their own models of Christian belief and monogamous domesticity. Not surprisingly, the missionaries recorded more disappointment than satisfaction with the attainment of such an ideal by the Duala elite. The successful examples tended to be relatively marginal figures, including the few African pastors such as John Deibol and especially Modi Din, men whose careers linked them intimately with the mission community. Among the laity, the major example of Christian virtue was David Mandessi Bell, already cited as the most successful merchant and planter among the Duala but also stigmatized among his own people as an ex-slave.[145]

Individuals such as Deibol, Modi Din and Mandessi had great influence over the political leadership of the Duala, particularly Manga Bell and his son Rudolf Duala Manga. However, Manga had already broken with formal Christianity before the Germans arrived by taking several wives, and was suspected of indulging in *losango* cult celebrations as well as making human sacrifices at the time of his father's death in 1897.[146] Duala Manga, who was educated in Germany and married Emily Engome Dayas, the daughter of an English merchant and a Duala mother, appears to have followed a more European lifestyle, although it is difficult to know what choices he would have made during a longer period of rule.

From a missionary viewpoint, the "backsliding" of Manga Bell and numerous other prominent Duala, including some former leaders within the church, simply represented a failure to achieve the moral status toward which all men should strive. We do not, unfortunately, have any indications from the Duala elite of their own, possibly more positive, definition of the way in which they had combined traditional and European modes of living. The existence of an independent Baptist church suggests one avenue for such a definition; but despite the tendency of the Baslers to label any effort at African ecclesiastical autonomy as "Ethiopianist," there is very little evidence of heterodox cultural content in the Christianity of even the most dissident African clergy in this era.[147]

The Duala confrontation with German colonial authorities and missionaries did produce a body of indigenous texts from which it might be possible to explicate a cultural self-definition; but again, this evidence is so mediated by European hegemony that its meaning remains elusive. Most mediated of all is that literature which seems, on the surface, quite "authentically" African namely the recording of oral narrative and proverbs. The most famous of these collections was made by a German government schoolmaster who claimed to know not only the Duala language but also the "real character of the people [*den eigentlichen Volkscharakter*]." This last, revealed in ancient folktales, was to be distinguished from the cunning, laziness and dishonesty displayed by the present-day commercial middlemen and would be restored as the basis for an eventual advance to civilization and Christianity once the Germans had broken the Duala monopoly on trade with the interior.[148] A Basel missionary folklorist took on the more ambitious project of recording for the first time several versions of the epic narrative of the Littoral, "Jeki la Njambe," but published the text only in fragmentary form many years later. In any case, this monumental work is itself less an assertion of Duala identity than a testimony to the ambiguity of precolonial middleman hegemony, as indicated in the narrators' preface to the German text: "Our fathers and forefathers often recited this epic but they could not discover its meaning or what it is supposed to teach us."[149]

The Basel Mission also produced a very extensive body of Duala-language literature, much (probably most) simply translating church doctrine but some undoubtedly worthy of closer further investigation than has so far been the case. Of the accessible works by Duala clergy that reveal something of self, such as Modi Din's autobiography or Joseph Ekollo's history of the local mission church, the theme seems to be one of a struggle toward Christian identity against the hostility of parents and dominant local authorities.[150] Thus, despite some suspicions of both these indigenous pastors for "Ethiopianist" assertiveness, neither seems to have derived (or at least revealed) any conscious positive identity from local culture.

Mpondo Akwa, the major object of suspicion by German secular authorities, was also associated with a literary project, the publication in both German and Duala of an independent illustrated monthly, *Elolombe ya Kamerun* (the Sun of Cameroon). The German language portion of this short-lived magazine has an interesting account of Duala musical skills;

otherwise it differs little from overtly colonialist writings in its condescend-
ing and denigrating references to the moral and other shortcomings of the
"Dualaman, not overly touched upon by culture." The Duala-language
sections are all either edifying accounts of German industriousness, etc. or
translations of European juvenile literature, However in the German-
language text, "From the Letters of a 'Savage'" a mission-educated Duala
provides some rich and ambiguous reflections on the dishonest reputation
of his own people, their relationship to a more socially and economically
secure past and the meaning of a sermon on Exodus for overcoming either
Duala moral weakness or (only implicitly) the oppressions of colonialism.
While this brief document fails to take into account the historical dilemmas
of Duala precolonial history as well as the achievements of the German era,
it does express quite poignantly the double middleman status of the
contemporary elite; their cultural role seems to have created not a new
identity but rather another poorly defined space between not only Africans
and Europeans but also between competing concepts of the self.[151]

The expropriation crisis: apotheosis of mythic politics

In 1910 the German administration of Cameroon drew up an elaborate
plan for the segregation of Douala into European and African quarters.
The Europeans were to occupy the land along the left bank of the Wouri
where the original Bell, Akwa and Deido "towns" had been located. Duala
inhabitants of this riverain zone were to move inland to new settlements
and would receive compensation for their land and houses at a rate fixed
by the government.

The chronology of the crisis that followed this initiative need only be
summarized here since it has been treated extensively in other historical
studies.[152] Immediately after the announcement of the expropriation plan,
late in 1911, the Duala, under the leadership of the Bell chief, Rudolf
Duala Manga, publicly protested. Although these complaints found some
echo among both official and private-sector Europeans, neither the local
Bezirksamt, the governor in Buea nor the Berlin Colonial Office would
accommodate the Duala. In 1913 Duala Manga Bell petitioned the Reichstag and also sent a personal envoy, Adolf Ngoso Din, to Germany, where
a lawyer was engaged. The Reichstag debated the expropriation question
at considerable length during the first half of 1914 but eventually a majority was won over to the government's position. Meanwhile, the authorities
in Douala completed (partly by force) the expropriation of the major Bell
area and then arrested Duala Manga Bell and various of his followers on
charges of high treason (seeking political support from foreign European

powers as well as other indigenous Cameroonian rulers). On August 8, 1914 – following the outbreak of World War I – Duala Manga and Ngoso Din were executed by hanging. In the following month British and French military forces captured Douala, thus terminating the German colonial regime in this region of Cameroon.

For present purposes the most striking aspect of the expropriation story is its empirical confirmation of the mythic qualities of the Duala–German encounter. Here in a set of documented events so dramatic as to seem implausible are compressed the defining contradictions of both the German colonial presence and, more importantly, Duala middleman transformations.

For the Germans, the expropriation project simultaneously represented the scientific reformism of the Dernburg era and a racism at least as brutal as anything practiced under von Puttkamer. For the Duala, the struggle against expropriation was at once an assertion of a "traditional" unified community with rights to a specific space in the Littoral, of "modern" educated elites claiming status as participants in a European parliamentary state, and of leadership in proto-nationalist politics contesting control over the entire territory of Cameroon with its colonial rulers. The ultimate irony of the German effort here was that it did effectively terminate the political and much of the economic power of the Duala while assuring this African community of a new heroic status that could at least appear to transcend such a material base.

German initiative and debate

Both Duala and European interpretations of local colonial history have tended to divide the European antagonists into "good" (trade-oriented, pro-African) and "bad" (pro-white settler, racist) Germans.[153] It is thus important to note that the original engineer of radical Douala segregation was Brauchitsch's successor as Bezirksamtmann, Herrmann Röhm; moreover, the project received full support from Governor Theodor Seitz, the chosen Cameroon instrument of Dernburg's reforms.[154] In approving this plan Seitz violated not only the explicit terms of the 1884 Duala–German treaty but also a personal promise he had made earlier that the government's acquisition of land for railroad construction did not imply any threat to the present main center of Bell residence on the Bali plateau, an area designated by Röhm as part of the "free zone" separating future European and African quarters.[155]

How can we reconcile Seitz's role in the expropriation project with his earlier proposal to create a racially integrated urban government in

Douala?[156] There is no immediate documentation for such a connection[157] but what appears to link the two plans is a sense that the changing role of Douala as the economic center of a more developed Cameroon had rendered the entire position of the local "tribal organization" anachronistic.[158] Given the failure of his more liberal effort at assimilating the Duala elite to this new order, Seitz appears to have contented himself with making sure that the community as a whole did not stand in the way of modernizing the urban landscape.

Another seeming incongruity of the expropriation proposal is its coincidence with a shift in German agricultural policy towards export production by Africans, a practice in which the Duala were, as noted, already well advanced by 1910. What German officials had in mind when promoting African agriculture, however, was not the kind of indigenous capitalism practiced by Duala planters but rather what they called *Volkskultur*: peasant production on small-scale units without any credit advances.[159] Governor Ebermaier even specified the basis of such cultivation as landholdings of one hectare cultivated by a single family and threatened to take action against the much larger Duala farms in the Mungo Valley.[160]

In this context the architects and enforcers of expropriation such as Ebermaier and Röhm do appear as "bad Germans" who would not even follow market economic principles in recognizing Duala middleman adaptability to the colonial economic situation. In both the *Volkskultur* view of indigenous agriculture and the expropriation plans, these officials found themselves in opposition to the very European merchants whose interests they presumably represented. Röhm tacitly recognized this contradiction when, in early 1914, he made a calculation of Duala Manga Bell's annual production of export goods (cocoa and timber) as well as his debts to local Europeans in order to conclude that not enough was at stake to induce the Douala merchant community to use its political influence against expropriation.[161] At the critical moment of decision in Berlin, the merchants' major metropolitan lobbying organization sided with the "bad Germans" to support expropriation, largely because it had been captured by a coalition of planters and rubber traders operating outside the Douala area.[162]

What most immediately motivated the expropriation plan was not the economic needs of the European private sector but rather the government's vision of an orderly and sanitary gateway to its West Central African domain. The Duala appeared to threaten this vision in both general terms, because of their very presence as an African group with claims to some standing beyond that of colonial subjects, and more specifically by harboring crime and disease.

Crime was not generally a great problem in early twentieth-century Douala but around 1910 there had been a series of thefts climaxing in a spectacular robbery by a Duala man of 65,000 marks from the Deutsch Westafrikanische Bank.[163] More importantly, the endemic health problems of Europeans in Douala were thought to be exacerbated by the proximity of their dwellings to those of Africans. Removal of the Duala from the Wouri river front would at once diminish the social and economic advantages they gained from possession of such a valuable geographical position and protect Europeans (numbering only 400 at this time) from further attacks upon their property and health.

Although the Douala business community soon overcame its concern over crime and recognized the hygienic nonsense of the government's proposed one-kilometer "free zone" between themselves and the African quarters of the city, no serious opposition to the expropriation plan came from this European sector. Instead, it was left for missionaries to play the local role of "good Germans," something they did with less than full gusto.

Unlike the earlier issue of plantation development in West Cameroon, the expropriation project did not represent an entire colonial "system" on which the more liberal Baslers and the more accommodationist Catholic Pallotiners could take clear and contrasting sides.[164] Both of the main missionary societies in the Littoral essentially opposed expropriation, at least in the drastic form sought by the government, but neither was able to take a strong public stand on this issue or influence it effectively from behind the scenes. The expropriation question arose in the midst of other controversies about the languages to be used in subsidized mission schools and possible boundaries between various Christian denominations; both Catholics and Protestants thus hesitated to offend a colonial regime which, in general, they viewed as reformist. As it turned out, the Pallotiners had potentially greater influence in Reichstag decisions through their ties to the Catholic Center Party, while the Baslers were divided between, on the one hand, their Swiss and Douala leaders, who strongly opposed expropriation, and on the other hand, the local head of the entire Cameroon mission, who wanted to stand by the government.

What this failure of the missions reveals from the viewpoint of the present study is that Duala aspirations to maintain some kind of effective middleman position under colonialism ultimately had no real support from any significant European group. In the final Reichstag showdown, the only opponents of expropriation were the stigmatized Social Democrat deputies (and not all of them) along with a prominent left-liberal journalist, Helmuth von Gerlach, who had lost his parliamentary seat in the "colonialist" 1907 election. From a European perspective, it is easy enough to read this story, with its disastrous outcome to an irrational policy, as yet another failure of German liberalism.[165] But what does it reveal about the Duala's own efforts to redefine their middleman role?

The Duala response

The single greatest irony of the expropriation crisis from a Duala viewpoint is the linking of its catastrophic conclusion with the one moment in the entire history of this community when true political unity was achieved. Moreover, because the primary target of the German project was Bonanjo, the precolonial Bell center, the ensuing protest immediately focused around Rudolf Duala Manga Bell, the figure best qualified for such a leadership role on grounds of lineage claims, political and economic position within the colonial system, and personal qualities of education and courage. Whether or not Duala Manga exercised the best possible judgment in playing this role is less clear, even from a position of extended hindsight, especially because such a powerful legend has been built up around his life and death.[166] At the very least, however, it is impossible for a historian to deny the tragic element in the violent demise of this critical Duala figure.

The absence of the usual segmentary divisions in the Duala response to this crisis is partly a credit to the capacities of Duala Manga but also an indicator of how far both earlier colonial developments and the specific threat of expropriation had themselves redefined the Duala situation. By the time the German plans were made known to the Duala, Akwa leadership had suffered its final blow – the exile of both Dika Akwa and his German-educated son Mpondo – so that no real basis for challenging Bell ascendancy was left.

Under the stewardship of Rudolf Duala Manga the Bell position seemed destined for even greater strength than in the times of his very successful grandfather and father, Ndumbe Lobe and Manga Bell. Duala Manga was, in European terms, one of the best-educated Africans in Cameroon, having completed the equivalent of an American high school in Germany.[167] At his accession to rulership in 1908 he inherited not only the full political jurisdiction of his father, but also considerable plantations in the interior as well as valuable real estate and modern buildings in Douala. These assets by no means made Duala Manga invulnerable to European pressures of various kinds. In 1910 he was summarily arrested and mistreated on completely unsupported suspicions of complicity in the great bank robbery of that year.[168] Manga Bell's urban construction projects, the cost of educating his children and grandchildren abroad and possibly his early plantation undertakings left his son with the not-inconsiderable debt of 7,000 marks at the moment of his succession. Although some of these liabilities were offset by the yield from eventually mature cocoa trees, Duala Manga had to rent his more prestigious buildings in Bonanjo to Europeans and shifted his own principal residence to Bali, an elevated area slightly away from the river.[169]

The Germans seem to have been surprised by resistance against their policies on the part of a local ruler whose own position had been built upon such close collaboration with the colonial regime.[170] Possibly they could have carried out their expropriation efforts more easily by indicating that they affected only the Bell quarters of the city, thus playing upon internecine Duala rivalries. Instead, the Germans sought to isolate their assault upon urban Duala land rights from all other political and economic concerns. Thus each riverside "town" was to have its own resettlement area and all would be provided with transport access to the Wouri for purposes of contact with inland constituencies, trading posts and agricultural settlements. One reason that Duala Manga could become the accepted leader of the entire community was that the economic and especially cultural issues at stake here affected all the Duala (other than those across the river in Bonaberi) with equal weight.

The economic issue centered mainly around the arbitrarily low prices placed by the Germans on the land that was to be surrendered. Not only the Bells but also the Akwas and particularly the successful Deido merchants had constructed a number of modern houses upon their properties near the Wouri. Although manifestly willing to sell or lease much of this real estate to Europeans, the Duala uniformly resented government insistence that in such transactions they were mere speculators, taking advantage of increased land values to which they had contributed no labor or investments of their own.

In cultural terms, expropriation attacked the very middleman identity that united the Duala but had never previously found expression in any lasting political organization. This identity, derived from the several centuries of coastal settlement, had both an indigenous aspect, based on the geography of riverain and inland habitation, as well as an external aspect, centered around access to things European.

The indigenous side of this identity goes back to the structural principles of Duala social mapping, which divided the African world into categories of free/noble (*wonja*) and slave (*bakom*).[171] The geographical correlatives of such a dichotomy linked free status with elevated areas overlooking waterways (*mudongo*) and slavery with enclosed inland areas (*koto*). By moving their main Duala habitations inland, the Germans were, in effect, demoting the Duala to the status of slavery. An argument of this kind would hardly have appealed to the Germans although it is implicit in

constant references to collective status in Duala arguments about expropriation and what one European witness called their "superstition" that
they would die if they moved inland.[172] But Ngoso Din, the Duala
emissary to Germany, linked the threatened "total destruction" of his elite
community to the fact that they were being consigned to "swampy areas,"
a situation that would certainly (although Ngoso Din does not say so) have
increased their own exposure to malaria.[173]

The stated modern grounds for opposing resettlement ostensibly did
appeal to colonial development goals although on a basis even more
objectionable to many Germans than notions of slavery. The Duala prided
themselves upon being closer to Europeans than other Cameroonians and
associated this status not only with their economic activities, but also their
physical presence near the Wouri, the modern houses that many of them
had built in the vicinity of Europeans already resident in the same areas,
and the education they received in mission schools also located in the older
sections of Douala. The effort to halt expropriation thus received the
support of all the Duala with advanced European education, regardless of
their segmentary affiliations or employment within the government
bureaucracy, the private commercial sector or the missionary churches. As
stated by the collective Duala chiefs, movement to the newly designated
native quarter of the city would mean "cultural ruin."[174]

Conclusion: the power of myth

Ironically culture, in terms of access to European learning, would be the
one advantage that the Duala retained over other Cameroonians throughout the colonial period and for some time afterwards. Expropriation
turned out to be less damaging in reality than in contemplation. However
the contemplation of expropriation fueled the political crisis which did
constitute an historical disaster for the Duala. In the end, therefore, the
importance of expropriation lay precisely in its evocation of mythic definitions of the Duala situation and it is these myths – both German and Duala
– which, in a critical sense, became the major actors in the very story they
sought to interpret.

To appreciate the power of such myths it is first necessary to recognize
the very small practical distance that separated the expropriation which
the Germans finally managed to carry out and the concessions which the
Duala were ready to make in their control over urban land. By 1914 the
Germans had only expelled Duala inhabitants from Bonanjo and immediately surrounding Bell areas, the zone in which government and European
commercial property was already concentrated. Plans for taking over land
in Akwa and Deido were postponed and the Bali plateau, where the Bell

leadership now resided, had not even been subjected to the first administrative steps preparatory to expropriation.[175] In private correspondence (known to the Germans, however) the Duala leadership had indicated that it would accept just such an outcome as a compromise solution to the entire conflict.[176]

To achieve a real compromise, however, it would have been necessary for the Germans to increase the prices they paid for the land evacuated by Bell people and for both Germans and Duala to declare publicly that they accepted this limited version of expropriation. No such steps were ever taken and events preceded on their course towards a confrontation whose immediate content was political rather than economic or cultural.

For the Germans, a major political factor preventing compromise over expropriation itself or even clemency towards the Duala protest leaders was its coincidence with the outbreak of international war.[177] However, World War I itself is difficult to separate from the nationalist politics that made the Germans unwilling to recognize Duala claims. The Duala lost in these events not only the life of Duala Manga but also the entire political structure over which he presided. Even before indicting him for treason, the Germans had stripped Duala Manga of the wide Littoral jurisdiction inherited from his father and the French would never reconstruct any of the Duala chieftainships on a comparable scale.

If the outcome of the expropriation crisis was political, its sources lie in the mutually incompatible and individually unworkable conceptions of their historical situation that the Germans and the Duala brought to this confrontation. The present study is not the place to elaborate on the internal contradictions of the Wilhelmian Reich, but the Duala expropriation crisis certainly presents a fine example of its explosive mixture of racist authoritarianism and advanced liberalism. Nowhere else in tropical Africa was urban segregation imposed in so brutal, elaborate and ultimately senseless a manner;[178] but in no other European metropole would the indigenous victims have received such an extended parliamentary hearing.

It is also possible, however, to see in the Duala conception of their middleman role at this time elements of both inattention to reality and racism. The Duala failed to recognize that after several decades of colonial development, the European regime was no longer dependent upon their intermediacy for the achievement of its own political and economic goals. Moreover, the claims made by the Duala against the Germans could be interpreted as privileges based upon their own identification with European superiority and a belief in the innate inferiority of hinterland Africans. As will be seen, such reproaches against Duala "pretensions" would remain a central element in French colonial ideology during the next period of European rule in Cameroon.

Although modern historians have read Duala Manga's appeals for support from Cameroonians of the interior as proto-nationalism, it is unlikely that any such radical action against the European regime was intended. There are no surviving direct records of Duala Manga and Ngoso Din's trial, which was held somewhat hastily owing to the awaited Allied attack on Douala.[179] The dossier that colonial officials were able to gather against Duala Manga indicates that he made efforts to gather funds in the Littoral hinterland and that news of the expropriation struggles was causing unrest in various parts of the interior.[180] Envoys were also sent to various Grassfields chiefs, although the only one documented in any detail is that to Njoya of Bamun, who was visited by an ex-slave bearing an oral message urging rebellion against German rule and appeal to Britain as an alternative colonial power.[181] Njoya immediately turned the envoy over to the German authorities and his testimony provided the most damaging piece of evidence against Duala Manga. The alleged Duala contacts with Britain and France (well before the crisis leading to World War I) derive from vague statements of intent to seek foreign support (possibly no more than publicity) and the alleged secret organization behind Ngoso Din's clandestine journey to Germany via Nigeria.

Whether or not the message to Njoya expressed any serious intent on Duala Manga's part (and there is good reason to doubt this), the undertaking itself constituted a major political error. The resulting accusations offered the government of Cameroon and the Colonial Office precisely the weapon they needed to stifle Reichstag opposition to expropriation. The situation was quite frankly assessed by the Duala Bezirksamtmann:

We are not confronted with any direct danger of some kind of violent action by the Duala. For now the main value of the statements from Ndane [the envoy to Njoya] lies in the fact that they contain material for proceeding against those chiefs who are guilty of actual deliberate agitation in refusal of the expropriation and of resistance that reaches all the way over to Germany.[182]

The climactic events of the German–Duala political connection parallel in a curious but also revealing manner their beginnings. In both cases the Duala reacted to local crises involving Europeans with a gesture that they seem to have understood as modifying rather than drastically transforming their situation: in the earlier case, requesting a more permanent foreign political presence; in the 1910s seeking a form of support and representation within the German colonial order. Just as that order had proven to be far more intrusive in their affairs than the Duala had originally bargained for, so later Duala interpretations of the political actions they could be permitted under colonialism proved tragically mistaken.

In both of these cases it was external forces essentially unrelated to

Africa – the international rivalries driving the Partition and World War I – that brought the most far reaching change. But the links between such historical processes are difficult to explain even from an academic ivory tower and for those experiencing them on the ground – whether Africans or Europeans – they are precisely the kind of events liable to be translated into myth. The German colonial regime would thus affect the most serious transformation of the Duala middleman position once the myths about the original colonial encounter transformed themselves into cataclysmic politics. But this catastrophe only gave birth to still further myths about the powers of both colonizers and colonized to bring about changes in Cameroon. In the later phases of their middleman role, however, the Duala would find themselves playing a smaller role upon a much enlarged Cameroonian stage.

5 Middlemen as ethnic elite: the Duala under French mandate rule, 1914–1941

On September 27, 1914 – exactly seven weeks after the execution of Duala Manga Bell – the Germans surrendered Douala to Allied forces and began withdrawing their forces from the entire Littoral. The Duala now moved from the "mythic" to the more "normal" phase of their colonial experience in which the expatriate rulers would be the same authorities responsible for the neighboring territories of French Equatorial Africa.

Normalization in this instance refers not only to the nationality of the Europeans in control but also the integration of what had for centuries been a coastal entrepot enclave into a fully Cameroonian political and economic regime, with its capital in the interior at Yaoundé. In formal political terms, the Duala now became marginalized: local chiefs had no authority over the rest of the Littoral and what little power they enjoyed within Douala was again divided between Akwa and Bell. Political struggles would continue to be waged at least through the early 1930s around two issues directly inherited from the German past: the mandate status of Cameroon (theoretically administered by France for the League of Nations); and the expropriated Bell land. Battles over these questions were fought with funds earned from a continuation of Duala enterprise in trade and particularly in cash-crop agriculture.

However, the most significant investment of previously accumulated middleman capital now took place in the domain of European education, which assured the Duala an elite position within Cameroon even after many of their other resources had been lost or devalued. With this shift in the Duala middleman role came also an increase in ethnic consciousness both real and mythic: real, in the sense of recognizing the place of Duala identity within an encompassing colonial state; mythic in terms of the aggrandized history that began to be constructed for the Duala people. Thus in the very period when their efforts at self-definition became less immediately tied to local political projects, the Duala began to confront some of the later dilemmas of Cameroonian nationalism.

The politics of a new colonial order

As in 1884, the establishment of colonial rule during the uncertainties of World War I and its diplomatic aftermath began with a good deal of confusion and improvisation. The heading of this chapter is technically inaccurate: French mandate rule did not officially begin until 1922 and ended only in 1946; between September 1914 and April 1916, moreover, Douala was administered by British military officers with only token French cooperation.[1]

This ambiguous situation encouraged Duala spokesmen to make very bold claims against European sovereignty throughout the early mandate period but it did not prevent the French, once firmly in charge, from imposing on Cameroon the form of colonial administration already well developed by them in other parts of Africa. The politics of this era thus constitute a dialogue between a European administration much firmer and more bureaucratically insulated than its German predecessor and a Duala leadership encouraged by what looked like a more hospitable climate to pursue both inherited grievances and new claims. It is a politics with many events but ultimately far less drama than that of German times. Its meaning, for both participants and detached historical observers, is not easy to link to its manifest form.

Establishing a French regime

The changing of colonial rules at the very climax of Duala–German conflicts would suggest a close connection between these events and an outcome vindicating the Duala position in their earlier struggle. For the Duala, as will be seen below, such continuity did exist just as the extreme punishment exacted upon Duala Manga Bell by the Germans had itself resulted from the circumstances of wartime. However, if we examine these developments from the perspective of the triumphant Allies, and especially the ultimately hegemonic French, Douala, and indeed all of Cameroon, seems to have been nothing more than a minor pawn in global struggles over much greater prizes.

The one moment of logical continuity in the changes brought by World War I was the eighteen months of British rule in Douala. The German annexation of Cameroon had always been seen by both Europeans and Duala as an interruption of previous British dominance in this area and it was Britain, from its key West African bases in the Gold Coast (Ghana) and Nigeria, which initiated the extension of World War I into both the neighboring colonies of German Togo and Cameroon. France joined the African campaigns against its own immediate interests, to protect "the honour of the flag."[2]

Once in possession of Douala, the British officers in charge, General Charles Dobell and Naval Captain Cyril Fuller put great energy into managing its civilian affairs as well as repairing the harbor, which Nigerian, Admiralty and Colonial Office officials considered a major strategic prize.[3] However the main energies of the British government during this period were directed towards driving the Germans from the rest of Cameroon, a task far more difficult than capturing Douala and one requiring extensive support from French forces. More importantly, once this immediate objective had been achieved, British policy makers determined that in return for consideration in areas of greater long-run priority (particularly East Africa), they would turn over the bulk of Cameroon, including Douala, to France.[4]

French rule in Douala thus began under the shadow of not only the defeated Germans but also the co-victorious British, whose own sliver of southern Cameroon mandated territory extended from the West bank of the Mungo river into portions of the Littoral well within the sphere of Duala commercial and agricultural expansion. Moreover, the authority of the French suffered both from the protracted postwar negotiations over the international status of territory taken by the Allies from Germany and its Ottoman ally and from the supervisory power over these dependencies ultimately granted to the League of Nations. Under the rules governing "Class B Mandates" France had, at a minimum, to report annually on Cameroon to the League's Permanent Mandates Commission in Geneva and also leave the territory more open to free trade and missionary activity than was the case in other French possessions.[5]

The substantive differences between Cameroon, as a mandated territory, and other French African colonies would be most evident in such areas as education policy, which will be discussed below. As far as local political institutions were concerned, however, the French proceeded, on the assumption stated by their chief colonial negotiator in the Peace Conference, that there was "no real difference between a colony and . . . [a] mandated area."[6]

Thus, despite the momentous war events and some very forward political initiatives on the part of the Duala (see below) their position within the French colonial system never achieved the prominence that it had under the Germans. With the exception of a brief postwar wave of excitement about colonial investments and some major efforts at reform in the late 1930s, tropical African colonies as a whole played little part in French metropolitan politics of this period.[7] More significantly for Duala protesters, no major party within the French National Assembly was interested in following the prewar German practice of using colonial affairs to attack the government.

As for the League of Nations, its Permanent Mandates Commission (hereafter PMC) should not be confused with the later United Nations Trusteeship Council, a body dedicated to dissolving colonial empires. In the PMC, by contrast, most representatives were colonial officials or ex-officials. The few exceptions, mainly Scandinavians (the United States never became a League member and the Soviet Union joined late), played a role similar to missionary societies, focusing on social rather than political issues. The Commission did take seriously complaints about the Cameroon administration's use of forced labor for railroad construction (no Dualas involved) and its deployment of budget surpluses, as well as urging the French to make greater moves towards British-type indirect rule. But even for such questions, the PMC could not send its own delegations to Africa and thus depended entirely upon the testimony of the administering powers. On broader political issues, no controversies arose; Class B Mandates were seen as falling very much within the conditions for continued dependency set forth in article 22 of the League of Nations Covenant: "inhabited by peoples not yet able to stand by themselves under the strenuous conditions of the modern world."

In Cameroon itself, the French continued the late German policy of shifting development efforts towards the interior. Douala had again become the capital under Allied occupation but in 1921 the French moved the site of territorial government permanently to Yaoundé, which was eventually connected to the coast through an extension of the central railway. By the 1930s the region around Yaoundé would also bypass the Littoral and Mungo Valley as the major source of Cameroon's African-produced cocoa. Douala remained the territory's main port and thus benefited from these changes through extensive construction as well as population growth. However, this growth came almost entirely from immigration and during the mandate period the Duala became an ethnic minority within their own city (see table 5.1).

In formal terms, the French regime made some gestures towards both its general mandate status and the special position of Douala. Thus the head of the administration was officially called Commissaire de la République rather than Governor, although the latter was his formal rank within the Colonial Ministry. The first civilian Commissaire, Lucien Fourneau, came to Cameroon from the position of Lieutenant Governor of Ubangi-Shari (Central African Republic) in the French Equatorial Africa federation (see table 5.2). The officer in charge of Douala, as chef de circonscription (later [Wouri] région), was the French equivalent of a German Bezirksamtmann although he usually carried the additional title of délégué for the management of territorial affairs pertaining to the city and its port.

Within this structure it is still conceivable that the Duala chiefs might

Table 5.1. *The population of Douala offical tabulations, 1916–56*

	Total	Duala	Other African	European
1916	15,225	13,101	933	?
1920	23,900	?	1,900	467
1921	25,000	?	?	415
1924	22,772	16,699	4,396	c. 600
1927	27,666	c. 14,000	?	819
1929	30,881	?	12,800[1]	
1931	26,761[2]	?	9,952	862
1933	27,186	15,839	8,870	?
1935	38,350	18,449	17,424	684
1937	41,812	21,022	18,181	939
1939	34,002	17,871	13,847	?
1941	36,232	c. 16,000	14,630	1,020
1944	37,751	20,692	14,151	1,050
1947	59,699	22,927	32,507	1,971
1949	67,925	?	46,006	?
1954	108,150		83,600	c. 6,000
1956/7	124,703	23,075	86,144	c.8,000

[1] An anti-sleeping sickness campaign of this year indicates that the actual count of immigrants may have been as high as 20,000, making them already a majority of the Douala African population; Douala Circonscription Annual Report, 1929, 25–6, ANC/FF APA 10005/A.

[2] A Protestant mission estimate of the Douala population for this year is 45,000 (*Journal des Missions Évangéliques*, 1931, 625ff). Even if this figure is somewhat high, it is based on sufficient independent information so as to suggest a total population of at least 35,000, a majority being immigrants.

Source: from Eckert, "Grundbesitz," 338; the figures given here consistently underestimate the immigrant African population, which included many residents whose illegal status would induce them to resist government registration; see ibid., 175; Derrick, "Douala," 355–60. This situation provides one explanation for the fact that for every year in which separate African groups are tabulated their sum falls below the total for the city; the more immediate reason for this discrepancy is that the figures in the various columns for a given year do not all come from the same source.

have enjoyed the kind of privileged political position they had held under the Germans until the expropriation crisis. The main obstacle to such power was not, as might be thought, the reputed French republican penchant for "assimilation" or "direct rule." Elsewhere in Cameroon African chiefs played as great a role as they had under the Germans or might have done under British "indirect rule."[8] The Duala instead came under very direct suspicion from the French because of their early and continuous protest activities, their small numbers, and eventually their ties (real or imagined) to various outside forces much feared by the new

Table 5.2. *French commissioners and high commissioners*

1916	General Georges Aymérich
1916–19	Governor Lucien-Louis Fourneau
1919–23	Governor Jules Carde
1923–32	Governor Théodore-Paul Marchand
1932–34	Governor August-François Bonnecarrère
1934–36	Governor Jules Répiquet
1936–38	Governor Pierre Boisson
1938–40	Governor Richard Brunot
1940	Colonel Philippe Leclerc[1]
1940–43	Governor Pierre Cournarie[1]
1943–46	Governor Hubert Carras[1]
1946–47	Governor Robert Delavignette
1947–49	Governor René Hoffherr
1949–54	Governor André Soucadaux
1954–56	Governor Roland Pré
1956–58	Governor Pierre Messmer
1958	Governor Jean Ramadier
1958–60	Governor Xavier Torre

[1]Office entitled "Governor" during this period between the effective end of the League of Nations Mandate and the beginning of United Nations Trusteeship.

Cameroon colonial regime: Pan-Africanists, Communists, and Germans. The loss of power by the Bells during the expropriation struggle as well as the personalities of those Duala in a position to take over the major chiefdoms after World War I also contributed, as will be seen, to this political weakness.

Again in formal terms, the French did recognize the rulers of all four major Duala segments (Bell, Akwa, Deido and Bonaberi) as chefs supérieurs. However, after debating what to do with these authorities the local administration decided, in 1921, to reduce their existing court jurisdiction in both Douala and the hinterland.[9] All official cases, both civil and criminal, were now to come before *tribunaux de race*, presided over by French administrators. Like their German predecessors (which had been courts of second instance), these tribunals included African Assessors, who were now to have a deliberative role in civil cases but only a consultative one in criminal cases.[10] Moreover, the African immigrant population of Douala, already numbering at least 2,000 by 1920, was removed entirely from the jurisdiction of the indigenous chiefs.[11]

As a counter-balance to this attack on Duala chieftaincy, the French did assure the Bell and Akwa rulers a position on the Chambre d'Homologation, which heard appeals from the administrative tribunal. The chiefs were also regular members of the district Conseil de Notables, and even of the territorial Conseil d'Administration, privileges which owed something to criticism from the League Mandates Commission but conferred nothing on Africans beyond a consultative role in government initiatives.[12] Moreover in 1933, belatedly and somewhat hesitatingly recognizing that immigrants formed at least one-third of the African population of Douala (in reality probably over a half; see table 5.1), the French created two *chefs supérieurs d'étrangers* (one for Cameroonians and one for foreign Africans) and appointed them to the Conseil de Notables.[13]

Along with limiting the political power of the Duala rulers, the French were quick to punish individual chiefs who stepped out of line. Thus the Akwa paramount, Dika Mpondo, who had been in exile at the German departure, was deposed again in 1916, as were in rapid succession his sons Diboussi, Din and Betote. The last of these dismissals, in 1921, was based on charges of illegal anti-witchcraft proceedings (possibly as a blow against the clandestine continuation of independent chiefs' courts) and finally landed Betote in prison.[14] The successor to Rudolf Duala Manga Bell, his brother, Henri Lobe, was also deposed in 1920 as was the Deido ruler one year earlier. This pattern of change in office would continue throughout the period of French rule indicating both the heavy hand of the European administration and the diminished worth of chieftaincy. Betote did reemerge – after the dismissal of his brother Hans Ngaka in 1931 – as an important figure in Duala affairs up until his death in 1976. But the most prestigious of all the hereditary elite during this time was the son of the martyred Duala Manga Bell, Alexandre Ndoumbe, a man who did not want or whom the French did not allow to take office until 1951.[15]

Duala protest: the politics of petitions

Between 1919 and 1931 the Duala despatched or had despatched on their behalf some twelve petitions to European or international bodies as well as several to the Cameroon French authorities (see Table 5.3). Because of their challenge to the entire political basis of French rule in Cameroon, these petitions have been seen by most historians as important precursors to the anti-colonial nationalism of the post-World War II era.[16] At the same time the protests of this time elicited far less response in either the metropole or Cameroon than the more restricted petitions of the Duala to the pre-World War I Reichstag. This apparent paradox epitomizes the new middleman politics of the Duala.

What emboldened the protests was the already mythologized history of Duala struggle against the Germans and its seeming link to the events of World War I. Indeed, the two issues that dominate the Duala petitions derive directly from this vision: the reversal of urban land expropriation and the renegotiation of the colonial status of Cameroon. The first of these is most closely connected to internal Duala affairs during the interwar era and will be discussed separately below. The present section will focus on the general politics of petitions and the question of mandate jurisdiction.

If the limited impact of their petitions suggest that the Duala were not very effective nationalists during this period, they also reveal what it meant to become an ethnic elite. Because of their extended history of contact with Europeans and their immediate educational assets, only the Duala could have attempted the kind of politics represented by the petitions. However, the very specificity of the group making the claims allowed the French to discredit them as unrepresentative of general Cameroonian aspirations.

Duala contentions that they could reopen the question of which foreign powers would rule over Cameroon and on what terms were not entirely new in the aftermath of World War I. There were suggestions of this kind in the two Reichstag petitions, but only for the purpose of holding the German authorities to the conditions of the 1884 protection treaty, a very local agreement in which the Duala themselves had been partners.[17] By contrast, the changes beginning in 1914 involved a succession of German, British and French administrations overlapping one another throughout Cameroon and manifestly linked to world-wide conflict and subsequent international peace settlements. While the Duala were much more aware of the scale and ramifications of these events than they had been during the Scramble for Africa, they now experienced them as distant and semi-passive observers. Thus Duala attempts to have some say over the new situation of Cameroon are at once more sophisticated and more hopeless than their earlier forays into world diplomacy.

These claims were first evidenced well before the earliest postwar petitions. Doo Dayas, a government interpreter and brother-in-law to Duala Manga Bell, is reported to have predicted in 1916 that the French would grant Cameroon self-government. At the time of the armistice, in November 1918, the Duala chiefs joined other Cameroonian notables in despatching a statement of congratulations to the French as well as gratitude for "having delivered us from the slavery and injustice in which we find ourselves." But they added "the Duala country refuses to choose a nation which will be the protector of the country before having seen the representatives of the allies who defeated the Germans."[18] In the next months the Duala chiefs continually resisted French pressure for a statement of support and made approaches to British representatives in Douala as well as the British administration in Buea to explore the possibility of coming under what they perceived as more liberal British control. However, the metropolitan British position was made very clear in a despatch from the Colonial Secretary instructing his Douala consul to "avoid any risk of

Table 5.3. *Interwar Duala petitions*

	Addressee	Petitioner(s)	Points	Major issues
1. June 19/27, 1919	Weimar National Conference/Reichs-kolonialministerium	M. Dibobé	1 + 32	German rule, full African civil rights, abolish abuses, veto over appointed German governor, ethnically elected African territorial officials, social services and compulsory education, expropriation invalidated, mixed marriages and mulatto children of Europeans recognized, no public segregation, minimum wage, Cameroonian rep. in Reichstag.[1]
2. August 18, 1919	Versailles Peace Conference	Bell, Deido chiefs	1 + 7 +1	Cameroon as neutral territory or dependency of self-selected power, civil rights, free trade, elected governor, communal self-government, invalidation of expropriation, compensation for war damages, investigation of Duala Manga Bell and Mpondo Akwa cases.[2]
3. Nov. 20, 1924	Commissaire (Yaoundé)	"Ncongo" Mbende (for "la population de Douala")	4	Abuses by police agents (of Betote Akwa among others), disease caused by immigrants, prisoners work Sundays, Duala corvée laborers clean streets.[3]
4. Jan. 20, 1925	Prime Minister of Britain	Joseph Bell (at head of 9+ co-petitioners)	1	Claim farms on west bank of Mungo sequestered by British administration because German maps show European ownership of the land.[4]
5. Sept. 6, 1926	League of Nations	Joseph Bell	1(?)	Expropriation
6. Dec. 22, 1926	Commissaire (Yaoundé)	Chiefs and Notables	8	Taxation, trade licenses, judicial system, schools, police, plantations, medical care.[5]
7. August 2, 1929	League of Nations	4 major chiefs (headed by Th. Lobe Bell)	5	Expropriation.[6]
8. Dec. 19, 1929	League of Nations	4 major chiefs (headed by Ngaka Akwa)	2 + 5 + 10 + 10	Ambiguity of mandate, abuses by German and French regimes of African rights and lack of development, proposal of internal sovereignty under League of Nations external protectorate as step towards eventual full independence.[7]

No.	Date	Addressee	Author	Signatures	Subject
9.	Sept. 5, 1930	League of Nations	Richard Bell	1(?)	Expropriation.
10.	June 19, 1931	League of Nations	Vincent Ganty, Betote Akwa	7+	Mistreatment of workers, peasants, women, schoolchildren, chiefs throughout Cameroon (Akwa quarter and chiefs in particular).[8]
11.	August 5, 1931	League of Nations	Ligue de Défense de la Race Nègre	1(?)	Women's demonstration.[9]
12.	August 14, 1931	League of Nations	Vincent Ganty, Betote Akwa	4+	Same as above plus missionaries vs. Native Baptists, international status of Cameroon, women's demonstration, conseils de notables, taxation.[10]
13.	August 21, 1931	League of Nations	Vincent Ganty	Very many	63 pages on status of Cameroon, condemnations for May 18, 1931 "plot."[11]
14.	May 9, 1938	League of Nations	J. Mandessi Bell (Union Camerounaise)	2+	Freedom of property in land, Cameroon as 'A' mandate.[12]

[1] Adolf Rüger, "Imperialismus, Sozialreformismus und antikoloniale demokratische Alternative: Zielvorstellungen von Afrikanern in Deutschland im Jahre 1919," Zeitschrift für Geschichtswissenschaft 23/2 (1975): 1293–308.

[2] ANSOM, AP II C615/1; German original text printed in Andreas Eckert, Die Duala und die Kolonialmächte (Hamburg: University of Hamburg, 1991), 306–9.

[3] ANC/FF APA 11875/17.

[4] ANC/BGA Od 1922/4.

[5] Carbon copies (unsigned) in Bell Family Archives, Douala.

[6] ANSOM, AP 615/1; printed in Eckert Die Duala; see also PMC XXIV (1931) for discussion of a petition on the same subject dated August 11, 1929, signed only by Ngaka Akwa and Lobe Bell.

[7] ANC/FF APA 10890; printed in Eckert, Die Duala, 316–21.

[8] ANC/FF APA 10187; printed in Adalbert Owona, "À l'aube du nationalisme camerounais: la curieuse figure de Vincent Ganty," RFHOM 56/20 (1969): 214–19.

[9] PMC XXII (1932), 214, 221–2, 299, 350–1.

[10] APA 10187; Owona, "À l'aube," 219–23.

[11] PMC XXIII (1932), 178–9.

[12] PMC XXIV (1938), 113, 131, 184, 213.

appearing to encourage the natives against the French administration."[19]

By the time the Duala made their first formal petitions, therefore, the European powers had not only settled among themselves the disposition of Cameroon but also completed the diplomacy needed to establish the groundwork of the post-war world order. It is true that the earliest of these appeals, the June 1919 petitions to the German authorities, were initiated just before the basis of the new Weimar republic had been decided and shortly after a near-unanimous demand by the Weimar conference for "the reinstatement of Germany's colonial rights."[20] The first Dibobe petition was also printed – but with all its reference to German abuses deleted – in a set of documents on the colonial question.[21] However, the petitioners never received any substantive response to their proposals and on June 28, 1919 Weimar representatives signed the Versailles accord, including its provisions for redistributing colonies. Indeed, these first petitions had little direct connection with politics in Cameroon. Their significance lies rather in their revelation of the extent, if not power, of Duala political connections in this period and provides at least a formal justification for early French anxiety concerning "the German question" in their mandated territory.[22]

The 1919 petition to Versailles, although composed after the peace conference with Germany had already disbanded, is more serious. For one it marked a recognition by the Duala that there were now international bodies which might receive such communications and thus set the precedent for later petitions to the League of Nations.[23] Moreover, the major issues addressed here would continue to be the subject of petitions although none, other than the expropriation question, would ever be seriously addressed by the colonial authorities. The petition marked a high point in the Duala agitation that was seen by both France and Britain (the Foreign Office received a copy) as a threat to the terms of their newly fashioned colonial settlement. However, as there was not yet any outside agency that could respond to the petitioners, nothing immediate came of their efforts.

During the ten years immediately following their first petitions, the Duala leaders appear to have accepted the basic conditions of French rule. This attitude is manifested not only in the absence of international appeals for major political change but also in the circumstances and content of the four petitions discovered for this period. The two from Joseph Bell to the British Prime Minister and League of Nations were never officially received by the addressees and are unrelated to the general Douala expropriation issue. Bell's 1925 appeal formed part of an ongoing struggle over land rights with the new British authorities which reveals, according to the best study of this topic "the fragility of the institutional or legal foundation upon which Duala agricultural enterprise was based."[24] The Permanent Mandates Commission explicitly rejected Bell's other petition on the grounds that all such purely personal appeals must come to them through administrative channels. Unlike the later Duala petitioners, who did eventually reach Geneva by this route, Bell seems to have abandoned his efforts once his urban property claim had been minimally investigated and he was given permission to travel to Europe.[25]

The other two petitions of this period do address communal issues but seem to have made little impact. The 1924 complaints of Ncongo Mbende did provoke an investigation by the French officials responsible for Douala but all the allegations were dismissed both on their own merits and because the author was completely unknown among either Europeans or those Africans he claimed to represent.[26]

It is also impossible to identify more specifically the Duala "Chiefs and Notables" who wrote to Yaoundé in 1926 since surviving copies of the document are unsigned. In all probability the petition was never delivered to the French authorities, whose own archives contain no record of its receipt. The text (a French translation from a Duala original) is also rather rough, with the various points presented out of their numerical order and many errors of language and typography. Nonetheless, the contents of this text do indicate a significant step back from the boldness of earlier and later communication to overseas bodies. Here nothing more is sought than an improvement in the internal conditions of French rule and the petitioners, who refer to themselves as "votre devoué population de Douala," insist that "nous n'avons point l'intention de nous opposer à l'ordre de l'administration de n'importe quel genre."

It must be kept in mind that this was the period not long after three of the four paramount chiefs, Henri Lobe Bell, Betote Akwa and Ekwalla Epee (Deido) had been deposed (the latter two with prison sentences). As is indicated by complaints about the treatment of chiefs in the 1924 and 1926 petitions as well as activities surrounding the expropriation issue and the Native Baptist Church (to be discussed below), Duala politics did not come to a halt during the 1920s. But energies were at least diverted from concerns with the formal structure of Cameroon's territorial governance.

The eruption of appeals to the League of Nations between 1929 and 1931 represents a very radical shift in Duala responses to both the general, longstanding issues of the 1926 petition and the more specific and recent question of urban land rights. The relationship between these factors in motivating the new level of Duala protests will be discussed below. For now we will concentrate upon the reactions of the French authorities and the PMC to the questioning of Cameroon's mandate status, a point raised explicitly in two of the four petitions, but implied in all of them by the very act of taking conflicts between African subjects and European rulers to an international supervisory body.

The combination of Duala voices and Cameroon-wide claims accounts for the historical fame of the petitions but at the time, also doomed them to failure. The only serious Duala issue that received even minimal attention from the Mandates Commission was expropriation (see below). As for the various requests to alter the basic conditions of the French mandate (even that of the 1938 petition, posed within existing League of Nations terms), the PMC simply refused to consider them. As the Commission stated in response to the first of these appeals: "It would be contrary to all our principles and rules of procedure to discuss such demands."[27]

In addition to counting on PMC repugnance for any radical changes in colonial governance, the French authorities could point to the ethnic provenance of the petitions as a basis for discrediting them. Governor Marchand seemed to feel no inhibitions about reviling the Duala in both despatches to the Colonial Ministry and public testimony at the Geneva PMC meetings. His response to the December 1929 petition included a counter-petition, signed by the chiefs of the region surrounding Yaoundé, denouncing Duala demands as the efforts of "a vicious race" to dominate yet-uneducated interior populations whose present "devotion and docility" earned them not only the immediate support of colonial authorities but also the eventual expectation of "hegemony when the question of our autonomous administration arises, that is to say, when the international jury has judged fit to examine the progress of the natives of Cameroon towards European civilization."[28]

The administration had even less difficulty in dealing with the series of petitions sent to the PMC in 1931 by Vincent Ganty.[29] Ganty, a French Guiyana citizen had entered Cameroon in 1922 as a junior customs official and, after resigning his position under a cloud, spent six years seeking a living at Kribi on the south coast in a range of careers as a planter, magician, masseur, "professeur hypno-magnétique," and finally founder of a "spiritualist" independent church. In 1930 Ganty was expelled from Cameroon, partly due to the accusations of fraud connected with his church but primarily, it seems, because he had clandestinely founded a local branch of the Ligue Universelle pour la Défense de la Race Nègre.[30]

While awaiting his ship in Douala, Ganty reestablished what were apparently earlier contacts with local chiefs and received an authorization to represent them in Europe. His subsequent petitions thus designated him as "Délégué en Europe des citoyens nègres camerounaises." As indicated in table 5.3, a number of the grievances that Ganty addressed related only to the interior and southern coastal populations of Cameroon. However it was the Duala chiefs, led now by the restored Betote Akwa, who provided him with formal powers of deputation (renewed in 1931 with a promise of payment for his expenses). It appears that Ganty's efforts represented a stream of protest based in Akwa rather then Bell, unrelated to the expropriation issue (note the names that head the two 1929 petitions), and thus reviving more radical claims against the mandate regime.

The explanations by the French authorities of Ganty's background as well as the fact that the major questions he raised had been dealt with previously made it easy for the PMC to dismiss his various petitions.[31] However one appeal of this period with which his name was not directly connected (although he probably instigated it) did arouse more extensive discussion and inquiry: the petition of August 5, 1931 concerning a women's demonstration in Douala. Here, and in other actions not reported to the PMC, French conflicts with the Duala brought about outright repression and violence. But did this climactic phase of interwar Duala protest constitute a real threat to the French regime?

The two events of the early 1930s that suggest such a threat are the women's demonstrations and the trial and arrest during 1930 and 1931 of several male Duala political activists. However, the connection between these phenomena themselves, as well as their mutual link to the main PMC petitions, is not at all clear. Ultimately, they tell us less about the substance of Duala politics than about how these were perceived and dealt with by the French.

The women's demonstrations should be discussed first because they are fairly well documented and touch on concerns that the Duala notables had themselves articulated in their 1926 petition to Yaoundé.[32] Tax collection and the harsh punishment of chiefs for not carrying it out had indeed been a problem since German times. In 1931, with the onset of the Great Depression, the Cameroon administration decided to increase its declining revenues by abrogating regulations that had exempted most women from tax responsibility. Hesitation in payment was dealt with, as usual, by the arrest of one of the paramount chiefs, Mbappe Bwanga of Bonaberi, ostensibly for embezzlement. However, in this case the government action elicited a series of actions by up to 1,000 Duala women around the Bonaberi police station and the Douala administrative headquarters. The climax to these events came on July 22, 1931 when three of the female leaders were arrested and a French gendarme fired upon another group which was marching along the main riverfront road, wounding three of them.

Sensational as they were, the women's demonstrations accomplished little other than the embarrassment of the French administration. No change was made in the tax rules and the female victims, lauded as heroines after their release from brief stays in jail and hospital, soon disappeared from the political scene. The French insisted on seeing the hand of clandestine male agitators behind these activities but could not support their allegations with any evidence.[33]

In May or June 1930 the administration had also taken action against visible male Duala political activists. The records of these efforts are unclear but apparently Daniel Siliki Same and Joseph Lea Elong, two well-known figures, and a few others were convicted at the inland town of Mbanga for "fraudulently" collecting political funds among the local Abo population.[34] There seems to be some link between these activities and the petitions of 1929 and 1931 as well as Ganty's general activities. The deposition of chef supérieur Ngaka Akwa in 1931 and his replacement by the now somewhat chastened Betote is probably also tied to the same events.[35] But the very obscurity of all these connections reveals the limited political impact of agitation.

There thus remains a major gap between the high politics of Duala petitions to the League of Nations and the discernible anti-French action of Duala chiefs or even the more marginal members of the educated elite. The French, apart from punishing (but not very severely) the few subversives they could find, would continually fill in this gap with speculations about wide-ranging conspiracies. These speculations, along with real dangers of returning Cameroon to Germany, were to bring the Duala back into a kind of international politics in the late 1930s, as will be seen at the end of this chapter. However a more general French paranoia also helps to explain the politics of the most enduring issue of the interwar era, the urban land question.

Expropriation: reformed, protested and extended

If the Duala struggle against German expropriation policies, concluding with the execution of Duala Manga Bell, can be seen as a genuine tragedy, its repetition under the French mandate follows Marx's well-known formulation by more closely resembling a farce. The basic elements remained the same and were played out in, if anything, an even wider arena with more elaborate props. However, the Duala were now inspired by their already mythic vision of the encounter with the Germans and their misreading of the postwar international situation to pursue protests far beyond the point of any practical gain. The French in turn were far more judicious than the Germans in formulating urbanization policies and negotiating them with the Duala; but at a critical moment they mishandled other issues in such a way as to contribute to the renewal and expansion of the conflict. Ultimately the French accomplished what they set out to do without inflicting violence upon the Duala, so there is nothing very tragic in the process; however the seemingly senseless elements in both Duala intransigence and French responses contributed in more serious ways to reshaping Duala middleman identity.

The significance of land questions in the new colonial order was first signaled by the Duala through the prominence given this question in their 1919 petition. However, for the next four years there is no evidence of any direct action by the Bell leadership to undo the effects of German expropriation. On the contrary in February 1920, three months after returning home to a hero's welcome, Alexander Douala Manga Bell effectively recognized the legality of the German policy by requesting the payment that had been offered for his executed father's sequestered land.[36] Many other Bell notables who had been forced by the Germans to move to New Bell now resettled closer to the river on the Bali plateau;[37] but this maneuver, as will be seen, accorded with eventual French plans.

It was rather the French, concerned with both urban development and the potential political costs of further conflict with the Duala, who took the first steps toward resolving the expropriation question. The Humblot inspection mission of 1919-20 concluded that the Germans had acted legally but also mistreated and insulted the Duala through their exaggerated and perhaps insincere belief in the need for total segregation of the African and European populations of the city. The French, with their "esprit moins absolu et plus libéral" would limit segregation to the older Bell and Akwa quarters and see that adequate compensation was paid (out of German war reparations) for all land lost.[38]

It took the French another two years to formulate a more precise policy for dealing with Douala land issues.[39] A report of the Service des Domaines in 1922 reviewed the German actions in detail and concluded that the French could exercise their property rights in the already expropriated Bell area (the Joss plateau, mainly Bonanjo), but should leave the development of the Akwa and Deido river front to "the free play of economic laws." As compensation for property already lost in Bonanjo but not paid for, the displaced Bell people should be offered rights to land on the Bali plateau.[40]

There is no record of an immediate government response to this study, but it does seem to have unleashed the first efforts to sell off sequestered properties. The renewed conflict over expropriation can be said to have broken out in 1924, when news of such sales elicited two letters from "the people of Bonanjo" claiming that their own rights to this land were still legally intact.[41] Instead of retreating, however, the French authorities now became even more active in pursuing their chosen policy. This goal was to be reached by three simultaneous efforts: developing a full plan for "Europeanizing" the entire Douala river front; selling and taking over for their own use still more of the properties under contention; and, finally, opening negotiations with the Bell protesters on the basis of the 1922 recommendations.[42]

During 1926 both sides in the dispute raised the stakes of confrontation. The Duala did so literally by bringing together a war chest of some 100,000 francs. With this money, as well as documents (apparently stolen from the old Bezirksamt) of German deviousness in the prewar expropriation, they were able to gain the active support of the newly established French Protestant Mission Society (Société des Missions Evangéliques de Paris, hereafter SMEP).[43] The French countered by sending a special inspection mission from Paris with an authorization to sweeten the Bali offer by including in it funds for the building of houses by the new (or newly legalized) Duala occupants as well as the provision of streets, squares and water supplies for the entire quarter. To keep other Duala from joining with the Bells, the French also promised publicly not to expropriate any property in Akwa or Deido except for very urgent public purposes.[44]

The Bells at first resisted giving up their claim to Bonanjo even for such compensation but changed their position after meeting with their missionary advocate, Charles Maître, through the entire night preceding the final scheduled negotiating session.[45] The convincing argument was less the generosity of the French offer than recognition of the inaccuracy of the main legal premise upon which the Duala had built their case: that the Reichstag had never voted to approve the expropriation in 1914.[46] The Bell delegation thus authorized Maître to sign, on December 8, 1926, an agreement accepting the French terms.

It is at this point that the anti-expropriation struggle begins to take on characteristics of a farce or perhaps a mystery. The Bells and the French continued, throughout 1927 and 1928 to negotiate details of the resettlement in Bali. In these discussions the French ultimately gave in on such points as formal Duala recognition of German expropriation of Bali and the rights of the new inhabitants to put up mat houses in anticipation of funds to build in more durable materials.[47] However, during this same time the Duala prepared to move the conflict to a still higher level. The former Bell paramount, Richard Din Manga, was sent to Paris as an official envoy while Richard's Douala successor, Théodore Lobe Bell, initiated a law suit over Bonanjo land ownership for the Cour des Contentieux in Yaoundé and drew up, together with his three fellow chefs supérieurs, the August 1929 petition to the League of Nations.

The key event triggering this new phase of resistance to the French was the resignation of Richard Bell in March 1927 and his subsequent departure for France. The letter announcing Richard's abandonment of the Bell paramountcy gave as an explanation only the abusive behavior of the new

Douala chef de circonscription, Louis-Julien Cortade and connected this not to the land issue in general but rather to the question of constructing mat dwellings in Bali.[48] Although the evidence is anything but clear, a good case can be made that the Bell people initially intended to maintain their acceptance of the main terms of their 1926 agreement but were driven to further and heightened opposition by Cortade's ill-timed revival of abusive behavior towards chiefs and notables. Richard Bell's resignation can be linked more directly to the list of grievances contained in the Duala petition of December 22, 1926 than to the expropriation issue, which was "settled" shortly before the writing of this petition and is not mentioned in it. It is possible, therefore that the expropriation question may now have taken on a more symbolic than substantive form;[49] it was a specific issue around which the Duala could focus all their frustrations with the French regime and their new position within it. The coupling of the PMC petition on expropriation with another, three months later, again calling for basic political change is thus not coincidental.

Cortade's conduct during the critical period of 1927–28 is also difficult to explain. It may simply be a function of his personality as well as general impatience with the protracted wrangling over an issue in which the French felt the Duala had little justification for their complaints. Another factor which seems to have entered the picture, however, is heightened fear that Duala discontent was being instigated by the Germans.

The French began keeping an elaborate watch on German activities in the regions neighboring Douala from 1925, shortly after the British rulers of West Cameroon allowed Germans to purchase plantations in this area.[50] In 1926, with the entry of Germany into the League of Nations, German trading firms, particularly the well-known Woermann house, reappeared in Douala. Among the Duala notables who now became suspect for their hospitality to "ex-enemies" was perhaps the most influential figure in the entire Bell community, the merchant, planter and godfather of the chiefly family, David Mandessi Bell.

Mandessi's name is not prominent in the expropriation documentation before 1927 although he was probably a major source of the funds raised to pursue the Bell case before the negotiations at the end of 1926.[51] He did, however, come into frequent contact with French authorities, particularly in exercising responsibility for his "son" Alexandre Douala Manga.[52] French attitudes towards Mandessi's role in the first years of the mandate varied considerably, from arguing that he was the member of the ruling Bell family best qualified for the chieftaincy (although obviously barred by his slave origin), to threatening him with arrest for "deceitful" business practices.[53] Somewhere near the end of 1926 Mandessi was briefly arrested for protesting the treatment of the driver of one of his trucks in an alleged hit and run accident. This, as well as a land case not related to Bonanjo, brought a protest to the Colonial Ministry from the Senegalese deputy and chair of the colonial committee in the French National Assembly, Blaise Diagne.[54] The French officials, including Cortade, immediately saw a connection between these matters and the stubbornness of the Duala on the expropriation issue. However, instead of trying to reconcile Mandessi, they now placed his house under surveillance in order to monitor contacts with German merchants and planters and concluded that he was "a German propaganda agent."[55] Such beliefs about a potentially moderating and certainly very realistic figure in the Bell community proved self-fulfilling; Mandessi now became a major supporter of Richard Bell's endeavors to fight the expropriation from Paris.[56]

Whatever their ultimate grievances, the dedication of the Bell population to resisting the 1926 land agreement was earnest. The French proceeded to carry out their side of the pact by drawing up a list of the lands lost in Bonanjo to the Germans and setting aside funds for title-holders to build houses in Bali. However, up to 1931 only four persons are known to have made use of these funds, among them again Alexander Douala Manga Bell, who had taken no role in the previous confrontations.[57]

This passive side of Duala resistance was complemented by the commitment of considerable funds and energies to more active but ultimately quite ineffectual efforts. Richard Bell, once established in Paris, raised more than 100,000 francs from Duala supporters and did attempt, in 1928 to lobby both the SMEP and Diagne. It quickly became evident that neither of these avenues would produce any results.[58] Yet in 1929 Richard Bell received a formal *procuration* to represent the Duala in their land affairs. In 1930 he submitted yet another petition to the PMC, but this was no more than the communication of a totally separate anti-expropriation endeavor within Cameroon to be discussed below.

For a time between 1929 and 1934 Richard Bell and two other Dualas living in Paris, Joseph Ebele and Gaston Kingue Jong, brought the expropriation issue, both directly and indirectly, into the more radical stream of Paris Pan-Africanist politics. In 1929 they formed a welfare organization, the "Association France–Cameroun," and began to publish a Duala-language newspaper, *Mbale* (Truth). The paper was at first banned from distribution in Cameroon by the French, then allowed to circulate, but it ceased publication anyway in 1930.[59] The content of *Mbale* was never actually very radical; however, between 1933 and 1934 Ebele, under the pseudonym "Doualaman" did publish three very vehement attacks on both German and French imperialism in Cameroon (with special attention to the expropriation question) in the leftist Pan-African journal *Le Cri des Nègres*.[60] None of these efforts did anything to advance the Duala case against expropriation nor do they seem to have provided any lasting prominence to Cameroonians in the Paris Pan-Africanist scene.[61]

Meanwhile at League of Nations headquarters in Geneva, the PMC did recognize that the issue of land policy, unlike changes in Cameroon's mandate status, fell within its jurisdiction. However, the lengthiest attention was given to expropriation not when the PMC received the August 1929 petition which focused on this issue, but rather around the non-received 1926 petition of Joseph Bell. When this earlier appeal was finally discussed in 1929 the PMC rapporteur established the principal that the Commission was not responsible for "injustices on the part of the German authorities."[62] The 1929 expropriation petition only reached the PMC in 1931, by which time the Cameroon Commissaire, Marchand, found himself in the curious position of being supported in his attack on the "childish presumption" of the Duala by the German PMC delegate and Cameroon expert, Julius Ruppel.[63] In any case, the petition hardly made a very good case for reversing French policy since it conceded the point of Reichstag ratification of the German measures and tied expropriation to a variety of unrelated land issues.

The most carefully prepared of the new Duala efforts was the Yaoundé court case of Theodore Lobe Bell. The claim to Bonanjo land was presented in a lengthy memorandum drawn up by a hired Guadeloupean lawyer, Henri Jean-Louis. However the main points of this argument were again either untenable or unusable. They included the discredited contention that the Reichstag had never approved expropriation, a dubious interpretation of Duala Manga Bell's will, and a new attack upon the entire basis of the mandate, claiming that it rested on the 1884 Duala–German treaty which was itself invalidated by expropriation.[64] When finally presented in Yaoundé in 1932 the court case was lost; another copy of the memorandum, submitted as a petition to the PMC by Richard Bell in 1930, was never even considered on the grounds that, by the time it reached the Commission, Duala capitulation to the French plan had rendered the issue itself moot.[65]

The end of effective resistance to expropriation came in 1931 when various holders of claims to land taken by the Germans in Bonanjo applied to exchange them for rights to plots in Bali and payments for use in constructing modern houses there. By the following year over 270 such transactions had been completed and there was no one left to protest.[66]

Another indicator of both the links between expropriation and general Duala protest and the bankruptcy of efforts to undo the 1926 agreement was the appointment in 1930 of Vincent Ganty as representative for the Duala in Paris. This move indicates early disillusionment with the efforts of Richard Bell and also a shift in Duala political leadership from the Bell to the Akwa community. The Akwa chiefs and intellectuals had previously supported the fight against Bonanjo expropriation but had no immediate stake in its outcome. Ganty himself, with his dubious background, his burst of new petitions to the PMC and his later lawsuit against the Duala for non-payment of promised funds, is a sufficiently dubious figure to provide a fitting coda to this affair. However, in the more limited but vital compass of Douala itself, the movement of indigenous populations from the river front would continue with its victims this time the very Akwas who had sent Ganty to Paris.

The final stage of Douala urban land struggles came only in 1937–38 when the French at last commenced the demographic and architectural transformation of Akwa (Deido was never to undergo such change). As already noted, the mandate regime planned from the early 1920s to extend the modernization of the city northward from Bonanjo but had also promised the Duala leaders not to undertake any more expulsions of the sort practiced by the Germans. The delay in carrying out this policy as well as the limited capacity of the Duala to protest it can be attributed in part to the effects of the world economic crisis which began in 1929. However, the means now used by the colonial authorities and the response of the African victims mark a change in Duala politics reflecting the impact of more general and enduring experiences.

Because it never became a major political issue, the Akwa move from their riverain base is not as well documented as its predecessor in Bonanjo. The terms of the policy were officially laid out in an *arrêté* of October 1, 1937 which stated only that Akwa (along with Bonanjo, Bali and parts of New Bell) were to be reserved for modern housing, with no construction permitted in non-durable materials, and no fields or cultivation allowed.[67] These measures did not amount to a direct expulsion of Africans from Akwa, since anyone who was willing to build a home in the prescribed form could stay there; moreover, there was no obligation to sell land as long as arrangements could be made (through rental if necessary) for bringing buildings upon it up to the new standards.

However, it was clear to all involved that this legislation amounted to what a government report called "the segregation of Akwa."[68] The decree was obviously anticipated since it had been preceded by considerable discussion of the public health problems presented by traditional African dwellings and even destruction of houses surrounded by diseased plants in some of the quarters.[69] On August 1, 1937 the Douala European newspaper *L'Eveil du Cameroun* contained an acrimonious exchange of views about expropriation between a party signing itself "Les Indigènes" and an anonymous friend of the editor. Two weeks later *L'Eveil* used the occasion of a particularly heavy rainfall to repeat the sanitary arguments in favor of expropriation and lay down what turned out to be the government conditions for "ségrégation mixte."

Following the 1937 decree, Commissaire Pierre Boisson came to Douala to meet with the Conseil de Notables and explain why his plan was not really an expropriation. Africans who could not modernize their property in Akwa would be compensated with both land in new areas of the city set aside for native settlement and payments for their abandoned "huts."[70]

Boisson's statement concluded with a warning that "despite how much he loves the natives" the government was prepared, in the case that the housing measures met any resistance "to repress it with all the means at our disposal." This threat came in response to a warning from the notables that expropriation might "lead to major agitation in the province." However, except for brief passive resistance in two quarters of Akwa in 1938, no such agitation occurred, and the majority of the Akwa population moved from its traditional lands on schedule. During this entire process the Akwa chiefs, and particularly their paramount, Betote Akwa, cooperated fully with the colonial authorities. Betote's boldest act was a request that the government loan money to Africans who wanted to build modern houses instead of leaving; the request was refused.[71]

Betote could probably not have done very much to resist the French measures. However his new preeminence among the Duala rulers lent a very powerful meaning to this weak posture, particularly in comparison with the earlier heroic role of Duala Manga Bell.[72] To make matters worse for Betote, Alexander Douala Manga Bell chose this same period to make a belated claim to eight of his father's properties in Bonanjo. Over the opposition of the Mandate administration the French Equatorial Africa court in Douala (1935) and the appeals court in Brazzaville (1937) agreed that these parcels of land had been excluded from the German expropriation procedure and did rightfully belong to Alexander.[73] Considering Alexander's role during the real struggle for Bonanjo land, this development is highly ironic but it helped – along with other developments discussed below – to maintain the power of myth in Duala politics.

Lotin Samé and the Native Baptist Church

The questions of Cameroon's international status and rights over urban land clearly constituted the dominant issues of Duala interwar politics. However, the most enduring source of friction between European authorities and Duala protesters during this period was another matter: that of the Native Baptist Church (NBC).[74] This conflict did not immediately involve politics in the normal sense; it took place entirely within the realm of Protestant church affairs, pitting French missionaries against a breakaway indigenous pastorate which wanted formal recognition of its Christianity, the right to proselytize, and access to existing church assets, again including real estate.

Although the Native Baptist controversy appears in one of Ganty's petitions and is generally connected with Duala proto-nationalism, all of the direct participants denied that they were engaged in politics. Thus the French administration never formally supported missionary efforts to suppress the NBC and the leader of the independent Baptists, Adolf Lotin Samé, insisted from the very moment of secession that his efforts were not political or anti-European.[75] Some aspects of this affair, particularly those concerning religious doctrine, need to be discussed below in a cultural rather than overtly political context. Yet the public controversies surrounding Lotin and his emergence as the most charismatic of the Duala protest leaders in the mandate era make it difficult not to consider the Native Baptist Church in political terms. Rather than a struggle for either secular or ecclesiastical power, the NBC controversy is best regarded as a form of political theater, but a theater that not only reflected existing lines of tension but also contributed to their definition.

An independent Duala Baptist church had existed, as noted in the last chapter, throughout most of the German period without arousing the kind of clamor evident in the 1920s and 1930s. The leader of this earlier movement, Joshua Dibundu, quarrelled with both the Basel Mission and later with the Berlin Baptists before his definitive schism in 1897, but after that time maintained a low profile while still holding together a significant congregation.[76] Lotin Samé first emerged as an African pastor after 1908 but within the ranks of the *bakala* (European i.e. Berlin), not the Native, Baptist church.

The conflicts that agitated Douala Protestant leaders in the immediate wake of World War I replicate in miniature the general Duala politics of this period.[77] After the fall of Douala in 1914, all local Germans, including missionaries, were removed by the British conquerors. This left responsibility for the continuation of church work entirely in the hands of African pastors, including Joseph Kuo, Joseph Ekollo and Jacob Modi Din for the former Basel congregations and Lotin Samé for those of the Berlin Baptists.

No European mission appeared to replace the Baslers and Berliners until 1917, when the Société des Missions Evangéliques de Paris (SMEP) arrived as the appointed successor of both German organizations. The attempt by a very small cadre of Europeans to reestablish control over African churches in such a situation was bound to cause difficulties. These problems were magnified by the rather authoritarian style of the head of the initial SMEP delegation, Elie Allégret, which disturbed even the Basel

African pastors, accustomed to a relatively centralized structure. Allégret recognized that the more autonomous tradition of the Baptists church in general, to say nothing of its local history of separatism, would present special problems; he thus assigned the organization of the new "United Baptist Churches" to Charles Maître, a missionary from the French Baptist church rather than the Calvinist SMEP. As seen above through his role in the expropriation affair, Maître had considerable sympathy for the Duala and his correspondence provides us with a record of Lotin's actions during a very critical period of conflict. But even he could not keep all of the Baptists within the SMEP fold.

Allégret was encouraged in his efforts at controlling the Baptists by the merging of the Berlin and Native congregations during the period of European absence. However, this change did not prevent the Natives, under Dibundu, from splitting off again at the first missionary effort to hold a Pan-Baptist conference in October 1917. Worse still from the European viewpoint, the temporary fusion of the two churches (it is even difficult to tell who belongs to which in this period) seems to have encouraged the *bakala* Baptists to consider further schism once they became too restive under the missionaries.

Unrest reached a critical level in 1920 when Allégret established a Missionary Conference, consisting entirely of Europeans, which was to supervise all church activities in the region. The political meaning of this practice to the Duala is best recorded in the words of a Basel Church elder: "Instead of aiding the [African] pastors, the missionaries have developed the habit of directing like governors."[78] But the most dramatic action was taken by the Baptists leaders, who met with their already independent co-religionists and decided to break away from those whites who "want us to listen to them in everything that they say or decide."[79]

Lotin Samé was not, apparently, the prime instigator of this secession but in 1921 he was elected head of the new Native Baptist Church, ostensibly for his seniority as an ordained minister but probably also because of his well-demonstrated gifts for speech, song and organization. The SMEP reacted angrily and threatened various actions against the dissident Baptist leaders, with the result that most of them, even those with the most established Native ties, returned to the mission fold. Lotin was thus left alone to guard what became a much harassed position.

The SMEP began its campaign against Lotin by banning him from most of the Baptist churches outside Douala as well, of course, as those under its direct control within the city. The next step was to expel him entirely. On March 19, 1922 placards were placed in the streets of Douala announcing a unanimous decision of the local European missionaries to deprive Lotin Samé of his title as pastor and all the functions that it implied.[80] The grounds given for this move included conducting private businesses (pro-hibited for pastors) and tolerating polygamy; but the key issues were political: "founding an association . . . independent of the missionaries" and "mix[ing] political questions (of race and clan) with religion."

Whatever its main motivations, this missionary action made Lotin into a major political figure. Indeed, the high point of his fame came right after his public denunciation when he preached in Douala without any regular church base, appearing all the more publicly at various celebrations and funeral wakes. In his sermons and self-composed hymns of this period, Lotin clearly did use religious images to speak out against European rule: "We suffer . . . under the weight of the foreigner; we have no more homes, they have taken everything from us."[81] Lotin's followers paraded on the streets of Douala singing: "The Germans have left; the French have come to replace them; they will likewise depart; if the English or the Americans take their place, it will be the same thing, until the day we have our liberty. While you wait, take my corpse and put it in the sepulchre: liberty will make its way. And despite everything, sing Alleluia."[82]

Lotin's most sensational subversive gesture during this period was to preside, in early May of 1923, over several meetings in Akwa between local notables (including Betote Akwa) and "John Smith" an African-American representative of the Garveyite Universal Negro Improvement Associ-ation.[83] The main agenda of these meetings was the establishment of a local branch of Garvey's Black Star shipping company. Betote's brother assured Pastor Maître that the meetings were not political: "we were promised that a great deal of money would be sent to us to struggle against European commerce but not against the government nor against the missionaries." However government sources claimed that at the last sessions "the Pan-African movement in America and in Africa was dis-cussed" and propaganda distributed. Lotin is also reported to have read out letters addressed to the French Parliament, the SMEP in Paris, the American government, the Federation of American Negro Churches, and the London Baptist Mission Society. All the letters. which were also passed on to Smith for delivery, demanded removal of the missionaries who oppressed Lotin and of government officials "who do not know anything about native justice."

What is most striking about the colonial authorities' response to this event is not the account of what transpired (in this case, probably accurate) but rather the limited action that followed. The government had been convinced since 1920 that the Native Church was behind opposition to French judicial policies and that beneath its religious facade lay "in reality, the political goal of turning Africa over to Africans alone."[84] Yet at a moment when Lotin was actually found to be engaged in actions confirming these suspicions, he simply received a warning that "severe sanctions would be taken" if he repeated such behavior.

The warning may, however, have had some effect because little was heard from Lotin or the NBC over the next several years.[85] In 1927 Lotin returned part way to the mission fold by accepting a position in the British Cameroons under his former mentor, the German Baptist, J. Hofmeister. There is no evidence of a direct government role in the suppression of the Natives[86] but there may be some connection to the jailing of Betote Akwa and the shift of Duala political activism to the camp of the Bells and their land claims. Akwa had been the main base of the Native Baptists since the time of Dibundu's break with the Berliners and it was only in the early 1930s, when Akwa again became the center of Duala anti-colonial protest, that the independent church re-emerged as a political issue.[87]

Even during its period of political dormancy in the latter 1920s the NBC seems to have maintained both a large following and confidence in its own future. Lotin himself refused several SMEP offers to integrate him back into the Douala mission church without the status of pastor. In 1930 the SMEP calculated that slightly under ten percent of the c. 15,000 Baptists in Cameroon belonged to the NBC; but, according to government evaluations, a majority of the rest were covert partisans of Lotin.[88]

The return of the NBC to the political limelight began in 1930, while Lotin was still in the British Cameroons, with a demand by African leaders within the missionary-affiliated Baptist church that the Natives be given formal recognition.[89] During the next year the NBC issue appeared in Ganty's second petition to the League of Nations and Blaise Diagne was requested to pass a communication from the Natives on to an English Baptist minister.[90] In 1932 Lotin officially returned to Douala (preceded by a printed edition of his hymns) and not only took over leadership of the NBC but also endowed it with a formal constitution. The Natives now took on the SMEP directly by instituting a lawsuit for the transfer of thirteen of the German-built Douala Baptist churches to their possession.

All of these actions concerned the colonial authorities, who in 1932 attempted, unsuccessfully, to broker a reconciliation between the Protestant missionaries and Lotin. During the entire mandate era, the government constantly sought out information on the subversive content of Lotin's sermons and his connections with other anti-French forces both in Cameroon and Europe.[91] In the face of such opposition and suspicion, the NBC failed to achieve either official recognition or control over church property. But Lotin could now at least remain in a public position of leadership, increasing his church's membership in both Douala and the wider Littoral and even ordaining pastors on his own. The only serious step taken against the NBC by the government came at the height of anti-German anxiety in 1938–39, when newly opened (and, of course, unauthorized) chapels in the Mungo valley were first banned and then destroyed.[92]

In contrast to the other Duala protest leaders of this period Lotin can at best be labeled *proto*-nationalist since he did not pursue any specific political goals. However through his religious endeavors he was able to articulate general resistance to French rule and also test the limits of free expression under the mandate system. Most paradoxical of all, although his messages were expressed in the Duala language their content appealed to both Littoral natives and immigrants, thus transcending the boundaries of even the larger Sawa Bantu ethnic base. Lotin Samé thus represents a uniquely successful development of the Duala political middleman role. But to understand both secular and religious aspects of Duala politics more fully, we must now turn to the economic and cultural transformations of the middleman situation.

Apogee and decline of middleman economics

The ability of the Duala to maintain their protest politics during the last part of the 1920s depended to a considerable extent upon monetary resources derived from the continued prosperity of their cocoa plantations. These enterprises flourished under the early French regime to an even greater degree than they had in the last decade of German rule. The collapse of protest in the 1930s can, in turn, be tied to the decline of Duala commercial agriculture in the wake of the Great Depression. But the role of agriculture as a support for politics is only one aspect of its function in defining the social space occupied by the Duala between European rulers and the interior populations. As owners of farms, the Duala retained a certain degree of autonomy from Europeans, although they still had to come to terms with the interior peoples upon whom they depended for labor. With the loss of income from cash-crop production, the Duala were forced to work out their identity within an urban setting more directly dominated by Europeans.

Apogee: the 1920s

The division of the northern Cameroon coast between French and British jurisdictions might be expected to have done serious damage to the Duala economic position. Many of the cocoa farms established by the Duala before World War I lay to the west of the Mungo River, which now formed the frontier between the two mandated territories.[93] For the French administration, however, the most serious economic cost of this new arrangement was the loss to Britain of the major Mount Cameroon plantation zones. Thus the authorities of French Cameroon recognized from a very early stage that "the future of the [Littoral] district lies incontestably with native cultivation."[94]

The most important policy consequence of the French commitment to African farming was the decision not to encourage new European plantations in the zones of interest to Duala entrepreneurs. Thus Africans produced 94.3 percent of goods exported from French Cameroon in 1920 and 82.4 percent in 1925, when small production of rubber and tobacco by European planters had begun.[95] Little was added to that European plantation production until the expansion of coffee and banana plantations in the 1930s.

The French also offered positive support to indigenous agriculture through some extension services such as advice on cocoa fermentation and drying.[96] However the most visible encouragement came through the institution of an official decoration, the Ordre de Mérite Indigène, awarded mainly to successful African farmers. Among the earliest recipients of this honor were the merchant-planter Sam Deido and the Paramount Chief of Bell, Richard Manga Bell.[97] On the negative side, the French came to depend far more heavily than the Germans on direct taxation of the Cameroon population for balancing their colonial budget.[98] This burden was more of an innovation for inland peoples than the Duala, who had been the first community to pay head tax under the Germans and initially benefited from the new pressure on interior groups to enter the labor market.

In the first decade of the Mandate, Duala plantation expansion thus continued along the lines established before World War I. An early French survey of the plantations within their own territory, found that the total number of trees on the Mungo had increased from 357,000 in 1913 to 450,000 mainly planted by Dualas. There were also at least 550,000 trees owned by Bell, Akwa and Deido planters along the other Littoral rivers. Some plantations now had over 50,000 trees, including one cultivated by Mandessi Bell "on the West Cameroon model." Dualas also retained their leading role in food cultivation, selling important quantities of maize, cocoyams and bananas to the government from their Mungo farms. The Douala Chef de Circonscription Chazelas further noted that "A Duala works in business, administration or workyards until he has saved up a sufficient sum to start and establish a plantation; then he lives off his plantation."[99]

In a pseudo-autobiographical account, based on the experience of real planters, the Duala journalist Iwiyé Kala-Lobe gave his own picture of a successful Duala of the 1920s, "Mun'a Moto" (= "son of man"), with farms in British Cameroons as well as on the French side:

Life was ideal on the plantations. There was no particular problem in obtaining manpower. The land laborers responded by themselves to the call of the soil. On the immense cleared spaces, every man had an acre of personal land where he grew foodstuffs . . . Among the men reigned the most harmonious community life. We knew nothing of end-of-the-month worries. Every family had enough to eat and sold its surplus of produce as it pleased.

Mun'a Moto had "fine masonry houses" in Douala, but "This city saw me only once or twice a year, at the time of the great cocoa sales."[100]

The idyllic working conditions described by Kala-Lobé are contradicted by French Protestant Missionaries, who claimed that laborers on the plantations were still slaves or treated little better than if they had been.[101] Kala-Lobe is surely closer to the truth, since Duala planters had no more means of recruiting slaves and laborers seem to have come to them voluntarily in preference to the employment available on European plantations in both the latter German and early French period. Real antagonism between immigrant workers, particularly Bamileke, and landowners in the Mungo Valley would only come after the shrinking of African farm revenues during the Depression of the 1930s.

Decline: the 1930s and before

The loss by the Duala of their prominent position in Cameroon export agriculture occurred in both absolute and relative terms. The absolute loss came during the 1930s and led to the abandonment of many farms and a retreat to urban sources of elite status. The decline in relation to other communities of Cameroonian cultivators began much earlier and in more irreversible form.

The key to both the rise and fall of Duala advantages in African agricultural enterprise was their control of the Littoral rivers. We have already seen how the trading stations established by various Duala groups along these waterways were converted into centers for growing cocoa and commercial food crops. The indigenous populations of the Littoral were never very numerous and seem to have had few qualms about ceding agricultural land to the Duala and their labor force, whether servile or free. However, the construction of colonial railroads by both the French and Germans allowed regions further inland with more dense populations to enter export agriculture and eventually overwhelm the Duala planters even without the intervention of the Depression.

This is not the place to chronicle the development of cash cropping in the non-riverain portions of the Cameroon "fertile crescent" whose "general curvature follows the railway line from Nkongsamba [at the edge of the Grassfields] to Bonaberi and from Douala to M'Balmayo [just beyond Yaoundé]."[102] However it is clear that the first step in launching this process was the extension of the German Nordbahn through the Mungo Valley but well beyond the navigable portion of the river up to Nkongsamba. The effects of this transport innovation did not make themselves felt until the Mandate period, because the Duala had not begun cultivating cocoa in the Lower Mungo region much before the railway was completed (1911); moreover, the Germans, as seen, took even longer to comprehend the significance of this phenomenon. However, by the latter 1920s cocoa and, more significantly, coffee cultivation in the Upper Mungo had taken off in a decisive manner, mainly under the control of indigenous farmers and immigrant groups other than the Duala.[103]

Cocoa growing among the Beti peoples of the Centre-Sud region of Cameroon took somewhat longer to develop since the Central Railway to Yaoundé was completed only in 1927. However once in place, this new artery provided the Centre-Sud, which possess the best ecological conditions for cocoa growing in Cameroon,[104] with the means to become the premier cocoa-producing region of the country. Moreover, the tax needs of the French administration and its political alliance with the authoritarian Beti chiefs under the leadership of Charles Atangana allowed cultivation in this region to increase even under the adverse market conditions of the Depression.[105]

Had the Duala been able to continue their own agricultural exports during the 1930s, it is possible that they would have moved beyond the position of growers to that of a new middleman role as major cocoa buyers and processors. Mandessi Bell, dissatisfied with his treatment by European intermediaries, contemplated such a shift in 1929 and official French evaluations of his prospects were quite positive.[106]

However, by the early 1930s cocoa prices took a drastic plunge and Duala planters found themselves hard pressed to find the cash revenues to cover the bills for wages and other costs. Administrative reports of the period thus describe the decay of Duala farms in the key Mungo valley area although some planters clearly hung on and Duala memory tends to date the permanent decline of the cocoa economy to the political turmoil of decolonization in the 1950s.[107] The economic effect of such a loss of revenue can be seen in the efforts of various Duala elites to capitalize their urban properties. However, this strategy could not be effectively implemented until the construction boom and easier access to the registration of landholdings which followed World War II.[108]

Within the region extending from the Grassfields to Douala through the Mungo Valley, the 1930s marks not only a Duala economic decline but also a rise in the numbers and influence of Bamileke immigrants. The Bamileke had long been present here, first as slaves (Mandessi Bell was one of them), and later as migrant laborers. During the 1930s this migration continued but many of the Bamileke laborers in the Mungo Valley now became landowners. Titles to farms were acquired either in default of wages, no longer payable under the low produce prices of the Depression, or by contracts made in advance for either labor services or the retail goods of petty Bamileke traders. While the Bamileke thus replaced the Duala as the major entrepreneurs in the Mungo Valley, the Duala themselves do not seem to have been the proprietors of much of the land now taken over. The Bamileke took no interest in acquiring defunct Duala cocoa farms along the navigable Lower Mungo, which remained abandoned. Instead, the Grassfield entrepreneurs concentrated on coffee and banana growing in lands farther north, where relatively few Duala had established themselves.[109]

The retreat from plantation agriculture thus had an important link to the changing position of the Duala as an "ethnic elite" but without involving them in direct conflict with either of the newly ascendent inland groups, the Beti and the Bamileke. On the contrary, those Duala (not an insignificant number) who maintained an interest in commercial farming joined with the Bamileke in directing their anger at newly established European planters in the Upper Mungo and the southern Grassfields, who benefited from government coercion in competing for labor.[110] Meanwhile in their urban sphere the Duala continued to exploit their educational advantages for both economic and cultural purposes.

Middleman status as ethnicity

It was during the interwar years of colonial rule that the Duala came to see themselves primarily as an ethnic group. This category of identity was not, of course entirely new. For Europeans the Duala, like all African peoples, were essentially a "tribe" whose pretensions to such "higher" institutions as kingship or modern nationhood could be derisively dismissed. The Duala also defined themselves at least in part as a group of lineages descended from a single ancestor, although even this "primordial" identity was consciously shared – in genealogical, linguistic and broader cultural terms – with the other Sawa Bantu-speaking peoples of the Littoral.

However, up until the late 1920s ethnicity, even its wider Sawa Bantu dimensions, had not provided the main basis for Duala relationships with the wider world. In their precolonial existence the Duala had thought of themselves as a community of free/*wonja* "men of water" dealing with the servile/*bakom* cultivator populations of the interior. Such regional categories directly contributed to the sharp internal divisions among the Duala, since the Bells regularly accused the Akwas and Deidos of being *"bakom"* and excluded them at times from the *jengu* cult.[111] Under German colonial rule the Bell lineage achieved political jurisdiction over much of the Littoral interior (both Sawa and Basaa/Bakoko-speaking) which again extended beyond and divided the "ethnic" community. During their various efforts to counteract colonial claims upon their original urban territory, the Bells made some appeal for Pan-Duala support but also attempted (with fatal results for Rudolf Duala Manga Bell) to speak for a wider Cameroon constituency.

By the 1930s all basis for these claims to economic and political hegemony over any portion of the Cameroon interior had severely receded and, with the reduced role of chieftainship, the divisions among the Duala had also become less significant. The Duala now became conscious of themselves as a group with a history of privileged interposition between Europeans and the rest of Cameroon. What remained of this middleman role, however, was precisely its history and the cultural advantages which survived from it.

The Duala continued to exercise influence over the interior population of the Littoral through their role as church leaders – both in the missionary Protestant organizations and as independent Native Baptists.[112] Moreover the role of these churches assured that the Duala language would remain a standard medium of liturgy, hymns, catechism instruction and general literacy throughout the region. The French regime was actually more adamant than its German predecessor about imposing its own language upon education throughout Cameroon. It thus built more government schools and also issued harsher decrees regulating missionary instruction. However, the mandate status of Cameroon gave the missionaries a stronger hand in combatting such measures than in other French territories and a compromise was reached which allowed the early level of mission schooling as well as the training of pastors to be carried out in vernaculars.[113] Duala, which the SMEP insisted could become "more civilized than the other [indigenous languages]"[114] thus spread even more fully into the interior, particularly the Mungo Valley where, ironically, it even became the medium for contracts by which Bamileke migrants acquired local land.[115]

Church leadership was only one of the areas where the educational advantages of the Duala placed them in a privileged position with regard to the rest of Cameroon's African population. Thus in a period when the vast majority of Cameroonians were still peasant farmers, herdsmen or unskilled migrant workers, at least half of the entire Duala population occupied positions involving some kind of skill, capital, education or political authority.[116] The Duala no longer monopolized such posts as government clerk-interpreter to the same extent that they had under the Germans but they were still heavily over-represented in these cadres.[117] Also those Cameroonians sent to Europe for education (in a few 1920s cases still Germany but by the 1930s entirely France) were overwhelmingly Duala.[118]

This continued domination of the educated ranks by the Duala now began to support the formation of a general ethnic consciousness as the recipients of such advanced schooling married among one another across the lines of earlier political divisions.[119] Some of the newly acquired skill in French was also used to write about Duala culture, particularly in the case of the clerk-interpreter Isaac Moumé Etia, who published six small books on Duala language, folktales, and customs.[120]

The most formal public use of the Duala language was in church activities but during the interwar years Duala was also the idiom for a whole new series of secular voluntary associations. These organizations operated at the level of chiefdoms as well as the entire Duala community (sometimes both simultaneously) but their main common feature was the cultivation of ethnic identity on a basis which was both modern, in its response to new conditions of colonial life, and "traditional" in its self-conscious evocation of the precolonial past.

The generic term for all such organizations was *muemba* (pl. *miemba*) a designation that, in the past, had only referred to age-grade associations. One set of the new *miemba* were actually formed by young people born within the same period of 3–4 years, but they were both perceived and organized on a different basis than their predecessors. Duala elders are still able to recite a list of twenty-five *miemba* stretching back to the 1840s with accompanying exegeses of their names and recital of the greetings for each age set.[121] The fact that this list always ends in 1916 is significant, because we know that named *miemba* were founded after that date. However, the post World-War I *miemba* were no longer linked to any kind of initiation ritual nor did they have any relationship to political function or authority within chiefdoms.[122] Instead their membership often cut across Duala sub-units and included individuals of less than pure *wonja* descent, including Dualaized immigrants and descendants of slaves. They were also organized on a rather bureaucratic basis, with formally elected officials, monetary dues and written constitutions.[123] Whatever the role of the *miemba* had been in precolonial times (and this is not entirely clear) they now served to provide both a symbolic link with that past and mutual (mainly financial) aid for such purposes as marriages and funerals. Considering the changing role of the Duala within their own city, it is not insignificant that organizations of this kind are most commonly associated, in Africa and elsewhere, with immigrants.

Another group of *miemba* was formed within each of the major Duala chiefdoms with the express purpose of promoting the social and cultural interests of its group. These associations displayed their modernity through the wearing of uniforms and declarations of concern for education and other forms of "progress" but they also collected and wrote down oral histories of their respective groups and of the Duala as a whole.[124]

The separate and collective nature of these identities became most visible during the *pembisan*, the semi-annual canoe races held on the Wouri. The large canoes themselves and even the practice of racing them publicly goes back well before colonial times, as does the belief that success in the races depended upon access to the power of *jengu* spirits.[125] However the occasion of the races were now determined by the European calendar (Bastille Day and Armistice Day under the French, the Kaiser's birthday in the German era) and the participation of the various Duala quarters (along with surrounding maritime communities such as Malimba and Bonandale) depended less upon mutual political and economic relations than upon their common submission to the *pax colonialis*.

Among the canoes regularly competing in the Douala races was one belonging not to any coastal community or sub-community but, rather, to the personal *muemba* of Prince Alexander Ndumbe Duala Manga Bell.[126] The sponsorship of a canoe was only one of the ways in which Alexander used the status of his family to transform politics into ethnicity while retaining a potential – as will be seen in the next chapter – for retransforming this charisma into politics.

As already noted, throughout the interwar decades Alexander stayed outside of formal politics – meaning chiefly office and the Bonanjo land expropriation dispute – through a combination of French suspicion and his own volition. He did undertake a few gestures of defiance against the regime – twice successfully suing colonial officers who had insulted him and winning a case for the return of his father's Bonanjo land. But at the same time he assured the new colonial authorities of his loyalty to them (guaranteed by a constant state of financial indebtedness) and in 1937–39 even enjoyed the rare privilege of a successful application for French citizenship.[127]

The most continuous and concrete base of Alexander's local power in this period was the *muemba* formed at his first return from Europe in 1919, then called the Alexanderbund and by 1937 given the less provocative title of *male ma N'Doumb'a Douala* and *Muemba ma Nyango Andre* (Alexander and Andre Associations [his wife's name was actually Andrea]). Alexander also profited from Duala cultivation of the memory of his martyred father. A hymn in Rudolf Duala Manga's honor, *Tet'Ekombo* (still popular today) was composed in 1929 and in 1935 the former chief's remains were reinterred behind his old house in Bonanjo; an obelisk was placed on the spot on August 8, 1936 the twenty-second anniversary of Rudolf's execution.

With his combination of advanced European education, a cultivation of local history and culture, along with a highly ambiguous political stance, Alexander Bell epitomized the new ethnic basis of Duala middleman identity. However, both for him and for other Duala elites, leadership within the larger Cameroon and Pan-African nationalist context had not yet been entirely abandoned.

Politics in a new key: the approach of World War II

If the collapse of efforts against land expropriation and the economic setbacks of the Depression had stifled Duala anti-colonial politics at the beginning of the 1930s, the rising threat of Nazi Germany from 1933 onwards brought a number of Duala leaders back into the center of at least French concerns about control over Cameroon. This new politics took two related forms: first, the persecution by the French of all Cameroonians (in this case, almost entirely Duala) suspected of pro-German sympathies; and second, French recruitment of Cameroonians (under Duala leadership) into an organization for the support of their own mandate claims, the Jeunesse Camerounaise Française (Jeucafra).

As already noted, French anxiety about German claims to Cameroon began not with Adolf Hitler's ascension to power but rather with the legal return of individual Germans to Cameroon as merchants and planters from 1925 onwards. In the course of the 1930s, however, the threat to French control of the mandated territory became real: in British Cameroon the German government had surreptitiously bought up plantations on behalf of its own citizens, who now (along with a large number of Germans in the Spanish colony of Fernando Po) came under Nazi control;[128] at home, French and British diplomats proposed the return of former colonies (particularly Cameroon) as an alternative to German expansion within Europe.[129]

One of the responses of the local French regime to these threats was to hunt down pro-German Dualas. Any real danger of political links between German-educated colonial subjects and the *Vaterland* had receded by this time since the Nazi regime was, to say the least, inhospitable to those Africans still living in Germany, especially as their political affiliations tended to be with the extreme left.[130] However in 1934 the French uncovered a truly pro-German organization in Douala, the KEDGV (Kamerun Eingeborenen [or Farbigen] Deutsch Gesinnten Verein [or für Deutsch [sic] Gesinnung]). This small group of about twenty members had corresponded with former Kamerun officials in Germany and in 1933 declared itself in favor of restored German rule, even requesting the enrollment of its members in the Deutsche Kolonialgesellschaft, Germany's official colonial propaganda association.[131]

The KEDGV was probably not much aware of – let alone seriously committed to – Nazi political goals (its members swore allegiance to the Kaiser). It certainly did not present any real menace to French interests, especially after six participants were arrested and the rest fled to the British Cameroons. However, the existence of such an association provided French Cameroon authorities with fresh fuel for their beliefs that some unlikely combination of German, Communist and Pan-Africanist forces was acting against them. Thus the German background of Lotin Samé, along with his connections to Germans in West Cameroon and some known Duala Germanophiles, was used to demonstrate "the very close links uniting various categories of opponents."[132]

French persecution of allegedly pro-German Dualas accelerated in the period immediately preceding World War II and reached even greater heights in 1941, when De Gaulle's Free French used Cameroon as a base for resistance against both the Germans (who now occupied most of France) and the Vichy collaborationist regime that claimed control of the French colonies. In January 1939 six Dualas were imprisoned and eighteen others subjected to exile for speeches "inciting to rebellion" by predicting a German return.[133] In 1941 sixty-one individuals, including Lotin Samé, were arrested although Lotin was eventually released along with forty-five of the other suspects. More dramatically, on March 19, 1941 Dikongue Meetom, a Duala who worked for a German planter on Fernando Po, was shot for attempting to pass military information to his employer.[134]

Meetom (whose name is even miswritten "Milton" in the announcement of his execution) was certainly no Duala Manga Bell, but his fate suggests a sad parallel between the end of the Mandate regime and that of its colonial predecessor. Despite the paranoia and diplomatic duplicity of the French, it would be cruel to refer to this replay of the 1911–1914 events as a farce: not only did Meetom and several of the imprisoned Dualas lose their lives but the Cameroon authorities cannot be blamed entirely for reacting so strongly to those Dualas who wrote letters of complaint to Hitler, spread rumors of a German return and are even reported to have suggested that the French and their African supporters would be treated like the recently annexed Czechs.[135]

The mandate regime did prove itself more liberal, or at least flexible, than the Germans in its efforts to balance repression by the organization of positive support among younger, French-educated Cameroonians through Jeucafra. Most accounts of Jeucafra stress its control by the colonial authorities and the fact that the majority of its members were government employees. The redeeming qualities of the organization, from a Cameroonian perspective, were its role in bringing together elites from various portions of the territory, thus overcoming the Duala-centered basis of previous African political life and also laying the groundwork for true nationalism after World War II.[136] Without disputing the general outlines of this standard interpretation, it must be noted that a more detailed study of the politics around Jeucafra reveals how central the Duala, in their capacity as an ethnic elite, remained to any serious confrontation between the French and their Cameroonian subjects.

Before Jeucafra was founded in 1938 the French became aware that Francophone Cameroonians in Paris had already founded a series of political organizations that simultaneously opposed any return of German rule and demanded some additional rights for Africans. The first of these bodies, the Comité (national[137]) de défense des intérêts du Cameroun (CNDIC) made its appearance in 1937 with a request by its president, Gottfried Chan, to lead a delegation to rally support in Cameroon against any reversion to German rule. Chan and most of the other officers of the CNDIC were not Dualas and it is significant that the Colonial Ministry decided that they "do not appear sufficiently educated to be used for propaganda purposes"; it was suggested that two more qualified Dualas be employed instead.[138]

The two individuals named by the Ministry, Jean Mandessi Bell and Moudoute Bell, belonged to prominent Duala families. Both were associated with Chan but in 1937 or 1938 left his group to form, along with another Duala studying in France, Léopold Moumé Etia, a new organization, the Union Camerounaise (UC). The UC also declared its loyalty to France over Germany and generally seemed moderate compared to the CNDIC; but its leaders did have specific ideas about reform in Cameroon, including education in local languages and, in a petition to the League of Nations, a change in the territory's mandate status from "B" (implying indefinite European rule) to "A" (implying very proximate independence).[139]

The French authorities in Paris, especially under the Popular Front government of 1936–38, had been reasonably hospitable to the CNDIC, even sending the Minister of Colonies, Marius Moutet, to one of its meetings in 1937 and giving money to Chan in 1938. However, the UC soon earned the reputation of all Duala political organizations, being feared for its quite manifest claims against the existing colonial order and also suspicion that its leaders were somehow pro-German.[140]

The Cameroon administration thus placed all its hope in Jeucafra, an entity over which it could exercise quite careful control. Nonetheless, in seeking a president for the new organization, originally decentralized in the various Cameroon regions under the supervision of local administrators, the government again had to turn to a Duala. The man chosen, Paul Soppo Priso, a young Public Works employee, appeared to be someone on whom the administration could rely. He was a clearly very intelligent individual but one with no patronage within his own community and limited formal education.[141] Yet the only extant document concerning Soppo's elevation to the leadership of Jeucafra indicates that Commissaire Brunot did not entirely trust him.[142] Later efforts by Soppo to take initiatives in collecting funds and particularly to demand the change of status of Cameroon, in this case from a mandate to a colony, were refused by the government because of their implications that Cameroonians could exercise some autonomy within the existing political order.[143]

Soppo's major role in nationalist politics was to come after World War II (see next chapter) but his Jeucafra position foreshadows the new status of the Duala in Cameroon. Their position between Europeans and their hinterland compatriots remained a powerful asset; but it was increasingly to depend for its material support upon real estate (the area of Soppo's extensive private enterprise) and for political leadership upon sophisticated individuals who knew better than any other Cameroonians how to deal with Europeans. Yet at the same time the Duala were becoming more aware of themselves as a community with an identity and "traditions" that had to be asserted against the demands of both Europeanization and other self-conscious Cameroonian groups who could never be subjected to Duala cultural influence. The Duala middleman formula was becoming diluted, but some of its strongest concoctions were still to come.

6   Between colonialism and radical
nationalism: middlemen in the era of
decolonization, *c.* 1941–*c.* 1960

The final phase of European rule in Cameroon provided the Duala with an opportunity to play out their own last actions as a collective historical force. In retrospect the failure of these efforts – at least in their own political and economic terms – appears inevitable. The fate of Cameroon would again be determined by international forces – this time linked to World War II, the struggles of West European recovery, and the global blocs of the Cold War – over which local communities could exercise little control. In the new territorial electoral politics, the indigenous peoples of the Littoral had to contend with much larger populations in other regions of Cameroon. Finally, within their own city the Duala had now clearly become a minority and could only act as bystanders to the most momentous local events.

However in the transition to independence, Duala individuals and organizations retained a surprisingly prominent role. They could do this because of the historical prestige of their hereditary rulers, the greater exposure to European education and modern institutions of their younger elite, and an even more growing ethnic consciousness, now articulated through their "Traditional Assembly," the Ngondo. Even if no elements of this last hurrah succeeded in retaining or restoring the power previously enjoyed by the Duala, they do reveal a great deal about the larger field of African experience that this middleman people still attempted to bestride.[1]

The uneven march towards independence

The great benchmarks of the terminal colonial period in Cameroon remain European decisions, even if these were now undertaken with at least as much of an eye on Africans as on the outside world. French policy throughout these years followed a rather ambiguous agenda of granting new freedoms to Africans while keeping them within some kind of political and economic union with the metropole. In Cameroon, as in many other colonial territories, this task was complicated by white settlers, who had gained new political and economic powers during the war. The ultimate

176

formal result was independence, but one involving considerable continuing dependence on France and arrived at through many – often violent – bumps and turns.[2]

At a conference held in nearby Brazzaville in 1944, the Free French regime committed itself to eliminating the most onerous features of colonial subjugation (forced public labor and a separate "native" legal system) while promising greater political participation to Africans in a postwar "French Union." This promise was at least partially realized in the 1946 constitution of the French Fourth Republic, which created the basis for electoral politics among Cameroonians with representatives to be chosen for both the National Assembly in Paris and an Assemblée Représentative Camerounaise (ARCAM later Assemblée Territoriale or ATCAM and after 1957 Assemblée Legislative or ALCAM) in Yaoundé.[3]

The first phase of these reforms severely limited the number of Africans who could vote and relegated all but the very few with full French citizenship to a "Second College," thus assuring a privileged position for European residents of Cameroon; moreover the power of ARCAM remained quite restricted. However, the Loi Cadre of 1956 removed most of these limitations and put French African territories on the same road to full sovereignty already evident in Asian and Mediterranean colonies as well as British West Africa. In the case of Cameroon this process was accelerated by the shift of international supervision from the League of Nations Mandate Commission to the Trusteeship Council of the new United Nations Organization. The latter body, in contrast to its predecessor, contained representatives of states actively hostile to colonialism (from both the Soviet Bloc and the ex-colonial "Third World") and was also empowered to send delegations directly to the territories under its jurisdiction.

Within Cameroon African electoral politics and party organization took some time to evolve. Initially, as will be seen, the only body approaching national status was the propaganda association, Jeucafra (Jeunesse Camerounaise Française) which, in 1945, changed its name to Unicafra (Union Camerounaise Française). By 1949 politics in the Littoral as well as the adjacent Grassfields and Basaa forest zone was dominated by the UPC (Union des Populations du Cameroun), a party with a very radical posture towards the achievement of full independence and the reunification of French Cameroon with the British-ruled western portions of the former German colony.[4] Whether or not the UPC had any potential for transcending its regional-ethnic base, the French succeeded in playing it off against parties based in the Beti-speaking Centre Sud and the Muslim North. By 1955 French hostility to the UPC had driven the party underground; in the years immediately preceding independence Cameroon national power thus passed first to a loose coalition led by the Beti Catholic, André-Marie Mbida, and later to the Northern Muslim, Ahmadou Ahidjo.

For Cameroon, like the rest of colonial Africa, the post-World War II years were a period not only of new political activity but also unprecedented levels of economic investment and urbanization. Douala and its region were particular targets for infrastructural development, including an expanded harbor, a bridge across the Wouri linking the main city more closely to Bonaberi along with the export agriculture of the Mungo Valley and finally a hydroelectric project at the navigable limits of the Sanaga River in Edea. The population of the city was also growing (overwhelmingly through immigration) at a vastly accelerated rate (see table 5.1).[5]

The Duala themselves now lost virtually everything that was left of their position as Mungo valley rural capitalists. European competition for labor was curtailed by the end of forced labor but this proved more of a boost to Beti and Bamileke cocoa and coffee growers than it did to the Duala. During World War II, restrictions on cocoa exports had added to the woes of the Depression. Then in the latter 1950s UPC violence throughout the Mungo region put a final nail in the coffin of Duala farming leaving only urban real estate holdings and relatively advanced education as a still very robust basis for maintaining some form of economic prominence. In terms of occupations and wealth the Duala thus remained an elite ethnic group, but a less enterprising one than in the past.[6]

The most dramatic political events within Douala during this period did not, therefore, involve the Duala community or its major leaders but centered rather on the majority and less affluent immigrant population. A further postwar reform – the licensing of formal African labor unions – produced the first major violent clash of the decolonization process: a 1945 railroad strike, which inspired riots among unemployed immigrants in the New Bell quarter and was met by a lethal response on the part of a right-wing white settler organization, affiliated to the Etats-Généraux de la Colonisation Française.[7] Very few of the strikers and none of the rioters were Duala.[8] The long-term significance of this event was to radicalize decolonization politics in the Littoral, thus assuring its dominance by leaders who could appeal directly to the immigrant urban masses. The UPC built itself upon this base and its founders were specifically concerned not to be identified with a tradition of Duala protest politics that was perceived as elitist.[9]

Demography and status also limited Duala participation in subsequent instances of urban violence involving the UPC: the riots of May 1955 that drove the party underground and a 1960 clash between Bamileke Upécistes and Hausa merchants that caused the burning down of fifteen hectares of New Bell.[10]

New Bell did represent a potential basis for direct conflict between the Bell/Bonadoo Duala, who still insisted that they owned it, and its restive immigrant population. However the French never allowed indigenous property rights in this quarter to be formally registered (as was now taking place throughout "Old Douala"), thus making it impossible for the Bell proprietors to collect rent. At the same time the Bonadoo were no more eager to settle there themselves than they had been when the Germans established this quarter as part of their pre-World War I expropriation plan; for Duala social geography New Bell was (perhaps now more than ever) *kotto*. i.e. low-lying inland territory fit only for inhabitation by bakom (slaves or any other peoples from the interior). This standoff made it impossible for the French to undertake any urban renewal measures in the very overcrowded and unsanitary New Bell; but it also allowed the Duala to be tolerated as a continuing, if more subdued, elite in post-colonial Cameroon.[11]

To understand the basis and limits of this position it is necessary to examine in some detail the more active aspects of Duala leadership during the last decades of colonial Cameroon.

History as electoral capital: the political career of Prince Alexander Ndoumbe Douala Manga Bell

Formal politics among the Duala had always revolved around their various chiefs. However, given both the segmentary character of the precolonial order and the attitude of colonial regimes since the pre-World War I expropriation crisis, these traditional rulers – more specifically the heirs to the dominant Bell and Akwa factions – did not appear likely to exercise much influence over events in the era of decolonization. French policies toward chiefs in and just before this process of change proved rather ambiguous, thus both eroding further such hereditary power and providing it with new avenues for exploitation.

As noted in the previous chapter, by 1933 the colonial authorities had established chieftainships as well as positions in the local Conseil des Notables and Chamber of Commerce for the immigrant communities of New Bell.[12] However the Dualas did regain some advantage from the elevation of their city to official urban status as a *commune mixte* in 1941; a new municipal council was created with two African members who, for most of the 1940s, consisted of the leading Duala chiefs Lobe Bell and Betote Akwa.[13]

But the most disturbing political changes did not come at this local level. It was rather the opportunity to elect Africans to represent Cameroon in France that most excited both the anxieties and ambitions of the Duala community. The first of such polls, in 1945, was for two delegates (one European and one African) to participate in drafting a constitution for the new French Fourth Republic.

This event touched upon a whole range of delicate issues.[14] Most generally, Duala leaders feared that the mandate status of the territory might be jeopardized in favor of either indissoluble integration with France or enhanced power for the very aggressive local white settlers. Unicafra (the successor to Jeucafra) was the logical base for promoting an African candidacy, but the organization could not agree on a single nominee so that the strongest figure to emerge was the vice-president of the organization, André Fouda (later Mayor of Yaoundé). Fouda was unpopular among the Duala elite for two reasons: his base among the Beti populations of the Centre-Sud region and his close association with government and settler policies.[15]

The impending elections were thus greeted in Douala by a wide range of protests: anonymous Duala-language pamphlets and posters, public meetings and petitions by the Duala chiefs and intelligentsia. In the popular statements the government initiatives (which included proposals to send other Africans to France for artisanal training) were associated with slave trade ("trafic d'indigènes")[16] and moves to "sell the country." All the protesters insisted that the elections, if not downright harmful, were illegitimate and urged a general Douala boycott.[17]

Such a reaction to what they saw as liberal initiatives constituted a serious embarrassment for the French. They thus promoted another African candidate for the Constituent Assembly, a man they probably did not trust entirely but over whom they had already established some hold and one who was sure to attract support in the Littoral: Alexandre Ndumbe Duala Manga Bell.[18]

Ndoumb'a Douala, as he was popularly known, not only won this election easily but in 1946 and again in 1951 and 1956 was chosen for the Cameroon African seat in the French National Assembly. In outward appearance, therefore, Alexandre had realized the potential of his father and grandfather, Rudolph Duala Manga Bell and Manga Ndumbe Bell, to build his Duala position into one of recognized national authority. Even the UPC leader Ruben Um Nyobé viewed the 1945 election results as "proof of great political maturity" on the part of the Cameroon population.[19]

Ndoumb'a Douala retained his popularity among local voters until his death in 1966. His only defeat at the polls came in 1947, when Paul Soppo Priso won the local seat in the Cameroonian Representative Assembly. However, in 1960 Alexander defeated Soppo in a contest for the new Cameroonian National Assembly, precipitating the latter's retirement from politics.

More knowledgeable participants in Cameroon public affairs of this era did not take long to become disillusioned with the leadership of the self-styled Prince.[20] As a legislator he became more renowned for his role as a Paris dandy than any serious efforts at lawmaking. Like in the interwar period, he produced a few memorable anti-colonial gestures and speeches, but more often (as at several United Nations appearances) he defended French positions against nationalist demands.[21] French influence over him appears connected to his now even more elevated lifestyle, which kept him in a continual state of financial indebtedness.

Alexandre Douala Manga Bell thus embodied in very powerful form all the qualities that kept the Duala prominent in Cameroon: education; urban real estate (see more below); and, above all, the aura of great precolonial status and colonial martyrdom. But in his persona (which did include considerable charm and artistic talent) these assets were only dissipated or, at best, endowed with a new layer of myth. Fortunately for the Duala, there were other means for building upon their past achievements that could produce more serious and even enduring results.

Middleman nationalism: the politics of Paul Soppo Priso

The other Duala leader to gain national prominence during the era of decolonization was also a holdover from the interwar period, although in this case a much younger man decidedly remote from the chiefly lineages. Although his formal schooling was actually quite limited Paul Soppo Priso is often discussed as a representative of the "educated" as opposed to the "traditional" Duala elite. It is perhaps more useful to view Soppo as a figure who attempted to combine some of the advantages of his Duala origin with a level of urban economic enterprise and supra-ethnic consciousness, which linked him to a broader Littoral and potentially Cameroon-wide constituency. In policy terms Soppo was also the consummate middleman, who consistently tried to steer a course between conservative French forces and the radical UPC.

As seen in the previous chapter, Soppo Priso's political career began in characteristically ambiguous fashion when the French reluctantly chose him to head Jeucafra, an organization designed primarily to defend the territory against pressures for its return to German rule. During World War II, as also noted, Jeucafra protested – with surprising success – against some of the more arbitrary measures instituted by the French administrators of Douala. As early as 1943 and 1944 the organization took on a more proactive posture and, while still professing loyalty to France, drafted petitions to René Pleven, the Free French Commissaire aux Colonies, demanding political, economic and social reform in Cameroon.[22]

Soppo Priso remained the guiding force behind these efforts. In 1945, when Jeucafra held its first autonomous national conference, reaffirmed its reformist platform and changed its name (as much on grounds of age as of ideology) to Unicafra, Soppo continued as president. His leadership – and that of other moderate Dualas such as Jacques Kuoh Moukouri – was only challenged in 1947 when a group with trade union ties took over Unicafra and renamed it Racam (Rassemblement Camerounais) thus in both form and substance abandoning any commitment to continued association with France. The new organization still had Dualas among its leaders, including the president, Gaston Kingue Jong. At a 1947 public meeting of regional elites at Yaoundé, Racam was even attacked as a Duala power conspiracy.[23]

The French colonial authorities also saw Racam as a major threat, and the organization proved unable to withstand the multiple but subtle pressures mobilized against it; by early 1948 it had ceased to exist. One of these undermining factors was the reluctance of men like Soppo and Kuoh – both still dependent on government employment for a major portion of their income and influence – to associate themselves with such a body. The longer-term result was the immediate replacement of Racam by the still more radical UPC, whose leaders, as already noted, consciously avoided any image of Duala "elitism."[24]

Soppo Priso himself remained very prominent in Cameroon politics, but from 1947 to 1954 these activities appeared to be dissociated from any organization. As the local French administration saw it, "in Douala, politics is not about parties, you are above all for or against Representative Douala Manga Bell or Councilor Soppo Priso . . . it is a matter more of personalities than of policies."[25] The above citation indicates that in addition to his seat in the Cameroon Representative Assembly, Soppo also held a position as Councilor of the Paris-based Assembly of the French Union, an advisory body of much less significance than the National Assembly to which Alexander Douala Manga Bell had been elected. During this period Soppo developed his tactics of steering between contending groups by avoiding affiliation with either the UPC (which seems to have wanted no public contact with him at the time) or the Duala ethnic partisanship of the Ngondo (see below). He is presented, in the best existing examination of his politics, as a spokesman for the new bourgeoisie of fonctionnaires and indigenous businessmen, seeking better opportunities for their collective advancement through removal of racial restrictions and privileges rather than radical political change.[26] This position allowed Soppo to retain close ties with many Dualas as well as aspiring Bamileke entrepreneurs, while the colonial authorities regarded him as an *interlocuteur valable,* loyal to the offical program of introducing reforms without breaking the political ties between France and Cameroon.

Soppo Priso's middleman politics took on a more nationalist and ambitious direction from about 1953. In February of that year he proposed to the Council of the French Union that indigenous Cameroonians be granted greater executive and legislative powers in the territorial government. More dramatically, Soppo's 1954 campaign for election to the newly constituted territorial legislature, ATCAM, was openly supported by the UPC. This alliance propelled Soppo to the presidency of ATCAM, thus making him the formally most powerful African figure in domestic Cameroonian politics. From this perch he continued to push the French to move beyond the changes advanced in their own initiatives, even claiming that the 1956 *loi cadre* (which, in hindsight, signaled the abandonment of all ambitions for political assimilation) failed to respect Cameroon's autonomy as a United Nations Trust territory.

The balance between principle and opportunism in Soppo Priso's new posture was much debated at the time and still remains unclear. Despite his territorial non-partisanship he had affiliated with the metropolitan Socialist Party (SFIO) in Paris and began his nationalist moves with some support from the Socialist governor, André Soucadaux, a man otherwise known for his hostility to the UPC. Soucadaux's replacement in 1955 by the even more repressive Roland Pré was opposed by Soppo, along with most other leading Cameroonian politicians.[27] It was Soucadaux's refusal to deal with the UPC that convinced leaders such as Um Nyobé to approach Soppo Priso, probably as early as 1952, and use him as their own *interlocuteur valable*.

When the UPC was driven underground by the violent events of 1955, Soppo reached the pinnacle of his own political trajectory.[28] In 1956 he co-founded the Mouvement d'Action Nationale Camerounaise (MANC), an alliance of the Ngondo and Charles Assate's Association Traditionnelle Bantu Efoula-Meyong. He also formed a broader (but short-lived) coalition of parties opposed to the *loi cadre*, the Courant d'Union Nationale (CUN). The goal of the CUN was quite avowedly to redefine Cameroonian nationalism on a centrist basis. Soppo hoped to win the 1956 ATCAM elections – the first based on a single democratic franchise and the potential prelude to an autonomous Cameroon government under a premier selected by a majority of the legislators – by joining together a still larger group of regional blocs, including the UPC.

Unfortunately for Soppo – and perhaps for Cameroon – this was a center that could not hold. While initially appearing as the one figure who could appeal to all the major forces in Cameroon politics, Soppo ended up trusted by none except the small Littoral constituency represented by the MANC (amounting, after the December 1956 vote, to 8 seats in a legislative body of 67). The French had been appalled by Soppo's entente with the UPC and successfully worked to draw the major components of the CUN into separate Northern and South Central regional groupings. The UPC, despite Soppo's embrace of their positions on independence and reunification, could not accept him as a substitute for their own full legalization. Instead, they opted for a boycott of the elections, enforcing this with a full commitment to violent opposition against the existing regime.

Both the public discourse of the election campaign (especially on the part of the Centre Sud leader and eventual first Cameroonian premier, André Mbida) and the private correspondence of French officials is full of language portraying Soppo and the Duala community he was now seen to represent as dangerous and parasitical tricksters with no valid claim to national leadership. Thus Soppo Priso, a leader who tried so hard to transcend the established forms and boundaries of Duala politics, was ultimately perceived by his fellow Cameroonians in ethnic terms, and terms that played negatively upon the small size of the Duala community and its history of privileged middleman status.

For Soppo himself the political aspect of this role ended soon after the failure of his great nationalist maneuver. He turned to cultivating economic interests based, like those of most Dualas, on real estate holdings. In Soppo's case, however, these holdings were not inherited but rather personally gained, apparently with at least some help from his earlier role in administration and politics.[29] Even in this domain Soppo (who died in 1996) stood apart from other Duala landlords not only by the extent of his wealth but also by his further investments in such enterprises as a private hospital (Polyclinique Soppo Priso – still the best such establishment in Douala) and private patronage of local artistic efforts.

Soppo Priso represents the fullest realization of Duala historical identity through an individual political and economic career. But the final instantiation of the Duala community was and remains a collective one, ultimately taking more a cultural than a material form.

From tradition as politics to politics as tradition: the Ngondo

The earliest documented references to the Ngondo – whose putative precolonial existence has been discussed in a previous chapter – occur in the 1940s. During the decade and a half between the end of World War II and independence, the Ngondo took on a succession of roles: first as a populist organization directed partially against chiefs; then as an instrument by which chiefs (and particularly Betote Akwa) represented Duala interests in the politics of decolonization; and finally (continuing into the present) as the basis for an annual festival celebrating Duala-Sawa cultural identity.[30]

The Ngondo first appears on record in a text dated February 27, 1947 with the title *Décision du Peuple* and containing a charter of the organization.[31] The only name to appear at the bottom of this document is that of Alfred Ebele Ekwalla (1890-1958) who, according to all available sources, was the key figure in creating the Ngondo of the 1940s.[32] Ebele Ekwalla, a Deido resident, was a member of the "educated" as opposed to "traditional" elite, who began his public life as an apparently faithful servant of various colonial institutions, including the German administration, the British mercantile firm of John Holt and the French-supervised Douala government courts.

Ekwalla's first known conflict with European rule came in 1940–41 when he was among those Dualas arrested, but never convicted, for allegedly pro-German sympathies. Among the other detainees was, it will be recalled, the independent Baptist Pastor Lotin Samé. It is very likely that during or around this incarceration Ekwalla learned of the Ngondo tradition from Lotin, who appears to have been its first proponent, if not inventor. In 1936, as a response to a government ethnographic inquiry, Lotin claimed (on the basis of no recorded precedent) that in the precolonial era a Grande Assemblée du Peuple judged Duala chiefs and had been responsible in the 1870s for the execution of Eyum Ebele/Charley Deido on the Ngondo sand bank (located but not named here). Lotin also described the annexation treaty with the Germans as an attempt by unspecified rulers to escape from the authority of this collective body. He further discusses a traditional system of judicial appeals from household through quarter chiefs to an Assemblée Générale du Peuple connected somehow with the cult of the *jengu* water spirit.[33]

The opposition between chiefs and people in the conception of Lotin's unnamed assembly remained central to the Ngondo propagated by Ekwalla. Thus the opening paragraphs of the February 1947 "Décision" (which also lacks the term "Ngondo"[34]), explicitly remind "the paramount chiefs . . . neglectful of their customary duties..."

de la procédure normale du règlement des affaires publiques de notre Collectivité, qui est de les soumettre à l'Assemblée Traditionnelle du Peuple, seule autorité compitent [*sic*] pour statuer valablement dans toutes les questions touchant l'ensemble du Peuple.[35]

From oral accounts it appears that the prelude to this published assertion of the Ngondo's prerogatives was a series of clandestine nocturnal meetings around 1944–45, mainly across the (yet unbridged) Wouri river in Bonaberi.[36] There is no evidence of any direct connection between the

Ngondo and the events surrounding either the railroad strike of 1945 or Duala protests against the election of Cameroonian delegates to a Paris constitutional convention. Subsequent identification of some of the petitions with the Ngondo[37] do nonetheless reflect the general atmosphere of apprehension surrounding the postwar renegotiation of Cameroon's colonial status. In fact the Ngondo, while tacitly accepting the sovereignty of *notre Gouvernement-Tuteur* in its first manifesto, soon afterwards claimed the right to choose its own "tutor" from among "all the nations of the UN."[38]

The colonial authorities could not feel very comfortable with the posture of the Ngondo toward either themselves or the established local chiefs. The immediate result of French concerns was the extensive surveillance which is the basis of much of our historical information. However, instead of either suppressing the organization or forcing the chiefs to sign its charter, the French appear to have brokered a reconciliation between the Ngondo and the traditional rulers. At a meeting of the Ngondo on August 17, 1947, the first with a large attendance, the major Duala chiefs did finally sign up with the Assemblée.[39]

From this moment onward, the politics of the Ngondo underwent a major shift. Ekwalla remained for a short time as secretary general but he gradually faded out of the picture in favor of the president of the organization, always a chef supérieur and from 1949 onwards, always Betote Akwa.[40] Moreover, whether or not the chiefs affixed their names to the text of the original charter, the Ngondo now concerned itself less with the forms of Duala internal governance and more with substantive community interests not mentioned in the founding document.

During the era of its greatest visible political activity (1947–1956) the Ngondo dealt both with the national and international affairs of Cameroonian decolonization and with local questions concerning Douala and its region. These two spheres are not entirely separable, but the present account will concentrate on the latter. The ambivalent relationship of the Ngondo to the radical political parties that dominated the Littoral, Racam and then the UPC, have been well-covered in previous writings as have its petitions and delegations to France and the United Nations Trusteeship Council.[41] Here the Ngondo functioned much like other ethnic blocs (but with limited success, due to its small population base) in pursuing general Cameroonian nationalist goals while assuring some place for Duala concerns and leadership in the new postcolonial order. Local politics, on the other hand, provide a better definition of these concerns and leadership and thus a more meaningful link to Duala history.

The local concerns of the Ngondo fall into three categories: landholding; inter-ethnic rivalry in the city of Douala; and internal rivalry among Duala elites. All these issues had specific political references in the decolonization era but their long-term common denominator is an attempt to define Duala identity in an effective form.

As already noted, urban real estate was (along with investment in education) the only remaining economic asset of the Duala and one that had been severely threatened by previous modernization efforts under both German and French colonial rule. There was good reason to think that the new development plans of the postwar era would have similar consequences.

The absence of any reference to land matters in the "Décision" of February 1947 may be due to the base of Ekwalla and his closest collaborators in Deido and Bonaberi, the two precolonial quarters of Douala that had been relatively undisturbed by earlier European projects. However, once the Akwa and Bell elites took over the Ngondo, land became a major concern: a commission was established to survey Duala holdings and regulations were passed forbidding any further sales to non-natives.[42]

In formal terms, Ngondo efforts to control land tenure failed entirely, as restrictions on real estate transactions could not be enforced and sales (mainly to Europeans) continued at a high level, reaching new peaks in 1950 and 1951. From 1952 to independence sales declined sharply, which may be partially the result of consciousness-raising on this issue by the Ngondo but certainly did not derive from any control over the process on the part of chiefs.[43]

Inter-ethnic politics would appear to provide the primary basis for the "invention" of the Ngondo. The key impetus here was the realization among Duala leaders that they now represented only a minority of the population in their own city. One means to deal with such a situation was to expand the definition of "Duala" so as to encompass not only the four major quarters of historical Douala (Bell, Akwa, Deido and Bonaberi) but also all the Sawa-Bantu speakers of the region as well as indigenous non-Sawa communities included in the same administrative unit as the city of Douala.[44] In political terms, none of this did much good as there was no definition by which the Duala could compete demographically with the Bamileke immigrants to the Littoral or their partners in the UPC, the Basaa of the adjoining Sanaga region.

The Ngondo did enjoy some temporary success in dealing with the issues of chiefly status and municipal government. In a petition to a 1949 visiting UN commission the Ngondo criticized the French for their system of "direct rule," through which traditional chiefs suffered "a decline in their prestige and authority " while "People who were of low social standing when they came to the Cameroons or Douala are promoted to the same rank as the dignitaries of the town . . . "[45] This attack on the immigrant communities of Douala as well as the general demand for a British-type indirect rule system in Cameroon created a rift between the Ngondo and Soppo Priso, who formally dissociated himself from the UN petition.[46] In his capacity as elected delegate to ARCAM Soppo did, however, respond to pressure from the Ngondo and opposed the conversion of Douala to a *commune de plein* or *moyen exercice* which would assure political control by the majority non-Duala urban population.[47] In these maneuvers, the Ngondo was in tacit alliance with Douala European settlers, who also feared local government reforms, but there is no evidence of any conscious complicity between the two groups.

At the end of 1955 Douala finally became a commune de plein exercice, so that Ngondo politics here achieved no more than a delaying action. However the reform – with its resultant loss of all privileged positions by the Duala chefs supérieurs and their subjects – appears to have been accepted without any significant protest.[48]

The most general political goal of the Ngondo, to provide a basis for political unity within the Duala community, was no more successfully met than its efforts regarding land legislation and municipal government. Soppo Priso's quarrels with the organization indicate how difficult it was to reconcile ambitions for national leadership with the particularist interests represented by the Ngondo. Fortunately for Soppo, by the time he made his most serious bid for primacy in Cameroon in 1956, the Ngondo ceased to be an autonomous political force.

The Ngondo likewise failed to contain the other key figure in local decolonization politics, Alexander Douala Manga Bell. Ndoumb'a Douala was criticized by the Ngondo for accepting French citizenship, supporting French and settler interests at various moments of conflict and not taking a strong stand on the land question.[49] In 1948 he made a brief stab at competing with the Assemblée by reviving the neo-traditional Muemba association that had supported him during the 1930s.[50] Alexander finally took over the Bell paramountcy in 1951, replacing his uncle Lobe Bell, who had briefly served as the Ngondo president. This change may well have been engineered by the French to weaken the Ngondo. Ndoumb'a Douala used the opportunity of local office to build up his own clientele within Douala. His major asset here was the control over even more millions of francs from real estate transactions, in this case based on government requisition of communal land to construct a new airport.[51]

For the Ngondo, the creation of an autonomous fiefdom among the Bells meant that the organization now became identified mainly with Betote Akwa. While such a position won Betote a seat in the immediate pre-independence national legislature and even a cabinet post ("Minister without Portfolio") in Ahidjo's first government, these were rather meaningless and short-lived offices. In the 1951 and 1952 elections to the French

National Assembly and ATCAM, when real influence on decolonization and national politics was still at stake, the Ngondo was never able to mobilize even 5 percent of the Douala voters.[52]

Bereft of a serious political function by the mid-1950s, the Ngondo was left with the role it still retains: a vehicle for the promotion and contemplation of Duala cultural identity.[53] In popular memory this appears to have been the purpose of the "new" Ngondo from the beginning, since many accounts date its founding only from 1949, when the first festival was held.[54] As already indicated, this public event actually followed several years of very intense Ngondo political activity and was labeled a *fête commémorative*, thus accenting the alleged earlier role of the organization in practical public affairs. Nonetheless, it is the ritual and celebratory aspect of the Ngondo that has survived and even thrived in postcolonial Douala.

At the center of the festival as it developed from 1949 and especially as it is observed now is a complex ritual of propitiating the local water spirit, *jengu*. On the night before the main public celebration a secret ceremony is enacted at the Wouri River island of Jebale and its surrounding waters in which various sacrifices (including living animals) are made to the water spirit and a container of further gifts is prepared for presentation near one of the main Duala beaches on the next day. In the daytime ceremony, this container is given to the *jengu* in the names of the major Duala chiefs as leaders of the Ngondo; but it is the Jebale ritual specialists who bring the offering to the chiefs and then carry it underwater to the spirit, who in return indicates how the community will fare in the following year.[55]

The link between the Ngondo and *jengu* is made in Lotin Samé's 1936 description of the Duala Assemblée Générale du Peuple. However there is no mention of any such spirit in the 1947 "Décision" or any of the French Sûreté reports on the subsequent five years of the Ngondo's activities. Other documents do, however, indicate that self-conscious efforts to link the organization with history and "coutume" were undertaken during these years.[56]

The *jengu* spirits have, of course, been the objects of various cults throughout the history of the Littoral. They are, like similar "Mamy Wata" figures elsewhere in Western Africa, most widely approached through "cults of affliction" in which most of the participants are women. Historically, *jengu* was also one of the *losango* cults that distinguished the Duala from inland populations and even enforced a divisive hierarchy among the Duala lineages themselves.[57] Finally, there appear to have been precolonial public celebrations in which the *jengu* was worshipped as a source of the triennial arrival of *mbeatoe* crustaceans (crayfish) in the Wouri, the end of the rainy season (very heavy in this part of Africa), success in canoe races, and to ward off epidemics.[58]

The Ngondo draws most directly on the last, most public, of these sets of *jengu* practices, although bringing in elements of all three. The secret and nocturnal role of Jebale specialists recalls their more frequent recourse to the water spirits in rituals of healing. During the public ceremony, at the crucial moment of the immersion of the communal gift, the assemblage cries out "*yai assu yai*"; this is a phrase in the secret language of the *jengu* cult which at least some of the participants understand quite clearly to be a declaration that only *wonja* (free indigenous Duala as opposed to *bakom*) are allowed to be present. Some conscious attempt to balance the affect of such an utterance is made by including in the celebration references to other *losango*, presumably representing not only all the Duala lineages but even inland communities and the descendants of actual Duala slaves.[59]

In its most manifest sense, the Ngondo festival thus attempts to draw on various aspects of Duala-Sawa culture and blend these into a "tradition" that can offend no one. But the very power of these practices and representations lies in their ability to evoke a history fraught with tensions: the appeal to *jengu* (even without a secret language) stresses the hegemony of the Duala, as water people over their inland compatriots who know that they are identified with *bakom*/slaves; at a deeper and more chronologically distant level it also recalls the dependence of the immigrant Duala upon the truly autochthonous coastal fishing populations represented by the Jebale islanders. Even the problematic historical narrative of the Ngondo tradition claims an earlier political unity while focusing on an event – the 1876 execution of the Deido chief Eyum Ebele – which most immediately recalls the segmentary conflict that characterized so much of precolonial Duala political life.

Conclusion: middlemen as historical paradigm

By the time of Cameroonian independence the Duala community had literally and figuratively become "history": they no longer constituted a major force in shaping their country's development but were now, perhaps more than ever, a critical element in the collective memory of all Cameroonians. This latter quality can be seen most immediately in the political career of Alexander Ndoumbe Duala Manga Bell, but more generally and lastingly in the prominence given the Duala in various textbooks on Cameroon past,[60] as well as the continued role of the Duala language in churches and Cameroonian pop music.

The prominence of the Duala depended entirely upon their position as middlemen. Since their numbers never grew to the scale of other self-identified ethnic groups (even with the pan-Sawa Ngondo) and they never produced the kind of precolonial political structures that could absorb outside communities, they were fated to remain a "minority" in Cameroon. The implications of such a history are both admiration and mistrust, seen most dramatically in the achievements of Soppo Priso and his failure to hold together a trans-regional nationalist party.

Politics in Cameroon has continued, as in many – perhaps most – African states to suffer from the ethnic divisions seen in the run-up to independence. In the case of Cameroon it is clear that French manipulation had as much to do with these fissures as any "primordial" African loyalty to kin and language over nationhood. However, in a larger sense "tribalism" and dependence on outside resources go beyond the immediate machinations of Europeans, whose economic stake in tropical Africa has receded steadily from the mid-1950s, if not well before then.[61] Cameroonians and other Africans have become involved in a "politics of the belly" based upon zero-sum competition between ethnically constructed and overseas-oriented patron–client networks because they have not yet developed confidence in their own capacities for generating the kind of wealth needed to maintain modern societies.[62]

As suggested in our introduction, all modern African leaders remain in some sense "middlemen," suspended across the chasms of a global hierarchy and appear incapable, even when they attain the kind of state power that always eluded the Duala elites, of creating a self-sustaining base for these positions. The history of the Duala is thus paradigmatic insofar as it encompasses such a long and active span of middleman roles.

The present study is historical, and thus throws direct light only upon the past, while offering no obvious lessons for the present or future. But one element in the contemporary African dilemma is the contestation of the continent's past in terms which oppose mythic grandeur to denigrating cynicism. Thus a sensitization to the longstanding dynamics and frustrations of a middleman experience like that of the Duala may at least provide an alternative perspective upon Africa's position in the world. It is a modest perspective and a modest claim on our part, but we hope that it is at least soundly based in the narrative we have presented.

Notes

1 INTRODUCTION

1 The argument here is consistent with the general consensus on such shifts from a broader West African perspective: see Robin Law (ed.), *From Slave Trade to "Legitimate" Commerce: The Commercial Transition in Nineteenth-century West Africa* (Cambridge: Cambridge University Press, 1995). The Duala case is not discussed in any detail in the Law volume but the specific issues it raises will be dealt with in chapters 2 and 3 below.

2 We were briefly tempted to define the commercially based intermediary role of the Duala through the term 'comprador," which has been utilized in other colonial or proto-colonial settings to describe indigenous merchants who seem to have served the interests of their foreign partners at the expense of local development. But "compradorism" has not proved to be a very useful concept elsewhere and is particularly problematic in the case of the Duala, who never enjoyed much opportunity to become a "national bourgeoisie." See Ralph A. Austen, "Compradorism in Africa," unpublished paper presented at the American Historical Association meetings, 1971; Robert Vitalis, "On the Theory and Practice of Compradors: the Role of 'Abbud Pasha in the Egyptian Political Economy," *International Journal of Middle East Studies* 22/3 (1990): 291–315.

3 Victor W. Turner, *The Ritual Process* (Chicago: Aldine, 1969); and "Myth and Symbol," *International Encyclopedia of the Social Sciences* (New York: Macmillan, 1968), X, 57.

4 Achille Mbembe, "The Banality of Power and the Aesthetics of Vulgarity in the Postcolony," *Public Culture 4/2* (Spring 1992): 1–30.

5 Homi K. Bhabha, *The Location of Culture* (Routledge: London, 1994); see especially chapter 4, "Of Mimicry and Man."

6 Ralph A. Austen, *The Elusive Epic: The Narrative of Jeki la Njambè in the Historical Culture of the Cameroon Coast* (Atlanta: African Studies Association, 1996); see bibliography of this work for further references.

2 FROM FISHERMEN TO MIDDLEMEN

1 For an analysis of such accounts which takes their content more seriously than we do, see M. Bekombo-Priso, "Essai sur le peuplement de la région côtière du Cameroun: les populations dites dwala," in Claude Tardits (ed.), *Contribution de la recherche ethnologique à l'histoire du Ca meroun* (Paris: CNRS, 1981),

503–10 and discussion in ibid., 575–7; for catalogue of and commentary on Duala oral traditions, see table 2.2 below.

2 The sometimes confusing similarity in the names of rivers in this region is based upon their common base in the local root term for water, *diba*.

3 Pierre de Maret, "A Survey of Recent Archeological Research and New Dates for Central Africa," *JAH* 26/2 (1985): 129–48. For more current data and skepticism about "linking archeology and historical linguistics" in this region, see Manfred K. H. Eggert, "Central Africa and the Archeology of the Tropical Rainforest," in Thurstan Shaw et al. (eds.), *The Archaeology of Africa* (London: Routledge, 1993), 322–3; also Jan Vansina, "New Linguistic Evidence and 'The Bantu Expansion'," *JAH* 36 (1995): 194.

4 The basis for this assumption appears to be the artefact of selective early publication of West Central African Bantu languages: Duala, one of the first to be written down by missionaries, was thus available for extensive comparison to Bakota by a French administrator in Gabon, Captain R. Avelot, "Recherches sur l'histoire des migrations dans le bassin de l'Ogöoué et la région litto rale adjacente," *Bulletin de Géographie Historique et Descriptive* 4 (1905), 357–412 (Avelot, unlike those Cameroonists who have cited him, does not postulate northward Bakota migration). Comparisons with Lingala have led Dika-Akwa (q.v. below) to postulate the "Dwala-Ngala" as a single historical super-ethnic group; Lingala is widely known in contemporary Africa as the idiom of recorded pop music (a status it shares with Duala) but in this form it evolved as a lingua franca only under Belgian colonial rule, as much out of Bobangi as the speech of the rather insignificant precolonial Mangala community; see William J. Samarin, "Protestant Missions and the History of Lingala," *Journal of Religion in Africa* 16/2 (1986): 138–63.

5 These studies place Duala and Basaa-Bakoko in a Bantu/Sanaga Group IV or Bantu "Group A" whose mutual affinities are much greater than those of either the languages in Bantu/Congo Group VIII or Groups B (including Bakota) and C (including Bobangi and Lingala); Malcolm Guthrie, *Comparative Bantu*, vol 3 (London: Gregg International, 1970), 11–12; Y. Bastin, A. Coupez and B. de Halleux, "Statistiques lexicale et grammaticale pour la classification historique des langues bantoues," *Bulletin de Séances de l'Académie Royale des Sciences d'Outre-Mer* 23/3 (1979), 375–87; Michel Dieu and Patrick Renaud, *Atlas linguistique de l'Afrique Centrale (ALAC): Atlas Linguistique du Cameroun (ALCAM)* (Paris: Agence de Coopération Culturelle et Technique, 1983), 45–60 (esp. 59); Bernd Heine, "The Dispersal of the Bantu Peoples in the Light of Linguistic Evidence," *Muntu* 1 (1984): 22–35. The most recent work on Bantu linguistics has challenged some of the Guthrie classifications upon which all this work is based but leaves intact both the Cameroon/Nigeria "cradle" concept and the (now Northwest) group to which Duala belongs (while also minimizing the role of massive movements in the spread of Bantu languages): Vansina, "New Linguistic Evidence," 173–95 (esp. 184–6).

6 See Bastin et al. and Heine in previous note.

7 In addition to the last item in table 1.2 see Gouellain, *Douala*, 31.

8 For an excellent discussion of the substantive and historiographic issues in understanding such migration, see Jan Vansina, "The Peoples of the Forest," in

David Birmingham and Phyllis Martin (eds.), *History of Central Africa* (London: Longman, 1983), I 79–83; also Vansina, *Paths through the Rainforest* (Madison: University of Wisconsin Press, 1990), 68–9 and "New Linguistic Evidence."

9 Ralph A. Austen, *The Elusive Epic: The Narrative of Jeki to Njambe in the Historical Culture of the Cameroon Coast* (Atlanta: African Studies Association, 1996), *passim*, see esp. 1, 26–7, 32–5, 50–52, 61–2.

10 See the discussion in chapter 3 below of the nineteenth-century Duala trade network for details on constructions of inland ethnicity.

11 Edwin Ardener, *Coastal Bantu of the Cameroons* (London: International African Institute, 1956), 21.

12 Ardener, *Coastal Bantu*, 22–7.

13 Edwin Ardener makes such a suggestion for the Kole: "Language, Ethnicity, and Population" in R. P. Moss and R. J. A. R. Rathbone (eds.), *The Population Factor in African Studies* (London: University of London Press, 1975), 48–56.

14 Compare Gust. Alf. Adams, "Die Sprache der Banoho," *Mitteilungen des Seminars für Orientalische Sprachen* 10/3 (1907): 34–83 with René Bureau, *Ethno-Sociologie religieuse des Duala et apparentés* (Yaoundé: Institut de Recherches Scientifiques du Cameroun, 1962), a special number of *Recherches et Etudes Camerounaises* 7/8 (1962–64): 316, and Madelaine Richard, "Histoire, tradition et promotion de la femme chez les Batanga (Cameroun)," *Anthropos* 65 (1970): 941–7.

15 See Shirley Ardener, *Eye-Witnesses to the Annexation of Cameroon, 1883–1887* (Buea: Ministry of Primary Education and West Cameroon Antiquities Commission) and Ralph A. Austen, with K. Jacob, "Dutch Trading Voyages to Cameroon, 1721–1759: European Documents and African History," *Annales de la Faculté des Lettres et Science Humaine, Université de Yaoundé* 6: 5–27, for fuller discussion of these documents.

16 Brun and Ulsheimer in table 2.2 are both Germans but sailed on Dutch ships.

17 Leers cited in Ardener, "Documentary and Linguistic Evidence," 102–3.

18 Johannes Loots, "Nieuwe gelyk groodige Pafkaart van een Gedeelte der Africaaanse Kust," Amsterdam, n.d. [appears 1700s], Bibliothèque Nationale, Paris, Map Collection, SH series, 109/3 2.

19 It should also be noted that even these accounts stress local rather than overseas trade as the incentive.

20 J. A. Alagoa, "Long-distance Trade in the Niger Delta," *JAH* 11/3 (1970): 319–29; Robert W. Harms, *River of Wealth, River of Sorrow: the Central Zaire Basin in the Era of the Slave and Ivory Trade, 1800–1891* (New Haven: Yale University Press, 1981); Robin Horton, "From Fishing Village to Trading State," in Mary Douglas and Phyllis Kaberry (eds.), *Man in Africa* (London: Tavistock, 1969); G. I. Jones, *Trading States of the Oil Rivers: a Study of Political Development in Eastern Nigeria* (London: Oxford University Press, 1963).

21 On the antiquity and importance of fishing, see J. E. G. Sutton, "The Aquatic Civilization of Middle Africa," *JAH* 15/4 (1974): 527–46; the present discussion tries to meet some of the challenges raised in Jean-Pierre Chauveau, "Une histoire maritime africaine est-elle possible: historiographie et histoire de la

navigation et de la pêche africaines à la côte occidentale depuis le XVème siècle," *CEA* 26/1–2 (1986): 173–235.

22 Vansina, "New Evidence," 191–2.

23 Johannes Ittmann, "Der kultischer Geheimbund Djengu an der Kameruner Küste," *Anthropos* 52 (1957): 135–76; René Bureau, *Ethno-Sociologie religieuse des Duala et apparentés* (Yaoundé: Institut de recherches scientifiques du Cameroun, 1962), 105–38.

24 Johannes Ittmann, "Der Walfang an der Küste Kameruns," *Zeitschrift für Ethnologie* 81/2 (1956): 203–17.

25 Interviews, Jebale, May 7, 1975; the IBB oral tradition (Bureau, *Ethnosociologie*, 319–22) presents Male as progenitor not only of the Jebale, but also of Ewondo and Basaa inland populations later displaced by the Duala.

26 One of the best-known examples is the Mande distinction between *dugu tigi* (village chief) and *dugu kolo tigi* (earth chief/priest); see also "Dual Sovereignty" in Rodney Needham, *Reconnaisances* (Toronto: University of Toronto Press, 1980), 41–62.

27 The Pidgin term for the Jebale ruler was "King Fish" (see Treaty between "Jeberret" ruler and German trading firms, July 15, 1884, Reichskolonialamt file (hereafter RKA) 4202, Deutsches Bundesarchiv, Potsdam: 92).

28 See discussion of the "Ngondo" below and in chapter 6.

29 Harms, *Rivers of Wealth*, 163ff.

30 J. v. Eitzen, "Die Eingeborenenfischerei von Kamerun" *Der Fischerbote* 6 (1916): 19–20, 58–9, 172–5, 200–2; Théodore Monod, *L'industrie des Pêches au Cameroun* (Paris: Société d'editions géographiques, maritimes et coloniales, 1928), 126–53; Austen various interviews, Cameroon Littoral, especially Estuary fishing villages, May 17–18, 1973, Bonaberi, July 14, 1973.

31 Interviews: Jebale, May 7, 1975; Bomono-ba-Jeru, April 18, 1975.

32 David Richardson, "Profits in the Liverpool Slave Trade: the Accounts of William Daven port," in Roger Anstey and P. E. H. Hair (eds.), *Liverpool, the African Slave Trade, and Abolition* (Liverpool: Historic Society of Lancashire and Cheshire, 1976), 66–7, 79–83.

33 Jean-Pierre Warnier, "Traite sans raids au Cameroun," *CEA* 29 (1989): 5–32.

34 For the Islamic trade, see Ralph A Austen, "The Mediterranean Slave Trade out of Africa: a Tentative Census," in *Slavery and Abolition* 13/1 (1992): 214–48.

35 Loots, "Pafkaart."

36 In contradistinction to the entire debate on changes in West African trade, it is here argued that the critical moment in precolonial commerce, at least for the Duala, comes with the transition from ivory *to* slaves. See Robin Law, "The Historiography of the Commercial Transition in West Africa," in Toyin Falola (ed.), *African Historiography: Essays in Honour of Ade Ajayi* (Lagos and London: Longman, 1993), 91–115; ibid., *From Slave Trade to "Legitimate" Commerce.*

37 Robert Bostock (shipowner) to various captains, 1787–90, Bostock Letter Book, Liverpool Public Library, Record Office, ms 387 MD54, 28, 78, MD55, 62.

38 C. W. Newbury, "Credit in Early Nineteenth Century West African Trade," *JAH* 13/1 (1972): 81–95.

39 Testimony of James Arnold and accompanying documents PP, 1789, XXVI (646A), Part 1, Report of the Lords of the Committee in Council, 50–8; trading log of Bristol brig *Sarah*, 30 May, 1790 ("Ivory taken as security for goods trusted to the following [Duala] traders"), Rogers Papers, Bundle 5 (1)

40 Arnold Testimony.

41 Arnold describes one slave as arriving at Bimbia after travelling "six moons" and several other being purchased at an inland market called Bunje.

42 P. Harter, "Le Ngondo," *Bulletin de l'Association Française pour les Recherches et Etudes Camerounaises* 3 (1968): 63–7; Maurice Doumbé Moulongo, *Le Ngondo: Assemblée traditionelle du peuple duala* (Yaoundé: Centre d'Edition . . . de l'Enseignement, 1972), 7–9; the Malobe story is also preserved in a canoe song that is still current and a proverb recorded before World War I (Friedrich Ebding, *Duala Sprichwörter* (Freiburg: Anthropos-Institut Micro-Bibliotheca, no. 31, microfilm, #142).

43 One Pongo account (recorded at Bomono ba Jeru, April 18, 1975) claims that after arriving in the New World, Malobe married and fathered children who were in turn the parents of Alfred Saker, the first European missionary in Cameroon (q.v. chapter 3); on the Ngondo assembly, see below.

44 G. I. Jones, "Time and Oral Tradition with Special Reference to Eastern Nigeria," *JAH* 6 (1965): 153–60; Jones also argues that this middle period should present its actors in elevated heroic form which, as will be seen, is not quite the case for the Duala.

45 The key sources for what follows here are Flad, Halbing, Ebding 1, Ekolo, IBB and Ngaka Akwa.

46 "Geschichte des Duala-Stammes," Ebding Nachlass, 12; in the same archive there is a "Geschichte des Mongo-Stammes" which states (7–8) that Doo Makongo was the biological father of Bele but took his mother without payment, thus giving rise to an asymmetrical system of marriages between the two groups (see more on this in chapter 3).

47 Relations between the Duala and the indigenous Basaa/Bakoko are described with the usual mixture of conflict and agreements but in this case all of the violence is attributed to the marginalized Priso.

48 Ewonde's son Kwane (7I) is said to have fled north of the estuary to Isuwu (Bimbia) where (a) the malevolent Priso a Doo was finally killed and (b) Kwane married Losenge (daughter of the Isuwu ruler, Mbimbi) producing a son, Bile a Kwane (8I), who later became the new ruler of Isuwu.

49 Duala sources, rather than concealing the European provenance of such terms, seem at times to exaggerate it: thus Priso's name is said to be based on the English "Prince" since his father, Doo, was the first Duala ruler to be called "King" (George or "Joss" from which the coastal plateau of Bonanjo and Bonapriso takes its name); as seen below, however, the English, who conferred the senior titles and names, rendered "Priso" as "Preshaw," "Preese" or "Peter."

50 All the documents cited in table 1.3 indicate that the Portuguese never entered the Wouri estuary; however "Portuguese" seem to represent less a specific

nationality than a trope for early Europeans in traditions throughout West Africa and their language is imprinted in the now more dominantly English lingua franca, Pidgin. Ironically, Dutch interlopers into territories first discovered by the Portuguese tended to canonize the Spanish versions of their place names, thus giving us "Cameroons River" ("River of Prawns" from Spanish *camerones* vs. Portuguese *cameroes*).

51 This was Manga Ndumbe Bell (see chapter 3 below); there is documentation of Africans from Calabar and even Gabon being educated in Europe or North America in the 1700s (David Richardson, private communication).

52 On ghost terms and references to maps, see Ardener, "Documentary and Linguistic Evidence," also Loots map, note 16 above.

53 See note 39 above.

54 See also King's Town and Peter's Town on 1790 map of "Cameroons River" by Captain Roger Latham, BN, SH series, 109/23 and 113/5/8D.

55 Treaty signed by Johan Pedar Wrisberg, Governor of Royal Danish Possessions in Guinea with chiefs Bimbia, May 3, 1800, Danish National Archives. For the context of these actions and full citation of the documents see Georg Nørregard, *Danish Settlements in West Africa* (Boston: Boston University Press, 1966), 182, 252.

56 Edmond Bold, *The Merchant Mariners' Guide to . . . West Africa* (London: no publisher, 1822), 82–5; James W. Holman, *Travels in Madeira, Sierra Leone . . .* (London: G. Routledge, 1840), 409–10; R. M. Jackson, *Journal of a Voyage to the Bonny River on the West Coast of Africa* (Letchworth, Herts: privately edited and printed by Roland Jackson, 1934), 101–27; G. A. Robertson, *Notes on Africa* (London; Sherwood, Neely and Jones, 1819), 321.

57 It should be noted that the presence of the Rogers papers in British archives is due to the fact that he entered into bankruptcy; William Davenport, the most active British slave trader to Cameroon, made an overall profit of about 8 percent on his voyages, Richardson, "Profits in the Liverpool Slave Trade," 69ff.

58 In addition to the events described in Arnold (see note 39 above), the 1800 Danish "occupation" of Bimbia was the unsuccessful result of efforts to recover debts (see note 55 above).

59 Mbela is associated with a more widely cited Duala proverb ("What the eagle holds, he never releases") but only the Akwa use it as a name; the present-day football team representing the Akwa quarter of Douala is called "Caiman".

60 Doumbé-Moulongo, *Le Ngondo*; Harter, "Le Ngondo."

61 Guillaume Bétotè Dika Akwa nya Bonambela, "Nyambéisme: pensée et modèle d'organisation des Négro-Africains." Thèse d'Etat, Université de Paris VII, 1985; for a convenient (and uncritical) summary of Dika Akwa's ideas, see Georges Balandier, "Economie, société et pouvoir chez les Duala anciens," *CEA* 15 (1975): 361–80. For some critique, see Austen, *Elusive Epic,* 62–4.

62 The entire issue of the Ngondo is dealt with at great length in Ralph A. Austen, "Tradition, Invention and History: the Case of the *Ngondo* (Cameroon)," *CEA* 32 (1992): 285–309.

63 Mpondo Dika Akwa fails to do so either in the general account cited in table 2.1 or the various statements recorded during his 1911 effort to create a large-scale

Duala political-economic organization based on his other notions of Duala political centralization (see chapter 4 below); there is reference to a "Grande Assemblée" or "Assemblée Générale du Peuple" with no name or extra-judicial function (but credited with the condemnation of Charley Deido) in Lotin Samé, "Etude concernant les coutumes Douala," June 20, 1936 (Yaoundé: Institut des Sciences Humaines, Dossier W201).

64 Malcolm Ruel, *Leopards and Leaders: Constitutional Politics among a Cross River People* (London: Tavistock, 1969).

65 Lotin Samé, "Etude concernant les coutumes Douala," does attribute a cross-cutting judicial function to the *losango* and they provide a reference point for Dika-Akwa's various conceptions of Duala culture; on the role of losango in nineteenth-century Duala trade networks and social conflicts, see below, chapter 3.

66 Nekes to Governor Ebermeier, May 27, 1914, ANC/FF TA6.

67 Manga Bekombo, "Conflits d'autorité au sein de la société familiale chez les Dwala du Sud-Cameroun," *CEA* 4/2 (1963): 317–29.

68 Vansina, "Peoples of the Forest," 84f.; and Vansina, *Paths*, 73f.

69 Ronald Cohen, "State Origins: A Reappraisal," in Henri J. M. Claessen and Peter Skolnik (eds.), *The Early State* (The Hague: Mouton, 1978), 31–77; Robin Horton, "Stateless Societies in the History of West Africa," in J. F. A. Ajayi and Michael Crowder, *History of West Africa* (London: Longman, 1971), 78–120.

70 K. David Patterson, "The Vanishing Mpongwe: European Contact and Demographic Change in the Gabon River," *JAH* 16/2 (1975): 217–38; Patterson sees virulent disease patterns as a characteristic of middleman historical experience although, unlike the Mpongwe, the Duala never appeared in danger of disappearing; for their response to becoming a minority within Douala, see chapter 4 below.

71 Alagoa, Harms, Horton and Jones.

72 See note 36 above; a separate analysis of the Duala case is attempted on a broad theoretical rather than comparative basis by Albert Wirz, *Vom Sklavenhandel zum kolonialen Handel: Wirtschaftsräume und Wirtschaftsformen in Kamerun vor 1914* (Zurich: Atlantis, 1972); "La 'rivière de Cameroun': commerce pré-colonial et contrôle de pouvoir en société lignagère," *Revue Française d'Histoire d'OutreMer* 60/2 (1973): 172–95; Wirz argues that changes in the spheres of circulation due to the export of low-prestige palm products during the nineteenth century upset the Duala social order; apart from the problematic status of such "substantivist" economics, the contention flies in the empirical face of crises induced under conditions of "high-prestige" slave exporting.

73 Jones, *Trading States*, 127–32, 186–7.

74 David Northrup, *Trade without Rulers: Precolonial Economic Development in Southeastern Nigeria* (Oxford: Clarendon, 1978).

75 Ruel, *Leopards and Leaders*.

76 The Mungo community, whose Sawa Bantu language is extremely close to Duala, do claim origin from Calabar rather than Piti ("Geschichte . . . Mongo," Ebding Nachlass), perhaps owing to awareness of Efik trade on the upper Mungo river.

3 HEGEMONY WITHOUT CONTROL

1 Historians have greatly modified earlier views of the end of the slave trade as a major rupture or "crisis" in West African society; see the previous chapter and Law, "Commercial Transition," and *From Slave Trade*.

2 David Eltis, *Economic Growth and the Ending of the Transatlantic Slave Trade* (New York: Oxford University Press, 1987), 3–28ff.

3 Ibid., 249 *passim.*

4 The Islamic slave trade drew particularly upon Northern Cameroon; see Paul E. Lovejoy, *Transformations in Slavery: A History of Slavery in Africa* (Cambridge: Cambridge University Press, 1983), esp. 157, 195–200.

5 Jackson, *Journal*, 126; a report from two years later describes Ngando Akwa's rather unrewarding participation in an 1820 or 1821 Spanish expedition to capture slaves directly at Fernando Po. See Holman, *Travels in Madeira,* 428.

6 In 1840 early missionaries found a Spanish slave trade establishment at Bimbia (testimony of Thomas Clark, PP 1850, IX, 107); 30 slaves were exported from Bimbia on a warning from Ngando Akwa just as the latter and Bebe Bell signed the 1841 abolition treaty (Capt. W. Tucker, report, May 25, 1841, FO84/384); in 1860 a Spanish vessel arrived at Douala expecting to receive 400 slaves from King Bell, although none was delivered (Acting Consul Laughland report, Aug. 31, 1860, FO84/1117); on slaves to the Portuguese at São Thomé and Principé (terminated by the buyers rather than Duala suppliers), see correspondence in Calabar Provincial Files, Nigerian National Archives, Ibadan (hereafter Calprof) 4/1/6, 1877; on early twentieth-century illegal labor exports to Fernando Po see ANC/FA Douala court transcripts, S1910/106.

7 Eltis, *Economic Growth*, 84–9; Christopher Lloyd, *The Navy and the Slave Trade* (London: Longmans, Green, 1949), 34–48; K. Onwuka Dike, *Trade and Politics in the Niger Delta, 1830–1885* (Oxford: Clarendon, 1956), 81–8.

8 Eltis, *Economic Growth*, 88; Eltis disputes Dike's account of an unratified 1839 treaty with Bonny (*Economic Growth*, 328 n. 36).

9 On the 1840 agreement, see testimony of Lt. Reginald Levinge, PP 1842, XI, 228; for the 1841 treaty and residual slave trade, Tucker report and Clark testimony, n. 6 above.

10 Dike, *Trade and Politics*, 55–60, 205; see more on Fernando Po below.

11 Marion Johnson, "Ivory and Nineteenth Century Transformation In West Africa," in G. Liesegang et al. (eds.) *Figuring African Trade* (Berlin: D. Riemer, 1986), 105, 116–22; however, the major oceanic outlet for Cameroonian ivory shifted in the course of the nineteenth century from Douala to Batanga in the south (Wirz, *Vom Sklavenhandel*, 96ff.)

12 Marion Johnson, "By Ship or by Camel: the Struggle for the Cameroons Ivory Trade in the Nineteenth Century," *JAH* 19 (1978): 539–49.

13 Jean-Pierre Warnier, "Histoire du peuplement et genèse des paysages dans l'ouest camerounais," *JAH* 25 (1984): 402; on the general economics of nineteenth century West African palm oil production and trade, see Ralph A. Austen, *African Economic History* (London: Currey, 1987), 97ff, 275.

14 Allan McPhee, *The Economic Revolution in British West Africa* (London: Routledge, 1926) 30–5.

15 Captain William Allen, *A Narrative of the Expedition . . . to the River Niger in*

1841 (London: R. Bentley, 1848), II, 249–50; interviews, Ngombe, May 15, 1973, Bonangando, April 15, 21, 1975; only in the first of these Wouri river villages did the inhabitants discuss slave settlements, apparently because the slaves had later been moved (see below, chapter 4); however internal evidence from the Bonangando interview (including the very name of the village) as well as testimony by Jacques Kouoh Moukouri, Akwa, Douala, May 16, 1973 attest to its servile history. On Kwa Kwa Akwa slaves, see Joseph Merrick report, *BMH*, 1844, 378.

16 Max Buchner, *Kamerun* (Leipzig: Duncker u. Humblot, 1887), 46.

17 The only Europeans with such ambitions were missionaries, but see below for the paradoxical results of their efforts.

18 See genealogical tables given in interviews, Ngombe village, May 15, 1973; there are also quarters within Douala whose founders are remembered as originally Basaa.

19 Interview, Ebenezer Penda Ngime, Dibombari, April 21, 1975; interview, Jebalé elders, May 7, 1975; see the previous chapter for discussion of the special status of Jebalé.

20 See above chapter 2, pp. 33–34.

21 Interview with Jean Ewondé Ebongo, Bwassalo, April 18, 1975 (for discussion of the latter conflict, see below).

22 Allen, *Narrative*, 251–60 (the date of observation is 1842).

23 Citation of a map in the possession of the British missionary, Alfred Saker, in Carl Heinersdorff (ed.), *Reinhold Buchholz' Reisen in West-Afrika* (Leipzig: Brockhaus, 1880), 88; George Grenfell, "The Cameroons District, West Africa," *Proceedings of the Royal Geographical Society* 4 (1882): 586 (report on 1875 journey).

24 Interviews at various Wuri and Bodiman villages, May–June, 1975; Consul Livingstone report, June 16, 1870, FO 84/1326; Consul Hewett report, Dec 17, 1883, FO 403/31, 8, enc. 1; Hugo Zöller, *Forschungsreisen in der deutschen Colonie Kamerun. Zweiter Theil: das Flussgebiet von Kamerun* (Berlin: Spemann, 1885), 29–31; Ramsay to Governor, May 21, 1886, ANC/FA 1/96 (AZ58).

25 Heinersdorff (ed.), *Buchholz*, 132f.

26 An entire thick dossier covering the first few years of German colonial rule is entitled "Abo-Palavern" ANC/FA 1(AZ58).

27 James Kaya, interview, Deido/Douala, May 14, 1973; for one version of the Dibombe crocodile legend which is directly connected with the Wuri-Bodiman war, see Bebe Njoh, "L'histoire de Difoum Ngango, le caiman du Wouri" in Gouellain, *Douala*, 36–8. In 1975 it was still difficult to get anyone to travel to Bangseng by canoe via the Dibombé.

28 Wuri and Bodiman traditions speak of a long-standing food trade with the Abo but European observers in 1881 (*BMS Annual Report*, 1881, 150) and as late as 1885 (Bernhard Schwarz, *Kamerun Reise in die Hinterlande der Kolonie* (Leipzig: P. Frohber, 1886), 47) report no Duala commerce on the Dibombé.

29 Interviews, Miang, Mangamba, Mandouka, Bessoung Kong (Abo), June 4–6, 1975; Bebe Njoh in Gouellain, *Douala*, 38–9. While most indigenous accounts attribute the war to the precolonial era, the first recorded indications of

troubles centering around commerce with Bangseng are found in the July 27, 1888 report of Sekretär Wallmut in ANC/FA1/96. The Abo missionary Friedrich Autenrieth, *Ins Inner-Hochland von Kamerun* (Stuttgart: Holland & Josenhans, 1900), 77–81 claims the war only began in 1893.

30 Max Buchner, *Aurora Colonialis* (Munich: Piloty & Loehle, 1914), 243–9 (Buchner even cites the price differentials for palm oil bought on the Abo and on the Mungo).

31 Fuller, "Recollections," 1882 and Fuller to Baynes, June 9, 1882, BMS Archives A5; *BMS*, 1879, 251–6 (on the general presence of the Baptist mission, see below).

32 Lovett Zephania Elango ("Britain and Bimbia in the Nineteenth Century," Ph. D. dissertation, Boston University, 1974, 98–122, 158f.) attributes Bimbia's decline to a combination of epidemics, internal dissension, and the shift of trade from west of the Mungo to the new mission settlement of Victoria (today Bota).

33 Heinersdorff (ed.), *Buchholz*, 155–6; Reinhold Buchholz, *Land und Leute in Westafrika* (Berlin: Habel, 1876), 45; Q. W. Thomson report, Feb. 14, 1878, *BMH*, 1878, 184–5.

34 Buchner, *Aurora*, 177–83; Schwarz, *Kamerun*, 242–366, *passim*; interviews at Mombo, December 16–18, 1975 by Elias Ngome, Theological College, Nyasoso.

35 Buchner, *Aurora*, 174; despite this evidence and that of Buchholz and Thomson in note 33 above, Balong oral traditions insist that there was no tension in Duala movement up the Mungo (interviews, Muyuka, Mundame, Mpondo, May 2, 3, 22, 1975). According to Fuller, "Recollections," Bell had promised the Balong a missionary teacher in return for letting him trade across their territory to Bakundu but had then reneged.

36 Schwarz, *Kamerun*, 318–19; G Valdau, "Eine Reise in das Gebiet nördlich vom Kamerungebirge," *Deutsche Geographische Blätter* 9 (1886), 125–40; in 1874 Buchholz (Heinersdorff, (ed.), *Buchholz*, 158) found Efik traders as far south on the Mungo as Muyuka.

37 Zöller, *Forschungsreisen*, 126, 209; interviews: Bonapoupa, Loungahé, May 15–16, 1975; Chief Bema Benoit (Bonapoupa), Douala, June 2, 1975; elders, Japoma, June 12, 1975; Grenfell, "Cameroons District," 587.

38 Grenfell, "Cameroons District," 587–8; Zöller, *Forschungsreisen*, 126, 209; Curt Morgen, *Durch Kamerun von Süd nach Nord* (Leipzig: Brockhaus, 1893), 139–40; interviews: Lobetal, April 26, 1975; Yadibo, Elogzogwout, April 27, 1975; Malimba, June 8, 1975; Cosme Dikoumé, Paris, June 23, 1975 (see chapter 4 on efforts of Duala traders to extend their trade to Edea in the German period).

39 On the navigational difficulties of trade at Malimba in 1864, see Consul Burton report, March 15, 1864, FO 84/1221.

40 Nicolls (Fernando Po Governor) report, Feb. 13, 1834, CO 82/7; see also Dike, *Trade and Politics*, 60–1.

41 The best record of these visits is provided in the eighteenth-century Middleburgh Commercial Company logs cited in Austen, "Dutch Trading Voyages;" for descriptions of nineteenth century practices, see McPhee, *Economic Revolution*, 70.

42 Testimony of John Arden Clegg, PP 1842, XI, nos. 1568–1640.

43 Nicolls reports, 1833–34, CO 82/6–7, *passim*; John Clarke, Diary, 1841, 200–1, BMS Archives A2; Senior Naval officer Bedingfeld report and enclosures, July 30, 1861, FO 84/1157; Consul Burton report, April 15, 1864, FO84/1221; see also Lilley's own testimony (concluding with arguments for sending indentured African laborers to the West Indies) in PP 1848, XXII, item 891, 15–24.

44 Report of Consul Beecroft, June 14, 1852, FO 2/7; there are also references to "agents" in the 1850 Duala-British treaty and to two "resident agents" in the February 1859 treaty (see table 3.1).

45 For accounts of merchant practices in these centers, see *Dike, Trade and Politics*, 108ff.; Jones, *Trading States of the Oil Rivers*, 74–83; A. J. H. Latham, *Old Calabar, 1600–1891* (Oxford: Clarendon, 1973), 56ff.; Martin Lynn, "Continuity and Change in the British Palm Oil Trade with West Africa," *JAH* 22 (1981): 331–48.

46 Consul Burton report, March 15, 1864, FO 84/1221; Johannes Thormählen (on 1868), in Max Esser, *An der Westküste Afrika* (Berlin: A. Ahn, 1898), 41–2; John Chandler Langdon, "Three Voyages to the West Coast of Africa, 1881–84 by 'Jerry'," typescript, Bristol Central Library, n.d. [1930, 1944]; Buchner, *Aurora*, 64.

47 For this general practice, see McPhee, *Economic Revolution*, 70; Lynn, "Continuity and Change," 332; for a Cameroon case in the early 1870s, John Harford, "A Voyage to the Oil Rivers Twenty-Five Years Ago," printed as appendix in Mary H. Kingsley, *West African Studies* (London: Macmillan, 1899), 375–82.

48 The status of Douala among West African ports is further indicated by the Bristol memoirs of "Jerry," who describes an 1881 voyage to lesser West African destinations in which the entire oil purchasing, processing and casking operation was still managed aboard the travelling vessel; Douala, the destination of Jerry's second voyage, is described as containing not only four hulks but also a "hospital ship," Langdon ms. (the "hospital" was undoubtedly the hulk of a British resident agent, George Allen, who also practiced medicine; see Ardener, *Eye-witnesses*, 55, n. 38).

49 Buchner, *Aurora*, 66; Zöller, *Forschungsreisen*, 7.

50 Dike, *Trade and Politics*, 114f.

51 Three Liverpool firms in PP 1850, IX, 219–21; the Bristol firm of R. & W. King seems to have arrived at this time according to Frederick Pedler, *The Lion and the Unicorn: a History of the Origins of the United Africa Company, 1787–1931* (London: Heinemann, 1974), 17–19; for the Dutch, John Clarke, "Diary", 2, 281, BMS archives, A5; J. H. van Boudyck Bastiaanse, *Voyage à la côte de Guinée...* (The Hague: Belifante, 1853), 268–80; P. J. Veth, "De Nederlanders in Afrika," *Tijdschrift van het Kon. Nederlandsch Aardrijkskundig Genootschap, Amsterdam* 10 (1893): 251–3.

52 Signatures on Jan. 14, 1856, treaty, FO 84/1001; Burton report, FO 84/1221.

53 Johannes Voss (German resident agent), report, n.d. [1884], Central Secretariat Office Files, Nigerian National Archives, Ibadan (hereafter CSO) 6/3/5.

54 Consul Hewett Report, Dec. 17, 1883, PP 1884–5, LV, 19; Zöller, *Forschungsreisen*, 123.

55 Buchner, *Kamerun*, 77, 104–6.

56 Consul Beecroft report, June 14, 1852, FO 2/7; for a more positive view of Scott and his background, see Martin Lynn, "Commerce, Christianity and the Creoles of Fernando Po," *JAH* 25 (1984): 257–78.

57 Burton report, March 15, 1864, FO 84/1221 (Burton does not distinguish very clearly between independent Sierra Leonean merchants and educated Gold Coast clerks, whom he does not much like either).

58 Craigie to Salmon, July 30, 1884 in Admiralty to Foreign Office Sept. 9, 1884, FO84/1689; the head of the Victoria Creole community, Samuel Brew, was functioning in the 1880s as the local agent of a German firm (Ardener, *Eyewitnesses*, 13).

59 No continuous records of any of these firms except for the Liverpool latecomer, John Holt (q.v. chapter 4) have been found; Pedler, *Lion and Unicorn*, 17ff., has used the records of the Bristol firm, R. and W. King, a business still active in modern Cameroon, and continuous with some form of eighteenth-century West African trade; on continuity between Cameroon oil and slave trade to Liverpool, see testimony of Thomas Tobin, PP 1848, XXII, no. 536, 1; Voss in CSO 6/3/5 provides the best account of German and late British firms but on the loss of both the Woermann and Jantzen & Thormählen records, see Helmut Washausen, *Hamburg und die Kolonialpolitik des deutschen Reiches* (Hamburg: H. Christians, 1968), 67, 75.

60 Burton report, FO 84/1221; Martin Lynn (private communication) suggests that the prevalence of Bristol firms, less efficient than their Liverpool colleagues and thus more concerned about short-term profits, may account for the disorderly situation at Douala.

61 Martin Lynn, "The 'Imperialism of Free Trade' and the Case of West Africa, c. 1830–c. 1879," *Journal of Imperial and Common wealth History* 15 (1986): 22–40; Austen, *Economic History*, 110–17; Eltis, *Economic Growth*, 1–28f.

62 Dike, *Trade and Politics* 126–7; Jones, *Trading States of the Oil Rivers* 77–8, 221–2; the best general account is Martin Lynn, "Law and Imperial Expansion: the Niger Delta Courts of Equity, c. 1850–85," *Journal of Imperial and Commonwealth History* 23 (1995): 54–76.

63 Beecroft report, June 30, 1852, FO 84/886.

64 Dike, *Trade and Politics* 199–202; Lynn ("Law and Expansion," 67f.) notes that even at this point the courts could not officially try non-British subjects.

65 Acting Consul Laughland report, Jan. 21, 1861 (Court functioning), FO 84/1147; Consul Burton reports, Jan. 14, 1862, March 15, 1864 (no Court at Douala), FO 84/1176, FO 84/1321; Consul Livingstone report, June 12, 1871 (1868 reorganization), FO 84/1343.

66 Minutes of Court proceedings, Ellis to Consul, March 7, 1869, Smith to Consul Dec. 2, 1871, Calprof 3/1; comments on Court, FO to Consul Livingstone, Jan. 24, 1870, Calprof 2/1/22, Consul Livingstone report, June 6, 1871 (Court rules broken, "members lacked common sense"), FO 84/1343; Collings (Douala merchant) to Consul Livingstone, June 18, 1872.

67 Consul Livingstone to Douala Court of Equity, June 28, 1872, Fo 84/1356; see also Consul Hopkins to Captain J. Ewart (chairman of Cameroons Court of Equity), Nov. 13, 1878, Calprof 3/2, Buchan to Consul, March 1883 (concerning the "old style" of the Court), Calprof 5/8/2.

68 The history and records of the Court of Equity in this era are reproduced (in German translation with commentary) by Buchner, *Kamerun*, 227–35.

69 See treaties, table 3.2 and various consular reports, FO 84 series.

70 The best account is in Jaap van Slageren, *Les origines de l'Eglise Evangélique du Cameroun* (Yaoundé: CLE, 1972), 17–37; see also Solomon Nfor Gwei, "The History of the British Baptist Mission in Cameroon with Beginnings in Fernando Po, 1841–1886" (Bachelor of Divinity dissertation, Baptist Theological Seminary, Rüschlikon-Zurich, 1966); Ardener, *Eye-witnesses*, 8–18; Gary Osteraas, "Missionary Politics in Cameroon, 1844–1914," (Ph. D. dissertation, Columbia University, 1972), 12–62.

71 For a good analysis of BMS efforts in these broader historical terms, see Lynn, "Commerce, Christianity and Creoles."

72 Gwei, "History," 121–4; figures in the BMS, *Annual Report*, 1885 vary only slightly from this total.

73 Alfred Saker, the chief missionary at Douala, refers to Manga as the son of King Bell "that I took to England," BMS *Annual Report*, 1871; however, while studying in Bristol Manga was sponsored by the Merchant firm R. & W. King and baptized as an Anglican; after his return to Douala he "lapsed" into large-scale polygamy as well as local dress, Admiralty to FO, Feb. 17, 1869, FO 84/1310; Buchner, *Kamerun*, 48–9; K. Stolz, "Tod des Königs Manga Bell," *Evangelische Heidenbote*, 1908, 81–2 (see much more on Manga below).

74 Fuller, "Autobiography," 63–70, BMS Archives; Fuller's claims are supported by his German successor at Bonaberi, Ernst Dinkelacker, *Bonaberi* (Basel: Missionsbuchhandlung, 1904), 23.

75 Court Protocol, June 10, 1872 (enc. in Consul Livingstone report, July 20, 1872), FO 84/1356.

76 Jean Comaroff and John Comaroff, "Christianity and Colonialism in South Africa," *American Ethnologist* 13/1 (1986): 1–22; see following chapters for the much more extensive Duala Christianization in the colonial era.

77 The prominence of black and mulatto Jamaicans among the BMS envoys accounts for the Pongo tradition which claims that Alfred Saker, a white Englishman, was descended from the enslaved giant, Malobe (see above, chapter 2, pp. 33–34).

78 Details of how slaves entered the Christian community are given in Robert Smith report, June 15, 1864, BMS Archives A4; *BMH*, 1869, 5; BMS *Annual Report*, 1871, 75–8; see also van Slageren, *Les origines* 31–2.

79 Lynn, "Commerce, Christianity and Creoles."

80 Austen, "Slavery among Coastal Middlemen," 321–2, *passim*; see more on Duala slavery below.

81 "the reason assigned by them [for learning reading] is that they will then become better traders and will not be so easily cheated as they hitherto have been," Joseph Merrick, report, *BMH*, 1844, 158. There is also some evidence of recording local political arrangements in writing, at least in the highly-missionized Bonaberi; see agreement of May 11, 1879 between the chiefs and elders (all unable to sign their names) of Bonaberi and a (now) subordinate offshoot settlement in Bell Family Archives, Grand Livre, 92 (copy supplied by Yvette Monga).

82 Van Slageren, *Les origines*, 30–1; S Ardener, *Eye-witnesses*, 9–11.
83 I. J. Comber to Baynes, April 1, 1877, BMS Archives, A12.
84 George Grenfell to Bailache, Nov. 6, 1877, BMS Archives, Box 21.
85 Van Slageren, *Les origines*, 35–6.
86 On economic and political grounds, Consul Livingstone (himself the brother of the most famous missionary-explorer of the century) characterized the BMS arguments for inland penetration as "unmitigated bosh" (report, June 12, 1871, FO 84/1343).
87 Van Slageren, *Les origines* 42–5.
88 The issues in this section are discussed with extensive documentation and insight in Wirz, *Vom Sklavenhandel*, 66–81; again, the approach here takes issue with Wirz's "substantivist" interpretation of the Douala exchange system.
89 It is ironic that such statistics are more readily available for the eighteenth century, when each trading voyage was a discrete business venture for which accounts had to be kept by the principal entrepreneur, than in the nineteenth, where the records of individual voyages are embedded in the apparently inaccessible records of more sophisticated merchant firms; see Martin Lynn, "Profitability of the Early Nineteenth-Century Palm Oil Trade," *African Economic History* 20 (1992): 78.
90 Bold, *Merchants' and Mariners' Guide*, 83–5 (for 1810); Voss report, CSO 6/3/5 (for 1870s–1884).
91 Latham, *Old Calabar*, 73–75, David Northrup, *Trade without Rulers: Precolonial Economic Development in South-Eastern Nigeria* (Oxford: Clarendon, 1978), 208–14; on the one important distinction, imports used as currency, see below.
92 See remarks of "Jerry" in Langdon ms., 3; Leonhard Harding, "1884–1984: Cent ans de relations commerciales," in Kum'a Ndumbe III (ed.), *L'Afrique et l'Allemagne: de la colonisation à la cooperation, 1884–1986 (Le cas du Cameroun)* (Yaoundé: Editions Africavenir, 1986), 396ff; contrast with Bold, *Guide*, 85 ("The guns must be very good for this river and high proof"); Consul Livingstone report, Jan. 11, 1873 (on quality choices in clothing and matchet demands) PP 1873, LXV; on similar behavior in 1884 see Carl Scholl, *Nach Kamerun!* (Leipzig: Cavaell, 1886), 48–56 (also cited in Ardener, *Eye-witnesses*, 30).
93 Austen, *Economic History*, 112, 275, 277.
94 Harms, *River of Wealth*, 43–7 (the general discussion of the impact of imports here is very valuable).
95 For further discussion of the economics of production in the Littoral, see chapter 4, in which the entry of the Duala themselves into agriculture will be taken up.
96 As expressed in the Duala proverb "Would you kill the whiteman and do without salt?", Betote-Guillaume Dika Akwa, *Bible de la Sagesse Bantoue* (Paris: Centre Artistique et Culturel Camerounais, 1955), 34–5.
97 Observations and interview in Estuary fishing camps, May 17, 18, 1973; interviews, Ngané Mbappe and Ekam Eyoumban, Bonaberi, July 14, 1973.
98 W. Arthur Lewis, "The Rate of Growth of World Trade, 1830–1973," in Sven Grassman and Erik Lundberg (eds.), *The World Economic Order: Past and*

Prospects (New York: St. Martins, 1981), 19–20.

99 Consul Burton report, April 15, 1864, FO 84/1221; *BMH*, 1864, 770 (3-month stoppage to August).

100 Voss report; Thomas Dayas, the merchant accused of thus breaking the price agreement, claimed he was not the only one to do so (Dayas to Consul Livingstone, June 15, 1873, Calprof 4/1/3).

101 Newbury, "Credit"; see also N. H. Stilliard, "The Rise and Development of Legitimate Trade in Palm Oil with West Africa" (M.A. dissertation, Birmingham University, 1938), 101–7.

102 Burton report, FO 84/1221; among other official invocations against trust see also Livingstone report, PP 1873, LXV; Buchner, *Kamerun*, 98–102; for merchants taking the same position, Robert Bostock, 1787, 1788, 1790 instructions to captains, ("trust . . . has been the defeat of many voyages"), Letterbook, I, 28, 78, II, p. 62, Liverpool Public Library, Record Office, 387 MD 54, 55: John Whitford, *Trading Life in Western and Central Africa* (Liverpool: Porcupine, 1877), 303.

103 Hamilton to Commander Jones, Feb. 6, 1846, enc. in Consul Beecroft report, July 16, 1849, FO 84/775; Dayas to Consul Wilson, March 30, 1869, Calprof 4//1/2; ibid. to Consul Livingstone, June 15, 1873, Calprof, 4/1/3; Voss also describes at some length his own failed attempts to avoid trust during the 1870s (Voss report); see chapter 4 for German colonial efforts to suppress trust and varying merchant reactions.

104 See table 3.1 and references; unfortunately we have no records of precise amounts of trust given out by Douala firms before the colonial period, although general indications, as in Buchner, *Kamerun*, 99, run into the thousands of pounds.

105 Helmlinger (*Dictionnaire*, 196) claims this word derives from the Portuguese "carta."

106 Interviews, Abo, Bodiman, Wuri villages, 1975.

107 See references in table 3.1 for treaties and various records of the Court of Equity cited above; for specific examples of cases involving Creoles and Europeans before the Court was established see 1852, FO 2/7; 1853, FO 2/9; 1855, FO 84/975; 1856, FO 84/1001.

108 Lynn, "Profitability," estimates very high rates of return before the introduction of steamships in the 1850s; the few commercial accounts found by Lynn do not include voyages to Douala, but he also notes the great wealth of several Liverpool merchants who regularly traded for oil in Cameroon.

109 Treaty of 1856, Art. XIII, XVI 1862, Art. IX, XII, Ardener, *Eye-witnesses*, 77, 80–1.

110 Dayas to Consul Wilson, March 30, 1869, Calprof 4/1/2; Agreement, Acting Consul Tait-Cameroons Court of Equity, Jan. 19, 1878, Calprof 5/7/2; Buchner, *Kamerun*, 102, 243–4 (for 1884).

111 Buchner, *Kamerun*, 103–4; Voss report; for a fuller discussion of the politics involved here, see below.

112 Latham, *Old Calabar*, 35–41; Ruel, *Leopards and Leaders*; Allen (*Narrative*, 240–1) describes what appears to be a Jengu ceremony and claims both that members "may pass unmolested into hostile countries" and that an elder

"affected to consider us as belonging to the 'Free Egbo' [pidginized version of Efik-Cross River *Ekpe*]"; however Allen may have been confusing Douala and Old Calabar, since such cross-ethnic links via *losango* are never mentioned in other European sources and were emphatically denied by all Littoral informants interviewed in 1975.

113 Buchner, *Kamerun*, 100 ("The only exchange relationship which has never yet been inhibited, even by the most serious stoppages, is free access to the daughters of the land."); the low reproduction rate of the nineteenth-century Duala population, despite constant slave immigration, also implies the spread of venereal disease resulting from sexual contact with outsiders (however, Buchner in his medical capacity, questioned contemporary beliefs that syphilis was rampant in Douala, saying "I have never observed an unambiguous case . . . among Cameroonians," *Kamerun*, 132); for a fuller examination of this issue elsewhere, see Patterson, "Vanishing Mpongwe."

114 On Lilley: affidavit of John Shower (claiming Lilley purchased his woman as a slave), Nov. 20, 1833, CO 82/6 (by 1841 he had eleven to twelve women, Clarke Diary, 200–1); on Schmidt: Buchner (describing "Martha" as brought up by the Baptist missionaries), *Aurora*, 88–9.

115 "Verkehr der Weissen mit eingeborenen Weibern und soziale Stellung der Mischlinge," ANC/FA 973; the father of one of these children, Thomas Dayas, played a key role in breaking a European price agreement in 1875 (see Voss report); the daughter, Emily, later married the Bell heir Rudolf Duala Manga (see chapter 4) and one Duala informant (Isaac Toko Priso, July 5, 1970) claims her mother was a "court lady" closely related to the Bell royal family, but this kind of oral evidence is both ambiguous (a euphemism for slave concubine?) and unreliable (Toko also confuses Dayas with Schmidt).

116 Buchner, *Aurora*, 88; domestic employment is here contrasted with the dishonorable outdoor labor for European firms, which was left to Kru immigrants; it would be useful to have more information about the Duala youths who undertook such service (there may be some analogy to Ngando a Kwa's service at the court of Bele in the oral tradition recorded by Flad (see table 2.1).

117 See travel accounts by Heinersdorff, *Buchholz*; Schwarz, *Kamerun*; Buchner, *Kamerun* and *Aurora*; et al.

118 Hypergamous marriages have only been studied systematically in South Asian caste societies, where wife-givers pay dowries to attain upward mobility; see Stanley J. Tambiah, "Dowry and Bridewealth and the Property Rights of Women in South Asia," in Jack Goody and S. Tambiah (eds.), *Bridewealth and Dowry* (Cambridge: Cambridge University Press, 1973), 64–72; for a practice in Africa comparable but not precisely parallel to that in the Littoral, see Caroline H. Bledsoe and William P. Murphy, "The Kpelle Negotiation of Marriage and Matrilineal Ties," in Linda S. Cordell and Stephen Beckerman (eds.), *The Versatility of Kinship* (New York: Academic Press, 1980), 145–63.

119 Various interviews, especially Jacques Kouoh-Moukouri, Douala, May 1, 1975; Johannes Thormählen, "Mitteilungen über Land und Leute in Kamerun" reports that *balalo* can trade in their motherlands even during wars, *Mitt. des Geog. Ges. in Hamburg* (1884), 334; there are frequent refer-

ences in contemporary sources to the commercial importance of King Ndumbe Lobe Bell's birth from an Abo mother.

120 Manga Bekombo, "La femme, le marriage et la compensation matrimoniale en pays dwala," *L'Ethnographie* 62–3 (1968–69): 179–88; Madelaine Richard, "Histoire, tradition et promotion de la femme chez les Batanga (Cameroun)," *Anthropos* 65 (1970): 407.

121 Austen, *Elusive Epic*, 35; for a pre-World War I inland oral tradition on the origin of hypergamous marriages see above, chapter 2, fn. 46.

122 Helmlinger, *Dictionnaire*, 156; Latham, *Old Calabar*, 76.

123 Buchner, *Kamerun*, 94 (Buchner's experience of seeing abandoned iron bars lying about in Douala was replicated in the 1970s interior, where they were sometimes used to hold down roof thatching).

124 Jan Hogendorn and Marion Johnson, *The Shell Money of the Slave Trade*. (Cambridge: Cambridge University Press, 1986).

125 Helmlinger, *Dictionnaire*, 269 (*mbamba*).

126 Buchner, *Kamerun*, 242–3.

127 For Cameroon, the first position is represented by Hans-Peter Jaeck, "Die deutsche Annexation," in Helmuth Stoecker (ed.), *Kamerun unter deutscher Kolonialherrschaft*, I (E. Berlin: Rütten & Loening, 1960) and the second by Wirz, *Vom Sklavenhandel*; Wirz and Austen, *African Economic History*, 2–8 provide references to the relevant theoretical literature.

128 Buchner, *Kamerun*, 97–8.

129 Bomono ba Mbengue, Apr. 24, 1975 (performance) ; Bomono ba Jeru, Apr. 22; Djouki, Apr. 19; FO 84/1343 Merchants to Hopkins (Hopkins-FO Aug. 2) July 28, 1871; Thormählen, "Land u. Leute," 330–1.

130 Loreto Todd, *Modern Englishes: Pidgins and Creoles* (London: Blackwell, 1984), esp. 35–48, 89ff.; note the Pidgin base of the currency terms discussed above.

131 E.g. Allen, *Narrative*, 246.

132 Todd, *Modern Englishes*, 3–4.

133 Thormählen, "Land u. Leute," 331.

134 On the early part of this period, see above p. 38; also Allen, *Narrative* and Clarke, "Diary"; succession conflicts of the 1840s and afterwards are treated at length in Wirz, "Rivière du Cameroun".

135 Clarke, "Diary", 272, 288.

136 See table 3.1; by 1850 "Dido" is listed as one of the four main political units of Douala (Consul Beecroft reports, Dec. 30, 1850, FO 84/816).

137 Cameroon European merchants to Consul Hutchinson, Jan. 4, 1856, enc. in Hutchinson report, Jan. 31, 1856, FO 84/1001; Hutchinson report, June 20, 1856, FO 2/16; Hutchinson, *Impressions*, 168; Léopold Moumé Etia, *Histoire de Bona Ebelé Deido* (Douala: B.P. 22, 1986), 11–15.

138 Contemporary accounts: Grenfell, *BMH*, 1877, 146–49; Voss, report (unfortunately, no British consul visited Douala during 1876); see also Moumé Etia, *Histoire*, 20–30.

139 Both Grenfell and Voss see him this way.

140 See invidious comparisons in Buchner, *Kamerun*, 47–54.

141 Voss report.

142 Dayas to Consul Wilson, March 30, 1869, Calprof 4/1/2; Agreement, Acting Consul Tait-Court of Equity, Jan. 19, 1878, Calprof 5/7/2; Buchner, *Kamerun*, 243–4.

143 Doumbé-Moulongo, *Le Ngondo*; Harter, "Le Ngondo"; Moumé Etia, *Histoire*, 20–30.

144 Dike, *Trade and Politics*, 209ff.; John E. Flint, *Sir George Goldie and the Making of Nigeria* (London: Oxford University Press, 1960).

145 This event is discussed in some detail in Austen, "Tradition," 288–90.

146 See statements (none very precise) in Grenfell, *BMH*, 1877, 147–8; Voss (who calls Eyum "the Old Pirate"); Moumé Etia; for earlier conflicts between Europeans and Eyum see Consul Wilson report, Jan. 15, 1869, Consul Livingstone report, Nov. 29, 1869 (by this time Ebule/Ned Deido seems to be dead), FO 84/1308; Consul Hopkins report, April 29 and July 30, 1872, FO 84/1356.

147 See previous note.

148 Consular reports, Feb. 10, 1873, FO 84/1377; ibid., March 17 and Oct. 27, 1874, FO84/1401; in 1878 Joss returned to Bell (Consul Hopkins report, Dec. 3, 1878, FO 84/1508).

149 Proceedings of April 7, 1883 Court of Equity plus commentary in Buchner, *Kamerun*, 229–30; see also Voss report.

150 There does not appear to have been a Duala term for these units. The preface "bona" is used to designate both "towns" and entire chiefdoms (see above, table 1.1) and simply indicates a descent group comprising something more than a single household.

151 Austen, "Slavery among Coastal Middlemen," *passim*.

152 As elsewhere on the Western African coast, the major Littoral concept of witchcraft, *ekong*, draws directly upon memories of the slave trade; see Ralph A. Austen, "The Moral Economy of Witchcraft," in J. and J. L. Comaroff (eds.), *Modernity and its Malcontents* (Chicago: University of Chicago Press, 1993), 89–110.

153 Hutchinson report, May 26, 1858, FO 84/1061; ibid., Dec. 23, 1859, FO 84/1087; Hutchinson, *Wanderings*, 4–6; above, table 3.1, 1858 treaty; *BMH*, 1871, 10–11. The 1858 and 1859 conflicts parallel similar actions by slaves in Old Calabar during the early 1850s (see Latham, *Old Calabar*, 93–6).

154 "Miango ma Bonebela[sic]/Die Geschichte von Bonebela," Part 4, Ebding Nachlass.

155 This is a point of agreement between the orthodox Marxist Jaeck, "Die deutsche Annexion," 37–8; the substantivist Wirz, "Rivière du Cameroun;" and (without specific references to Cameroon) the liberal A. G. Hopkins, *An Economic History of West Africa* (New York: Columbia University Press, 1973), 124–6 (for Hopkins' more recent position, see below).

156 See various cases involving trade stoppages with inland peoples in Court of Equity proceedings, 1883–84, Buchner, *Kamerun*, 227–35.

157 The best treatment is in Wirz, "Rivière de Cameroun," 172–8, 193–4.

158 For this earliest episode, reported by Captain F. A. Close of HMS *Trident*, see A. F. Mockler-Ferryman, *British West Africa* (London: Swan Sonnenschein, 1900), 433.

159 Bell and Akwa to Gladstone, Nov. 6, 1881, this and the 1879 Akwa letter can

be found on the opening pages of PP 1884–85, LV; all that survives in manuscript in FO 84/1617 is a March 8, 1881 Bell letter to Consul Hewett using virtually identical language; internal memos within the same file indicate that the original of the Bell and Akwa letter was lost sometime after its first printing in FO 403/18.

160 Wirz, "Rivières," 175–6; Ardener, *Eye-witnesses*, 19.

161 This meeting is not described in detail by Hewett himself, who became ill immediately afterwards and lost his notes (Hewett report, June 7, 1883, FO 84/1634); the transactions are reported by the Baptist missionary W. K. Collings (transmitting an oral account from Fuller, who was present), letter to Gladstone, 27 Sept. 1883, PP 1884–85, LV; also Voss report, CSO 6/3/5.

162 See Article X in the April 1883 treaty requiring the restoration of runaway slaves.

163 Andrew Porter, "The Berlin West Africa Conference of 1885–85 Revisited: a Report," *Journal of Imperial and Commonwealth History*, 14 (1985): 84; see also Lynn, "Imperialism of Free Trade." Hopkins now seems to place less emphasis upon internal African crisis than upon the failure/unwillingness of African polities to meet the perquisites of British "development"; however he also notes the very marginal role of Africa in the "true" (largely financial) British Empire of the later nineteenth century: see A. G. Hopkins, "The 'New International Economic Order' in the Nineteenth Century: Britain's First Development Plan for Africa," in Law, *From Slave Trade*, 240–64; P. J. Cain and A. G. Hopkins, *British Imperialism: [I] Innovation and Expansion 1688–1914* (London: Longmans, 1993), 351–62, 381–96.

164 John D. Hargreaves, *Prelude to the Partition of West Africa* (London: Macmillan, 1963), 282–322 (esp. 311); the French never appear to have exercised the claim on Batanga created by their 1842 treaty or its 1845 and 1869 follow-ups, but they now showed renewed interest not only in this area but also the Campo region immediately to its south (see table 3.1).

165 William G. Hynes, *The Economics of Empire: Britain, Africa and the New Imperialism, 1870–95* (London: Longman, 1979), 29–37, 57–68; Barry M. Ratcliffe, "Commerce and Empire: Manchester Merchants and West Africa," *Journal of Imperial and Commonwealth History* 7/3 (1979): 293–321.

166 Hans-Ulrich Wehler, *Bismarck und der Imperialismus* (Cologne: Kiepenhauer & Witsch, 1969), 298–314.

167 See notes 65–67 above; a German, Mersmann, even represented one of the British firms at Douala; there are still complaints about occasional inequities by Thormählen (Esser, *Westküste*, 41–4) and in the 1884 report of Thormählen's agent, Voss (CSD 6/3/5).

168 Consul Hewett report, Dec. 17. 1883, PP 1884–85, LV, 19.

169 "Denkschrift des Handelskammer über die deutschen Interessen in West-Afrika," Hamburg, July 6, 1883, *Das Staatsarchiv*, 43 (1885): 226–43.

170 Adolf Woermann, "Kultur-Bestrebungen in West-Afrika," "Über Tauschandel in Afrika," *Mitteilungen der Geographischen Gesellschaft in Hamburg*, 1878–79, 58–71, 1880–81, 29–43; the generally defensive character of the Hamburg business community's conversion to colonialism is documented in Klaus J. Bade, "Imperial Germany and West Africa: Colonial Movement, Business Interests, and Bismarck's 'Colonial Policies'," in Stig Förster, Wolf-

gang J. Mommsen and Ronald Robinson (eds.), *Bismarck, Europe and Africa* (Oxford: Oxford University Press, 1988), 127–32.
171 Hewett report, Jan. 14, 1882, PP 1884–85, LV.

4 MYTHIC TRANSFORMATION AND HISTORICAL CONTINUITIES

1 As noted below, some of the most mythic views of precolonial Duala history have their origin in the German period.
2 These myths may serve as a guide to the most prominent secondary works on this period. Harry R. Rudin, *Germans in the Cameroons* (New Haven: Yale University Press, 1938), the first archival-based study of any modern colonial regime in Africa, owes its very existence to a collaboration of American revisionist liberalism and German Nazi-era nationalism in reassessing a colonial achievement that had been unfairly impugned after World War I; Stoecker's two-volume edition *Kamerun unter deutscher Kolonialherrschaft* (vol. 2, Berlin: Deutscher Verlag der Wissenschaften, 1968), is a self-conscious effort to recover all the oppressive dimensions of the regime glossed over by Rudin (see I, 10–12) particularly so in the very valuable chapter by Adolf Rüger, "Die Duala und der Kolonialmacht, 1884–1914: Eine Studie über die historische Ursprünge des afrikanischen antikolonialismus" II, 181–257. The Duala view of this period as a golden age runs through the oral accounts cited below as primary sources but the degree to which this interpretation has been institutionalized is best indicated by a local Baptist pastor, born only in 1913, who reported having preached to his congregation that "we should love Jesus as the Duala love the Germans" (Paul Mbende, interview, Akwa/Douala, July 1, 1970).
3 This point was first made by John Iliffe, *Tanganyika under German Rule, 1905–1912* (Cambridge: Cambridge University Press, 1969), 30–9; but for the present case, see also Karin Hausen, *Deutsche Kolonialherrschaft in Afrika: Wirtschaftsinteressen und Kolonialverwaltung in Kamerun vor 1914* (Zurich: Atlantis, 1970), 50–1.
4 Rudin, *Germans*, 32, 39, 120–6; Jaeck, "Annexion," 81–3; Wehler, *Bismarck*, 320–4; efforts at "para-statal" colonialism via various chartered and concessionary companies were actually common to all European powers in tropical Africa during the late nineteenth century and early twentieth, and all proved abortive (Austen, *African Economic History*, 123–5).
5 Woermann to Bismarck, Oct. 15, 1884, RKA 4447 (this official was to be given the title of governor but would operate through a council including the local merchant firm heads and one native representative).
6 Rudin, *Germans*, 43–55; Ardener, *Eye-witnesses*, 25–31, 41–5.
7 The December events, including subsequent German actions, are extensively documented in Jaeck, "Annexion," 71–6; Ardener, *Eye-witnesses*, 31–40; the Bonaberi and Joss rebels stated that their immediate motive was Bell's failure to share with them his payment from the Germans .
8 For the following general account of German Cameroon administration, see Rudin, *Germans,* 126ff.

9 See the lengthy reports of these campaigns in *inter alia* RKA 3381-84 and ANC/FA 23/K, 58.

10 Adolf Rüger, "Der Aufstand der Polizeisoldaten (Dezember 1893)," in Stoecker, *Kamerun* I, 91–147 (see 137–45 on Reichstag criticism); Rudi Kaeselitz, "Kolonialeroberung und Widerstandskampf in Südkamerun (1884–1907)," in Stoecker, *Kamerun* II, 13–54 (see 25–6 on the Reichstag); Adjai Paulin Oloukpona-Yinnon, *La Révolte des esclaves-mercenaires: Douala, 1893* (Bayreuth: Bayreuth University, 1987).

11 Rüger, "Polizeisoldaten," 123–4; Oloukpona-Yinnon, *La Révolte*, 53–7; the son of one of the government interpreters of this era described the notorious acting governor Leist as a "good German" because he opposed the Abo and the Dahomeans, not the Duala (interview, Ferdinand Edingele Meetom, Akwa/Douala, June 26, 1970).

12 See below for details of these positions.

13 A very rich personal account of German administration in the latter portion of this period (1895–99) is given in Theodor Seitz, *Vom Aufstieg und Niederbruch deutscher Kolonialmacht* (Karlsruhe: Müller, 1929), I, *passim.*

14 The role of Puttkamer as creative demiurge and oppressor will be evident below; his association with sentimental African attachment to the German era is attested by the celebration, in a 1985 Yaoundé historical conference on German–Cameroon relations, of Madame Else Njinjie, a Bamun woman alleged (inaccurately, it appears) to be Puttkamer's daughter (Kum'a Ndumbe [ed.], *L'Afrique et l'Allemagne*, 429.

15 For excellent accounts of these undertakings, see Hausen, *Deutsche Kolonial-herrschaft*, 216–29, 274–90, 310–15; Wirz, *Vom Sklavenhandel*, 165–201; William Gervase Clarence-Smith, "From Plantation to Peasant Cultivation in German Cameroun," in Peter Geschiere and Piet Konings (eds.), *Proceedings/Contributions: Conference on the Political Economy of Cameroon – Historical Perspectives* (Leiden: African Studies Centre, 1989), II, 483–502.

16 The use of "D(o)uala" rather than "Kamerun" or "Kamerunstadt" as the name for the city dates from this event.

17 Protocol of Colonial Minister Solf meeting with Mittelkamerun Chamber of Commerce, Sept. 10, 1913, ANC/FA 600, 13–14; Seitz to Berlin, June 2, 1910, RKA 4427, 4–6; see also Rudin, *Germans,* 190.

18 The real coastal loser in these shifts was the more southern port of Kribi which, with the booming rubber trade of its hinterland, actually accounted for a greater ad valorem percentage of Cameroon's exports during most of the German period than did Douala; however, Kribi did not have the natural harbor or access to inland rivers of Douala and, although no one recognized this at the time the railroad decisions were made, its *landolphia* wild rubber exports would soon lose their market to superior *hevea* varieties from Southeast Asian plantations.

19 Douala Bezirksamt proclamation on Nordbahn railroad expropriation, Jan. 25, 1907 and ff., ANC/FA 1230 "Enteignung von eingeborenen Besitz in Bonaberi und Bonasoma" (these measures are to be distinguished from the later and more general expropriation of Duala urban land to be discussed at length below).

20 Woodruff D. Smith, *The German Colonial Empire* (Chapel Hill: University North Carolina Press, 1978), 183–219.

21 Buea–Berlin correspondence, Dec. 25, 1907–Nov. 11, 1911, RKA 4279, 4–46; Seitz had served in Douala from 1895 to 1899 as second-in-command to the governor and as the first Bezirksamtmann (Seitz, *Aufstieg*, I, *passim*, II, 54–8, 92).

22 Howard Wolpe, *Urban Politics in Nigeria: a Study of Port Harcourt* (Berkeley: University of California Press, 1983); on German discussions about applying at least an Indonesian model of indirect rule to the Littoral, see Dr. Plehn (Buea) to Douala Bezirksamt, May 9, 1902, ANC/FA 1501.

23 As will be seen below, segmentary Duala politics now consisted essentially of direct rivalries between Bell and Akwa; however, the old Priso-Bell conflicts (with Bonaberi now apparently supporting Bell) did continue as late as 1908 in the form of street brawls and hut burnings; see extensive reports in ANC/FA 1369.

24 Hausen, *Deutsche Kolonialherrschaft*, 169.

25 Rüger, "Die Duala," 188–9; RKA 3823, *passim*; see below for the economic issues involved in this change.

26 Soden report of July 17, 1885 meeting with chiefs, ANC/FA 333, 3–7.

27 ANC/FA 333, *passim*.

28 [Julius] Ruppel, *Die Landesgesetzgebung für das Schutzgebiet Kamerun* (Berlin: E. S. Mittler u. Sohn, 1912), 853–4; see also Joseph Gomsu, "Problématique de la collaboration: les chefs traditionnels du Sud-Cameroun dans l'administration coloniale allemande," in Ndumbe (ed.), *L'Afrique et l'Allemagne*, 135–8; Gotthilf Walz, *Die Entwicklung der Strafrechtspflege in Kamerun unter deutscher Herrschaft, 1884–1914* (Freiburg: K. Schwarz, 1981), 113–20.

29 Seitz, *Aufstieg*, I, 50 indicates the significance of alternating Bell and Akwa majorities in the Duala Schiedsgericht; for the later Bell domination of the entire Littoral native court system, see below.

30 See Duala Bezirksamt annual reports, for 1904–1908, ANC/FA 397, 912, 859.

31 See above, pp. 88–90.

32 E.g. Gomsu, "Problématique."

33 For typical invidious comparisons see Buchner, *Kamerun*, 47–58; Johannes Voss, "King Bell und King Akwa," *Mitterlungen der Geographischen Gesellschaft und des Naturhistorisches Museum in Lübeck*, 3 (1891), 109–119; on Mpondo, see Ralph A. Austen, "Cameroon and Cameroonians in Wilhelmian *Innenpolitik*: Grande Histoire and Petite Histoire," in Ndumbe (ed.), *L'Afrique et l'Allemagne*, 217–21.

34 See the census by Nachtigal of Nov. 12, 1888 in RKA 4208, 399 and of Zimmerer in 1894 in ANC/FA 333, 245–50; of the other two recognized Duala *Oberhäuptlinge* (Paramount Chiefs) in this period, Deido appears to have functioned as a loyal subordinate of Akwa while Bell exercised less influence over Bonaberi.

35 On Alfred, see Austen, "Grande histoire," 216–17 and Joseph Gomsu, "La formation des Camerounais en Allemagne pendant la period coloniale. Alfred Bell: le refus de connaissances objectives aux colonisés," *Cahiers d'Allemand et d'Etudes Germaniques* (Yaoundé) 1/2 (1985): 58–69.

36 Soden to Berlin, March 28, 1889, ANC/FA 333, 92–93.

37 Soden to Berlin, Nov. 6, 1888, ANC/FA 333, 65.

38 Soden to Berlin, March 24, 1889, Berlin to Soden, June 29, 1889, ANC/FA 333, 88–91, 114 (Soden's letter of Nov. 6, 1888 cited above was written on stationery of the Zintgraff expedition); see more on these economic issues below; for Soden's interest in Buea plantations, see Clarence-Smith, "From Plantation to Peasant Cultivation," 485–6.

39 Leist to governor, Aug. 28, 1891 ANC/FA court records/Dibumbadi (on Manga's assistance in inland affairs); on Manga's support of Leist during the mutiny see Oloukpona-Yinnon, *La Révolte* 55–7; an administrative colleague of Leist described Manga as someone willing "even to hand over his own people" (Vallentin diary, in Franz Giesebrecht, "Tagebuchblätter eines in Kamerun lebenden Deutschen," *Neues deutsches Rundschau*, 1894, 348); on Manga's relations with Seitz and Brauchitsch, see below.

40 ANC/FA Court Files 1894/1/#167; ANC/FA 942, 61ff.

41 Kaeselitz, "Eroberung," 21–5; see more on Sanaga trade below.

42 The Schiedsgericht was thus the institution most resembling the Ngondo of Duala legend discussed in chapter 2 above.

43 Duala traders were exempted from the jurisdiction of inland chiefs but not of the Schiedsgerichte; in the case of Bodiman, a representative of the "autonomous Duala settlements" was granted membership in the appeals court.

44 Seitz to governor, Jan. 6, 1898, Colonial Department Decree, Sept. 22, 1898, RKA 3824, 16–17, 23.

45 Seitz to governor, March 29, 1898, ANC/FA 208, 12; the income from such appeals cases is specified in van Brauchitsch memo, May 5, 1906, RKA 3823, 101–2.

46 Seitz correspondence, July 27–August 17, 1898, ANC/FA 23K.

47 Bezirksamtmann Röhm to governor, March 14, 1909, ANC/FA 43; see more on Duala Manga Bell, the martyr of 1914, below.

48 Rüger, "Die Duala," 196–219; on Mpondo see Austen, "Metamorphoses," 20 and "Cameroon and Cameroonians," 217ff.

49 Dobritz to Berlin, Jan. 18, 1906, RKA 4435, 40.

50 Horst Gründer, *Christliche Mission und deutscher imperialismus, 1884–1914* (Paderborn: Schöningh, 1982), 141–8.

51 For his obituary plus elaborate local funerary observances, see *Amtsblatt für das Schutzgebiet Kamerun* 1 (1908), 78, 91.

52 On agriculture, see below; even Akwa informants, who had reason to resent Brauchitsch's actions, recall him in very positive terms.

53 For debate over Brauchitsch's actions in precisely these terms, see *Verhandlungen des Reichstags* (hereafter RT) 216 (March 19, 1906), 2146–7, 2155; it is thus ironic that one of the most provocative aspects of the Akwa petition was its general demand that "*assessorismus*" (the standard German epithet for bureaucratic formalism) be replaced by a revived "consulate."

54 Unless otherwise indicated, all references here and below to the Brauchitsch modernization project as well as controversial incidents of German and Akwa behavior are cited from the two Reichstag white papers on the Akwa complaints, RT 222 (1905/06), 3387–3420; RT 241 (1907), 1832–69; the Reichstag

floor debate cited in the previous footnote also notes irregularities by Brauchitsch not mentioned in the Akwa petition.

55 Three dealt with taxation, twelve with general complaints about administrative behavior (including the taking of local women by Brauchitsch and a German judge), and five with specific Akwa issues.

56 See details of this issue (no. 16 in the petition) in RT 241, 1848–50.

57 In addition to the sources cited in Rüger, "Die Duala," see the explanation and chronology of events given by the missionary, K. Stolz in his report to Basel, July 5, 1906, BMG Kamerun, 1906 I/922.

58 In addition to the two white papers cited above, see the lengthy references to the petition (along with other questions about both Puttkamer and Brauchitsch) in the course of the deliberations on railroad construction and the general budget for Cameroon, Jan. 18–19, March 19–20, 1906, RT 214, 630–75, RT 216, 2137–2171, *passim*.

59 See letters and testimony of Bell, Deido and Bonaberi chiefs, Nov. 18, 27, 1905, RT 222, 3405, 3408; the most extensive response to the petition from Puttkamer, who hated the Duala in general (see below) designated "the intelligent and energetic . . . Manga Bell" as "paramount chief of the entire tribe," n.d. [1906], ibid., 3417.

60 See Austen, "Cameroon and Cameroonians," 218–21; the major documentation is newspaper clippings in Hamburger Staatsarchiv, "Polizeibehörde: Politische Polizei, S 1365, bd. 29, "Verwaltung deutsche Besitzung in Afrika: Prinz Akwa u. andere Häuptlinge"; see also the derogatory pamphlet of Heinrich Liesemann, "*S.K.H. Prinz*" *Ludwig Paul Heinrich M'pundo Njasam Akwa: ein Betrag zur Rassenfrage* (Berlin: Schwetschke, 1907).

61 Rüger, "Duala," 216–19; Ralph A. Austen, "Duala vs. Germans in Cameroon: Economic Dimensions of a Political Conflict," *Revue Française d'Histoire d'Outre-Mer* 64/4 (1977): 493–4; ibid., "Metamorphoses," 20; for a time some Akwas believed that Mpondo was not really dead and would some day return, like Barbarossa, to lead his people back to glory (interview, Albert Mpondo Dika, Akwa/Douala, June 28, 1970); these rumors may have been encouraged by the claims of a sailor to be Mpondo (see correspondence of 1920–21 in Archives Nationales, Section d'Outre-Mer, Aix-en-Provence [hereafter ANSOM] APA II/29–30).

62 Seitz, *Aufstieg*, I, 76.

63 August Heinrich Kobler, *Einst in Berlin* (Hamburg: Hoffmann u. Campe, 1956), 134–5; see also the interview with Mpondo reported in Hamburg *Nachrichten*, June 11, 1907, Hamburger Staatsarchiv.

64 For Mpondo's 1906–1911 correspondence as well as reports of meetings and activities after his return, see AN/FA 1539, *passim*; Mpondo's views of the precolonial Duala state are recorded in Mpundo [sic] Akwa to Governor Ebermaier, n.d. (*c*. Jan.–Feb. 1914, French translation), ANC/FF TA6.

65 Jan S. Hogendorn, "Economic Initiative and African Cash Farming: Precolonial Origins and Early Colonial Developments," in Peter Duignan and L. H. Gann (eds.), *Colonialism in Africa, 1870–1960. Volume 4. The Economics of Colonialism* (Cambridge: Cambridge University Press, 1975), 283–328.

66 Texts in Rudin, *Germans* 423; Stoecker, *Kamerun* II, 259.

67 See above, pp. 101f.

68 Rüger, "Die Duala," 188–9.

69 In 1901 five out of the ten European merchant houses in Douala were still British: RT, 196 (1900–1903), 5417; by 1912, Germany accounted for 79.5 percent of total imports into Cameroon and Britain only 16 percent but the latter country did provide 31 percent of imported textiles, the commodity still of greatest relevance to African consumers; RKA, *Die deutsche Schutzgebieten in Afrika und der Südsee, 1912/1913* (Berlin: Mittler, 1914), 236–8, 256–8.

70 See above.

71 Probably explained by the brief rise in demand for palm products in the mid-1880s and a renewed decline in the latter part of the decade; see Colin Newbury, "On the Margins of Empire: the Trade of Western Africa, 1875–1890," in Förster et al., *Bismarck, Europe and Africa*, 41–5.

72 Governor v. Zimmerer to Duala chiefs, Nov. 18, 1892, ANC/FA 333. 223; in later statements German officials frequently claimed that the Duala used trust to purchase wives instead of the export products contracted for Seitz to Berlin, Sept. 11, 1896, RKA 3828, 11–12; Seitz, *Aufstieg*, I, 54 (more on this below).

73 On trust disagreements, see Kusserow to Berlin, Nov. 6, 8 1885, RKA 3826, 8–10; see also correspondence of Nov.–Dec. 1886 in RKA 3413, "Syndikat für West-Afrika," 1–43.

74 Soden to Berlin, Dec. 20, 1885, RKA 3826, 53–7.

75 C. Woermann and Mervyn King to Berlin, Feb. 1, 1886; Jantzen and Thormählen to Kusserow, Feb. 27, 1886, RKA 3826, 68–72.

76 Ruppel, *Landesgesetzgebung*, 1021–4.

77 The various phases of these efforts are documented in RKA 3827, 3828 misleadingly entitled "Die Aufhebung [abolition] des Trustsystems."

78 Governor Ebermaier to Berlin, Dec. 6, 1913, RKA 3828, 87–8; in 1914 the German organization of West Africa merchants did endorse a widened prohibition of trust although the reference point here was the now catastrophic rubber trade of southern Cameroon: report of meeting between Ebermaier and Verein Westafrikanische Kaufleute, Berlin, Mar. 2, 1914, ANC/FA 10/1.

79 Kusserow to Berlin, June 22, 1886; Soden to Berlin, June 4, 1886, Feb. 2, 1887, RKA 3814, 6–9, 13–20, 68–71 (Rüger, "Die Duala," 187–8, sees Soden's 1886 compromise as a major victory over the Duala; however, as with much of his analysis of these trade conflicts, Rüger pays more attention to the rhetoric of German intentions than to the more balanced economic outcome).

80 1891, 1903 agreements in John Holt Papers, Rhodes House, Oxford; 10/7, 1/9; 1899 agreement, RKA 3816, 160–72; agreements (and their breakdown) 1910–1912, Sanaga [Malimba/Edea factory] correspondence, Woermann Papers, ANC/FA.

81 Sanaga correspondence, 1908–12, Woermann Papers; Cameroon correspondence, 1907–10, John Holt Papers, 27/1–5.

82 Krabbes to Governor, June 30, 1886, ANC/FA 23/K "Palavern 1886, Abo u. Wuri"; see also various files cited in note 9 above.

83 On Sanaga expeditions, Rüger, "Die Duala," 191–2; on Duala traders in Edea, RKA 4325, *passim*.

84 Wallmut to Governor, July 27, 1888, ANC/FA 58 plus other cases in this and parallel files.

85 Duala chiefs to Governor, Oct. 29, 1892, ANC/FA 333, 211–17.
86 See Rudin, *Germans,* 80–7 for a good overview of these expeditions and their relationship to both Cameroon territorial policy and international colonial rivalries.
87 Eugen Zintgraff, *Nord-Kamerun* (Berlin: Paetel, 1895), esp. 343–93; for the earliest connections between Zintgraff and the Jantzen and Thormählen , see Kusserow to Berlin, June 25, 1889, RKA 3827, 84–85; on Soden's role, see above, p. 104.
88 ANC/FA 51 "Expedition Zintgraff," 1891–92, *passim*; Puttkamer to Berlin, Dec. 9, 1890; Zimmerer to Berlin, Dec. 14, 1892, RKA 3815, 33–4, 42–67; Zintgraff and Jantzen and the Thormählen firm shifted their energies after 1892 into developing plantations in West Cameroon with labor supplies from Bali (Clarence-Smith, "From Plantation to Peasant Cultivation,"486).
89 Kaeselitz, "Kolonialeroberung," 17–20; Woermann to Berlin, May 12, 1890, RKA 3814, 116–17; Pfeil to Berlin, July 6, 1890, RKA 3815, 17–8.
90 See Sanaga correspondence, 1908–12, Woermann Papers, ANC/FA; the Douala-Edea-Yaoundé axis also became the key line of commercial and political contact between the coast and the Muslim north.
91 Bohner report, Sept. 27, 1892, BMG Kamerun, 1892/169.
92 Puttkamer to Berlin, July 10, 1895; Seitz to Puttkamer, June 26, 1895, ANC/FA 791 (ironically the officer in charge of searching for percussion caps – he found only one – was voan Brauchitsch).
93 See the pathetic plea for reinstatement by Joss traders, May 8, 1896, ANC/FA 797, 130–1.
94 In 1908 Brauchitsch – with no ultimate success – supported a request by Manga Bell to allow Duala traders re-entry into Edea, ANC/FA 345, *passim.*
95 ANC/FA 58, *passim.*
96 Seitz, Aufstieg, I, 77–8, 93; AN/FA 260, 1–5; ironically, Yabassi did become a key entrepot for Hausa merchants from northern Cameroon, although this contact proved to be of ambiguous value for German interests: Wirz, *Vom Sklavenhandel,* 196–201.
97 ANC/FA 1226, *passim*; ANC/FA 260, 40, 64 (on Mandessi, see below).
98 Seitz, *Aufstieg,* I, 90–1.
99 Buthut to governor, Nov. 20, 1906, ANC/FA 297, 160–6; ibid., Dec. 9, 1908, ANC/FA 260, 87–93; Oberleutnant Buthut, "Der Handel in Kamerun," *Zeitschrift für Kolonialpolitik, Kolonialrecht u. Kolonialwirtschaft* 11 (1909), 577–602.
100 Report of Nov. 21, 1908 meeting with merchants, Yabassi Bezirksleiter von Stein to Governor, Jan. 1, 1909, van Stein papers, ANC/FA.
101 E.g from April 1 to Dec. 31, 1912 the Douala Bezirksamt issued 805 *new* licenses, the vast majority to Dualas, mostly working for themselves rather than European firms, *Amtsblatt* 5 (1912), 49–53, 58, 330–5.
102 A 1907 German expedition found Akwa merchants well beyond Bonapoupa, their precolonial end-point on this river, dealing in ivory, rubber and cattle (*Deutsches Kolonialblatt,* 1908, 530).
103 It could be argued that colonial investment in roads for motor transport – today the main carriage system and a possibility in the early twentieth century – would have allowed more entree for the Duala and similar African entrepre-

neurial groups owning and operating their own vehicles: Austen, *Economic History*, 124–9.

104 See anxious remarks in Edea to Hamburg, Feb. 2, 1912, and the announcement that the Malimba factory would be closed and Edea placed under Douala supervision (thus terminating this entire file), Hamburg to Edea, Oct. 7, 1912, Sanaga correspondence, ANC/FA Woermann Papers.

105 The issues in the following section have already been dealt with at some length in Wirz, "Der Anbau von 'Cash Crops'," in *Vom Sklavenhandel*, 202–22; Austen, "Slavery," 323–6; Austen, "Germans vs. Duala," 486–90; Austen "Metamorphoses," 16–17; Clarence-Smith, "From Plantations to Peasant Cultivation," and Yvette Monga, "Les entrepreneurs duala, ca. 1890–ca. 1930" (Doctoral dissertation, University of Provence, 1996).

106 See above, p. 57.

107 In addition to items cited in note 105, see Hausen, *Deutsche Kolonialherrschaft*, 216–24, 274–90, 310–15; Marc Michel, "Les plantations allemandes du mont Cameroun," *Revue française d'histoire d'Outre-Mer* 57 (1970), 183–213; and above.

108 For documentation of this attitude, see Clarence-Smith, "From Cocoa Plantations," and Wirz, "Cash Crops," *passim*.

109 Wirz, "Cash Crops," 203–4; Clarence-Smith, "From Cocoa Plantations," 487.

110 Seitz, *Aufstieg*, I, 60 describes the refusal of Manga's slaves to grow cocoa in 1895.

111 Gärtner Mattner report, Nov. 20, 1911, ANC/FA 1385.

112 Chiefs to Reichstag, March 8, 1912, RT 305, 3308; Duala oral informants also uniformly credited Brauchitsch with the development of cocoa cultivation.

113 Brauchitsch, Annual Report for 1907/08, Douala, March 4, 1908, ANC/FA 859, 91–92.

114 Austen, "Slavery," 324–5; Clarence-Smith, "From Cocoa Plantations," 489 (in contrast to Clarence-Smith's inference, it could be argued that early plantations were not hidden by the Duala from local German authorities, but rather by the latter – especially the rough-and-ready Brauchitsch – from their superiors and the missionaries).

115 On such labor recruitment in the German period, see Monga "Entrepreneurs," 264–70.

116 Mattner, Nov. 11, 1911; Frommhold, Oct. 26, 1913, ANC/FA 1385.

117 See letters and memoranda of 1908–13 ANC/FA 1210, 5-21; letters from clerks Hugo Etoa and Lobe Manga, July 31, 1911, Feb. 17, 1912, July 18, 1912, BGF B36 VIA3 Spec. 1.

118 See the inquiry about African cash-crops in Dernburg to Buea, Nov. 7, 1906, BGF VI B4.

119 Se ANC/FA 925, *passim*; Ngange Nduma to Buea, Jan. 16, 1911, BGF IV B 34 1.

120 Wirz, "Cash Crops," 207–18.

121 Agricultural Assistant Berger report, Feb. 22, 1914, ANC/FA 1210, 35–9.

122 See Frommhold report, April 13, 1913, ANC/FA 591.

123 Interview, Ngombe village, May 15, 1973.

124 Monga, "Entrepreneurs," 208–51.

125 Ralph A. Austen and Rita Headrick, "Equatorial Africa under German and French Rule," in David Birmingham and Phyllis Martin (eds.), *A History of Central Africa* (London: Longman, 1983), II, 63–75.

126 Rudin, *Germans*, 353–82; Erik Hallden, *The Culture Policy of the Basel Mission in the Cameroons, 1886–1905* (Uppsala: Uppsala University Press, 1968); Hausen, *Deutsche Kolonialherrschaft*, 175–83; van Slageren, *Les origines*, 38–73; Rudolph Stumpf, *La politique linguistique au Cameroun de 1884 à 1960* (Berne: Peter Lang, 1979), 19–78, appendix 3–23; Madiba Essiben, *Colonisation et Evangélisation en Afrique: L'Héritage scolaire du Cameroun (1885–1956)* (Berne: Peter Lang, 1980), 25–102; Gründer, *Christliche Mission*, 135–59.

127 See chapter 5 for a discussion of the Native Baptist Church, which only became a significant factor during the French Mandate period.

128 Heinrich Berger, *Mission und Kolonialpolitik; die katholische Mission in Kamerun während der deutschen Kolonialzeit* (Immensee: Neue Zeitschrift für Missionswissenschaft, 1978).

129 Puttkamer to Berlin, Nov. 11, 1896, RKA 4073, 133–4.

130 Account of private conversation, Spellenberg report to Bruderkonferenz, April 1905, BMG Kamerun 1905, I/62.

131 Articles 2 and 3, Schulordnung, April 25, 1910, Ruppel, 1142; on negotiations see Dinckelacker commentary on ordinance draft, n.d., BMG Kamerun 1909, I/26–7; ibid., March 7, 1910, BMG Kamerun 1910, I/17.

132 Stumpf, *La politique linguistique*, 66–8.

133 Spellenberg report, April 1905, BMG Kamerun 1905 I/62.

134 A major theme here was the continuation of BMS battles against *losango* and other local cults; see Keller, Mangamba report, Jan. 1, 1898, BMG Kamerun, 1898 II/144; Stolz, Bonaku [Akwa], report, Sept. 29, 1904, BMG Kamerun, 1904 I/107; the positive ethnographic value of these campaigns is the preservation of large number of Littoral cult objects at the society's Missionhaus in Basel; while modern Duala music owes much of its development to Christian churches, the Baselers seem to have contributed far less to this than the Baptists as shown in Christaller's observation that German folksongs would have to be translated because "the Duala Negroes have neither rhythmic nor unrhythmic songs" (Report on Schooling in Cameroon, May–Sept. 1887, RKA 4070).

135 Bohner (Duala Mission) to Basel, June 6, 1891, BMG Kamerun, 1891/67 (in this letter Bohner also stresses the geographic importance of a Douala base and the Gold Coast mission experience that coastal peoples made the best school pupils).

136 Marcia Wright, "Local Roots of Policy in German East Africa," *Journal of African History* 9/4 (1968): 621–30.

137 For the wide use of Pidgin and official disapproval, see Erlass: betrifft Negerenglisch (Pidgin), *Amtsblatt für Kamerun*, Apr. 29, 1913, 165, reprinted in Stumpf, *La politique linguistique*, Appendix, 6–7.

138 See the proceedings of an April 7, 1914 language policy conference organized in Berlin by Governor Ebermaier, reprinted in Stumpf, *La politique linguistique*, Appendix, 16–19.

139 Statistics in ANC/FA 1373 (the Duala constitute 304 of the 319 pupils in the

Douala school and 9 of the 281 in Victoria; the only other ethnic group with over 15 pupils are the "Bakum" (= Bamileke) with 159 in Victoria; published statistics for the previous year indicate that these two coastal schools accounted for 74 percent of all enrollment in Cameroon (*Die deutschen Schutzgebiete in Afrika u. der Südsee, 1912/13*, 80).

140 See above, pp. 104, 113; Puttkamer, in his tirade against Duala education, insisted that the more talented of the new graduates were "refined thieves and rascals," citing the case of Lotin Ewane, an interpreter who was caught in "gross fraud" and other misuse of his powers (Puttkamer to Berlin, Nov. 11, 1896, RKA 4073, 132).

141 John Deibol was ordained in 1901, Joseph Kuo, Joseph Ekollo and Jacob Modi Din in 1912, van Slageren, *Les origines,* 64, 126.

142 Max Klein, "Zur Frage des Zwischenhandels in Kamerun," *Deutsche Kolonialzeitung,* 18 (1901): 290–1; Puttkamer to Lutz, Aug. 8, 1905, BMG Kamerun, 1905 I/115; there are no statistics for this sector but in interviews with Duala who finished school in the German period, several did report working for merchant firms during this time, usually after government employment (Ernest Betote Akwa, Akwa, Douala, July 14, 1970; Henri Ebose Etoke, Akwa, Douala, Sept. 5, 1972).

143 Interviews: James Kaya, Deido, Douala, May 14, 1973, June 15, 1975; Gaston Kingue Jong, Deido, Douala, March 29, 1973; Johannes Sam Deido, Deido, Douala, Sept. 29, 1972 (the houses of these Deido families have inscriptions indicating the dates of construction and Kaya also has German-era papers).

144 Cf. Kristin Mann, *Marrying Well: Marriage, Status and Social Change among the Educated Elite in Colonial Lagos* (Cambridge: Cambridge University Press, 1985); the first Duala professional was the architect Ekwe Bell, who qualified sometime around 1914 (see blueprints for a Deido merchant's house of April 1914 in ANC/FA 1061).

145 Deibol obituary (his last name and the early Baptist affiliation of his father also suggest servile origin), June 5, 1908, BMG Kamerun, 1908 II/130; Modi Din's autobiography accompanies his June 20, 1911 request for ordination, BMG, Kamerun, I,1911, #128/29; Mandessi is mentioned throughout the Basel records but see especially a description of Christmas celebrations at his home and its contrast with general Duala life in Desselberger to Basel, Jan. 1, 1913, BMG Kamerun, 1913 II/1.

146 Manga Bell to Johann Albrechtshöhe [Kumba] Station, Jan. 2, 1898, Seitz to ibid., Jan. 20, 1898, ANC/FA, 242; Seitz, *Aufstieg,* I, 60, 72.

147 Van Slageren, *Les origines,* 63, 126 (the alleged Ethiopianists here were Basel church leaders); as will be seen in the next chapter, similar patterns characterized the more assertive Native Baptist Church during the Mandate period.

148 Wilhelm Lederbogen, "Duala Märchen," *Mitteilungen des Seminars für Orientalische Sprachen* 4 (1901): 154–5.

149 Friedrich Ebding, "Duala Märchen," *Mitteilungen der Ausland-Hochschule an d. Univ. Berlin* 41/3 (1938): 36–102; see also Austen, *Elusive Epic.*

150 Modi Din, June 20, 1911, BMG, Kamerun, 1911 I/128–29; Joseph Ekollo speech, April 21, 1912, BMG Kamerun, 1912 II/1.

151 The one number of *Elolombe* (Jan. 1908) and administrative correspondence

(Feb.–April 1908) connecting its German publi sher, Hans Mahne-Mons to Mpondo in RKA 4069/1; the link to Mpondo's later efforts at neo-Duala empire building can be seen in the use of the titles "Niaziam" and "Biscomta" in the Duala translation of a German fairy tale, "The Severed Hand"; for a different interpretation of *Elolombe* and its contents, see Rüger, "Die Duala," 216–17.

152 Austen, "Duala vs. Germans"; Rüger, "Die Duala," 120–53; and Rüger, "Die Widerstandsbewegung des Rudolf Manga Bell in Kamerun," in Walter Markov (ed.), *Etudes africaines/African Studies/Afrika Studien* (Leipzig: Karl Marx University Press, 1967), 107–28.

153 Austen, "Duala vs. Germans," 478–80.

154 Seitz to Berlin, June 2, 1910, RKA 4427, 3–4.

155 For 1884, see article 3 in Rudin, *Germans*, 425; on Seitz's promise, Bonanjo Mission Annual Report, BMG, Kamerun 1909 II/14; Seitz, *Aufstieg*, II, 44.

156 See above, p. 100.

157 In his memoirs Seitz glosses over his role in the expropriation, claiming that it might have been avoided if the government had taken up an idea he put forth in 1898 for acquring vacant Deido land (*Aufstieg*, I, 41–2).

158 Ibid., II, 54, 91–2.

159 Kurrle (Kribi) to Buea, Aug. 26, 1912, BGF VI B4a; see also Monga, "Entrepreneurs," 183–5.

160 Governor to Mittelkamerun Chamber of Commerce, Sept. 29, 1912; Governor to Douala Bezirksamt, n.d. (*c*. Sept. 1912), BGF B36 VI A3.

161 Röhm to Buea, Jun. 1, 1914 BFA.

162 Memorandum of *Verein Westafrikanische Kaufleute*, March 23, 1914, RT 305, 3367; Hausen, *Deutsche Kolonialherrschaft,* 287.

163 ANC/FA court records 1910/291; the event is cited in Seitz to Berlin, June 2, 1910, RKA 4427.

164 For extensive treatment, see Gründer, *Christliche Mission,* 161–9; Osteraas, "Missionary Politics," 280–96.

165 Austen, "Cameroon and Cameroonians," 207–15.

166 For a version of Duala Manga's life richly based on such local traditions, see Iwiyé Kala Lobe, *Douala Manga Bell: héros de la résistance douala* (Paris: ABC, 1977).

167 Unfortunately no details are available on Duala Manga's career at the gymnasium of Ulm during the 1890s but German officials in Douala granted him the status of "Ein-Jähriger," i.e. holder of a certificate beyond primary school but below that of the *Abitur* (baccalaureate) awarded at the full termination of secondary school studies; Helmuth von Gerlach, *Rechts nach Links* (Zurich: Europa, 1937), 219. A vague recollection from an Ulm classmate also speaks of an *"einjährigezeit"* in 1896 (Fritz Funcius to AA, May 5, 1935, RKA 4301, 42).

168 ANC/FA court records, 1910/291.

169 Duala Manga Bell to Bezirksamt and Bezirksamt to Buea, Sept. 26, 1909, ANC/FA 942, 65–67; Missionary Vohringer (Douala) to Lutz (Buea), (Duala Manga's debts now down to 3,000 marks) July 13, 1912, BFA.

170 At least one local official insisted (without evidence) that the anti-expropri-

ation agitation had been initiated by Mpondo Akwa, thus forcing similar action upon the otherwise "reasonable" Duala Manga (Wipfler to Colonial Office, Feb. 2, 1912, RKA 4427, 71).

171 Austen, "Slavery among Coastal Middlemen," 307–11.

172 Testimony by the Catholic missionary Vieter in a meeting with Colonial Undersecretary Conze, May 2, 1914, RKA 4430, 246–47 (the Bali plateau, as high ground near – if not immediately adjacent to – the river, qualified as mudongo).

173 Interview in *Berliner Tageblatt*, March 8, 1914, RKA 4432, 47.

174 Petition to Reichstag, March 8, 1912, RT 305, 3308.

175 Röhm to Buea, Dec. 23, 1913, RKA 4427, 194; Enteignungskontrolle (list of land blocks and actions taken), ANC/FA 765.

176 Ngoso Din, travel report, Feb. 22, 1914, RKA 4430, 298–9.

177 Ebermaier is reported to have turned away missionary pleas for the lives of Duala Manga and Ngoso Din only on the grounds of war; see Philip Hecklinger, *Tagebücher über Krieg and Kriegsgefangschaft in Kamerun und England* (Stuttgart: Evangelische Missionsverlag, n.d.), 4.

178 This is not to say that the Douala case was entirely unique: see Albert Wirz, "Malaria-Prophylaxe und koloniale Städtebau: Fortschritt als Rücktritt?," *Gesnerus* 37 (1980): 215–34.

179 A recollection of the trial by the official defense attorney is filled with inaccuracies and racist sentiment but does attest that Duala Manga (in contrast to the writer's own belief) never admitted guilt (Dr. Alfred Etschel to Colonial Office, Nov. 9, 1927, RKA 4431, 43ff.).

180 RKA 4430, 288ff; see also accounts of the trials of lesser Duala leaders in ANC/FA 1444.

181 Statements by Njoya, Ndane (Bell envoy), Missionary Geprägs, Fumban, April 28–29, 1914; RKA 4430, 183–9.

182 Röhm to Kuti Agricultural Station [where Ndane was held], May 6, 1914, RKA 4430, 190.

5 MIDDLEMEN AS ETHNIC ELITE

1 On details of wartime administration and diplomacy. see Wm. Roger Louis, *Great Britain and Germany's Lost Colonies, 1914–1919* (Oxford: Clarendon, 1967); Akinjide Osuntokun, *Nigeria in the First World War* (Atlantic Highlands, NJ: Humanities Press, 1979); C. M. Andrews and S. Kanya-Forstner, *The Climax of French Imperial Expansion, 1914–1924* (Stanford: Stanford University Press, 1981); Lovett Elango, "The Anglo-French Condominium in Cameroon, 1914–1916; The Myth and the Reality," *International Journal of African Historical Studies* 18/4 (1985): 657–73.

2 Osuntokun, *Nigeria,* 172–4; Andrew and Kanya-Forstner, *The Climax,* 61.

3 Osuntokun, *Nigeria,* 207ff., esp. 230; for the weak French efforts at sharing control of this effort, see correspondence of Colonel Mayer, July 18, 1915–March 13, 1916 in Archives Nationales du Cameroun, Fonds Français (hereafter ANC/FF) NF 3856.

4 The best overview of this diplomacy is Louis, *Great Britain,* 58–62ff.

5 Ralph A. Austen, "Varieties of Trusteeship: African Territories Under British and French Mandate," in Prosser Gifford and William Roger Lewis (eds.), *France and Britain in Africa: Imperial Rivalry and Colonial Rule* (New Haven: Yale University Press, 1971), 515–41.
6 Henry Simon, cited in Wm. Roger Louis, "The United States and the African Peace Settlement: The Pilgrimage of George Louis Beer," *JAH* 4 (1963): 421.
7 Ralph A. Austen and Rita Headrick, "Equatorial Africa under German and French Rule," in David Birmingham and Phyllis Martin (eds.), *A History of Central Africa,* vol. 1 (London: Longman, 1983), 61, 82–3; Andrews and Kanya-Forstner, *The Climax* 209–13, 226–8.
8 Philippe Laburthe-Tolra, "Charles Atangana" in Charles André Julien et al. (eds.), *Les Africains* (Paris: Jaguar, 1977), V, 109–41; Philip Burnham, "'Regroupement' and Mobile Societies: Two Cameroon Cases," *JAH* 15/4 (1975): 577–94; Daniel Abwa, "The French Administrative System in the Lamidate of Ngaoundéré," in Martin Njeuma (ed.), *Introduction to the History of Cameroon: Nineteenth and Twentieth Centuries* (London: Macmillan, 1989), 137–69.
9 Report of Inspector Humblot, March 25, 1920, in file on Douala expropriation, Archives Nationales Section Outre-Mer, Carton Cameroun (hereafter ANSOM), AP II 29; Douala Annual Report 1920, ANC/FF APA 11873, 6f.
10 See appendix to "Rapport au Ministére des Colonies sur l'administration des Territoires Occupés du Cameroun de la Conquête au 1 Juillet 1921," *Journal Officiel de la République Française*, Sept. 9, 1921, annexe, 418; *Journal Officiel du Cameroun* (hereafter JOC), June 1, 1921.
11 Douala 1920 Report, ANC/FF APA 11873.
12 League of Nations, Permanent Mandates Commission, Minutes (hereafter PMC), I (1921), 12–13; ibid., III (1923), 22–3, 62; Lovett Z. Elango, "The Councils of Notables and the Politics of Control in Cameroon under French Rule, 1925–1949," *Transafrican Journal of History* 16 (1987): 24–46.
13 Commissaire Bonnecarrère to Colonial Ministry, Dec. 15, 1933, ANSOM AP II 28 (this communiqué also discusses – although the policy was never carried out – substituting for the Douala chiefs "whose powerless no longer needs to be pointed out, a system of more direct administration . . . ").
14 Douala circonscription report, cited in Gouellain, *Douala,* 201.
15 For conflicting accounts of Alexander's role in the ousting of his uncle Henri Lobe, see Commissaire Carde to MC, March 29, 1920, ANSOM AP II 29; interview Jonathan Derrick w. Albert Bebe Bell, Douala; there is no information connecting Alexander with the change in Bell chieftaincy of 1927 (q.v. below), although he was reported to have refused the chieftaincy in this period as well "for multiple reasons," Douala administrator to Yaoundé, Dec. 13, 1938, ANC/FF NF 781; see also Richard A. Joseph, "The Royal Pretender: Prince Douala Manga Bell in Paris, 1919–1922," *CEA* 14 (1974): 339–58.
16 Emmanuel Ghomsi, "Résistance Africaine à l'impérialisme Européen: le cas des Douala du Cameroun," *Afrika Zamani* 4 (1975): 157–202, *passim*; the same applies to Eckert, "*Die Duala* and Jonathan Derrick," "Douala under the French Mandate, 1916 to 1936" (Ph.D. dissertation, University of London, 1979).

17 The Akwa petition of 1905 had made some reference to a preference for a "consulate" implying the abrogation of the protectorate, but this was used as grounds for accusations of treason by the Germans and never pursued by the Akwa leaders.

18 Douala chef de circonscription to Commissaire, May 31, 1919, Gouellain, *Douala* 172 (no archival reference given); there is another version of this meeting, with a date of December 1918 but similar content, in Fourneau to Governor-General of AEF, Jan. 22, 1919, ANSOM AP II C28.

19 Lord Milner to Consul Holder, March 3, 1919; see also reports of Duala maneuvers in Holder to Foreign Office, Dec. 22, 1918, John Holt to Foreign Office, Feb. 4, May 8, 1919, all in FO 371/3774/166 and Commissaire to MC, July 22, 1919, ANSOM II 29 (on Lobe Bell's mission to Buea).

20 Hans Poeschel, *Die Kolonialfrage im Frieden von Versailles: Dokumente zu ihrer Behandlung* (Berlin: Mittler, 1920), 87, 94.

21 Ibid., 244–5.

22 The French monitored Cameroonian activity in Germany and knew of the 1919 Weimar petitions (Colonial Ministry to Cameroon, Nov. 5, 1920, ANC/FF 10038); for more on this issue see below and Richard A. Joseph, "The German Question in French Cameroun, 1919–1939," *Comparative Studies in Society and History* 17/1 (1975): 65–90.

23 A copy was enclosed in the August 1929 petition to the League.

24 Monga, "Entrepreneurs duala," 291–3.

25 PMC minutes, XV (1929), 140; see also correspondence, 1926–29, in ANC/FF 10890.

26 Délégué (Douala) to Commissaire, March 5, 1925, ANC/FF APA 11875/17.

27 PMC minutes, XIX (1930), 196 (official report on Dec. 19, 1929 petition); see also PMC minutes cited in table XIII and letter of E. De Haller, Directeur de la Section des Mandats, to Ngaka Akwa and other dignitaries, Feb. 7, 1931, ANC/FF APA 10890.

28 Charles Atangana and other Yaoundé-Bané notables, April 4, 1931, ANC/FF 10890 (printed in Ghomsi, "Résistance," 201–2).

29 On Ganty's career, see Owona, "A 'l'aube du nationalisme;" also Jacques Serre, "Vincent Ganty (1881–1957): douanier guyanais et homme politique camerounais," *Comptes rendues . . . Académie des Sciences d'Outre-Mer* 36 (1976): 105–20.

30 Duala relations with such international anti-colonial organizations will be discussed below.

31 PMC, XXIII (1932), 178–9.

32 Details and documents of this event can be found in ANC/FF 11217/B; PMC XXII (1932), 350–1; Derrick, "Douala," 326–33; Léopold Moumé Etia, "La révolte des femmes en 1931," *Wife* 6 (April 1973): 12–16 [based on accounts by participants].

33 Cortade (Douala administrator) to Yaoundé, July 27, 1931, ANC/FF APA 11217/B.

34 Special Police Commissioner to Marchand, Douala Aug. 1, 1930, ANC/FF APA 11202; Marchand to Minister, May 22, 1930, Jan. 19, 1931, ANSOM AP II 29 & 30; Douala Circonscription Annual Report 1930, ANC/FF APA

10354/A; JOC April 15, 1932; interview, Johannes Sam Deido, Douala.

35 Ghomsi, "Résistance," 186 reports a tradition (without citations) that Betote brought about this change by informing the administration of Ngaka and Edinguele Meetom's leading role in the Ganty affair.

36 Bell to Chef de Circonscription, Feb. 12, 1920, in a report by Inspector-General Meray, April 24, 1920, ANSOM AP II 29.

37 interviews, Albert Bebe Bell, Doumbe-Mouloby.

38 Meray report, Apr. 22, 1920; Humblot report, March 25, 1920; Commissaire Carde to MC, March 2, 1920, ANSOM AP II 29; the reparation idea was rejected by the Cameroon authorities out of fear that it would be used by the Germans "to propagate here 'indemnités de propagande'" (Joseph, "German Question," 73).

39 In a letter to the Colonial Ministry of Feb. 3, 1926 (cited in Gouellain, *Douala,* 227) the mandate regime claimed that in 1920 it made an offer of payment to the Duala, who refused it; but there is no direct evidence of such negotiations at this time.

40 Report of March 11, 1922, cited in Gouellain, *Douala,* 224.

41 Letters of April 16, 23, 1924, Affaires Domaniales, Douala Archives, ANSOM AP II 29.

42 Douala–Yaoundé–Paris administrative correspondence, cited in Gouellain, *Douala,* 225–7.

43 Pastor Charles Maître to Preiswerk (BMS. Basel), Oct. 10, 1926, BFA. The Bell Family Archive, which includes most of Maître's papers as well as the Bezirksamt material, is the main source for the history of these events. Detailed accounts of the second expropriation struggle can be found in Eckert, *Die Duala,* 238–56 and especially Derrick, "Douala under Mandate," 250–331 *passim.* On other aspects of SMEP-Duala relations (particularly concerning the Native Baptist Church) see below.

44 Transcripts of these negotiations can be found in BFA and ANSOM AP II 29.

45 The meeting is described in Maître to Daniel Couve, SMEP Paris, Dec. 13, 1926, BFA.

46 Maître convinced the Duala by reading to them the official Reichstag proceedings but the point seems to have been es tablished earlier by the SMEP's lawyer in Paris (see memo of André Gouin, Nov. 26, 1926, BFA).

47 Details in Derrick, "Douala," 265ff.

48 Richard Bell to Marchand, March 7, 1927.

49 The symbolism, in this case, would no longer be linked to the association of riverside land with free vs. slave status (see chapter 4), since the Bali plateau to which the Bells had now moved is an elevated terrain that seems to have been acceptable even before World War I. Bali is clearly differentiated from the previously designated and low-lying New Bell, already established by the 1920s as an immigrant quarter.

50 Joseph, "German Question," 76–9.

51 Mandessi is mentioned in a Sept. 20, 1926 letter of protest (BFA) as someone who would have signed had he not been absent on his Mungo plantations.

52 See citations in Joseph, "The Royal Pretender."

53 Acting Commissaire to Paris, July 22, 1919, ANSOM AP II 29; Commissaire

Carde to Paris, March 29, 1920, ibid.

54 The correspondence connected with these matters can be followed in ANSOM AP II 30; for marital and other ties between Mandessi's family and the Senegalese community in France, see Maria Diop, *Biographie du David Léon Mandessi Diop* (Paris: Présence Africaine, 1980).

55 Cortade to Yaoundé (with accompanying police report), Dec. 31, 1927, ANSOM AP II 30.

56 According to French intelligence, Mandessi contributed 40,000 francs to the funds put at Richard's disposal (unsigned note for Directeur des Affaires Politiques), June 7, 1928, ANSOM AP CII 29).

57 Arreté, Sept. 11, 1928, JOC, Oct. 1, 1928; Douala Circonscription annual report, 1929, ANC/FF APA 10005/A.

58 The continuing Bell-SMEP discussions are documented in BFA; contacts with Diagne's in Commissaire to Paris, March 21, 1928, ANC/FF, APA 10572/N; and ibid., May 21, 1928, ANSOM AP II 29; Diagne's main queries on Douala expropriation are found in his 1927 correspondence concerning Mandessi Bell (ANSOM AP II 30).

59 Circular on revolutionary activity, Paris, May 30, 1929, 17, ANC/FF APA 10367.

60 For general references on this journal and facsimiles of Ebele's articles, see Eckert, *Die Duala*, 273–4, 322–4.

61 On the role of Mandessi Bell's grandchildren (more Senegalese than Cameroonian) in the later Negritude movement, see Diop, *David Diop, passim* and Austen, *Elusive Epic*, 58–62.

62 PMC XVI (1929), 183–4.

63 PMC XXI (1931), 141.

64 Mémoire, July 10, 1930 ANSOM AP 615/2.

65 PMC XXIV (1933), 122.

66 France, *Rapport annuel au Conseil de la Société des Nations sur l'administration sous mandat du territoire du Cameroun*, 1931, 30; Douala circonscription annual report, 1932, ANC/FF APA 11757.

67 JOC, Oct. 15, 1937.

68 Anonymous and undated report, Institut des Sciences Humaines, Yaoundé (hereafter ISH) W 2ER, W ANA, V LER; this text, apparently written by an official with access to government documents, provides the best general record of the Akwa events.

69 Procès verbal de la réunion des chefs et notables de la Région de Wouri, May 2, 1937, ISH W 2ER.

70 Procès Verbal de la réunion du Conseil de Notables de la Région de Wouri, Oct. 8, 1937, ISH W 2ER.

71 Ibid.

72 Betote's action is described as the "depersonnification de l'homme douala" in the very pro-Akwa unpublished manuscript of Jacques Kuoh Moukouri, "Le Cameroun et ses reférences: l'âme du peuple Duala," 70.

73 Commissaire to Paris, Dec. 16, 1938, and related handwritten note, ANSOM AP II 29; for details see Eckert, "Grundbesitz," 215–16.

74 The account that follows, unless otherwise noted, derives from van Slageren,

Les Origines, 47–52, 131–54, 188–96, 231–2; Richard A. Joseph, "Church, State and Society in Colonial Cameroon," *International Journal of African Historical Studies* 13/1 (1980): 20–31; Anne Dentan, "Lotin a Samé et la Native Baptist Church," *Genève-Afrique* 28/2 (1990): 136–64.

75 Lotin to Yaoundé, Dec. 15, 1921, ANC/FF APA 11188.

76 Dibundu's "Church a Duala" troubled the German Baptists somewhat and Dibundu himself was briefly jailed in the early 1900s for "embezzlement and instigation" (J. Hofmeister, *Erlebnisse in Missionsdienst in Kamerun*, vol 2, Dill-Weis senstein, [1923], 7, 68) but there is very little about him in German government records; in 1914 both Baptist churches had about 3,000 members.

77 See additionally for this period Carl Jacob Bender, *Der Weltkrieg und die christlichen Missionen in Kamerun* (Cassel: Oncken, 1921)

78 Letter to Missionary Conference, June 3, 1920, in van Slageren, *Les origines*, 150.

79 Transcript of a meeting of Oct. 20, 1920 from archives of Pastor Mathi-Mathi in Dentan, 48.

80 Text in van Slageren, *Les origines*, 192.

81 Maître to Allégret, May 1, 1923 in Dentan, "Lotin a Samé", 51 (for more citations like this, see ibid., 53–5).

82 Sung in 1923, recorded *c*. 1926 in Raymond Buell, *The Native Problem in Africa* (New York: Macmillan, 1928), II, 304.

83 There is a misdated account of this meeting in Buell, *Native Problem*, II, 304; the best reports (from which the following material is taken) are Maître to Allégret, May 8–9, 1923 in Dentan, *Lotin a Samé*, 55–6; Commissaire Marchand to Paris, July 9, 1923, ANC/FF APA (the last document is to be reprinted with commentary in Robert A. Hill (ed.), *The Marcus Garvey and Universal Negro Improvement Association Papers* vol. 8, (Berkeley: University of California Press, forthcoming).

84 Douala annual reports, 1921 cited in Gouellain, *Douala* 201.

85 The SMEP Douala Station report of 1925 claims that the NBC no longer controlled any churches and that Lotin wanted to be reinstated as pastor (Archives of the Eglise Evangelique du Cameroun, Douala).

86 See "Etude Historique" of *c*. 1937 (ANC/FF 11183) in which government policy (fully documented in this voluminous file) is summed up as consistent refusal to recognize the NBC as a legal entity combined with its toleration as a "collection des fidèles."

87 The documents on the early 1930s in ANC/FF 11188 show a consistent pattern of Akwa support for the NBC and hostility on the part of the Bell leadership.

88 Douala circonscription to Yaoundé, Sept. 2, 1930; Pastor Rusillon to Circonscription, May 20, 1931, ANC/FF APA 11188.

89 Transcript of meeting of Administrator and Baptist church members, Aug. 22, 1930, ibid.

90 Diagne to Yaoundé, March 28, 1931 (Diagne was by now the Colonial Undersecretary and promised to work with the SMEP to avoid trouble).

91 ANC/FF APA 11188, *passim*; official persecution of Lotin for pro-German activities is discussed below.

92 Joseph, "Church, State," 28–9.

93 See reports of Duala landholdings in British mandated territory; Lobe Bell, March 9, 1915, Buea British Files, Cameroon National, Archives (hereafter BBF) Qc/f 1915/1; A. R. Whitman, Aug. 14, 1922, BBF Qf/e 1922/1; on the obstacles (apparently overcome fairly easily) to exporting this cocoa through Douala see Monga, "Entrepreneurs duala," 295–300.

94 Douala Annual report, 1920, ANC/FF APA 11873.

95 Gouellain, *Douala* 215–16.

96 Monga, "Entrepreneurs duala," 304–9.

97 JOC May 15, 1924, Jan. 1, 1925.

98 Jane Guyer, "Head Tax, Social Structure and Rural Incomes in Cameroun, 1922–37," *CEA* 20 (1980): 305–29.

99 Annual Report 1920, 7 *passim*, ANC/FF APA 11873; for statistics showing vast increases in Douala cocoa exports (not all emanating from French-controlled territory) see Monga, "Entrepreneurs," 302–4.

100 I. Kala-Lobe, "The Greatness and Decline of 'Mun'a Moto'," *Présence Africaine* 37 (1961), English version: 69ff.

101 Van Slageren, *Les origines,* 144–5; Idelette Dugast, *Rapport sur les Travailleurs Recrutés*, 1943 report in Yaoundé archives cited in J.-L. Dongmo, *Le Dynamisme Bamiléké* (Yaoundé: CEPER, 1981), 262–3 (Dugast was a missionary turned government anthropologist).

102 *Climats* 2 (July 1953), 17 cited in Joseph, *Radical Nationalism*, 106.

103 J. C. Barbier, J. Champaud and F. Gendreau, *Migrations et développement: la région du Moungo au Cameroun* (Paris: ORSTOM, 1983), 97–100, 110–11.

104 J. Champaud, "L'économie cacaoyère du Cameroun," Cahiers ORSTOM, sér. Sci. hum., 3 (1966): 106.

105 Jane Guyer, "The Administration and the Depression in South Central Cameroun," *African Economic History* 10 (1981): 67–79.

106 Agence Economique du Territoire sous Mandat to Yaoundé, Aug. 2, 1929, ANC/FF APA 11223/B.

107 Compare "Tournées Mbanga, 1931–37," ANC/FF APA 1797/C with responses to a 1938 "Enquête sur l'alimentation indigène," ISH W V. 22, 42; Kala-Lobé, "Mun'a Moto," pp. and Gaston Kingue Jong, interview, Deido/Douala, March 29, 1973; Monga ("Entrepreneurs," 341f.) notes that for those plantations which kept going during the 1930s, foodstuff and timber sales began to replace cocoa.

108 French observers during this era write of the Duala as "feckless people, [who] mortgage their possessions to obtain money which they waste" (Douala Annual Report 1932, 28ff., ANC/FF APA 10005/A); however, Eckert's careful study of Douala real estate transactions ("Grundbesitz," 207–10) indicates very few mortgages, rentals or land sales during the 1930s. For the difficulties now encountered by the Duala elite in meeting such established cash expenditures as the support of children studying in France, see ANC/FF APA 11220/B and ANSOM Agence FOM C1002.

109 Austen, "Metamorphoses," 18–20; Barbier et al., *Migrations,* 111.

110 Complaints in Wouri (Douala region) Conseil de Notables, April 23, 1938, cited in Gouellain, "Résistance," 255–6; for a continuation of such concern after World War II see Joseph, *Radical Nationalism*, 122–3, 142–3.

111 See above, chapter 2.

112 Van Slageren, *Les origines,* 155–200, 230–6 *passim* (note especially the role of Modi Din and other Duala Protestant missionaries in the evangelization of the Grassfields).

113 Stumpf, *Politique linguistique*, 81–100, Ax 24–41; van Slageren, *Les origines,* 197–8.

114 Stumpf, *Politique linguistique*, 90.

115 Jacques Binet, "Droit foncier coutumier au Cameroun," *Monde non Chrétien* 18 (1951): 161.

116 See a survey of Douala circonscription occupations in 1930 Douala Annual Report, ANC/FF APA 10005/A, 2, 10, 40ff. and again in the 1935 report, APA 108208 (here only 8,000 of *c.* 20,000 Dualas are categorized in the "traditional" occupation of fishermen).

117 See statistics on Duala clerks in Douala Annual Report, 1930 ANC/FF APA 10354/A; in a 1938 list of "Commis d'Ordre et de Comptabilité" (the highest position in the African clerical ranks) 13 of 23 were Duala, ANC/FF NF 806/3.

118 See the names in ANC/FF APA 11220; for references to many more Dualas studying in France during this period, see Diop, *David Diop, passim.*

119 Derrick, "Douala," 382–4.

120 See Mark W. and Virginia H. DeLancey, *A Bibliography of Cameroon* (New York, Africana: 1975), entries 1319, 3290, 4894–7.

121 Johannes Ittmann, "Bemerkungen zu den Altersklassen der Duala and ihrer Nachbarn." *Afrika und Übersee* 39/2 (1955), 83–8; various interviews, Douala.

122 Manga Bekombo-Priso, "Les classes d'âge chez les Dwala (Cameroun)," in Denise Paulme (ed.), *Classes et associations d'âge en Afrique de l'ouest* (Paris: Plon, 1971), 286–307 (little is known about what, if any, initiation rituals were associated with precolonial Duala age grades).

123 "Note au sujet des sociétés d'âge à Douala," ISH Yaoundé Wouri III 131, 1934.

124 Jonathan Derrick, "Colonial Elitism: The Duala in the 1930s," in Martin Njeuma (ed.), *Introduction to the History of Cameroon* (London, Macmillan: 1989), 115–16.

125 Pierre Harter, "Les courses de pirogues coutumiers chez les Dualas ou pembisan a myoloo Duala," *Recherches et études camerounaises* 1 (1960): 71–91; on precolonial practices, see Wilcox, "Maritime Arts," 76–7, 112–16.

126 Derrick, "Colonial Elitism," 118–19, 127–9; Joseph, "Royal Pretender." In an article probably written by Alexander in *L'Eveil du Cameroun* of November 23, 1937, he even claimed that the canoe races were "invented" by his supporters in 1919, a contention which cuts against the usual arguments between historians and upholders of "tradition" and apparently explains a similar error in Harter's otherwise excellent study of the *pembisan.*

127 Joseph, "Royal Pretender," 355–6; the application for citizenship is in ANC/Ff 1AC 2846.

128 Adolf Rüger, "Die kolonialen Bestrebungen der deutscher Imperialismus (vom Ende der ersten Weltkrieg bis zu Locarno-Konferenz)," Habilitationsschrift, Humboldt University, Berlin, 1969, 254–64; Emmanuel Tchum-

tchoua, "Aux sources de l'Union des Populations du Canmeroun (UPC): la Jeucafra, l'Unicafra et le Racam (1938–1948)," Thèse de Doctorat de 3e Cycle, University of Yaoundé, 1993, 48–52.

129 Andrew J. Crozier, *Appeasement and Germany's Last Bid for the Colonies* (New York: St, Martins, 1988), esp. 136–48, 172–84; Hitler ultimately refused to make any concessions in return for colonies and the negotiations were abandoned.

130 See the file on Joseph Ekwe Bile ANC/FF APA 11201/K.

131 Joseph, "German Question," 84–5; Jonathan Derrick, "The 'Germanophone' Elite of Douala under French Administration," *JAH* 21/2 (1980): 266–7; Leonard I. Sah, "Présence et activités allemandes au Cameroun pendant la période de l'entre-deux guerres (1924–1946)," in Kum'a Ndumbe (ed.), *L'Afrique et l'Allemagne*, 296–309; Tchumtchoua, "Aux sources,"53–8.

132 Yaoundé to Paris, June 9, 1934, ANC/FF APA 11188; see also in same file an Aug. 16, 1934 report of the Sûreté to the Douala Délégué describing an NBC-sponsored meeting in which Edinguele Meetom, a key Ganty supporter and KEDGV member, allegedly tried to form a Communist "cell."

133 Commissaire Brunot to Paris, April 7, 1939, ANC/FF APA 10124/B.

134 Report of July 5–31, 1941 court case, ANC/FF APA 10599 (Lotin and other released suspects belonged to an apolitical group of Germanophones called "*Bund der Freunde*"); see also Jonathan Derrick, "Free French and Africans in Douala," *Journal of the Historical Society of Nigeria* 10/2 (1980): 53–70; Tchumtchoua, "Aux sources," 123–8 (this otherwise valuable account confuses Dikongue with Edinguele Meetom, q.v. note 132. The latter was a much more important figure in Duala politics and a valuable informant for both of the present authors on, among other matters, Dikongue's execution).

135 Letters to Hitler in Sah, 300–301 and RKA 4301, 44; on general rumors see Jacques Kuoh Moukouri, *Doigts noirs: je fus écrivain-interprete au Cameroun* (Montreal: Editions à la Page, 1963), 64–73; on threats, Commissaire Brunot to Paris, April 7, 1939, ANC/FF APA 10124/B; we can never be sure of the accuracy of all the French accusations since most Dualas with personal papers in the German language destroyed them during this period.

136 On the history and early historiography of Jeucafra see Joseph, *Radical Nationalism*, 39–44; Tchumtchoua's unpublished work has the richest account of the organization and, as will be seen mainly in the next chapter, notes the relatively autonomous character of its Douala leadership.

137 This critical term is used in some of the Comité's correspondence and in other cases omitted or expressed only as "N."

138 Correspondence in ANSOM AP II 28, beginning Jan. 1, 1937; see especially note by Conseiller d'Etat attached to Paris to Yaoundé, Feb. 10, 1937. For more on Chan (who had a colorful and rather radical past) see: ANSOM AP II 30, *passim*; Léopold Moumé Etia, *Cameroun: les années ardentes* (Paris: Jalivres, 1991), 97–98; Tchumtchoua, "Aux sources," 66–71.

139 See table 5.3 and documents reproduced in Moumé Etia, *Cameroun*, 98–105.

140 The accusations are based on complaints by the Cameroon "plenipotentiary" of the UC, the senior clerk Isaac Moumé- Etia, about both Jeucafra and the imprisonment of Germanophiles in 1939 as well as vague allegations against

Mandessi Bell by, among others, Chan; see correspondence Feb. 3 to March 7, 1939 in ANC/FF APA 10124/A; cf. Moumé Etia, *Cameroun*, 46–8, 105–10.

141 The teenage Soppo's request for support to study overseas of June 20, 1930 was ignored by the government, ANC/FF APA 11220/B; Moumé Etia (*Cameroun*, 48) remembers Soppo in 1939 as someone who "had a library and not only for show"; Soppo's ancestry is undistinguished and he is sometimes rumored in Douala to be of servile origin.

142 Brunot to Douala administrator, March 18, 1939, ANC/FF NF 742/2.

143 Jeucafra proposed poster and government comment, Sept. 3, 1939; proposal for collection of funds and government reply, Dec. 8, 27, 1930, ANC/FF APA 10400/A.

6 BETWEEN COLONIALISM AND RADICAL NATIONALISM

1 Because developments during this period have been covered at some length in Austen, "Tradition" and Eckert, "Grundbesitz" (to be published in 1998 with the same title by Franz Steiner Verlag, Stuttgart) the narrative here will be less detailed than in previous chapters.

2 Ralph Austen and Rita Headrick, "Equatorial Africa under German and French Rule," in David Birmingham and Phyllis Martin (eds.), *A History of Central Africa* (London: Longman, 1983), II, 82ff.

3 For a fuller definition of these bodies and the powers they involved, see Joseph, *Radical Nationalism*, 74; Mark W. DeLancey and H. Mbella Mokeba, *Historical Dictionary of Cameroon* (Metuchen, NJ: Scarecrow Press, 1990), 28–9.

4 On the UPC and this whole period see Joseph, *Radical Nationalism*.

5 On the motivations structure, and scale of these investment programs from a European and Africa-wide perspective, see Austen, *African Economic History*, 200–2, 206–10; for Douala, Gouellain, "Grundbesitz," 271ff.

6 Eckert, "Grundbesitz," 170–1, 229ff.

7 Richard Joseph, "Settlers, Strikers and Sans-Travail: The Douala Riots of September 1945," *JAH* 15 (1974): 669–87.

8 The major exception was the then trade unionist and later political candidate Léopold Moumé Etia (see his *Cameroun: les années ardentes*, 53–68).

9 Richard Joseph, "National Politics in Post-war Cameroun: The Difficult Birth of the U.P.C.," *JAH* 2/2 (1975): 223–4.

10 Joseph, *Radical Nationalism*, 263–88; Austen, "Metamorphosis," 22.

11 Eckert, "Grundbesitz," 262–71; the insistence on interethnic conflict between the Duala and immigrants mars the otherwise very useful essay by David Gardinier, *Political Behavior in the Community of Douala, Cameroon. Reactions of the Duala People to Loss of Hegemony, 1944–1955* (Athens, OH: Ohio University Papers in International Studies, No. 3, 1966).

12 *Journal Officiel du Cameroun*, Aug. 15, 1933; Jan. 1, 1934.

13 Gardinier, *Political Behaviour*, 8–10; Eckert, "Grundbesitz," 240–1 (in 1949, African membership in the municipal council was increased to eight with four Dualas and four immigrants).

14 The best account is in Tchumtchoua, "Aux sources," 178–80, 202–3, 212–14.

15 Among other issues, Fouda was responsible for a 1941 statement by the

Yaoundé branch of Jeucafra dissociating itself from the defense, organized by Soppo Priso, of those Duala accused of pro-German sympathies (Tchumtchoua, "Aux sources," 128–9; see above, p. 173.

16 Apparently some 100 Cameroonians had been dispatched to the newly liberated west of France to make up for a deficit of French industrial labor (Tchoutchoua, "Aux sources," 107).

17 See documents in ANC/FF APA 10209/3 and Gouellain, *Douala*, 316–17; the events are discussed at some length in Austen, "Tradition," 296 and Joseph, *Radical Nationalism*, 78–83; Tchumtchoua, "Aux sources," 212–13.

18 Kuoh-Moukouri, a Unicafra leader and civil servant of the time, names the local French administrator, Léon Salsac, as the man who chose Alexander (*Doigts noirs*, 106–7).

19 Joseph, *Radical Nationalism*, 82–3.

20 The best accounts of Alexandre Bell's politics can be found in Eckert, "Grundbesitz," 238–40; Joseph, *Radical Nationalism*, 79–84; Moumé Etia, *Années ardentes*, 72–4.

21 Moumé-Etia, *Années ardentes*, 72, even claims that Ndoumbe initially opposed the abolition of forced labor, one of the reforms for which he later (unjustifiably in any case) claimed credit.

22 Tchumtchoua, "Aux sources," 133–6; Joseph, *Radical Nationalism*, 70–3, 351–3.

23 Tchumtchoua, "Aux sources," 254 (the attack was orchestrated by the Ewondo chef supérieur Martin Abega Atangana).

24 On Unicafra and Racam, see Joseph, *Radical Nationalism*, 84–91; Tchumtchoua, "Aux sources," 140–260 *passim*.

25 Annual Report, Wouri Region, Douala Subdivision, 1949 (cited in Gouellain, *Douala,* 323).

26 Joseph, *Radical Nationalism*, 153–5. For the entire scope of Soppo's career in this period, see ibid., 179, 184–6, 300–1, 308–31 *passim*, 347; Eckert, "Grundbesitz," 353–5.

27 Joseph, *Radical Nationalism*, 245.

28 For this aspect of Soppo's career, see also Jonathan Derrick, "Douala's Landlord Politician" [obituary of Soppo Priso], *West Africa,* July 1, 1996.

29 For details of the real and rumored connections between Soppo's private wealth and his public career see Eckert, "Grundbesitz," 210, 227, 289–92.

30 Most of this section is drawn from Austen, "Tradition."

31 French version and undated, not quite identical Duala language text (both unsigned copies), in Archives of Léopold Moumé Etia, Deido, Douala (ALME).

32 The only written accounts on the Ngondo for this period other than the "Décision" are weekly reports of the French Sûreté, beginning May 3–10, 1947 (ANC/FF APA 10182); there are also citations to 1947 Ngondo documents, of which the originals could not be found, in the lengthy report by the Sûreté director, P. Divol, "Le Ngondo ou Assemblée Traditionnelle du Peuple Douala," Aug. 28, 1952 (ANC/FF 2-AC 124/A). Other information comes from interviews with participants in the 1940s Ngondo: Richard Din Samé (July 14, 1991), Gaston Kingué Jong (July 12, 1991); Léopold Moumé Etia

(July 8, 1991); the most detailed data on Ekwalla's career comes from an interview with his son, Dr. Simon Eboko Ebelé (July 20, 1991).

33 A. Lotin Samé, "Etude concernant les coutumes Douala," 1936 (Yaoundé: Institut des Sciences Humaines, Dossier W201).

34 It does appear in the Duala version of this document but the latter, without date or place for signatures, may well be newer than the French text (ALME); the first dated mention is in an August 1947 Sûreté report.

35 " . . . the normal procedure for the regulation of the political affairs of our Collectivity, which is to submit them to the Traditional Assembly of the People, the only authority with valid legislative juridiction over all questions concerning the People as a whole."

36 Interviews with Din Samé (a participant in the meetings) and Dr. Eboko Ebelé, who helped his father with French correspondence at this time.

37 For a discussion of these accounts, see Austen, "Tradition," 296.

38 Nta Lobé at May 7, 1947 Ngondo meeting (Divol, *Le Ngondo*, 5).

39 Sûreté reports Aug. 16–23, 1947, ANC/FF APA 10182; for evidence that the French authorities helped bring about this meeting see P. Harter unpublished ms. cited in Gouellain, *Douala,* 325.

40 Ebele Ekwalla's name is absent from a list of the Comité des Directeurs dated Jan. 3, 1950 in ALME; he was particularly hostile to the chef supérieur of his own Deido quarter, Ekwalla Essaka, who now became vice-president of the Ngondo.

41 Joseph, *Radical Nationalism, passim*; Robert Fankem, "Le rôle du Ngondo dans la décolonisation du Cameroun" (Yaoundé: Ecole normale supérieure, mémoire de maîtrise, 1990).

42 Report of August 17, 1947 Ngondo meeting, Sûreté reports, Aug. 16–23, 1946, ANC/FF APA 10182; see also a request "that non-Cameroonians should be forbidden to purchase land in the Territory," "Petition from the Ngondo, *Assemblée traditionnelle du Peuple*, Duala, concerning the Cameroons under French and under British administration," United Nations Trusteeship Council, *Official Records*, Annex, vol. II, Fourth Year, Sixth Session (1949–50), T/Pet/5/56–T/Pet/4/31, 265; another Ngondo ruling against land alienation is reported by Vallier, Commissaire Général de Yaoundé, June 6, 1951, ANC/FF APA 12406.

43 Eckert, "Grundbesitz," 274ff.; Gouellain, *Douala* 301–2.

44 The organization/festival did not formally change its name to "Ngondo'a Sawa" until its (re)revival in 1991.

45 Ngondo Petition, 262.

46 Soppo Priso to Ngondo, Nov. 26, 1949, "Petition," 272; Moumé Etia, *Années ardentes*, 89–91.

47 Gardinier, *Political Behaviour,* 19–29; for Ngondo pressures on an apparently reluctant Soppo Priso concerning the commune reforms, see Sûreté reports, April 3–12, 17–24, 1948, ANC/FF APA 10182.

48 There was some serious political tension around the Ngondo in 1972 (although not leading to its suppression); see Jean- François Bayart, *L'Etat au Cameroun* (Paris: Fondation Nationale des Sciences Politiques, 1979), 128–9. With the opening to multiparty politics in the 1990s, there have been demonstrations by

Duala and other Sawa groups demanding the reservation of some positions within local government: see Florent Ndjicki, "A Douala: Autochtones contre Allogènes," *Africa International*, 293 (April 1996): 18–20: on the muted role of the Ngondo in these politics, see Peter Geschiere, "Chiefs and Colonial Rule in Cameroon: Inventing Chieftancy, French and British Style," *Africa* 63/2 (1993): 168–9.

49 The formative Aug. 17, 1949 Ngondo meeting ruled that any Duala with French citizenship would lose all local property rights (Sûreté reports, Aug. 16–23, 1949, ANC/FF APA 10182); Between 1944 and 1947 Ndoumbe Duala Manga sold to Europeans eighteen parcels of land, worth over 4.8 million francs (Eckert, "Grundbesitz," 479).

50 Sûreté report, March 20–27, 1948, ANC/FF APA 10182.

51 Eckert, "Grundbesitz," 238–8, 306–11.

52 Divol, "Le Ngondo" 12, 13.

53 The Ngondo was banned by the Ahidjo government in 1981 as an unrecognized "association tribale" but revived again in 1991.

54 Maurice Doumbé Moulongo, *Le Ngondo: assemblée traditionelle du peuple duala* (Yaoundé: Centre d'Edition et de Production de Manuels et d'Auxiliaires de l'Enseignement, 1972), 13, 31; Jacques Soulillou, *Douala: un siècle en images* (Paris: chez l'auteur, 1982), 88.

55 Harter, "Le Ngondo," 83–93 provides the best of several published descriptions; Ralph Austen witnessed the public ceremony in 1973.

56 See committee on "histoire" in Ngondo meeting of June 2, 1948 (ALME) and one for "coutume" in a March 30, 1953 meeting (Gaston Kingue Jong Papers, Douala); Harter ("Ngondo," 83) gives a lengthy account of the deliberations preceding the 1949 festival.

57 See above, chapter 2, pp. 41–42; also Edwin Ardener, "Belief and the Problem of Women," in J.S. La Fontaine (ed.), *The Interpretation of Ritual* (London: Tavistock, 1972), 145–53; Eric de Rosny, *Healers in the Night* (Maryknoll, New York: Orbis, 1985); Ralph Austen, fieldwork, Kribi, Cameroon, July 1991.

58 Friedrich Ebding, *Duala Sprichwörter* (Freiburg: Anthropos-Institut Micro-Bibliotheca, no. 31), microfilm, 1959), #305; Harter, "Courses de pirogues"; Eric de Rosny, "La lutte contre le choléra à Jebalé (Cameroun)," in Sylvie Devers (ed.), *Pour Jean Malaurie* (Paris: Plon, 1990), 635–45.

59 This deliberate muting of the history of slavery can also be seen in the other, far less effective, monument of Duala-Sawa culture, the oral epic of Jeki la Njambè (Austen, *Elusive Epic*; ibid., "Inventing and Forgetting Traditions on the Cameroon Coast: The Ngondo Council and the Jeki Epic," *Passages*, 7 (1994): 8).

60 E.g. Engelbert Mveng, *Histoire du Cameroun* (Paris: Présence Africaine, 1963), 108–79 *passim*.

61 Austen, *African Economic History*, esp. 5, 198ff.

62 It is perhaps no coincidence that one of the classic works on this dilemma was written by a specialist on Cameroon: Jean-François Bayart, *The State in Africa: The Politics of the Belly* (London: Longman, 1993).

Bibliography

1 ORAL INTERVIEWS

(Dates do not cover all the occasions upon which we drew upon these individuals and groups for historical information.)

A INDIVIDUALS

Akwa, Ernest Betote: Akwa/Douala, July 14, 1970; March–June, 1972.
Bebe Bell, Albert: Bali/Douala, July 1, 1970, Feb.–June 1972, Sept. 25, 1972.
Bema, Benoit (Bonapoupa chief): Douala, June 2, 1975.
Dikoumé, Cosme: Paris, June 23, 1975.
Din Samé, Richard: Bonaberi/Doula, July 14, 1991.
Doumbe-Mouloby, Rudolf: Bonanjo/Douala, June 30, 1970, Feb.–June, 1972, Dec. 23, 1972, May 12, 1973.
Eboko Ebelé, Dr. Simon: Akwa/Douala, July 20, 1991.
Ebose Etoke, Henri: Akwa/Douala, Sept. 5, 1972.
Edingele Meetom, Ferdinand: Akwa/Douala, June 26, 1970, April–June, 1972.
Epée, Michel: Bali/Douala, 1972.
Ewondé Ebongo, Jean: Bwassalo, April 18, 1975.
Eyoumban, Ekam and Ngané Mbappe: Bonaberi/Douala, July 14, 1973.
Kaya, James: Deido/Douala, May 14, 1973, June 15, 1975.
Kingue Jong, Gaston: Deido/Douala, Feb.–June, 1972, March 29, 1973, July 12, 1991.
Kuoh Moukouri, Jacques: Akwa/Douala, Feb.–June, 1972, May 16, 1973.
Mandessi Bell, Sam: Bonanjo/Douala, 1972.
Mbende, Paul: Akwa/Douala, July 1, 1970, Feb.–June, 1972.
Moumé Etia, Léopold: Feb.–June, 1972, Deido/Douala, July 8, 1991.
Mpondo Dika, Albert: Akwa/Douala, June 28, 1970, Feb.–June, 1972.
Penda Ngime, Ebenezer: Dibombari, April 21, 1975.
Sam Deido, Johannes: Deido/Douala, April–May, 1972, Sept. 29, 1972.
Soppo Priso, Paul: Bonanjo/Douala, 1972.

B VILLAGE ELDERS

Abo (Miang, Mangamba, Mandouka, Bessoung Kong), June 4–6, 1975.
Bomono-ba-Jeru, April 18, 1975.
Bonangando, April 15, 21, 1975.
Bonapoupa, May 15, 1975.

Estuary fishing camps, May 17, 18, 1973.
Mombo, December 16–18, 1975 (interviewed by Elias Ngome, Theological College, Nyasoso).
Mpondo, May 2, 1975.
Mundame, May 3, 1975.
Muyuka, May 3, 1975.
Ngombe, May 15, 1973.
Japoma, June 12, 1975.
Jebalé, May 7, 1975.
Lobetal, April 26, 1975.
Loungahé, May 16, 1975.
Malimba, June 8, 1975.
Wuri and Bodiman, May–June, 1975.
Yadibo, Elogzogwout, April 27, 1975.

2 ARCHIVES

CAMEROON

Archives Nationales du Cameroun, Yaoundé.
Archives of the Eglise Evangélique du Cameroun, Douala.
Archive of Léopold Moumé Etia, Douala.
Bell Family Archives, Douala.
Cameroon National Archives, Buea.
Institut des Sciences Humaines, Yaoundé.

ENGLAND

Baptist Missionary Society, London.
James Rogers Papers, Public Records Office (photocopies as well as catalogue of contents provided by the Perkins Library, Duke University).
John Holt Papers, Rhodes House, Oxford.
Bristol Central Library.
Liverpool Public Library, Record Office.
Public Record Office, London/Kew.
William Davenport Papers, University of Keele Library (copies of relevant sections provided by James Rawley of the University of Nebraska).

FRANCE

Archives Nationale, Section d'Outre Mer, Aix-en-Provence (previously rue Oudinot, Paris).
Bibliothèque Nationale, Paris, Map Collection.

GERMANY

Deutsches Zentralarchiv (now Deutsches Bundesarchiv), Potsdam, Germany.
Seminar für Afrikanische Sprachen und Kulturen, Hamburg.

NIGERIA

Nigerian National Archives, Ibadan.

SWITZERLAND

Basler Missionsgesellschaft Archives, Basel.

3 OFFICIAL PUBLICATIONS

Amtsblatt für das Schutzgebiet Kamerun.
Annual Report, Baptist Missionary Society.
Baptist Missionary Herald.
Bulletin de la Chambre de Commerce du Cameroun Français.
Calendar of State Papers, Colonial Series. Great Britain, Public Record Office,
    vol. 7. London: HMSO, 1889.
Deutsches Kolonialblatt.
Die deutsche Schutzgebieten in Afrika und der Südsee.
Hertslet's Commercial Treaties, Lewis Hertslet.
Journal des Missions Evangéliques.
Journal Officiel du Cameroun.
Minutes, Permanent Mandates Commission, League of Nations.
*Rapport annuel au Conseil de la Société des Nations sur l'administration sous mandat
    du territoire du Cameroun,* France.
Recueil des traités de la France. M. de Clerq and Jules de Clerq, vol. 14. Paris:
    Durand et Pedone-Lauriel, 1886.
Sessional Papers (Parliamentary Papers), Parliament, House of Commons, Great
    Britain.
Verhandlungen des Reichstags (Reichstag debates and papers), Germany.

4 PUBLISHED PRIMARY SOURCES

Adams, Captain John. *Remarks on the Country Extending from Cape Palmas to the
    River Congo . . .* London: Whittaker, 1823.
Allen, Captain William. *A Narrative of the Expedition . . . to the River Niger in
    1841.* London: R. Bentley, 1848.
Autenrieth, Friedrich. *Ins Inner-Hochland von Kamerun.* Stuttgart: Holland &
    Josenhans, 1900.
Bender, Carl Jacob. *Der Weltkrieg und die christlichen Missionen in Kamerun.*
    Cassel: Oncken, 1921.
Bold, Edmond. *The Merchant Mariners' Guide to . . . West Africa.* London: no
    publisher, 1822.
Bostock, Robert. *Bostock Letter Book.* 1787–90. Liverpool: Liverpool Public
    Library, Record Office, ms. 387 MD54, 28, 78; MD55, 62.
Boudyck Bastiaanse, J. H. van. *Voyage à la côte de Guinée . . .* The Hague, 1853.
Buchhholz, Reinhold. *Land und Leute in Westafrika.* Berlin: Habel, 1876.
Buchner, Max. *Kamerun.* Leipzig: Duncker u. Humblot, 1887.
    Aurora Colonialis. Munich: Piloty & Loehle, 1914.

Buthut, Oberleutnant. "Der Handel in Kamerun," *Zeitschrift für Kolonialpolitik, Kolonialrecht u. Kolonialwirtschaft* 11: 577–602, 1909.

Dinkelacker, Ernst. *Bonaberi.* Basel: Missionsbuchhandlung, 1904.

Diop, Maria. *Biographie de David Léon Mandessi Diop.* Paris: Présence Africaine, 1980.

Donnan, Elizabeth. *Documents Illustrative of the Slave Trade to America.* Vol. 2, New York: Octagon, 1969.

Ebding, Friedrich. "Duala Märchen," *Mitteilungen der Ausland-Hochschule an d. Univ. Berlin* 41/3 (1938): 36–102.

Duala Sprichwörter. Freiburg: Anthropos-Institut Micro-Bibliotheca, no. 31, 1959. Microfilm, # 142.

Esser, Max. *An der Westküste Afrika.* Berlin: A. Ahn, 1898.

Flad. "Zur Geschichte der Vergangenheit der Dualla," *Mitteilungen aus den Deutschen Schutzgebieten* 4 (1891): 39–47.

Gerlach, Helmuth von. *Rechts nach Links.* Zurich: Europa, 1937.

Giesebrecht, Franz. "Tagebuchblätter eines in Kamerun lebenden Deutschen," *Neues deutsches Rundschau* (1894): 348.

Grenfell, George. "The Cameroons District, West Africa," *Proceedings of the Royal Geographical Society* 4 (1882): 586.

Halbing, Aug. "Genealogie des Duala, Sohns des Mbedi," *Mitteilungen des Seminars für Orientalischen Sprachen* 9/3 (1906): 259–77.

Harford, John. "A Voyage to the Oil Rivers Twenty-Five Years Ago," in Mary H. Kingsley (ed.), *West African Studies.* London: Macmillan, 1899.

Hamer, Philip (ed.). *The Papers of Henry Laurens.* Vol. 1, Columbia: University of South Carolina Press, 1968.

Hecklinger, Philip. *Tagebücher über Krieg and Kriegsgefangschaft in Kamerun und England.* Stuttgart: Evangelische Missionsverlag, n.d.

Heinersdorff Carl (ed.). *Reinhold Buchholz' Reisen in West-Afrika.* Leipzig: Brockhaus, 1880.

Hofmeister, J. *Erlebnisse in Missionsdienst in Kamerun.* Vol. 2, Dill-Weissenstein, 1923.

Holman, James W. *Travels in Madeira, Sierra Leone . . .* London: G. Routledge, 1840.

Jackson, R. M. *Journal of a Voyage to the Bonny River on the West Coast of Africa.* Letchworth, Herts: privately edited and printed by Roland Jackson, 1934.

Klein, Max. "Zur Frage des Zwischenhandels in Kamerun," *Deutsche Kolonialzeitung* 18 (1901): 290–1.

Kuoh Moukouri, Jacques. *Doigts noirs: je fus écrivain-interprete au Cameroun.* Montreal: Editions à la Page, 1963.

Lederbogen, Wilhelm. "Duala Märchen," *Mitteilungen des Seminars für Orientalische Sprachen* 4 (1901): 154–5.

Liesemann, Heinrich. "*S.K.H. Prinz*" Ludwig Paul Heinrich M'pundo Njasam Akwa: ein Betrag zur Rassenfrage.* Berlin: Schwetschke, 1907.

Makembe, Peter. "Duala Texte," *Zeitschrift für Eingeborenen-Sprachen* 11 (1921): 179–80.

Mockler-Ferryman, A. F. *British West Africa.* London: Swan Sonnenschein, 1900.

Morgen, Curt. *Durch Kamerun von Süd nach Nord.* Leipzig: Brockhaus, 1893.

Moumé Etia, Léopold. *Cameroun: les années ardentes.* Paris: Jalivres, 1991.

Pauli, Dr. "Anthropologisches und Ethnologisches aus Kamerun," *Correspondenz-Blatt der Anthropologische Gesellschaft* 32 (1901): 112–17.

Robertson, G. A. *Notes on Africa.* London: Sherwood, Neely and Jones, 1819.

Ruppel, Julius. *Die Landesgesetzgebung für das Schutzgebiet Kamerun.* Berlin: E. S. Mittler u. Sohn, 1912.

Scholl, Carl. *Nach Kamerun!* Leipzig: Cavaell, 1886.

Schwarz, Bernhard. *Kamerun. Reise in die Hinterlande der Kolonie.* Leipzig: P. Frohber, 1886.

Seitz, Theodor. *Vom Aufstieg und Niederbruch deutscher Kolonialmacht.* Vols. 1 & 2, Karlsruhe: Müller, 1929.

Stolz, K. "Tod des Königs Manga Bell," *Evangelische Heidenbote* (1908): 81–2.

Thormählen, Johannes. "Mitteilungen über Land und Leute in Kamerun," *Mitteilungen der Geographischen Gesellschaft in Hamburg* (1884): 334.

Valdau, G. "Eine Reise in das Gebiet nördlich vom Kamerungebirge," *Deutsche Geographische Blätter* 9 (1886): 125–40.

Whitford, John. *Trading Life in Western and Central Africa.* Liverpool: Porcupine, 1877.

Woermann, Adolf. "Kultur-Bestrebungen in West-Afrika," *Mitteilungen der Geographischen Gesellschaft in Hamburg* (1878–9): 58–71.

"Über Tauschandel in Afrika," *Mitteilungen der Geographischen Gesellschaft in Hamburg* 4/5 (1880–1): 29–43.

Zintgraff, Eugen. *Nord-Kamerun.* Berlin: Paetel, 1895.

Zöller, Hugo. *Forschungsreisen in der deutschen Colonie Kamerun. Zweiter Theil: das Flussgebiet von Kamerun.* Berlin: Spemann, 1885.

5 SECONDARY SOURCES

Abwa, Daniel. "The French Administrative System in the Lamidate of Ngaoundéré," in Martin Njeuma (ed.), *Introduction to the History of Cameroon: Nineteenth and Twentieth Centuries.* London: Macmillan, 1989, 137–69.

Adams, Gust. Alf. "Die Sprache der Banoho," *Mitteilungen des Seminars für Orientalishe Sprachen* 10/3 (1907): 34–83.

Alagoa, J. A. "Long-distance Trade in the Niger Delta," *Journal of African History* 11/3 (1970): 319–29.

Andrews, C. M. and S. Kanya-Forstner. *The Climax of French Imperial Expansion, 1914–1924.* Stanford: Stanford University Press, 1981.

Ardener, Edwin. *Coastal Bantu of the Cameroons.* London: International African Institute, 1956.

"Documentary and Linguistic Evidence for the Rise of Trading Polities between the Rio del Rey and Cameroons, 1500–1650," in I. M. Lewis (ed.), *History and Social Anthropology.* London: Tavistock, 1968, 81–126.

"Belief and the Problem of Women," in J. S. La Fontaine (ed.), *The Interpretation of Ritual.* London: Tavistock, 1972, 145–53.

"Language, Ethnicity, and Population." in R. P. Moss and R. J. A. R. Rathbone (eds.), *The Population Factor in African Studies.* London: University of London Press, 1975, 48–56.

Ardener, Shirley G. *Eye-Witnesses to the Annexation of Cameroon, 1883–1887*. Buea: Ministry of Primary Education and West Cameroon Antiquities Commission, 1968.

Austen, Ralph A. "Varieties of Trusteeship: African Territories Under British and French Mandate," in Prosser Gifford and William Roger Lewis (eds.), *France and Britain in Africa: Imperial Rivalry and Colonial Rule*. New Haven: Yale University Press, 1971, 515–41.

"Compradorism in Africa," unpublished paper presented at an American Historical Association meeting, 1971.

With K. Jacob. "Dutch Trading Voyages to Cameroon, 1721–1759: European Documents and African History," *Annales de la Faculté des Lettres et Sciences Humaines, Université de Yaoundé* 6 (1974): 5–27.

"Duala vs. Germans in Cameroon: Economic Dimensions of a Political Conflict," *Revue Française d'Histoire d'Outre-Mer* 64/4 (1977): 493–4.

With Rita Headrick. "Equatorial Africa under German and French Rule," in David Birmingham and Phyllis Martin (eds.), *A History of Central Africa*. Vol. 2, London: Longman, 1983.

"Cameroon and Cameroonians in Wilhelmian Innenpolitik: Grande Histoire and Petite Histoire," in Kum'a Ndumbe (ed.), *L'Afrique et l'Allemagne*, 217–21.

African Economic History. London: Currey, 1987.

"The Mediterranean Slave Trade out of Africa: A Tentative Census," *Slavery and Abolition* 13/1 (1992): 214–48.

"Tradition, Invention and History: The Case of the Ngondo (Cameroon)," *Cahiers d'Etudes Africaines* 32 (1992): 285–309.

"The Moral Economy of Witchcraft," in J. and J. L. Comaroff (eds.), *Modernity and its Malcontents*. Chicago: University of Chicago Press, 1993, 89–110.

"Inventing and Forgetting Traditions on the Cameroon Coast: The Ngondo Council and the Jeki Epic," *Passages* 7 (1994): 8.

The Elusive Epic: the Narrative of Jeki la Njambe in the Historical Culture of the Cameroon Coast. Atlanta: African Studies Association, 1996.

Avelot, Captain R. "Recherches sur l'histoire des migrations dans le bassin de l'Ogôoué et la région littorale adjacente," *Bulletin de Géographie Historique et Déscriptive* 20 (1905): 357–412.

Balandier, Georges. "Economie, société et pouvoir chez les Duala anciens," *Cahiers d'Etudes Africaines* 15 (1975): 361–80.

Barbier, J. C., J. Champaud and F. Gendreau. *Migrations et développement: la région du Moungo au Cameroun*. Paris: ORSTOM, 1983.

Bastin, Y., A. Coupez and B. de Halleux. "Statistiques lexicale et grammaticale pour la classification historique des langues bantoues," *Bulletin de Séances de l'Académie Royale des Sciences d'Outre-Mer* 23/3 (1979): 375–87.

Bayart, Jean-François. *L'Etat au Cameroun*. Paris: Fondation Nationale des Sciences Politique, 1979.

The State in Africa: The Politics of the Belly. London: Longman, 1993.

Bekombo-Priso, Manga. "Conflits d'autorité au sein de la société familiale chez les Dwala du Sud-Cameroun," *Cahiers d'Etudes Africaines* 4 (1963): 317–29.

"Les classes d'âge chez les Dwala (Cameroun)," in Denise Paulme (ed.), *Classes et associations d'âge en Afrique de l'ouest*. Paris: Plon, 1971, 286–37.

"Essai sur le peuplement de la région côtière du Cameroun: les populations dites dwala," in Claude Tardits (ed.), *Contribution de la recherche ethnologique à l'histoire du Cameroun*. Paris: CNRS, 1981, 503–10.

Berger, Heinrich. *Mission und Kolonialpolitik: Die katholische Mission in Kamerun während der deutschen Kolonialzeit*. Immensee: Neue Zeitschrift für Missionswissenschaft, 1978.

Bernd, Heine. "The Dispersal of the Bantu Peoples in the Light of Linguistic Evidence," *Muntu* 1 (1984): 22–35.

Bhabha, Homi K. *The Location of Culture*. London: Routledge, 1994.

Binet, Jacques. "Droit foncier coutumier au Cameroun," *Monde non Chrétien* 18 (1951): 161.

Bledsoe, Caroline H. and William P. Murphy. "The Kpelle Negotiation of Marriage and Matrilineal Ties," in Linda S. Cordell and Stephen Beckerman (eds.), *The Versatility of Kinship*. New York: Academic, 1980, 145–63.

Boogaart, Ernest van den and Pieter C. Emmer. "The Dutch Participation in the Atlantic Slave Trade, 1596–1650," in Henry A. Gemery and Jan S. Hogendorn (eds.), *The Uncommon Market: Essays in the Economic History of the Atlantic Slave Trade*. New York: Academic Press, 1979.

Buell, Raymond. *The Native Problem in Africa*. Vol. 2, New York: Macmillan, 1928.

Buhan, Christine with Etienne Kange Essiben. *La mystique du corps: jalons pour une anthropologies du corps, les Yabyan et les Yapeke, Bakoko, Elog-Mpoo ou Yamban-Ngee de Dibombari au Sud-Cameroun*. Paris: L'Harmattan, 1979.

Bureau, René. *Ethno-Sociologie religieuse des Duala et apparentés*. Yaoundé: Institut de Recherches Scientifiques du Cameroun, 1962 (special number of *Recherches et Etudes Camerounaises* 7/8).

Burnham, Philip. "'Regroupement' and Mobile Societies: Two Cameroon Cases," *Journal of African History* 15/4 (1975): 577–94.

Cain, P. J. and A. G. Hopkins. *British Imperialism: Innovation and Expansion 1688–1914*. London: Longman, 1993.

Champaud, J. "L'économie cacaoyère du Cameroun," *Cahiers ORSTOM, series Sciences Humaines* 3 (1966): 106.

Chauveau, Jean-Pierre. "Une histoire maritime africaine est-elle possible: historiographie et histoire de la navigation et de la pêche africaines à la côte occidentale depuis le XVème siècle," *Cahiers d'Etudes Africaines* 26 (1986): 173–235.

Clarence-Smith, William Gervase. "From Plantation to Peasant Cultivation in German Cameroun," in Peter Geschiere and Piet Konings (eds.), *Proceedings/Contributions: Conference on the Political Economy of Cameroon. Historical Perspective* (Leiden: African Studies Centre, 1989), II, 483–502.

Cohen, Ronald. "State Origins: a Reappraisal," in Henri J. M. Claessen and Peter Skolnik (eds.), *The Early State*. The Hague: Mouton, 1978, 31–77.

Comaroff, Jean and John Comaroff. "Christianity and Colonialism in South Africa," *American Ethnologist* 13/1 (1986): 1–22.

Crozier, Andrew J. *Appeasement and Germany's Last Bid for Colonies*. New York: St. Martins, 1988.

DeLancey, Mark W. and Virginia H. *A Bibliography of Cameroon*. New York: Africana, 1975.

DeLancey, Mark W. and H. Mbella Mokeba. *Historical Dictionary of Cameroon.* Metuchen, NJ: Scarecrow, 1990.

Dentan, Anne. "Lotin a Samé et la Native Baptist Church," *Genève-Afrique* 28/2 (1990): 136–64.

Derrick, Jonathan. "Douala under the French Mandate, 1916 to 1936." Ph.D. dissertation, University of London, 1979.

"Free French and Africans in Douala," *Journal of the Historical Society of Nigeria* 10/2 (1980): 53–70.

"The 'Germanophone' Elite of Douala under French Administration," *Journal of African History* 21/2 (1980): 266–7.

"Colonial Elitism: The Duala in the 1930s," in Martin Njeuma (ed.), *Introduction to the History of Cameroon.* London: Macmillan, 1989.

"Douala's Landlord Politician" [obituary of Soppo Priso], *West Africa,* July 1, 1996.

Dieu, Michel and Patrick Renaud. *Atlas linguistique de l'Afrique Centrale (ALAC): Atlas Linguistique du Cameroun (ALCAM).* Paris: Agence de Coopération Culturelle et Technique, 1983.

Dika Akwa nya Bonambela, Guillaume Bétoté. "Nyambéisme: pensée et modèle d'organisation des Négro-Africains." Thèse d'Etat, Université de Paris VII, 1985.

Dike, K. Onwuka. *Trade and Politics in the Niger Delta, 1830–1885.* Clarendon: Oxford, 1956.

"Un Douala Français." "La Fédération Ancestrale des Piroguiers de Douala," *L'Eveil du Cameroun* Nov. 23, 1937.

Doumbé Moulongo, Maurice. *Le Ngondo: Assemblée traditionelle du peuple duala.* Yaoundé: Centre d'Edition . . . de l'Enseignement, 1972.

Eckert, Andreas. *Die Duala und die Kolonialmächte.* Hamburg: University of Hamburg, 1991.

"Grundbesitz, Landkonflikte und kolonialer Wandel. Douala 1880 bis 1960." Ph.D. dissertation. University of Hamburg, 1995.

Eggert, Manfred K. H. "Central Africa and the Archeology of the Tropical Rainforest," in Thurstan Shaw et al. (eds.), *The Archaeology of Africa.* London: Routledge, 1993, 322–3.

Eitzen, J.v. "Die Eingeborenenfischerei von Kamerun," *Der Fischerbote* 6 (1916): 19–20, 58–9, 172–5, 200–2.

Elango, Lovett Zephania. "Britain and Bimbia in the Nineteenth Century." Ph.D. dissertation, Boston University, 1974.

"The Anglo-French Condominium in Cameroon, 1914–1916: The Myth and the Reality," *International Journal of African Historical Studies* 18/4 (1985): 657–73.

"The Councils of Notables and the Politics of Control in Cameroon under French Rule, 1925–1949," *Transafrican Journal of History* 16 (1987): 24–46.

Eltis, David. *Economic Growth and the Ending of the Transatlantic Slave Trade.* New York: Oxford, 1987.

Essiben, Madiba. *Colonisation et Evangélisation en Afrique: L'Héritage scolaire du Cameroun (1885–1956).* Berne: Peter Lang, 1980.

Fankem, Robert. "Le rôle du Ngondo dans la décolonisation du Cameroun." Yaoundé: Ecole normale supérieure, mémoire de maîtrise, 1990.

Feinberg, Harvey M., and Marion Johnson. "The West African Ivory Trade during the Eighteenth Century," *International Journal of African Historical Studies* 15/3 (1982): 435–53.

Flint, John E. *Sir George Goldie and the Making of Nigeria.* London: Oxford University Press, 1960.

Gardinier, David. *Political Behavior in the Community of Douala, Cameroon. Reactions of the Duala People to Loss of Hegemony, 1944–1955.* Athens, OH: Ohio University Papers in International Studies, no. 3, 1966.

Geschiere, Peter. "Chiefs and Colonial Rule in Cameroon: Inventing Chieftaincy, French and British Style," *Africa*, 63/2 (1993): 151–75.

Geschiere, Peter and Piet Konings (eds.). *Proceedings/Contributions: Conference on the Political Economy of Cameroon. Historical Perspectives.* Vol. 2, Leiden: African Studies Centre, 1989.

Ghomsi, Emmanuel. "Résistance africaine à l'impérialisme européen: le cas des Douala du Cameroun," *Afrika Zamani* (Yaoundé) 4 (1975): 157–202.

Gomsu, Joseph. "La formation des Camerounais en Allemagne pendant la période coloniale. Alfred Bell: le refuse de connaissances objectives aux colonisés," *Cahiers d'Allemand et d'Etudes Germaniques* (Yaoundé) 1/2 (1985): 58–69.

"Problématique de la collaboration: les chefs traditionnels du Sud-Cameroun dans l'administration coloniale allemande," in Kum'a Ndumbe (ed.), *L'Afrique et l'Allemagne,* 1986, 135–8.

Gouellain, René. *Douala: ville et histoire.* Paris : Institut d'ethnologie, Musée de l'homme, 1975.

Grunder, Horst. *Christliche Mission und deutscher Imperialismus, 1884–1914.* Paderborn: Schningh, 1982.

Guthrie, Malcolm. *Comparative Bantu.* Vol. 3, London: Gregg International, 1970.

Guyer, Jane. "Head Tax, Social Structure and Rural Incomes in Cameroun, 1922–37," *Cahiers d'Etudes Africaines* 20 (1980): 305–29.

"The Administration and the Depression in South Central Cameroun," *African Economic History* 10 (1981): 67–79.

Gwei, Solomon, Nfor. "The History of the British Baptist Mission in Cameroon with Beginnings in Fernando Po, 1841–1886." Bachelor of Divinity dissertation, Baptist Theological Seminary, Rüschlikon-Zurich, 1966.

Hallden, Erik. *The Culture Policy of the Basel Mission in the Cameroons, 1886–1905.* Uppsala: Uppsala University Press, 1968.

Harding, Leonhard. "1884–1984: cent ans de relations commerciales," in Kum'a Ndumbe (ed.), *L'Afrique et l'Allemagne,* 1986, 392–413.

Hargreaves, John D. *Prelude to the Partition of West Africa.* London: Macmillan, 1963.

Harms, Robert W. *River of Wealth, River of Sorrow: The Central Zaire Basin in the Era of the Slave and Ivory Trade, 1800–1891.* New Haven: Yale University Press, 1981.

Harter, Pierre. "Les courses de pirogues coutumiers chez les Dualas ou pembisan a myoloo Duala," *Recherches et études camerounaises* 1 (1960): 71–91.

"Le Ngondo," *Bulletin de l'Association Française pour les Recherches et Etudes Camerounaises* 3 (1968): 63–7.

Hausen, Karin. *Deutsche Kolonialherrschaft in Afrika: Wirtschaftsinteressen und Kolonialverwaltung in Kamerun vor 1914.* Zurich: Atlantis, 1970.

Hill, Robert (ed.). *The Papers of Marcus Garvey and the Universal Negro Improvement Association*, Vol. 8, Berkeley: University of California Press, forthcoming.

Hogendorn, Jan S. "Economic Initiative and African Cash Farming: Precolonial Origins and Early Colonial Developments," in Peter Duignan and L. H. Gann (eds.). *Colonialism in Africa, 1870–1960. Volume 4. The Economics of Colonialism*. Cambridge: Cambridge University Press, 1975, 283–328.

With Marion Johnson. *The Shell Money of the Slave Trade*. Cambridge: Cambridge University Press, 1986.

Hopkins, A. G. *An Economic History of West Africa*. New York: Columbia University Press, 1973.

"The 'New International Economic Order' in the Nineteenth Century: Britain's First Development Plan for Africa," in Robin Law (ed.), *From Slave Trade to "Legitimate" Commerce: The Commercial Transition in Nineteenth Century Africa*. Cambridge: Cambridge University Press, 1993, 240–64.

Horton, Robin. "From Fishing Village to Trading State," in Mary Douglas and Phyllis Kaberry (eds.), *Man in Africa*. London: Tavistock, 1969.

"Stateless Societies in the History of West Africa," in J.F.A. Ajayi and Michael Crowder (eds.), *History of West Africa*. London: Longman, 1971, 78–120.

Hynes, William G. *The Economics of Empire: Britain, Africa and the New Imperialism, 1870–95*. London: Longman, 1979.

Iliffe, John. *Tanganyika under German Rule, 1905–1912*. Cambridge: Cambridge University Press.

Ittmann, Johannes. "Bemerkungen zu den Altersklassen der Duala and ihrer Nachbarn," *Afrika und Übersee* 39/2 (1955): 83–8.

"Der Walfang an der Küste Kameruns," *Zeitschrift für Ethnologie* 81/2 (1956): 203–17.

"Der kultischer Geheimbund Djengu an der Kameruner Küste," *Anthropos* 52 (1957): 135–76.

Jaeck, Hans-Peter. "Die Deutsche Annexation," in Stoecker (ed.), *Kamerun unter Deutscher Kolonialherrschaft* I (1960): 29–5.

Johnson, Marion. "By Ship or by Camel: The Struggle for the Cameroons Ivory Trade in the Nineteenth Century," *Journal of African History* 19 (1978): 523–78.

"Ivory and Nineteenth Century Transformation In West Africa," in G. Liesegang et al. (eds.), *Figuring African Trade*. Berlin: D. Riemer, 1986, 105–22.

Jones, Adam. *German Sources for West African History, 1599–1669*. Wiesbaden: Franz Steiner, 1983.

Jones, G. I. *Trading States of the Oil Rivers: A Study of Political Development in Eastern Nigeria*. London: Oxford, 1963.

"Time and Oral Tradition with Special Reference to Eastern Nigeria," *Journal of African History* 6/2 (1965): 153–60.

Joseph, Richard A. "The Royal Pretender: Prince Douala Manga Bell in Paris, 1919–1922," *Cahiers d'Etudes Africaines* 14 (1974): 339–358.

"Settlers, Strikers and Sans-Travail: The Douala Riots of September 1945," *Journal of African History* 15 (1974): 669–87.

"National Politics in Post-war Cameroun: The Difficult Birth of the U.P.C.," *Journal of African Studies* 2/2 (1975): 223–4.

"The German Question in French Cameroun, 1919–1939," *Comparative Studies in Society and History* 17/1 (1975): 65–90.

Radical Nationalism in Cameroun: Social Origins of the U.P.C. Rebellion. Oxford: Oxford University Press and New York: Clarendon. 1977.

"Church, State and Society in Colonial Cameroon," *International Journal of African Historical Studies* 13/1 (1980): 20–31.

Kaeselitz, Rudi. "Kolonialeroberung und Widerstandskampf in Südkamerun (1884–1907)," in Stoecker (ed.), *Kamerun unter deutscher Kolonialherrschaft* II (1968): 13–54.

Kala Lobe, Iwiyé. "The Greatness and Decline of 'Mun'a Moto'," *Présence Africaine* 37 (1961): 69ff. English version.

Douala Manga Bell: héros de la résistance douala. Paris: ABC, 1977.

Kobler, August Heinrich. *Einst in Berlin.* Hamburg: Hoffmann u. Campe, 1956.

Kuoh Moukouri, Jacques. Unpublished manuscript. "Le Cameroun et ses références: l'âme du peuple Duala."

Kum'a Ndumbe III, Alexandre (ed.). *L'Afrique et l'Allemagne: de la colonisation à la coopération, 1884–1986 (Le cas du Cameroun).* Yaoundé: Editions Africavenir, 1986.

Laburthe-Tolra, Philippe. "Charles Atangana," in Charles André Julien et al. (eds.), *Les Africains.* Volume 5, Paris: Jaguar, 1977, 109–41.

Lamb, D. P. "Volume and Tonnage of the Liverpool Slave Trade, 1772–1807," in Roger Anstey and P. E. H. Hair (eds.), *Liverpool, the African Slave Trade, and Abolition.* Liverpool: Historic Society of Lancashire and Cheshire, 1976 91–112.

Latham, A. J. H. *Old Calabar, 1600–1891.* Oxford: Clarendon, 1973.

Law, Robin (ed.). *From Slave Trade to "Legitimate" Commerce: The Commercial Transition in Nineteenth Century Africa.* Cambridge: Cambridge University Press, 1993.

"The Historiography of the Commercial Transition in West Africa," in Toyin Falola (ed.), *African Historiography: Essays in Honour of Ade Ajayi.* Lagos and London: Longman, 1993, 91–115.

Lewis, W. Arthur. "The Rate of Growth of World Trade, 1830–1973," in Sven Grassman and Erik Lundberg (eds.), *The World Economic Order: Past and Prospects.* New York: St. Martins, 1981, 11–26.

Lloyd, Christopher. *The Navy and the Slave Trade.* London: Longman, Green, 1949.

Louis, Wm. Roger. *Great Britain and Germany's Lost Colonies, 1914–1919.* Oxford: Clarendon, 1967.

Lovejoy, Paul E. "The Volume of the Atlantic Slave Trade: A Synthesis," *Journal of African History* 23 (1982): 473–501.

Transformations in Slavery: A History of Slavery in Africa. Cambridge: Cambridge University Press, 1983.

Lynn, Martin. "Continuity and Change in the British Palm Oil Trade with West Africa," *Journal of African History* 22 (1981): 331–48.

"Commerce, Christianity and the Creoles of Fernando Po," *Journal of African*

History 25 (1984): 257–78.

"The 'Imperialism of Free Trade' and the Case of West Africa, *c*. 1830–*c*. 1879," *Journal of Imperial and Commonwealth History* 15 (1986): 22–40.

"Law and Imperial Expansion: The Niger Delta Courts of Equity, *c*. 1850–85," *Journal of Imperial and Commonwealth History* 23 (1995): 54–76.

Mann, Kristin. *Marrying Well: Marriage, Status and Social Change among the Educated Elite in Colonial Lagos*. Cambridge: Cambridge University Press, 1985.

de Maret, Pierre. "A Survey of Recent Archeological Research and New Dates for Central Africa," *Journal of African History* 26/2 (1985): 129–48.

Mbembe, Achille. "The Banality of Power and the Aesthetics of Vulgarity in the Postcolony," *Public Culture* 4/2 (1992): 1–30.

McPhee, Allan. *The Economic Revolution in British West Africa*. London: Routledge, 1926.

Mettas, Jean. *Répertoire des Expéditions Négrières françaises au XVIIIieme siècle*. Volume 2, Paris: Société Française d'Histoire d'Outre-Mer, 1978, 1984.

Michel, Marc. "Les plantations allemandes du mont Cameroun," *Revue française d'histoire d'Outre-Mer* 57 (1970): 183–213.

Monga, Yvette. "Les entrepreneurs duala, ca. 1890–ca. 1930." Doctoral dissertation, University of Provence, 1996.

Monod, Théodore. *L'industrie des Pêches au Cameroun*. Paris: Société d'editions géographiques, maritimes et coloniales, 1928.

Moumé Etia, Léopold. "La révolte des femmes en 1931" *Wife* (Paris) 6 (1973): 12–16.

Mveng, Engelbert. *Histoire du Cameroun*. Paris: Présence Africaine, 1963.

Ndjicki, Florent. " Douala: Autochtones contre Allogènes," *Africa International* (Paris) 293 (1996): 18–20.

Needham, Rodney. *Reconnaisances*. Toronto: University of Toronto Press, 1980.

Newbury, Colin W. "Credit in Early Nineteenth Century West African Trade," *Journal of African History* 13/1 (1972): 81–95.

"On the Margins of Empire: the Trade of Western Africa, 1875–1890," in Stig Förster et al. (eds.), *Bismarck, Europe and Africa: The Berlin Africa Conference 1884–85 and the onset of Partition*. London: Oxford University Press, 1988, 41–45.

Nørregard, Georg. *Danish Settlements in West Africa*. Boston: Boston University Press, 1966.

Northrup, David. *Trade without Rulers: Precolonial Economic Development in Southeastern Nigeria*. Oxford: Clarendon, 1978.

Oloukpona-Yinnon, Adjai Paulin. *La Révolte des esclaves-mercenaires: Douala, 1893*. Bayreuth: Bayreuth University Press, 1987.

Osteraas, Gary. "Missionary Politics in Cameroon, 1844–1914." Ph.D. dissertation, Columbia University, 1972.

Osuntokun, Akinjide. *Nigeria in the First World War*. Atlantic Highlands, NJ: Humanities Press, 1979.

Owona, Adalbert. "A l'aube du nationalisme camerounais: la curieuse figure de Vincent Ganty," *RFHOM* 56/20 (1969): 214–19.

Patterson, K. David. "The Vanishing Mpongwe: European Contact and Demographic Change in the Gabon River," *Journal of African History* 16/2 (1975): 217–38.

Pedler, Frederick. *The Lion and the Unicorn: A History of the Origins of the United Africa Company, 1787–1931.* London: Heinemann, 1974.

Porter, Andrew. "The Berlin West Africa Conference of 1885–1985 Revisited: A Report," *Journal of Imperial and Commonwealth History* 14 (1985): 84.

Postma, Johannes Menne. *The Dutch in the Atlantic Slave Trade, 1600–1815.* Cambridge: Cambridge University Press, 1990.

Ratcliffe, Barry M. "Commerce and Empire: Manchester Merchants and West Africa," *Journal of Imperial and Commonwealth History* 7/3 (1979): 293–321.

Richard, Madelaine. "Histoire, tradition et promotion de la femme chez les Batanga (Cameroun)," *Anthropos* 65 (1970): 941–7.

Richardson, David. "Profits in the Liverpool Slave Trade: the Accounts of William Davenport," in Roger Anstey and P. E. H. Hair (eds.), *Liverpool, the African Slave Trade, and Abolition.* Liverpool: Historic Society of Lancashire and Cheshire, 1976, 66–83.

de Rosny, Eric. *Healers in the Night.* Maryknoll, New York: Orbis, 1985.

"La lutte contre le choléra à Jebalé (Cameroun)," in Sylvie Devers (ed.), *Pour Jean Malaurie.* Paris: Plon, 1990, 635–45.

Rudin, Harry R. *Germans in the Cameroons.* New Haven, CT: Yale University Press, 1938.

Ruel, Malcolm. *Leopards and Leaders: Constitutional Politics among a Cross River People.* London: Tavistock, 1969.

Rüger, Adolf. "Der Aufstand der Polizeisoldaten (Dezember 1893)," in Stoecker (ed.), *Kamerun unter deutscher Kolonialherrschaft,* I (1960): 91–147.

"Die Widerstandsbewegung des Rudolf Manga Bell in Kamerun," in Walter Markov (ed.), *Etudes africaines/African Studies/Afrika Studien.* Leipzig: Karl Marx University Press, 1967, 107–28.

"Die Duala und der Kolonialmacht, 1884–1914. Eine Studie über die historische Ursprünge des afrikanischen antikolonialismus," in Stoecker (ed.), *Kamerun unter deutscher Kolonialherrschaft,* II (1968): 181–257.

"Die kolonialen Bestrebungen der deutscher Imperialismus (vom Ende der ersten Weltkrieg bis zu Locarno-Konferenz)." *Habilitationsschrift.* Berlin: Humboldt University Press, 1969.

"Imperialismus, Sozialreformismus und antikoloniale demokratische Alternative: Zielvorstellungen von Afrikanern in Deutschland im Jahre 1919," *Zeitschrift für Geschichtswissenschaft* 23/2 (1975): 1293–308.

Sah, Leonard I. "Présence et activités allemandes au Cameroun pendant la période de l'entre-deux guerres (1924–1946)," in Kum'a Ndumbe (ed.), *L'Afrique et l'Allemagne,* 1986, 296–309.

Samarin, William J. "Protestant Missions and the History of Lingala," *Journal of Religion in Africa* 16/2 (1986): 138–63.

Serre, Jacques. "Vincent Ganty (1881–1957): douanier guyanais et homme politique camerounais," *Comptes rendues . . . Academie des Sciences d'Outre-Mer* 36 (1976): 105–20.

Simon, Henry. "The United States and the African Peace Settlement: the Pilgrimage of George Louis Beer," *Journal of African History* 4 (1963): 421.

Smith, Woodruff D. *The German Colonial Empire*. Chapel Hill: University of North Carolina Press, 1978.

Soulillou, Jacques. *Douala: un siècle en images*. Paris: chez l'auteur, 1982.

Stilliard, N. H. "The Rise and Development of Legitimate Trade in Palm Oil with West Africa," M.A. dissertation, Birmingham University, 1938.

Stoecker, Helmuth (ed.). *Kamerun unter deutscher Kolonialherrschaft*. Volume 1, E. Berlin: Rütter and Loening, 1960.

Kamerun unter deutscher Kolonialherrschaft. Volume 2, Berlin: Deutscher Verlag der Wissenschaften, 1968.

Stumpf, Rudolph. *La politique linguistique au Cameroun de 1884 à 1960*. Berne: Peter Lang, 1979.

Sutton, J. E. G. "The Aquatic Civilization of Middle Africa," *Journal of African History* 15/4 (1974): 527–46.

Tambiah, Stanley J. "Dowry and Bridewealth and the Property Rights of Women in South Asia," in Jack Goody and S. Tambiah (eds.), *Bridewealth and Dowry*. Cambridge: Cambridge University Press, 1973, 64–72.

Tchomtchoua, Emmanuel. "Aux sources de l'Union des Populations du Cameroun (UPC): la Jeucafra, l'Unicafra et le Racam (1938–1948)," Thèse de Doctorat de 3e Cycle. University of Yaounde, 1993.

Todd, Loreto. *Modern Englishes: Pidgins and Creoles*. London: Blackwell, 1984.

Turner, Victor W. "Myth and Symbol," *International Encyclopedia of the Social Sciences*. Volume 10, New York: Macmillan, 1968, 57.

The Ritual Process. Chicago: Aldine, 1969.

Vansina, Jan. "The Peoples of the Forest," in David Birmingham and Phyllis Martin (eds.), *History of Central Africa*. Volume 1, London: Longman, 1983, 79–83.

Paths in the Rainforests: Toward a History of Political Tradition in Equatorial Africa. Madison: University of Wisconsin Press, 1990.

"New Linguistic Evidence and 'The Bantu Expansion'," *Journal of African History* 36 (1995): 173–95.

van Slageren, Jaap. *Les origines de l'Eglise Evangélique du Cameroun*. Yaoundé: CLE, 1972.

Veth, P. J. "De Nederlanders in Afrika," *Tjidskift van het Kon. Nederlandsch Aardrijkskundig Genootschap, Amsterdam* 10 (1893): 251–3.

Vitalis, Robert. "On the Theory and Practice of Compradors: The Role of 'Abbud Pasha in the Egyptian Political Economy," *International Journal of Middle East Studies* 22/3: 291–315.

Walz, Gotthilf. *Die Entwicklung der Strafrechtspflege in Kamerun unter deutscher Herrschaft, 1884–1914*. Freiburg: K. Schwarz, 1981, 113–20.

Warnier, Jean-Pierre. "Histoire du peuplement et genèse des paysages dans l'ouest camerounais," *Journal of African History* 25 (1984): 395–410

"Traité sans raids au Cameroun," *Cahiers d'Etudes Africaines* 29 (1989): 5–32.

Washausen, Helmut. *Hamburg und die Kolonialpolitik des deutschen Reiches*. Hamburg: H. Christians, 1968.

Wehler, Hans-Ulrich. *Bismarck und der Imperialismus*. Cologne: Kiepenhauer and Witsch, 1969.

Williams, Gomer. *The Liverpool Privateers with an Account of the Liverpool Slave*

Trade. London: Heinemann, 1897.

Wirz, Albert. *Vom Sklavenhandel zum kolonialen Handel: Wirtschaftsräume und Wirtschaftsformen in Kamerun vor 1914*. Zurich: Atlantis, 1972.

"La 'rivière de Cameroun': commerce pré-colonial et contrôle de pouvoir en société lignagère," *Revue Française d'Histoire d'Outre-Mer* 60/2 (1973): 172–95. "Malaria-Prophylaxe und koloniale Städtebau: Fortschritt als Rücktritt?", *Gesnerus* 37 (1980): 215–34.

Wolpe, Howard. *Urban Politics in Nigeria: a Study of Port Harcourt*. Berkeley: University of California Press, 1983.

Wright, Marcia. "Local Roots of Policy in German East Africa," *Journal of African History* 4 (1968): 621–30.

Index

OTHER BOOKS IN THE SERIES